DATE DUE

FE 22 '94			
NO 23 '99			

The Rise of the Spanish Empire
by R. B. Merriman

The Jews in Spain

VOLUME TWO

A Social-Cultural Study

Title-page of Joshua ibn Shu'aib's *Derashot*, part II,
from a manuscript of the 15th century

(see p. xi)

THE MORRIS LOEB SERIES

THE JEWS IN SPAIN

THEIR SOCIAL, POLITICAL AND CULTURAL LIFE DURING THE MIDDLE AGES

BY

ABRAHAM A. NEUMAN

VOLUME II

A Social-Cultural Study

1969

OCTAGON BOOKS

New York

Reprinted 1969
by special arrangement with The Jewish Publication Society of America

OCTAGON BOOKS
A DIVISION OF FARRAR, STRAUS & GIROUX, INC.
19 Union Square West
New York, N. Y. 10003

LIBRARY OF CONGRESS CATALOG CARD NUMBER: 70-105964

TABLE OF CONTENTS

VOLUME II

CHAPTER XI

Family relationship as index to social morality—Strict enforcement of family purity—Severe treatment of rumor-mongering—Rabbinic utterances—Contrast to laxity of Spanish background—Observations on the moral condition of their times by Ibn Adret and Rabbi Asher—Contrasting personalities and viewpoints—Social differences between Aragon and Castile—Influence of slavery and concubinage—Sexual relation between Jews and Christians a capital crime—Prostitutes—Crimes of violence infrequent—Executions—Gaming and gambling—Religious vows to strengthen moral will—King's defense of gamblers—Morals and religion identified—Filial love and duty.

CHAPTER XII

Amorous courtship discouraged—Parental control of marriage—Child marriages—Talmudic attitude differentiating between male and female minors—Relapse in the Middle Ages—Social and moral causes—Marriage standards—Prevention of mock or hasty marriages—Parental responsibilities—Engagement ceremonies—Gifts and festivities.

CHAPTER XIII

Few references to marriage customs and ceremonies—Two stages of wedding ceremony: *erusin* and *nissu'in*—Looseness of marriage ceremony contrasted with difficulty of annulment or divorce—Abuses illustrated—Protective measures—Reasons for and against lapse of period between *erusin* and *nissu'in*—Influence upon concubinage—

Countries in which concubinage was tolerated—Status of concubine in
biblical and rabbinical literature—*Erusin* as quasi-marriage creating
legal status for concubine—Denounced by rabbis—The *ketubah*—
Legal provisions—Ethical purpose—Provision against bigamy—Use
against feminine caprice—Ruled essential for conjugal relationship.

CHAPTER XIV

Early marital difficulties—Paternal attitude of Jewish court—
Problems due to migration of head of family—Remedial measures—
Plural marriages—Validity of ban of Rabbenu Gershom questioned
in Spain—Monogamy the rule—Abandoned under exceptional
circumstances—Royal license required—Levirate marriage preferred to *halizah* in Spain—Frequent protest by widow—Woman's
status in divorce proceedings—"Rebellious" wives—Compulsory
divorce—Legal protection of economic status of woman—Theory
versus practice—Laws of inheritance.

CHAPTER XV

Communal duty to provide public instruction—Provisions for
elementary and secondary education through private initiative—
Higher education communally endowed—Educational measures in
Castilian statutes of 1432—Religious motive of Jewish education—
Vacations not favored—Basis of educational program: Hebrew
prayers, Bible and Talmud—Detailed curricula—Elaborate pedagogical programs of philosophical theorists—No corresponding
schools—Few Jews in Christian and Mohammedan universities—
Secular education self-acquired—*Yeshibah* as community institution
of higher learning—The *yeshibah*, historic background—Content
and method of *yeshibah* studies—Importance of rector—Extra-
rabbinical attainments of teachers and disciples—Conflicting
attitudes—Personality of rector—Dominating moral figure—
Talmid hakam defined—His privileges and prerogatives—Community counselor and spiritual leader—Relation to *Bet Din*—
Remuneration of rector discussed—Maimonides' opposition—
Influence of his idealistic teaching—Changes due to economic
deterioration in fourteenth century—*Yeshibah* students—Number
and character—Foreign students—Language of study—Affectionate
relation between students and teachers—Supply of textbooks—
Books as objects of public interest—Libraries and bibliophiles.

CHAPTER XVI

CHAPTER XVII

CHAPTER XVIII

CHAPTER XIX

CHAPTER XX

LIST OF ILLUSTRATIONS

VOLUME II

xi

Volume Two

A Social-Cultural Study

CHAPTER XI

MORAL CONDITIONS

A TRUE index of the social morality of a group lies in its concepts and ideals of the family relationship. Individual violations of the moral code will occur among every group and in every age. But the collective conscience of the organized community is the chief criterion for moral judgment, and this lies in the accepted norms of family morality and the enforceable laws by which they are safeguarded. Thus appraised, the mediaeval Jewish communities could rightly boast of standards so superior to those of their environment as to defy their adversaries with the challenge that the truth of a religion is proved by the morality of its adherents.[1]

To maintain scrupulously high standards of family purity and personal chastity was the supreme duty of the Jewish courts and the communal authorities. Unfaithfulness was strongly denounced in the husband,[2] but the mere suspicion of infidelity in the wife, if seriously entertained by the husband, resulted in the separation of the family by the Jewish court even against the will of both the husband and the wife.[3] For the married state was sacred. Its sanctity was not rooted in the will of the man and the woman; its violation was nothing short of desecration, or a profanation of the Holy Name. Surely this could not be overlooked by a community that looked upon life as a discipline to sanctify the Holy One of Israel.

If rumor implicated a prospective bride concerning a previous betrothal, that rumor had to be traced to its source and disproved before the marriage ceremony could take place.[4] When the report was too vague to be traced, the rabbi ordered the public reader, the *hazzan,* to make a proclamation at the Sabbath service in the synagogue, calling upon those who had any knowledge in the matter to appear before the court as witnesses—the penalty for withholding information being excommunication.[5] Only if no damaging information was forthcoming even then, would the rabbi permit the marriage ceremony to be performed. No whisper of suspicion, no scandal was to besmirch the fair name of the family. "Put away from thee frowardness of mouth, and perverseness of lips put far from thee," was the text with which Ibn Adret supported a colleague who had refused to permit the marriage of a widow to a man with whom she had been on scandalous terms during the lifetime of her husband.[6] If a man showed cause to doubt the fidelity of his wife, they were no longer fit to live together nor even to effect a reconciliation.[7] Even the removal to another city was of no avail, for the unhappy story of their blighted family life would find its way to their new abode, and the Jewish authorities would be compelled to part them.[8] If, on the other hand, a man believed in the innocence of his wife in spite of suspicious circumstances, and if he remained unshaken in his belief despite the direct testimony of one witness and in the face of a strong persistent rumor, he then was permitted to live with her; for then only the formal, incontrovertible testimony of two witnesses appearing before a properly constituted *Bet Din,* incriminating the woman of adultery, could disrupt the family.[9]

Cruel and harsh the court's strict decree of separation sounded, no doubt, to the married couple who were willing to forgive and forget. But the moral conscience of the Jews was strict to the point of tragedy. Once, therefore, the sacredness of the marriage tie was violated, it was declared irrevocably broken, and no course was left to the unhappy family but to resign themselves to the grim consequences. The blow to the family often struck innocent members as well as the guilty and, at such times, the rabbis were painfully reluctant to pronounce the harsh decree.[10] As far as was consistent with truth and their sacred responsibility, they strained every effort to vindicate the innocence of the accused persons or to resolve favorably any doubt.[11] Thoroughly humane was the special considerateness shown by the rabbis to the accused woman if she was a mother.[12] She was spared the shame and defamation of being publicly striped with the lash, which would have been her fate if she had had no children.[13] Where no legal defense was possible, however, the rabbis were inexorable. In instructing another judge how to act, Solomon ibn Adret wrote categorically, "Know that the court must withdraw from the husband, even with the lash, any woman whose legal status disqualifies her as wife."[14] The relentless consistency with which the religious heads enforced their conviction in regard to family purity, no matter how great the sacrifice, gives striking emphasis to the moral fiber of mediaeval Jewry.

No commentary could more vividly portray the scrupulous regard for family honor than the following curious document emanating from a Jewish court:[15]

I certify over my signature to all whom this document may reach that witnesses appeared before my teacher, Rabbi Isaac, son of R. Eliakim, who was presiding at the court session, and that he received proper and legal testimony from aged and venerable men of the country concerning the family of the brothers David and Azriel, to the effect that they were of pure descent, without any family taint, and that they could intermarry with the most honored families in Israel; for there had been no admixture of impure blood in the paternal or maternal antecedents and their collateral relatives.

Jacob Issachar, son of R. Shalom.

The family in question was one of the most highly respected in the community. David was distinguished for his learning; Azriel was the philanthropist of the community. With his own funds he maintained *yeshibot* and supported their students. He was deeply devoted to the cause of learning. He assisted the rabbis liberally with money and with all the personal influence that he could exert in their behalf. Members of the Jewish aristocracy eagerly associated and intermarried with the families of the two brothers. Against this influential and highly respected family, a wicked calumniator — he is so described by the defendant as well as the rabbi — arose and, supported by perjured witnesses, it seems, cast aspersions on the brothers by asserting that one of their ancestors had been a slave. That the charge was unfounded and was plotted in vindictiveness was soon evident. No one was able to recall anything suspicious with regard to the family. On the contrary, as far back as the memory of most could travel, the parents and grandparents of the two brothers were highly respected and their children had married into the best families. Some of the most aged and venerable members of the community appeared before the Jewish court and submitted formal testimony completely clearing the family of any shadow of suspicion. Thereupon, the court officially vindicated the genealogical purity of the two brothers David and Azriel, and condemned, in the most denunciatory terms, the vileness of the attempted calumny. But so seriously was the matter regarded, and so deeply grieved were the brothers, that they could not rest with the verdict of the local rabbis and invoked the aid of all the prominent rabbis in their vicinity, begging them to confirm with the weight of their authority the sentence already pronounced. The written opinions of these rabbis, all of whom uniformly confirmed the sentence of the first court, were received and sent to Rabbi Solomon ibn Adret in Barcelona, and this renowned authority was asked to add the dignity of his great name to the formidable array that now supported the spotless reputation of the injured family.

The entire responsum is charged with deep emotion. The fact that a blemish had been cast on an innocent family in Israel was regarded with horror as an act of monstrous villainy. Ibn Adret wrote:

> When your letter reached me and I opened it, I stood terrified. The author of this wicked rumor, whatever his motive, has sinned grievously and deserves severer punishment than one who slaughtered his victim in cold blood. For a murderer slays but two or three souls, but this man has defamed thirty, forty souls and the voice of the blood of the whole family cries from the earth, groaning aloud. The defamer should be excommunicated. While the sages of the Talmud stated long ago, "He who calls his neighbor slave shall be considered an excommunicate," it is not sufficient to leave the culprit under the general reproach of the ancient ban, but he should now be excommunicated

by a living court, and I shall confirm their act and affix my signature to such a document.

This feeling of family sensitiveness was not peculiar to the wealthy and learned alone. Thus we read in another responsum[16] of a rich man who, in a fit of anger, heaped abuse upon a respected youth by calling him "bastard son of a bastard." Here, it seems, there was not even the danger that the coarse insult would be taken seriously as a reflection on the youth's family. Nevertheless, it was regarded as a serious offense and the rabbi wrote:[17]

> It is a great iniquity and one deserving of severe punishment to stretch one's hand against the holy ones in the earth. Let the blasphemer take heed. Let him repent and afflict himself through fasts, flagellation and the dispensing of charity; perhaps he will be forgiven; peradventure there is hope for him and it may yet be well with him.

How significantly this intense feeling for chastity and family purity stands out on the background of mediaeval Spain! The absence of any social stigma attached to illegitimate birth was one of the noted features of Spanish society in the Middle Ages.[18] Illegitimacy was no bar to the throne of Spain,[19] and the same leniency applied to private families. Some of the most powerful and celebrated families in Andalusia were founded by bastards; and, indeed, of the two rivals for the dukedom of Medina-Sidonia, both were illegitimate. For a long time, birth out of wedlock was considered no disgrace in Castile.[20] Yet in a Jewish community living amidst such an environment the mere abusive epithet "bastard" was considered an offense calling for the severe penance of contrition, fasting, flagellation and the dispensing of charity.[21]

Needless to say, reality fell short of the ideal and revealed many blots and stains.[22] The rabbis and moralists were quick to detect them and passionate in their denunciation. Thus Rabbi Asher in Toledo exclaimed, "Woe to our sins! The daughters of Israel have become bold in our days."[23] In another instance, he argued against the enforcement of the geonic ordinance by which the husband was compelled to grant his wife a divorce upon her demand. He reasoned sadly: "The daughters of Israel in this generation are not to be trusted. If any woman could free herself from her husband by merely saying, 'He pleases me not,' not one of them who traces her descent from Abraham our father would be found dwelling with her husband; for the women would soon set their hearts upon strangers and rebel against their husbands."[24] His son and successor, R. Judah, living in the same territory, complained bitterly: "I have observed the land and, lo, it is corrupt. The women have cursed the land. They invent lies to free themselves from their husbands."[25] Rabbi Solomon ibn Adret, on the other hand, living in Barcelona, in northeastern Spain, was more charitable to Jewish womanhood: "I see that the number of men who are breaking down the bounds of morality is increasing today, and there is none in the land to rebuke the wicked one and to say to him who corrupts his place 'wherefore hast thou done so?' The daughters of Israel are modest. It is the generation which brings them into ill repute."[26] In striking contrast to Rabbi Asher, Ibn Adret was jealous of the good name of Jewish womanhood: "It is the duty of the Jewish court to remove all stumbling blocks and leave no room for would-be transgressors to defame the fair name of the daughters of Israel and to contaminate the land."[27]

Speaking of his own country, Rabbi Solomon ibn Adret exclaimed:

> Praised be the Lord for the purity of the generations
> of these parts. The daughters of Israel are chaste.
> They will not break with propriety and take unto
> themselves secretly men of their own choice without
> the consent of their parents and without public cele-
> bration while their fathers are alive. Such imputa-
> tions are not true of the daughters of the land, and
> who will hearken unto them?[28]

The difference in outlook of these authorities is, no doubt, partly to be explained on the grounds of personal tempera- ment. Undoubtedly, the kindly and genial Rabbi Solomon, native of the sunny land of Spain, would be less harsh a critic of his country's morals than the new settlers, R. Asher and his son R. Judah, both hailing from Germany where the persecution and the intolerance of the ruling classes had narrowed the interests of the oppressed Jews and intensified their feelings of right and wrong. It is understandable, too, that a few flagrant cases of immorality would make a deep impression upon a newly arrived immigrant and color his views of the people among whom he had come to live. One may readily see how, in a burst of righteous indigna- tion, R. Asher would thunder a sweeping denunciation against all classes, and his dark outlook is therefore not to be taken as a true reflection of his time. A careful analysis of the responsa of these rabbis, however, would seem to show that there was actually a marked divergence between the moral standards of the Jewish communities of north- eastern Spain and those in Castile and Leon.

Even a cursory reading of the responsa of Ibn Adret and of R. Asher reveals an unmistakable difference in the political, social and moral atmosphere of the two countries represented by their authors. The one reflects the civilization of Christian Aragon in which the spoken language was either Catalan or Castilian. The other, where R. Asher lived, at Toledo, in central Spain, in the kingdom of Castile and Leon, was inhabited by a population largely Mohammedan, Arabic in tongue and civilization,[29] whose moral and cultural standards undoubtedly influenced the ruling Christian population. It is not surprising, therefore, that these racial and cultural differences should also be reflected in the social and moral standards of the Jewish inhabitants, and the responsa furnish much evidence corroborative of this conclusion.[30]

The prevalence of slavery created conditions which were bound at times to lead to moral laxity between master and slave.[31] Concubinage was the natural result; but in order to receive even a grudging social recognition and tolerance, the master was compelled first to liberate the slave, convert her to Judaism and then wed her in semi-marriage.[32] Far more serious were the instances of alleged illicit relationships between Jews and Christians.[33] While Jewish sentiment was shocked by such revelations, in mediaeval Christendom this relationship was regarded as carnal sin, which even marriage could not absolve save through baptism. It is true that the famous French Rabbi, Moses of Coucy, who traveled through Spain in 1236, was much exercised over the number of intermarriages between Jews, Christians and Mohammedans.[34] But his testimony is unique and otherwise unsupported. Perhaps he wrote in an excess of preacher's fervor or in an exaggerated pride of his role as a reincarnated Ezra, through whose influence Jewish husbands sent away their heathen wives. The penalty for sexual intercourse between Christians and non-Christians

was death by fire.[35] But evidently love and passion, then
as now, laughed at death and hazarded life and fortune.
The extreme penalty was not always exacted, but rarely
was it possible for the Jewish offender to escape the confiscation of his wealth.[36] As this proved a tempting bait, charges
were frequently invented for their revenue yield and were
easily disproved when a fair trial was held.[37]

The sins of individuals were visited not only upon the
guilty persons but upon their families and, indeed, the entire
aljama.[38] The transgressions of one person frequently stirred
the wrath of the mob or officialdom and brought retribution upon a whole community. The Jewish authorities,
therefore, showed great zeal in discouraging dangerous
propinquity between men and women of different faiths.[39]
They dealt severely with the Jewish offender.[40] In exceptional cases, as in Calatayud, the *aljama* had also the power
to arrest the Christian corespondent in adultery, whose
punishment was limited to a fine of three hundred *morabatins.*[41] What a sad commentary that some of the communities actually connived at the existence of Jewish prostitutes in the *judería* in order to keep dissolute youths from
consorting with Christian prostitutes and thereby endang-
ering the entire Jewish population.[42]

Crimes of violence, even murder, were less antisocial
in consequence, for their punishment was usually limited to
the perpetrator and the immediate conspirators.[43] Only a
cause célèbre had distant repercussions.[44] Cases involving
informers were notorious examples of such reverberations.[45]
Minor offenses, lesser aggravated cases of assault and bat-
tery, were the subjects of communal enactments which
prescribed relatively heavy penalties. Thus, in one community, there was a penalty of one hundred gold *maravedís*

for assault.[46] In another community, an alternative of imprisonment was provided for one who was unable to meet the fine, at the rate of one *maravedí* per day.[47] In this enactment, it was specified that the fine was to be divided equally among the plaintiff, the court and the charities. On the other hand, Alfonso III claimed the entire fine of 500 *morabatins* from Joseph del Rab for fighting in the synagogue.[48]

More serious crimes were usually judged by general principles of law rather than local enactments. How the Jewish courts treated the entire field of criminal jurisprudence was previously indicated.[49] The king frequently injected himself or his designated representative into murder trials, but as a rule applied the principles of Jewish law with the aid of a rabbinical consultant.[50] Despite the notorious crudity of these courts, many were acquitted and a still greater number escaped with heavy fines.[51] Judging by the number of murder charges, it must be obvious that Spanish Jews frequently carried armed weapons.[52] In a number of instances, these acts of violence were committed by court sycophants, highhanded courtiers, who abused their power, or they were acts of revenge against that class by those whom they victimized.[53] When the death penalty was carried out, the execution was generally by hanging.[54] Out of deference to Jewish sentiment, it was forbidden to hang the victim near the Jewish cemetery.[55]

In so turbulent a country as Spain and in an age of brigandage and violence, robbery was virtually an unknown crime among Jews and theft was extremely rare.[56] Nor did they share in the popular vice of clipping the coinage and passing counterfeit money.[57] Those who were guilty of theft were treated as "thorns in the vineyard."[58] They were disfranchised religiously. They were disqualified to take an oath or to bear testimony, so that, for instance, a bill of divorcement which was attested by one guilty of theft was declared invalid.[59] Even prayer, fasting and good conduct did not restore a thief to his former status, unless he first made restitution to his victim.

The Jewish authorities had far more occasion to be concerned with the minor vices of gaming and gambling and, what was from a religious viewpoint extremely serious, the popular addiction to take vows in haste, to repent at leisure and to seek religious absolution which could not be granted. All shades of human frailty connected with the timeless passion for games of chance are mirrored in the rabbinic responsa. Losses ranged from small amounts to one thousand gold *maravedís*.[60] In one instance, a man pawned his wife's clothing to pay his loss in dice.[61] Not unlike modern times, women were then also victims of their husbands' gambling habits.[62] The rabbis were painfully aware of the effects of this vice on character deterioration and denounced its ravages in no uncertain terms.[63] Gambling debts were not collectible at court.[64] On the contrary, the victim could sue the winner and obtain restitution of his losses.[65] But neither in their capacity of preachers and moralists nor as judges and lawmakers did the rabbis succeed in extirpating an instinct that seems so deeply imbedded in human nature.

Despite the severe ban which the Talmud placed on gambling and its votaries, the populace did not seem to be much affected by it and the mediaeval rabbis were not more successful in disturbing this indulgent, tolerant attitude. Nevertheless, from time to time, a wave of reform swept over the community, and the authorities attacked the problem with great zeal. Severe penalties were added to

the local ban and both were vigorously enforced.[66] Realizing
the shifting nature of public opinion, the legislators usually
set a time limit to these enactments. But inevitably a
reaction followed and public protest frequently forced the
authorities to repeal hastily the reforms which they had inaugurated. Against this course, the rabbis interposed
strenuous objections on grounds of ethical policy as well as
religious law.[67]

More eloquent of human frailty were the faltering attempts of weak-willed habitués to reinforce their virtuous
resolutions by means of a religious vow.[68] With full understanding of human weakness, the rabbis discouraged these
attempts to bolster a weak will with a shaky religious prop.[69]
When the admonition was not heeded, the result was moral
frustration and a double sense of guilt.[70] The cases all ran
pitifully true to form. Thus a scion of a noble family took
an oath not to play any game for money. In addition, he
vowed that if he broke the oath, he was to be in a state of
excommunication, ostracized by his fellow Jews, his very
bread deemed contaminated. But temptation proved too
strong. He yielded to his weakness and contritely he
appeared before the rabbi, seeking absolution from the
vow which he was unable to keep. But he soon found that
there was no easy way out of the dilemma. The oath could
not be repealed, and for the broken vows of the past he
suffered flagellation. To spare the family public humiliation,
the flagellation was administered in privacy.[71] In another
case, a man who took a similar oath became insane, with
occasional rational intervals. When it was found that gaming had a good effect upon him, a way was found to annul
the oath.[72]

The king turned the human weakness of some of his

Jewish subjects to the profit of his coffers.[73] The *aljamas*
were not averse to this procedure. On the contrary, they
welcomed the royal cooperation of which they were thus
assured. But it was a high price to pay, and the communities
later had occasion to regret it. With the royal house, favoritism stood higher than law and public policy. Consequently,
it is not surprising to find the Infante Don Juan protecting
some of his Jewish favorites from the anti-gambling ordinances of their respective *aljamas* Saragossa and Valencia.
He ordered that they were not to suffer the prescribed penalties of fine and excommunication. He specifically granted
the *familiar*, Jacob Zambell, the right to play dice anywhere
with Christians, Jews or Saracens for any stakes he pleased.
When the *aljama* of Valencia ignored the royal command,
they were sternly threatened with a fine of one thousand
morabatins.[74]

Owing to the curious rabbinic mode of using archaic
talmudic terminology, all the games played for money are
referred to as "dice," so that we have scant information in
our sources concerning the character of the mediaeval games
of chance. Mention is made of games played with fruit or
eggs like pellets in place of balls, these being regarded as less
baneful than dice.[75] There is also reference to a game איסקונדרי,
a name used in the Talmud, which is described as being
played on a tablet which an artist painted with figures.[76]
But as the details of the game had no legal pertinence they
are not described.

There is an interesting description of a wrestling match
in which the object of the wrestler was to throw his opponent.
The rabbi understood the game well, and he properly freed
the victor from damages in the unfortunate accident in
which the vanquished opponent lost an eye as he was thrown

to the ground.[77] No opprobrium was attached to the sport. On the other hand, acting was associated with immoral living. To entertain actors in one's home was like inviting women for immoral purposes, a cause for expulsion from the membership of a Jewish benevolent fraternity.[78] Nevertheless, Jewish actors and musicians enjoyed favor in the royal courts.[79]

To the mediaeval mind — Jewish, Christian or Mohammedan — morals and religious practices were inseparable. They were both branches of the same tree. The violation of either was a sin, and the same disciplinary authorities censored the morals as well as the religious observances of the people. They were appropriately called ברורי עבירות, vice, or sin commissioners. They invariably showed equal zeal in cleansing the community of either type of offense, the punishment ranging from fines, excommunication and expulsion from the community to imprisonment, corporal and even capital punishment.[80] How extreme these penalties were at times has been described elsewhere.[81]

In conclusion, it may be pertinent again to revert to the family ideal. Filial reverence was one of its noble, notable characteristics.[82] In all the responsa of the Spanish rabbis, there is only one case of a son who was hailed to court for the nonsupport of his father.[83] In defense, the son claimed that his father had outstanding loans on which he could draw, while he, on the other hand, had his own children to support. Because of the rarity of such cases, Jewish law made no special provision to compel a son to support his father. Nevertheless, Ibn Adret recommended in such cases the expedient of social ostracism and especially exclusion from public worship. Jewish law furthermore endowed the father with the power to excommunicate his son. In the case

just cited, the father, in a burst of anger, did so. Despite
the religious homage which the father commanded, love of
man stood higher than filial duty. A man who commanded
his son to hate his enemy and not to speak to him or to
forgive him was reprimanded by Rabbi Asher, for no parent
had the right to command his son to hate his fellow in
defiance of the precepts of the Bible.[84]

CHAPTER XII

COURTSHIP AND MARRIAGE

LOVE and romance rarely find their way into state doc-uments or court records, and our sources form no ex-ception to the rule. Indeed, one may rightly suspect that mediaeval chivalry with its jousts, tournaments and courts of love, and the ribaldry and the excesses that accompanied them, were totally alien to the Hebrew spirit, which stressed the religious purpose of marriage rather than the indulgence of love. What we may reasonably expect to find in our records — and in this we shall not be disappointed — is an account, in the prose of fact and legal concept, of the social ideals and ethical standards which made of the family a true index of the moral conscience of mediaeval Jewry.

Unlike the turbulent and stormy nature of Jewish life throughout the Middle Ages, the romantic prenuptial period of youth was in most cases disappointingly placid. Amorous courtship was not countenanced in good Jewish society.[1] Love songs were denounced by earnest preachers as un-Jewish and as lewd and lustful, although the vehe-mence of the preacher's language would show how difficult it was to convey this sense of sinfulness to the Jewish maid-ens who learned to sing them in childhood.[2] Life evidently was too brief and too stern for sentimental indulgences. The plans for matrimony were not to be traced to the secret plottings of two youthful hearts, for not with them was the choice.[3] Marriage was too serious a step to be under-

19

taken by children of their own accord,[4] for children they truly were in numberless cases.[5] It was the great privilege and the duty of parenthood to arrange for the proper marriage of the children and the matrimonial settlement was measured by the sober standards of parental valuation rather than by the sentimental promptings of youth.[6]

The part taken by the mother in the matrimonial deliberations was important, but her opinions carried persuasive power rather than official authority. The sole right to bind in marriage was vested in the father. His rule in the house may have been kindly in spirit, but it was absolute in legal power. During the minority of the children, he was invested with the sole right to betroth them and to give them in marriage with or without their consent. The right was exercised frequently, so that child marriages were a common occurrence. This was a strange reversion from the more liberal and advanced attitude which found expression in earlier practice as recorded in the Talmud.

Talmudic law recognized, in the first place, a sharp distinction between the status of the son and the daughter. At no time was the son's legal independence seriously threatened. During his minority, the father was naturally his guardian. In any civil transaction, he could act in his son's behalf as the custodian of his rights and interests. But in marriage, where the assertion of the will is fundamental, the father could not substitute his will for that of his son. No marriage arraned by the father could, therefore, be legally valid until the son attained to majority, which was thirteen years.[8] At that age he attained complete independence in respect to marriage and did not legally require the sanction of parental consent. In point of fact, however, it appears that in talmudic times marriage normally took place several years after the age of majority, when the boy had matured and developed to early manhood. "Eighteen years is the time for marriage," reads the dictum in the *Ethics of the Fathers*.[9]

In the case of the daughter, on the other hand, the condition was totally different. The talmudic teachers recognized the earlier biblical law which invested the father with the right to give his daughter in marriage during her minority to any candidate of his own choice, even against her own expressed desire and protest. But in characteristic fashion, they sublimated this legal right to the plane of an ethical principle. In law and in precept they taught that it was not a right or privilege to be exercised as a whim or in self-interest, but that it was a sacred duty calling for devotion and self-sacrifice. "The father is obliged to dress his daughter generously and to provide her with a suitable dowry, so as to make her attractive to would-be suitors."[10] Furthermore, the famous Babylonian teacher, Abba Arika, or Rab, of the third century, ruled that "it is prohibited to betroth one's daughter during her minority. It is incumbent upon the father to wait till his daughter grows up and can herself declare 'this man is my choice.'" This ruling was accepted as a precedent in the Talmud and in the later codes of medi-aeval Jewish authorities.[11] With this provision in force, the rabbis virtually emancipated the daughter from the legal control of the father. For no sooner did she attain to majority, which, in Jewish law, is twelve years and six months for girls, when she at once passed out of the legal jurisdiction of her father and was subject to no authority save the moral influence of her parents.

Thus, compared with talmudic conditions, the Middle Ages witnessed a decided reaction toward the less liberal

and more rigorous conception of the relation between parents
and children. In the mind of Ibn Adret, there was no doubt
but that the father should marry his daughter, a child not
yet twelve years old, to a man against her will, rather than
break the pledge he had made to him under oath.[12] The
difference in spirit between the view thus advanced by a
rabbi, who was undoubtedly liberal in his time, and the
statement uttered by a teacher one thousand years earlier
is as clear as the transitory stages between the two views
are obscure.

For talmudic opinion itself is not uniformly of one tone.
While none of the rabbis would encourage marriage between
children appreciably under age, some were also averse to
delaying the marriage much beyond the period of puberty.[13]
In Babylonia, scholars married at an earlier age than in
Palestine[14] and, while this does not point to marriage of
minors, proof is not wanting in geonic literature to show that
the tendency among Jews in the following centuries was to
reduce the standard age of marriage.[15] Nor was this tendency confined to any one country. Marriages between
Jewish children were customary in all European countries
in the Middle Ages. Certainly in Spain, in the thirteenth
and fourteenth centuries, child marriages were matters of
everyday occurrence and excited no comment.[16] That this
practice was contrary to the spirit and the letter of talmudic
precedents did not, strangely enough, disturb the learned
rabbis or the general population.[17] Ibn Adret stood alone
in protest against the validity of a marriage entered into by
a father for his son under thirteen years of age.[18] He was
moved to oppose the prevailing custom for purely halakic
reasons, but did not seem to have succeeded in impressing
his views upon his contemporaries.[19] In those parts of Spain

which were not under his immediate jurisdiction, therefore, the marriage of boys under thirteen years of age met with as little opposition as the marriage of girls at a still earlier age.

The relapse of social custom in this regard is thus explained by a Franco-German source of the twelfth century, which has been widely quoted:

> And as to the custom that prevails among us to betroth our daughters before they are twelve years old [which is contrary to talmudic teaching], we are compelled to follow this course by the fate of our exile which we are made to feel more painfully every day. Thus, if a man have it in his power today to endow his daughter with a dowry, who can tell but that the following day he will be robbed of his fortune, and his daughter might forever remain unmarried.[20]

This reason, which reflects faithfully the precariousness of Jewish life during the period of the Crusades, could only have been a contributory cause in Spain, where the condition of the Jews was relatively more stable. Furthermore, it would argue for greater frequency of early marriages among the wealthier classes and in periods of increasing persecution, a hypothesis extremely unlikely.[21]

The cause is, at least in part, to be sought in the moral sensitiveness of the Jewish people, in the feeling that love is holy and passion beastly. It lay in the stern conviction that moral purity was essential to godly living and that the way to attain it was not to brave the dangers of temptation, but to avoid its pitfalls. Said Rab Hisda, "If I am better than my friends, it is because I married when I was only sixteen years old, and if I had been married at fourteen, I would have said boldly to Satan, 'Behold, I defy thee.' "[22] In this attitude of the rabbinic teacher, the trend of subsequent development is clearly foreshadowed. The married state, the rabbis taught, was the haven of safety against the tempests attendant upon the period of youth. It was exalted and ranked in importance with the supreme duty of the Jew to study the Torah; and the father was in duty bound to provide for the one as well as for the other.[23] From the rabbinic conception that it is the duty of the father to "secure a wife for his son"[24] to the mediaeval custom of child marriage is but a step.

Needless to say, the communal mind which for moral reasons sanctioned the betrothal of children by their parents also affected the conditions of marriage among adults. Ulterior motives, it was held, desecrated the sacredness of the marriage tie.[25] A young man could be restrained by the Jewish officials from marrying an aged woman when his motive was glaringly mercenary.[26] If such a marriage was consummated, the husband could not invoke pious motives to free himself of his wife when disillusionment followed.[27] Love was the religious basis of a woman's marriage — such was the view of R. Nissim Gerundi.[28]

On the other hand, outward display of strong emotion by a youth or maiden for one another was frowned upon as a breach of decorum, and a girl's insistence upon her love contrary to the will of her parents was a breach of maidenly modesty.[29] It was an unheard-of matter and, on this ground alone, Ibn Adret acquitted a defendant in Estella from forfeiting the bond which he had pledged in behalf of his granddaughter when she subsequently refused to wed the bridegroom selected for her by that contract. "He could not have foreseen the possibility of his granddaughter's refusal, as all girls, with rare exception, abide by the wishes of their parents or relatives." By communal enactments,

secret marriages were often declared null and void.[30] In
any event, they were considered highly disreputable and
were rare.[31] A quorum of ten persons, at least, was required
at the wedding ceremony in order to give it the nature of a
public function,[32] and the bride's parents or, in case of
death, other relatives were by communal statute required
to be present as a sign of the family's consent and sanction.[33]
Ibn Adret scornfully rejected the notion that any Jewish
maiden would be found in the land so bold as to choose her
own husband without consulting her father.[34] Thus it was
through moral pressure that youth waived its rights before
age, and the marriage contract became a family deed.

No marriage was considered respectable which was not
preceded by preliminary negotiations,[35] or espousals, when
the date of the wedding and the terms of the marriage
settlement were agreed upon with due ceremony. In other
countries, these negotiations were facilitated by a professional go-between, the so-called *shadkan*, a much lauded
and much abused person.[36] In Spain, his mediation was
dispensed with.[37] In the numerous cases of matches made
and unmade, of which our sources bear record, the *shadkan*
played no role.[38] The effacement of this naturally obtrusive
person can lead only to the conclusion that he was nonexistent.

Upon the father fell the brunt of carrying on the preliminary negotiations, and only in his absence or death
were these responsibilities transferred to the mother and
the elder brother.[39] That matchmaking was often a battle
of wits between the elders is illustrated in a realistic tale
of a father's thwarted ambition. The scene is laid in Mont-
clus. Simon was the father of two sons; Isaac was endowed
by heaven with two daughters. Could anything be more

natural and desirable than for these two families in Israel
to be symmetrically matched and interlinked? Such thoughts
presumably, and others more practical perhaps, moved
Simon to decide upon the only course of action that seemed
both obvious and proper. Accordingly, he supplied himself
with rings and shoes and headed straight for the house of
the father with the two daughters. What was his chagrin
and astonishment, however, when Isaac turned a deaf ear to
his proposals and would have nothing to do with the arguments and entreaties which Simon pressed so urgently. A
less resourceful person would have acknowledged defeat and
would have retired from the scene. Not so Simon. Knowing
the weakness of feminine nature, he abandoned the hard-
headed father and resorted to the more pliable mother.
"Your husband is immovable, it seems; but we have been
such intimate friends," he pleaded, "do accept these gifts
from me for your daughters, anyhow." She was pleased and
accepted the gifts in good faith. They were, however, part
of a plot by which Simon hoped to carry out his matrimonial
plans. He left and soon afterward continued to press his
attentions upon Isaac and, when the latter still remained
inexorable, Simon resorted to a ruse by asserting that the
girls were already betrothed to his sons, for there were the
rings and shoes which he had dèlivered as tokens of betrothal.
He proclaimed this high and low, and the wheels of gossip
were set in rapid motion. Serious complications threatened
to follow; but fortunately, he was speedily brought to justice
and effectively silenced by the Jewish court.[40]

The intrigue and its abortive outcome must not be taken
as typical of mediaeval matchmaking. Matrimonial proposals being in theory, at least, mutually beneficial, the differences were generally smoothed over by the politic parents,

who soon reached an amicable settlement and the engagement was then celebrated with public ceremony. It was a notable social function. All the friends and the relatives of the families were invited.[41] The entire community seemed to participate in the festivities. For the time being, the young couples found themselves to be the center of social attention and their happiness was shared by the whole community.[42] It was considered a peculiarly Jewish merit to extend a helping hand to a poor bride, and many a maid was decked in bridal finery and presented with perhaps a more attractive dowry directly from the communal treasury.[43]

The important feature at the engagement ceremony was the interchange of a solemn pledge between the bride and the bridegroom, or persons representing them, by which the young couple were pledged to present themselves in good faith on a fixed date for the betrothal and wedding ceremonies. The pledge took on the double form of an oath and a substantial fine.[44] The items of the dowry were carefully stipulated and the method and the date of payment were specified.[45] Usually the dowry consisted of money[46] or deeds of loan;[47] sometimes houses and gardens were included.[48] In some instances it was also specified that the bridegroom was not to take a second wife while he was still married to the first. When the affianced lived in different cities, the place of marriage was specified; otherwise, it was to be the city in which the bride lived, for this was the prevailing custom.[49] "It is customary for a man to go in search of a wife, but it does not behoove the woman to go after a husband,"[50] Ibn Adret reminded a remonstrating groom.[51]

While these matters were no doubt arranged in private, the legal formalities were carried out in the presence of the entire assembly.[52] The full agreement was drawn up in

writing, formally witnessed,[53] and the document deposited
with a third party as trustee,[54] to be surrendered to the one
party if the other defaulted.[55] It was customary, in addition,
for the two parties to deposit with the trustee bills of in-
debtedness also to be surrendered in case of default.[56]

It may be assumed that those who gathered for the cele-
bration displayed but little interest in the legal proceedings.
Even the bride, for the most part, remained passive during
the formal proceedings. She was seated in the midst of the
gay assemblage and the *hazzan* arose and proclaimed in
sonorous tones that Reuben has engaged his daughter to
Simeon. Then the bride witnessed the formalities of symbolical delivery, pledging both parties to adhere to the marriage contract, after which she arose before the assembly
and was presented to the bridegroom. He thereupon bestowed upon her a number of presents, which he placed in
her lap.[57] All the guests then repaired to a banquet, and the
festivities of the engagement ended with a hearty repast.[58]

Eager as the parents were to have their children engaged
and their matrimonial plans settled, they did not on that
account hasten the period between the engagement and
the betrothal or the wedding proper. The marriage date
was sometimes set more than two years after the engagement[59] and, in one instance,[60] the "parents were to present their daughter to her fiancé for marriage within four
years." Under a social scheme in which young people were
betrothed at parental behest although hardly known to one
another, sometimes without having seen each other,[61] these
long intervals were certainly a providential arrangement.
For it was during these long periods that they came to
know each other, and the foundations were laid for the love
which was to carry them through life. Not infrequently, of

course, a closer acquaintanceship revealed disagreements and disharmony of purpose in the two characters. In such cases, the engagement could be dissolved without serious impediment.[62] For while they were pledged to each other by oath and the penalty of a fine, it could legally be shown that, under sufficiently provoking circumstances, the oath was not binding and the fine was not to be forfeited.[63] Ibn Adret's decisions were consistently of this tendency,[64] and the numerous instances of broken engagements that occur in the judicial records show that such revocation was feasible when desirable.[65] Undoubtedly, many of the knots that were thus disentangled were those originally tied too eagerly and carelessly, and a great deal of human suffering was averted in good time.

The young man coming gallantly to visit his fiancée would not present himself empty-handed. Delicacies of food, costly dresses and dazzling jewelry were the valued marks of his attentions.[66] The mediaeval young lady seemed to be no less partial to rings with precious stones than her sisters of today.[67] Naturally these expensive compliments were reciprocated by the bride or her family with equally valued presents. A complete outfit of a mule, rabbits' skins, dress and jewelry made up a father's gift to his daughter's fiancé in Toledo.[68] Most of these gifts were indeed luxurious[69] and our young couples must have gloried in their display. Thus the frequent visits and the better understanding of each other, aided by the interchange of costly presents and the consciousness that they were henceforth to share all the fortunes of life in common, knitted the two hearts together and prepared them for the great event when marriage was to unite them permanently in body and soul.

CHAPTER XIII

MARRIAGE CUSTOMS AND CEREMONIES

THE responsa offer but few of the colorful details of the wedding customs and ceremonies. Occasionally a glimpse of a picturesque scene breaks through the legalistic writings. Thus we learn that in Jativa, the betrothal ceremony was preceded by the rhythm of the dance and the beating of drums.[1] Elsewhere it was the custom after the *huppah* ceremony for the bridegroom, saddled on a costly mule, to gallop to the country at the head of a mounted band of friends.[2] We learn something of the treasures and gifts that were bestowed upon the bride at the great feast on her wedding day.[3] One can observe also, as Maimonides did, a streak of superstition in the fact that so many weddings were set for days when the moon was full, a custom defended by the mystical Nahmanides.[4] The subdued spirit that marked the marital union of a widow or divorced woman was in refined contrast to the gay animation that characterized the wedding of youth and virgin.[5] It was the custom of widows, when marrying, quietly to enter the house of the bridegroom on the night of the fifth day of the week and the benedictions were recited on the following morning.[6] But, on the whole, few local embellishments left their traces in the legalistic sources, a loss to the folklorist rather than to the historian.

A strange anachronism persisted in the mediaeval marriage ceremony of the Jews in Spain. This was the ancient custom of separating the wedding into two stages: the preliminary stage of betrothal, or *erusin*, and the wedding proper, called *nissu'in* (taking in). In the talmudic period, this was the universal custom and twelve months were generally allowed to intervene between the two stages to permit the bride sufficient time for the preparation of her trousseau. Unlike the engagement described in the preceding chapter, the betrothal bond of *erusin* was considered a sacred religious union. The betrothed became formally husband and wife, but they were not permitted to live conjugally. With but minor variations, the betrothed couple were bound by the same laws regarding fidelity that applied to those fully married. Dissolution of this bond could be effected only by means of a *get*, or bill of divorce.

Theoretically, the betrothal ceremony could be performed in one of three ways: by the ceremony of the ring or any other gift of the value of a copper coin, accompanied by the statement, "Behold thou art betrothed unto me according to the law of Moses and Israel;" by a written instrument containing the same formula; or by cohabitation. In practice, however, only the first method was used, the second not being much in vogue and the last being rigorously condemned.[7] The presence of two legal witnesses was required, but no religious functionary was needed.[8] Either the bride, the bridegroom or both might be represented by proxy.[9]

The nuptial ceremony, following a year after the betrothal and designated by the term *nissu'in* or *likuhin*, meaning the act of "taking in," constituted the second, the final stage of the wedding. In this ceremony, the groom and the bride went under the cover of the *huppah*, or the canopy, to symbolize the isolation of the bridal chamber and marital union, the benedictions were pronounced and, henceforth, the couple were fully husband and wife. It was customary to recite appropriate benedictions both during the preliminary ceremonies of the *erusin* as well as during the *nissu'in*, but they were not an essential part of the ritual.[10]

Unfortunately, the looseness of the prescribed forms of marriage was hardly compatible with the strictness of the Jewish conscience in all matters pertaining to marriage and family integrity. Thus, on the one hand, the marriage laws were noted for their laxity. The performance of the marriage rite did not require the presence of any special functionary, nor was any particular marriage formula essential. A mere understanding was sufficient.[11] The method of betrothal might be the usual one of bestowing a ring, which was customary[12]— the ring containing no stone[13]— or else by presenting a prayer book,[14] a loaf of bread,[15] a pair of shoes,[16] a coin[17] or a citron.[18] Now, paradoxical as it may seem, this very laxity connected with the ceremony was the height of severity in disguise. A young couple might suddenly find themselves legally united as the result of a jest or mock ceremony.[19] Many an unsuspecting girl was trapped into betrothal by a wily plotter who knew the vulnerability of Jewish law on this point.[20] For it was not even necessary to prove that the betrothal was strictly legal. So exacting was the Jewish conscience in all that touched family life[21] that a mere doubt of marriage hanging over the head of a woman subjected her to all the restrictions of the married state.[22] It required a *get*, or legal divorce, to release her, and this necessity left her exposed virtually to the mercies of her "betrothed." The scandal arising from such cases was always injurious to the cause of morality, and it was obviously necessary to amend these laws if they were not to defeat their own purpose.[23]

We may well turn for illustration to some of those plain, unadorned tales so vividly portrayed in our sources. In one of these, we are introduced to a household where a number of guests were gathered.[24] One of the guests arose and, presenting the daughter of the host with a loaf of bread, said in the hearing of two persons, "Be thou betrothed unto me herewith." The loaf was accepted lightheartedly by the girl who paid no attention to his declaration. Some time later, she was unsuspectingly married in the usual way to an apparently more conventional suitor. But to the consternation and despair of all concerned, the former suitor suddenly appeared before a Jewish court and raised the specter of the fateful loaf of bread which had bound him to the now unlawfully wed bride. The case was only too well proved and the sentence was clear. The unfortunate woman had to leave her husband and to be legally divorced from him as well as from the man whose quaint prank had caused all this misery and ruined her life. Her life was indeed in all probability ruined. For the law strictly forbade her remarriage with her husband, and no reconciliation was ever possible.

What wonder then that the mere thought of such a plight virtually frightened a girl into an hysterical fit, as we learn from the following story: Leah said to Reuben, "Pay me now the debt you owe me." In response, he gave her three *dineros* but also added: "Be thou betrothed unto me." No sooner did Leah hear these words than she angrily flung the money away from her and shrieked, "I do not wish to be betrothed to you." She tore her hair, scratched her face and cried, "Woe that this should have happened to me."[25] Excelling in pathos the sad plight of Hannah in the *Children of the Ghetto* was the fate of an unmarried heroine related in

the prosaic language of a legal work.[26] The story concerns
the not unusual occurrence of a girl breaking an engagement
to one fiancé and becoming engaged to another, who, as
it happened, was a *kohen*. The girl's father, who was an
ignorant man, was persuaded by well-meaning friends to
secure a divorce for his daughter from her first fiancé, so
that no improper rumors could be circulated regarding her.
But, lo and behold, it was soon discovered that this divorce
now made a union between her and her fiancé, the *kohen*,
forever impossible.

Such matters threatened to become dangerous when they
reached the ears of the governmental officials. For the
king was only too eager to interfere in the internal matters
of the community whenever there was fair promise that
an offense could be proved and a fine collected from the
guilty person.[27] Thus the royal personage himself, in one
instance, showed surprising solicitude in the case of a widow
who was claimed in betrothal by one of her relatives,
but against whose claim she protested vehemently, charging him with deliberate fraud and deceit. The king not
only ordered the rabbi personally to investigate and to
pass upon the widow's charges, but he appointed a special
deputy, representing the Crown interests, who was to impose
a fine upon the guilty man if her charges should be sustained.
It, therefore, behooved the communal authorities to devise
effective means to check this evil before it reached alarming
proportions. Accordingly, various plans were submitted to
Ibn Adret for approval, and his advice on this matter was
sought by distant communities.

The problem was universally the same; the solution was
uniformly ineffective. No vigorous attempt was made on
any appreciable scale to meet the question in the manner it

deserved. Ibn Adret believed the evil could be remedied by devices of a legal character: "Every person should train his household and teach his daughters to deny themselves by solemn vow the use or benefit of any valuables that would ever be given to them as a means of betrothal, unless it be in the presence of certain specified persons." Such had been the custom, according to Ibn Adret, in no less venerable a family than that of Sherira Gaon. "Thus have I taught the daughters of our city at different times," were his concluding words.[28]

Mere advice, however, is no reform; and this purely personal suggestion did not have the force of a communal measure. Various enactments accordingly were adopted in order to render impossible the clandestine marriage, in which the woman was always placed at a disadvantage, and to protect the community generally from the demoralization caused by unscrupulous men. In many places it was decreed by communal statute that no marriage was valid unless it was sanctioned by the presence and consent of the bride's parents, if living, or else her nearest relatives.[29] In some communities, the presence of a public functionary, like the *hazzan*, or the *ne'emanim*, was also made a fundamental requirement.[30] To declare the marriage invalid, it was necessary to confiscate the money or other gift of betrothal, and the man consequently found himself doubly beaten.[31] Sometimes, however, the Jewish court awarded him financial restitution.[32]

On the whole, these protective measures were eminently unsatisfactory. For, in the last analysis, owing to the timidity of the rabbis in interpreting the law, the very strictness of the Jewish conscience in matters of matrimony was bound to defeat itself. Though irregular courtships and marriages were banned as invalid by these ordinances, could it for a moment be thought that a marriage ceremony performed according to the law of Moses and Israel, but not complying with the local ordinance, was to be totally disregarded and the couple set free without a divorce?[33] Consequently, the problem remained unsolved, and the proposed solutions were, to say the least, of problematic value. At best, they served only as a deterrent influence.[34]

The abuses described thus far were connected, in the main, with the early marital stage of betrothal, known as *erusin*. Had it been possible to abolish this preliminary form of quasi-marriage, many of the abuses would have been prevented. Such abolishment was not attempted, but a tendency gradually developed to combine the betrothal and the marriage into one ceremony, a process which marked a distinct social advance.[35] For in any event, it must have been obvious that an arrangement which provided for a married state, from which marital life was excluded, reduced the social barrier between the betrothed and fostered intimacy under circumstances in which the keenness of the moral dictate was apt to be blunted.[36] But even this improvement was not vigorously pressed. Throughout the Middle Ages — indeed, as late as the fifteenth century — the older custom still persisted[37] side by side with the tendency to merge the two stages of marriage into one ceremony.[38] Several centuries elapsed before this social innovation was made a mandatory measure by communal statute.

Perhaps the older custom was not without its uses. It must be conceded that it served as a convenient medium for child marriages when it was not desirable for the young couple to live maritally.[39] It also made possible marriages by proxy, which the migratory condition of Jewish life naturally fostered.[40] These advantages, however, did not compensate for the potential abuses which inhered in the arrangement, nor for the greater indictment which may be brought against it for having facilitated in some countries a system of concubinage similar to that which prevailed among the non-Jewish population and, we may add, with similarly unhappy consequences.

The status of concubinage has not received due treatment in the social history of Europe.[41] In Christendom during the early Middle Ages, the concubine was legally recognized by Church and State as a sort of quasi-wife, provided that there was no legal wife with prior claims.[42] In the later period, the concubine was regarded as a necessary concession to the enforced celibacy of the priesthood. Thus the Church Council of Valladolid, in 1322, complained bitterly of the parishioners who compelled their priests to take female consorts in order to protect the virtue of their families.[43] Among the Jews, the institution of concubinage had a totally different origin. As celibacy had no standing in Jewish ethical doctrine, there was no room for a counterfeit substitute of marriage. By example as well as by doctrine, the rabbis taught that marriage was the ideal state and was indispensable for holy living. In those countries where monogamy was the existing order, the concubine was ruled out from public consideration. It was only in Mohammedan countries, where polygamy was still tolerated, or even in Christian Spain where, under extenuating circumstances, the rabbis would permit a second marriage, that concubinage was at least a legal possibility. Even under these favorable conditions, however, the Jewish conscience would not countenance unsanctified cohabitation. But when the concubine was married by means of the preliminary marriage of "betrothal," or *erusin*, the question of public policy became a debatable subject.

The rabbis dealt with the subject characteristically by the process of legal interpretation. At the outset, they were handicapped by the fact that the Bible countenanced the concubine, or *pilegesh*, without censure. This difficulty was also encountered by the earlier rabbis of the talmudic period. But with these, the subject was purely academic, since concubinage was then nonexistent among Jews. Consequently, they were not very helpful to their rabbinical successors who were compelled to face the problem realistically in later ages.

Their treatment of the question centered almost wholly on the definition of the Hebrew term *pilegesh*, or concubine. Although in the Bible the term is obviously used unrestrictedly, the talmudic teachers could not conceive of the Bible tolerating a union of the sexes without the sanctification of religious ceremonial. In characteristic fashion, therefore, they proceeded to read into the Bible their own definition of *pilegesh*, by which the free concubine of Bible days was converted into a quasi-legal wife who was betrothed in a religious ceremony, but was unprovided with a *ketubah*, or marriage contract, according to R. Meir, or with the additional stipulations customary in the marriage settlement, according to R. Judah.[44] As indicated, this discussion was purely theoretical. The institution itself was unknown, as can be judged from the fact that no concrete instance of concubinage is to be found in the Talmud.

Unfortunately for the mediaeval rabbis, this clear but unreal definition of *pilegesh* was recorded in the Jerusalem Talmud but not in the Babylonian version. In the latter, which was better known and more authoritative, only a later tradition of the early Amoraim is mentioned, to wit: a wife is one who had been duly betrothed and been given a *ketubah*; a *pilegesh*, or concubine, is one who had neither been betrothed nor given the necessary *ketubah*.[45] The definition was obviously inadequate, for it failed to determine the status of the one type that troubled the public conscience — the semi-wedded concubine who was blessed by the ceremony of *erusin*, but who had not the consummating sanction of the *nissu'in* and the *ketubah*.

Emphatically, the concubine, who was a mistress living in unsanctified cohabitation,[46] constituted no problem. Only a few instances of such relationships occur in the responsa and these were summarily repressed by the communal authorities as soon as they became known. Thus R. Asher said: "Not only has the family of the girl (who was said to live as concubine with her master) a right to protest against her remaining in his employment, but the Jewish court on its own initiative is constrained to compel the man to discharge her."[47] Such a woman was free to abandon her consort at will and, likewise, he was under no conjugal obligations to her.[48] No marital relationship existed between them, so that a man's mistress could afterward become his brother's legal wife.[49]

It was quite different, however, with the "betrothed concubine." A correspondent of Rabbi Asher testified that in his town, "It is quite customary to betroth women and then to dwell and cohabit with them without the wedding ceremony of the *huppah* and the sanctification of the marriage benedictions."[50] R. Asher referred to a concubine in the unusual phrase, a woman "who was betrothed unto him in concubinage."[51] Finally, the popular frame of mind is shown in the attitude of a Toledo Jew who set his Moorish

slave free, converted her to Judaism and then lived with
her after the betrothal ceremony. Although public sentiment was aroused against him and, indeed, there was a
communal ban against such a practice, he insisted on his
right to live with her, stating that he was committing no
wrong but that, if Ibn Adret would consider mere betrothal
insufficient, he would wed her properly and make her his
wife.[52] This, it should be remembered, was the conscientious
reply of a law-abiding citizen.

The task of the rabbis was a delicate one. With one
voice, they denounced the practice of concubinage with or
without *erusin*. In a community where knowledge of the
law was not the exclusive monopoly of a caste, this was by
no means a simple matter. For the rabbis, faithful to the
law, could not and would not deny that the Bible did not
discountenance concubinage, while the talmudic teachers
had no occasion to abrogate it. Maimonides, however,
resorted to the ingenious theory that the Pentateuchal
instances of polygamy reflected pre-Sinaitic custom which
was abrogated by the Law,[53] while the examples of polygamy in the later books of the Bible reflected the exclusive
prerogative of royalty.[54] To the nation at large, he ruled,
concubinage was strictly forbidden. But this apparently
clear dictum was promptly thrown into confusion by the
commentators who could not agree as to which form of
concubinage Maimonides thus proscribed. Much more difficult was the position of Nahmanides, who by legal reasoning was forced involuntarily to the conclusion that concubinage was both biblically and rabbinically lawful, but
was nevertheless aware of its harm to social morality.
He thus ended a plea to his colleague and correspondent,
R. Jonah: "But thou, O teacher, the Lord grant thee life,

in thy place thou shalt warn them carefully against the practice, for if its lawfulness should be generally accepted, it will lead ultimately to immoral intercourse, and the laws of purity will not be observed."[55] From whatever angle they viewed the legal theory, Ibn Adret, Rabbi Asher, and also Barfat at the close of the fourteenth century, denounced the practice in precept and exhortation.[56] An ethical teacher of the fourteenth century, in a code which was addressed especially to the upper classes, deplored the growing custom of taking concubines in betrothal, stating that it would be less reprehensible to keep a mistress or resort to polygamy.[57]

If the rabbis did not succeed in completely abolishing the practice of concubinage, their influence no doubt led to its gradual elimination. In the last resort, concubinage was a modified form of polygamy and existed only in those provinces where the latter was tolerated.[58] It justified itself in the popular mind as being less aggravating than the state of polygamy where the plural wives were equal rivals.[59] The practice of concubinage was sometimes invoked with pious intention even in the monogamous parts of Spain, when a marriage proved childless after ten years.[60] Under these circumstances, it was a convenient substitute for remarriage, which might have necessitated the divorce of the childless wife. Finally, in some communities, concubinage, semi-sanctified through betrothal, took on the form of a trial marriage, so that, if children resulted from the union, the complete, sanctified wedding followed.[61] It was in contributing toward this situation that the persistence of the old talmudic division of the wedded state into two stages, removed from each other by a long interval of time, proved injurious to the moral well-being of the Spanish communities.

A discussion of the Jewish marriage ceremony is incomplete without reference to the *ketubah*, or marriage contract. The *ketubah*, literally a written instrument, was the marriage agreement which the bridegroom handed to the bride after its contents were read aloud by the religious functionary, or *hazzan*, during the benedictions under the canopy.[62] This document may be described as the rabbinic charter of woman's rights. Both in form and content, it represented an evolution of over a thousand years' development. Its origin can be traced to Babylonian and Hebrew roots. Though it was an integral part of Hebrew tradition, it had striking parallels in pagan custom. Its development may be traced continuously through the Bible, the Apocrypha and Hellenistic literature to its final rabbinic composition in the quaint Aramaic language.[63]

Technically, the *ketubah* was a deed transcribing in official legal language the terms of the marriage agreement. It included various provisions required by biblical and rabbinical legislation and, in addition, other settlements which the wife received from the husband, either as a result of local custom or through special agreement among the interested parties. The husband pledged in simple but dignified words:

> I shall work for thee, honor, support and maintain thee in accordance with the custom of Jewish husbands who work for their wives and honor, support and maintain them in truth.

The duty to fulfill the more intimate marital relationship was then stated:

> And I shall go with thee according to the ways of the world.

The essential feature of the *ketubah*, however, was the clause which guaranteed to the wife her dower rights. In case of divorce or widowhood, she was awarded a sum of money which, by rabbinical ordinance, was fixed as two hundred *zuzim* for a virgin and half of this amount for one previously married.[64] This was the fixed minimum to which the poorest woman in Israel was entitled.[65] If it was within the means of the husband, propriety required that he should make an additional settlement (תוספת כתובה) on his wife.[66] With a similar object in view, it was customary already in tannaitic days to include in the *ketubah* an itemized statement of all her property and personal belongings, which she transferred as dowry to the husband for the use of the family, and for the principal of which the husband declared himself responsible to her and her heirs.[67] Social vanity soon established the naive custom in many communities to represent the value of the articles mentioned in the inventory at double and treble their real worth, though it was clearly understood by all that the husband's liability extended only to the actual and not the inflated value.[68] With becoming but inexpensive generosity, the husband added a personal endowment toward his wife's settlement, which euphemism required to be at least equal to the stated "value" of the dowry which she brought to his household.[69] Under such circumstances, his real obligation was usually commensurate with the actual worth of her dowry, but not infrequently this additional settlement was merely a social formality involving no financial obligation.[70] The consequence of these manipulations was to inflate the value of the *ketubah* to its maximum and, as conditions varied bewilderingly with time and place, the reduction of the *ketubah* to its true value became at times a complicated fiscal problem.[71]

This strictly legal instrument with its detailed monetary provisions was converted by the rabbis into a subtle instrument that served an ethical purpose. It was deliberately designed by them as a safeguard for the wife and mother, and as an anchor in troubled marital seas. Because talmudic law adopted the lenient view of Hillel that the husband was permitted to divorce his wife at will and rejected the stricter opinion of Shammai, which recognized adultery as the only ground for divorce, the rabbis felt it incumbent upon them to counteract the abuses rendered possible by the husband's arbitrary power. They were morally sensitive to the danger which threatened the relationship between husband and wife when they were both aware that he could practically divorce her at will. They therefore seized upon the *ketubah* as a wholesome check upon masculine arbitrariness. Without curtailing his power in theory, they declared it mandatory for all the provisions of the *ketubah* to be met in advance as an indispensable condition of the divorce.[72] In many cases, this made divorce economically impossible. In any event, the settlement of its numerous provisions involved elaborate financial adjustments which required much time, thus affording the distracted couple a psychological period for the peaceful solution of their marital difficulties.

The *ketubah* was also a convenient instrument for the insertion of other clauses in the interest of the woman. One of these provisions, as we shall see, was the all-important renunciation by the husband of his right to marry another woman while he was wedded to his present wife. This was particularly important in countries where the ban of R. Gershom against polygamy was not legally recognized.

On the other hand, the *ketubah* was an instrument that could also be used against feminine caprice and willfulness. Thus, if the woman refused to perform her wifely duties or if she violated the code of honor — "if," in mishnaic phraseology, "she transgressed the Mosaic law or womanly etiquette" — she forfeited the provisions of the *ketubah*, in whole or in part.[73] Consequently, in all conjugal disputes, whenever a divorce was proposed or contested either by the husband or the wife, the *ketubah* was the focusing point of the contending arguments; and the court's verdict directing that the *ketubah* be honored or canceled was interpreted also as its judgment on the legal and moral issues of the contest.

We may thus understand the rabbinical insistence that no marriage was proper without the *ketubah*. Without this document, they declared, the wife was reduced to the level of a concubine.[74] Rabbi Meir, famous *tanna* of the second century, was authority for the statement that without the *ketubah* the union of husband and wife was unhallowed cohabitation.[75] This view prevailed even when the husband was stripped of the power to divorce his wife at will. When the Jews of France, robbed of all their possessions, were expelled en masse by Philip the Fair, in 1306, and flocked to the Provence, the word of Ibn Adret in Spain went forth to them that every man should deliver a new *ketubah* to his wife, for "thus have the sages ordained formerly for the exiles in Gerona."[76] Conjugal relationship among the exiles was virtually suspended until they complied with this ordinance.[77]

Yet it is obvious that the *ketubah* alone did not solve all the problems of one-sided divorces and further checks had to be devised to prevent frequent abuses. Nevertheless, it was

a factor of the greatest ethical import and was turned to
ingenious use to raise the status of the woman in marriage
and to create healthy resistance to the disruptive elements
that threatened the integrity and stability of family relationships.

CHAPTER XIV

DOMESTIC LIFE

IN VIEW of the many youthful marriages,[1] it will be readily perceived that the period of domestic life included a stretch of years of family dependence. It was a natural expedient for the parents of either the bride or the bridegroom — it was the parents of the latter usually — to house and maintain the young family for a number of years,[2] a social practice which later was highly developed among Jews in Eastern Europe. This arrangement often proved embarrassing to the young housewife and led to many family disturbances. Thus the responsa, which reflect the pathos of much of the family unhappiness that is bound to appear in a court, while showing comparative freedom from the serious complaints of marital infidelity,[3] often reveal the keen suffering of the young wife from the tongue of an exasperating mother-in-law[4] or sometimes, though far less often, from the reproaches of an inconsiderate father-in-law.[5] The Bet Din usually showed sympathy for the young woman and invariably acted in the interest of the peace and happiness of the wedded couple.[6] No complaint was refused a solicitous hearing. Each case was carefully investigated, and neighbors as well as discreet and indiscreet relatives were called upon to testify regarding what they knew about the domestic quarrels and their origin. In the eleventh century it was a widespread practice of the Jewish courts to appoint a woman investigator to live for a time with the

47

troubled family in order to ascertain by personal observation
the true cause of the domestic infelicity.[7] If the interest of
peace required the removal of the couple from the parental
roof, the court ordered the husband to establish an independent household.[8] In the meantime, he had to pay for
his wife's maintenance under the more favorable shelter of
her own parental home.[9] If he refused to comply with the
recommendation of the court, he was compelled to grant his
wife a divorce upon her demand and to pay the full settlements of the marriage contract, or *ketubah*, as well as to
make complete restitution of her dowry.[10]

A woman who left her husband because she found her
home with his parents intolerable was defended by Ibn Adret
with this declaration:

> The husband has no right to hurt and afflict his wife.
> It is her duty to live with him but not to suffer under
> him. Indeed he must hold her dearer than himself.
> If the husband seeks to place the blame on the wife,
> the court should investigate the matter and if they
> find that she deserted him because of cruel treatment,
> they should vindicate her, for no person can be com-
> pelled to live with a serpent in a cage . . . It is the
> duty of the court to reprimand and to chastise the
> husband and to warn him that, upon repetition of the
> offense, he would be compelled to divorce his wife and
> make payment of the *ketubah* . . . Moreover, if the
> wife declines to live on the same premises with her
> husband's mother, she may say to him, "I will not
> live with people who provoke me and cause ill feeling
> to exist between me and my husband."[11]

Thus, with kind but firm hand, the *Bet Din* exercised
paternal vigilance and helped to solve some of the initial
marital difficulties. There were, however, adverse circum-

stances attending Jewish life in the Middle Ages, beyond
the control of local agencies, which proved inherently hostile
to the peace of the Jewish household. First and foremost,
there were the hazards of Jewish life itself. While feudalism
rooted the general population to the soil, the Jew was pre-
eminently the wanderer. Persecutions, precarious economic
conditions, the enmity of a rapacious official or the inevitable infractions of the numerous restrictive regulations of
the Crown forced many a Jewish family out upon the highways, braving the perils that attended distant travels in
those days, particularily for Jews.[12] The brave woman
loyally followed her husband and shared his dangers, but
it was not always possible to do so. This led to family
desertion and at times also to repeated marriages in countries where, as in Spain, the bar against polygamy had only
limited application.[13] Far more frequently, death, shrouded
in mystery and unknown to the anxious family, prevented
the return of the wanderer.[14] The helplessness of the family
during the protracted absence of its head, the plight of the
woman who remained for years in suspense about the fate
of her husband have left their sad traces in the responsa of
every age and country. Countless women whose husbands
left, never to return, were compelled to end their days in
marital solitude, as there was no legal means to declare them
free. This gave rise to the tragic figure of the 'agunah, who
was neither wife, widow nor divorcée, and whose sorrowful
fate has haunted the pages of Jewish social history. She is
to this day the victim or the sacrifice offered on the altar of
the Jewish conscience.

Many methods were attempted to remedy this lurking
danger. A communal statute of the eleventh century ruled
that "he who betrothed a maiden in this town must declare

in advance that the marriage was conditional and that, if
he absented himself for a full year, the marriage was to
stand annulled and his wife was to be free to remarry without
a divorce."[15] This drastic measure is to be understood only
in the light of the political and religious upheaval in Spain
and North Africa toward the end of the eleventh century.[16]
Later the conditional marriage was substituted by the conditional divorce. Thus, in the early part of the fourteenth
century, if a man undertook a distant journey, the court
compelled him to draw up a conditional divorce which took
effect automatically if he did not return by a specified date.[17]
Indeed, it was a widespread custom of considerate husbands to perform this act of kindness on their own initiative.[18] At times, the young bridegroom was requested by
the bride's father on the day of the wedding to take a
solemn oath never to leave the city without his permission[19]
or, more reasonably, not to remain out of the city more than
three or four months during the year.[20] Moreover, the
man who removed from the domicile of his wife without
her consent was subject to a considerable fine. This was
considered an old established rule in all the Spanish countries
as early as the eleventh century.[21] But this precautionary
measure availed little later in life when serious reverses set
in. It became necessary then to invoke the firm hand of the
law and to be guided by its standards. The husband could
be legally restrained from removing to another town if his
wife objected to it.[22] Not even the longing for the Holy
Land was permitted, according to R. Nissim Gerundi, to
supersede the pleadings of the wife.[23] Only if unable to
earn a livelihood did the husband have the right to call
upon her to settle with him in a place where there were
better opportunities.[24] Even then there were limitations to

the extent to which she was legally obliged to follow her husband's wanderings.[25] If he made unlawful demands upon her, she could, through the *Bet Din,* obtain a divorce from him as well as the payment of her *ketubah.*[26] It is a significant tribute to the loyalty of the Jewish woman that these marital difficulties appear in far fewer cases than the circumstances actually warranted and that they belonged mainly to the more troubled periods of the Middle Ages.

The Spanish archives as well as the responsa yield occasional references to plural marriages which were sanctioned by Jewish law and for this reason allowed by the king.[27] From this it is not to be inferred that polygamy was normally tolerated in all the Spanish communities. Undoubtedly custom varied considerably in this regard, the degree of tolerance to plural marriages being an indication of the relative strength of the Mohammedan influence in the community. In Castile and the adjacent territories under Moorish control, polygamy was tolerated by law and not unknown in practice.[28] In the responsa of Alfasi, reflecting the Mohammedan background of the eleventh century, polygamy is depicted as a not uncommon state.[29] Thus, in a heated quarrel with his wife, a man vowed not to return to his home until he had the means of marrying a rival wife. It is true that when, in the course of events, neither fortune nor maid could be cajoled to smile favorably on him despite his desperate wooing of both, he appeared penitently before a rabbi, wishing to retract his hasty oath. It is also true that the rabbi not only reprimanded him but pointed out that there never was any validity to the oath which violated his sacred obligations as husband. Nevertheless, the sanction of polygamy under more favorable circumstances is not impugned in any phase of the discussion.[30] Maimonides,

who prohibited concubinage, permitted polygamy in theory.[31] In the territory which had strong Mohammedan
influence, plural marriages continued also in the thirteenth
and fourteenth centuries.[32]

As the Moorish influence declined, tolerance of polygamy
waned. In the kingdom of Aragon and Catalonia, therefore,
polygamy was forbidden and unheard of except under
special, extenuating circumstances.[33] Ibn Adret thus ruled
that Maimonides' sanction of polygamy was not valid where
popular practice tacitly rejected what the codifiers permitted.[34] To be sure, it was still an open question in the
time of Ibn Adret whether and to what extent the ban
against plural marriages, promulgated in France and Germany by Rabbenu Gershom in the eleventh century, applied
to Spain.[35] But Ibn Adret's teaching and testimony were
clear and emphatic. Normally monogamy was strictly the
rule in Aragon and Catalonia. Only when the first marriage
proved childless after a period of ten years did the question
arise whether bigamy was not the lesser evil, if the other
alternative was the divorce of the first wife. Ibn Adret
stated the law in his reply to a distant community where a
case of bigamy aroused deep resentment:

> God forbid [he exclaimed], it has never happened in
> our midst that a man should be guilty of such an
> offense — not even the most disreputable man —
> to sin openly with his slave, to proselytize her and to
> marry her; especially, as in this case, to repel on her
> account the wife of his bosom. The altar of God sheds
> tears for such as these. Already in olden times the
> Gaon Rabbenu Gershom, the Light of the Exile —
> may his memory be for a blessing — pronounced the
> ban against any one who, while wedded to his wife,
> would marry another woman — even a woman who

ranked as the equal of his first wife — how much more
so a woman of this character. In only two or three
instances has it happened in these parts that a
man married a second wife, and in each case it was
because the first wife bore her husband no children.
Even under these extenuating circumstances, however, the man did not presume to act thus except after
numerous entreaties of his first wife, and I have not
yet seen any of these marriages end happily.[36]

So severe was the attitude toward bigamy in the northern
provinces that, at times, the state declared it a capital
crime,[37] although consistency was hardly to be expected of
Spanish kings.[38] Even in Castile and in the Mohammedan
provinces, however, plural marriages were comparatively
rare exceptions. Without reference to the famous ban of the
Franco-German rabbi, the custom developed in these countries to insert a clause in the engagement contract (שטר
שידוכין), and in the ketubah as well, in which the husband
solemnly covenanted not to marry another woman during
the lifetime of his wife.[39] This custom covered as with a
network all the communities which had not joined in the ban
of Rabbenu Gershom. Notwithstanding the theoretical
sanction of his code, Maimonides fathered communal enactments which effectively eliminated plural marriages in
Egypt.[40]

When the marital union proved childless after ten years,
however, an inevitable clash of loyalties ensued. Was the
marriage to be preserved when it failed of its main purpose?
Was the rabbinical ban of polygamy or the private marriage
agreement to supersede the divine purpose of marriage, the
first and primary command of the Bible, "Be fruitful and
multiply?" Obviously, if the biblical exhortation was to
be given primacy, there were only two alternatives: com-

pulsory divorce, if monogamy was to be adhered to, or permission to the husband to marry another woman. In Spain,
popular opinion favored the latter course and it found
weighty rabbinic support, notwithstanding the fact that in
the Talmud barrenness was clearly recognized as a legitimate
cause for divorce.[41] Thus, when a correspondent from
Castellón asked Ibn Adret whether the ban against polygamy was also intended to apply in cases where the wife was
childless, he replied:

> Whatever may have been the intention of its formula-
> tor, this enactment, in the strict interpretation that is
> proposed, has not been accepted within our borders.
> Moreover, we have not heard of its acceptance even
> in the domains of the Provence, although they border
> directly on France. In actual life, we have observed
> scholars and leading men of the community as well as
> many others married to second wives (when the first
> wife was childless) and no one has ever questioned the
> propriety of their acts.[42]

R. Asher wrote similarly that, talmudic law notwithstanding, it was an established custom not to divorce the wife
who bore her husband no children.[43] In the same strain,
his son and successor, R. Judah, wrote: "While we do not
compel a childless wife to accept a divorce and the payment
of her *ketubah*, we do permit the husband to marry another
woman." For it was not the intention of R. Gershom to
include this class in the prohibition, adds the German-born
rabbi.[44] The clearest statement on the subject, strangely
enough, is contained in the royal license issued to no less a
personage than the famous philosopher and rabbi of Saragossa, Hasdai Crescas, on May 18, 1393, permitting him to

marry a second wife, "inasmuch as Hebrew law views this course as not only permissible but obligatory."[45]

A royal permit was requisite for all second marriages and was granted frequently.[46] The penalty for entering into such a marriage without official license was severe — the death penalty is mentioned in a responsum.[47] What is of primary significance, however, is the fact that the compromise with the ideal of monogamy under these circumstances originated from a deeply religious and moral conviction, and was attributable in part to kindly and tender feeling for the first wife. The sympathy that was felt for the unfortunate woman is noticeable in nearly all the rabbinic decisions, and it is also evident how often the husband's resolve to marry another woman was reached only after a long inner struggle between duty and affection.[48] Full consideration was taken of the painful position of the woman and various measures were adopted to alleviate what was at best a hard lot. According to the code of Maimonides, she had the right to demand maintenance in a separate home.[49] If she preferred, on the other hand, to be totally released from the painful embarrassment of sharing with another woman the rights over her husband's person, he was promptly instructed to grant her a divorce and honorably to meet every provision of the ketubah.[50] In a surprising number of instances, she took this spirited, heroic course rather than submit to a life that was a reproach and humiliation to her even with the tenderest of husbands.

The religious motive of begetting children also entered as a complicating factor when the husband died without issue. The Bible provided two alternatives: the more ancient levirate marriage wherein a brother of the deceased took the widow to wife, or the later substitute ceremony of *halizah* which was the equivalent of divorce and is described in Deuteronomy.[51] Although levirate marriages were distinctly discountenanced in the Talmud,[52] they continued in Spain as a common practice throughout the Middle Ages, even when the levir was married, thus giving rise to another category of bigamous marriage.[53] This was in marked contrast to the custom in France and Germany where *halizah* was substituted for the levirate marriage as a matter of course.[54]

The lot of the woman who was thus called upon to continue the marital bond was trying indeed. The new claimant that was assigned to her by the decree of heaven — as the rabbis phrased it — was at times a grotesque mate for the woman, owing to differences of age or stature, not to speak of more serious blemishes.[55] The ideal of establishing the name of the deceased was not without pathos, but popular belief cynically discredited the notion that an unselfish or holy motive ever inspired levirate unions.[56] The fact that by entering into marriage with his brother's widow he became the sole heir of his estate[57] gave an unfortunate touch of plausibility to the popular skepticism.[58] At best it was but poor comfort for a bereaved woman to find herself in duty linked to a man who claimed her on the basis of a biblical commandment.

What wonder then that in the majority of cases the woman violently objected to the levirate marriage?[59] If the brother consented, the biblical ceremony of *halizah* was duly performed, and the widow became a free divorced woman. This was the usual course and met with the hearty approval of the rabbinic teachers. But with an unscrupulous man, the woman was placed at a fearful disadvantage. She could not be coerced into marriage, but she could be forced into a position of "revolt." By taking this stand, she not only forfeited her *ketubah*, which represented her entire fortune, but she ran the risk of remaining in a sort of bonded widowhood.[60] It is significant that the only threat of suicide mentioned in the thousands of rabbinic responsa of Spain was made by a desperate woman who clamored to be freed by the ceremony of *halizah*.[61] In this respect, the Spanish Jewess fared worse than her sister in Germany. In the latter country, the Jewish court coerced the *yabam*, or levir, to free his brother's wife;[62] but in Spain, where the view prevailed that the levirate marriage was more in harmony with the spirit of the Bible than *halizah*, which was only an evasion, the rabbis could not consistently use compulsion to enforce the performance of the less meritorious act.[63] Nevertheless, they attempted by earnest exhortation and prudent counsel to accomplish the object for which they would not use force. If necessary, they even advised the woman to hold out tempting offers of money to move her brother-in-law from his fixed purpose, offers which she was not in duty bound to honor later.[64] It was only when the court recognized that his motive was one of sheer cruelty or deliberate extortion that it used the full power at its command to compel him honorably to free the widow by submitting to the *halizah* ceremony.[65] Fortunate indeed was the woman whose husband spared her these trying ordeals by preparing a conditional divorce for her at the first sign of approaching death. This thoughtful and considerate act, inspired by love, was not uncommon.[66]

No permanent advance in the status of woman was possible through marriage reforms without a corresponding change in the laws of divorce. For the view which prevailed in talmudic law conferred upon the husband the arbitrary right to divorce his wife freely without cause and even against her will. This alone would have been sufficient to nullify whatever gains she might otherwise have won. It was therefore an indication of wise social planning when the progressive abolition of polygamy was accompanied simultaneously by steps leading to the removal of the husband's arbitrary powers in divorce. Thus, in France and Germany, the same edict which put polygamy under the ban also nullified the man's right to divorce his wife without her consent. In Spain, the course taken was less drastic. Reform by legislative fiat on a nation-wide scale was not congenial to the individualistic spirit of the *aljama*. The same goal, however, was effectively attained by the more experimental method of diversified local ordinances, supported by the aid of the government. Thus an early communal enactment imposed a heavy fine on the husband who divorced his wife without her consent and compelled him to pay this penalty to his wife in addition to all the provisions and settlements of the marriage contract.[67] In another community, at a later date, a more logical enactment provided that no divorce was to be written without the authorization of the *kahal* officials,[68] thus subordinating the will of the individual to the judgment of the public authorities. In addition to these and other communal ordinances, the aid of the government was invoked and a compulsory divorce was strictly forbidden under the penalty of fines and corporal punishment.[69] In one instance, at least, it was declared a crime for which the punishment was death.[70] Rabbi Nissim Gerundi, in the middle of the fourteenth century, was therefore able to make the sweeping assertion, "This prohibition (against compulsory divorces) has spread among all Jewries. We have never seen or heard of a woman being divorced against her will."[71]

The development of the woman's status in divorce was not solely negative, however. Her right to be freed from an intolerable marital state was also recognized. Although Jewish law did not confer upon a woman the right to give her husband a writ of divorce, the Mishna recognized various grounds by reason of which the woman could properly seek relief and have the Jewish court compel her husband to grant her the desired divorce.[72] The causes recognized in the Mishna were denial of the woman's conjugal rights, cruelty and improper encroachment upon her personal liberty.[73] As human nature cannot always govern its likes and dislikes on the basis of legal classification, the Mishna also treated the case of the "rebellious" wife, who refused to live with her husband out of malice or anger or who denied herself to her husband because his person was revolting to her in an uncontrollable manner.[74] Such an attitude could not be condoned and the woman, after due warning, was penalized by a gradual confiscation of her *ketubah*.[75] In this classic Mishna, no mention is made of the divorce. It is implied that with the confiscation of the *ketubah* the husband would of his own accord grant the woman her divorce, but evidently he was under no compulsion to do so. A surprising development, however, ensued early in the geonic period. By special ordinance, known as the *takkanah* of the geonim, it was decreed that even the "rebellious" woman was entitled to a divorce upon demand, that the *ketubah* was to be paid her in full, and that the court was in duty bound to use force upon the husband if he proved recalcitrant.[76] This was indeed an astonishing legal coup. The *takkanah* was incorporated in Alfasi's code and it became law in many parts of Spain.[77]

Maimonides did not concede the *ketubah* to the "rebel,"but
he upheld her right to the divorce, "as she was no captive!"[78]
When therefore the husband's right to divorce his wife at
will was curtailed, the woman really enjoyed an unequal
advantage. But her triumph was brief. A reaction inevitably followed. Ibn Adret in Aragon and Rabbi Asher in
Castile opposed the measure with great vigor. The former
wrote to a correspondent in Saragossa: "The *takkanah* never
spread to any of these lands and was possibly framed by the
geonim only for their own generation." R. Asher was provoked to more emphatic expression:

> I believe, moreover, that the geonim who adopted
> the *takkanah* did so in answer to an immediate need
> of their own times respecting the daughters of Israel.
> Since then the situation has changed completely.
> The women of this generation are not to be trusted.[80]
> Know thou that it is an evil custom to compel the
> man to give a bill of divorce except in the cases speci-
> fied by our sages, as I have already written elabo-
> rately in my code.[81] From the day that I arrived in
> this country, I have exerted my influence in all of
> Castile to restrain them from such acts of compulsion.[82]

He therefore condemned the elders of the city who impris-
oned a man upon his refusal to divorce his wife at her
request, and who kept him in chains, afflicting him nigh
unto death, and persistently persecuted him after he had
once made good his escape.[83] "Nevertheless," he wrote in
another responsum, "my decision has reference only to the
present and the future; but as to the past, if the courts
relied on the authority of Maimonides, their decisions
stand."[84] The efforts of these two eminent authorities were
crowned with success, and the issue was no longer raised in

the responsa of the succeeding Spanish rabbis.[85] Thus the talmudic position was regained for the wife but not for the husband, and the two partners in marriage became mutually dependent in matters of divorce.

As these decisions indicate, Jewish law interfered only with the compulsory dissolution of the marriage bond when it was at the behest of one party. The rabbis deplored the occurrence of divorce as ethically tragic. Picturesquely and poignantly, a teacher of the third century painted the sorrows of a broken home: "The altar of God sheds tears for one who divorces his first wife."[86] Nevertheless, Jewish teachers also recognized the need and validity of divorce. If, therefore, despite all efforts at conciliation, both husband and wife were convinced that peaceful life was forever impossible between them, a divorce was regarded as frankly desirable and no objection was interposed by the Jewish authorities.[87] The elimination of such homes emphasized the qualities of the ideal household. Furthermore, if the adultery of the wife polluted the family hearth, Jewish law sternly demanded the complete severance of the marital tie. Even the united passionate pleading of husband and wife could not avail then. A home desecrated was irrevocably disrupted. A compulsory divorce, ordered and decreed by the court, completed the act.[88] The excessive punctilious formalism that attended the writing and the delivery of the divorce was but the legalistic expression of a deep moral conviction of the sanctity of the wedded state.

Disintegrated family life naturally occupies a disproportionate place in the records of court proceedings. Needless to say, however, Jewish law was equally concerned with the protection of the personal and economic rights of the woman in marriage and with measures for safeguarding the interests of the widow and the dependent orphan. Unless the wife was guilty of desertion, the husband was responsible for her support and medical care, even if she became insane, and he was not permitted to evade these responsibilities by charging the costs to her wealthy father or by deducting them from the *ketubah*.[89]

He could not lay claim to her jewelry or clothing even if she deserted him.[90] Likewise the burial rites and the erection of a suitable tombstone in her memory were duties that devolved upon him and were enforced, if necessary, by the Jewish court.[91] On the other hand, her property rights were narrowly restricted in talmudic legislation. Her earnings, if she had any, belonged to the husband in lieu of her support.[92] Theoretically, too, she had almost no independent property rights. The possessions which she acquired prior or subsequent to her marriage were hers only in title. The principal belonged to her, but the interest or usufruct belonged to her husband, unless the donor specifically excluded him as a condition of the gift.[93] In Lerida—and in other communities too, no doubt—all gifts from the husband were treated as belonging to the latter category and were at her free disposal.[94] But she could not validly make such reservation for gifts from other sources.[95] As a result, she was virtually not liable for damages.[96] It was seriously questioned whether it was permissible to accept charitable donations from a married woman without her husband's knowledge and consent.[97] Despite these narrow restrictions, which were never abrogated in theory, it was common for women to be in control of their husband's fortunes[98] and occasionally to be sufficiently skilled in commerce or professional work to become the sole means of the family support.[99]

The *ketubah,* supplemented by rabbinic legislation and local custom, made detailed provisions for the widow and the orphan daughters. While the husband was the sole heir of his wife, the widow did not inherit from her husband; but she had the option to maintain the home and receive support from the estate or to reclaim the *ketubah,* with all the provisions of the marriage settlement, the gifts and possessions and all the property which constituted the dowry. The *ketubah* had first lien on the estate with priority even over the costs of the husband's burial.[100] For support, the widow was entitled to all the requirements of her customary standards, including a retinue of servants, if her own family station warranted it.[101] The daughters did not inherit from their father when there were sons, but their support and dower were, for this reason, a preferred charge upon the estate.

There was always a wide divergence between the standard of the Jewish woman in law and her rank in life. The Jewish wife and mother was always safeguarded by love and reverence more than by law. One principle in particular, taken precisely from the law, may be chosen to end this chapter fittingly. The woman rises to higher dignity in marriage; she does not stoop to a lower level by assuming the duties of a wife.[102]

CHAPTER XV

SCHOOLS, CURRICULA AND
EDUCATIONAL IDEALS

IN A remarkable statute which was drawn up by a
council of Jewish delegates from all the communities of
Castile, in the city of Valladolid in the year 1432,[1] the first
chapter, or "Gate," opens with this striking introduction:

> "This is the gate of the Lord, the righteous shall
> enter into it."[2] The opening of our words and the
> beginning of our ordinances are to support those
> who occupy themselves with our Holy Law; for it
> is the Torah which upholds the world; as our sages,
> may their memory be for a blessing, expressed it:
> "The world is based on three things: study, divine
> service and the practice of charity."[3]

The duty to provide and support public instruction, so
forcefully enunciated in this preface, was from ancient times
recognized as the sacred obligation of the Jewish community,[4]
ranking higher in importance than even the maintenance
of institutions of divine worship.[5]

No Jewish settlement was considered complete without
proper teachers for young children.[6] Universal compulsory
education, however, although an early Palestinian institution,[7] was not attempted in the mediaeval Jewish communities. The existence of illiteracy was recognized and
had occasionally to be reckoned with in the communal
statutes.[8] Nevertheless, complete ignorance of Hebrew read-

ing and writing was certainly unusual among the male population. An interesting reference to a teacher of little girls occurs in an Arabic autograph responsum of Maimonides, which seems, however, to belong to Egypt rather than to Spain.[9] From the same source we also learn of the existence of expert women teachers, but again this reflects Egyptian rather than Spanish conditions.[10] In Spain, as elsewhere, however, ample provisions were made for the education of the children even in the smallest communities. The Jews of Cervera were too poor to own a cemetery, but they could boast of their schools and educational funds.[11] Community schools, where such existed, were supported by public assessments levied upon the wealth of the inhabitants.[12] In the main, however, elementary and secondary education was carried on by private initiative rather than through communal endowment. The official generosity of the *kahal* was reserved for the higher talmudic academy over which the chief scholar, usually the rabbi of the community, presided.[13] The instruction of children, on the other hand, was a duty directly incumbent upon the parents[14] and they arranged for private, limited classes for their sons by annual agreement with the teachers.[15] Pupils of means were taught by private tutors who, as a class, formed an educational factor of the highest importance throughout the Middle Ages.[16] The support of indigent pupils and teachers was a favorite object of donations and bequests.[17] In one instance, a single patron paid for the instruction of all the poor children of his community.[18] Men of piety and wealth often established talmudic academies in their own homes and supported them with liberal generosity.[19]

In the fourteenth century, we find societies under the name of *Hebrat Talmud Torah* which were organized to support the study of Torah.[20] In Perpignan, the *Hebrat Talmud Torah* was one of the five major organizations of the community.[21] Through these auxiliary channels the facilities of elementary and secondary education were extended freely to the children of the poor. Even in the fourteenth century, the *kahal*, as a rule, was not called upon to establish communal schools for elementary or secondary education.

The persecutions that darkened the end of the fourteenth century and cast a heavy shadow over the fifteenth, however, wrought a sad transformation in the educational as in other aspects of Jewish life in Spain.

As we behold [reads the joint resolution of the Castilian communities in 1432] that the hands of the learned in most places are benumbed and that the scholars are but meagerly supported; and for this reason the students of the Talmud are diminishing, while the pupils of the primary schools are decreasing because the poverty of the parents does not enable them to pay the fees of the teachers, and thereby the teachings of God are in danger of being forgotten in Israel; therefore, in order to restore the ancient glory, that there may again be found scholars versed in the law and that students may again abound in our communities, be it resolved that, in the entire kingdom of both Castiles, the members of every community be obligated to take measures to raise contributions for a Talmud Torah fund in the following manner: for every head of large cattle that shall be slaughtered among them ritually for their own use, a tax of five *maravedís* for Talmud Torah shall be levied; for every calf and every heifer of one hundred pounds, or twenty *arreldes*, two *maravedís*; for every small head of cattle as lamb, sheep, buck or goat, one *maravedí*; for one goat or one lamb less than sixteen pounds, one *cornado*, and of sixteen pounds or more, five *dineros.* A tax of three *dineros* shall be levied on the sale of retail wine from one to five jugs.

A tax was also fixed upon the wholesale distribution of wine, to be paid by the purchaser, and also on wine sold to Christians, payable by the seller. A tax of ten *maravedís* was levied on weddings and circumcisions. Upon the death of a member of the community, male or female, from the age of ten upward, the heirs were to contribute a garment of the deceased person or ten *maravedís*. "In all these cases," adds the statute, "no limitation upon the generosity of the giver is intended." Dependents on charity, or those who would be qualified to receive it, were to be exempted at the discretion of the administrators of the educational fund from the tax on weddings and circumcisions as well as the contributions in cases of death.[22]

The proceeds of the Talmud Torah fund were sequestered from the general treasury of the *kahal* and were entrusted to specially appointed administrators. The funds were placed under the general control of the chief rabbi at the king's court for the purpose of subventioning elementary and secondary schools in all the communities of Castile. It was not designed to destroy the basis of the older school system which rested on the private initiative of parents and teachers. The payment of tuition fees still prevailed, but the proceeds of the Talmud Torah fund were used to supplement the teacher's income when it was inadequate. With the consent of the chief rabbi, it was also permitted to apply the fund toward the salary of the local rabbi and the support of his scholars, but it could not be diverted to any other cause. A community which had fifteen families was morally obligated to engage at least one elementary teacher. *Aljamas* of forty families had also to provide

advanced instruction, and it was deemed proper, in such
communities, to apply the Talmud Torah fund toward the
maintenance of talmudic academies where rabbis were
engaged specifically to teach the laws (*halakot*) and the
ethics (*aggadot*) of Judaism. Here too the plan was merely
to supplement the allotment from the general community
chest (*hekdesh*) and the special income which was derived
from excises on wine and meat. With the aid of the Talmud
Torah fund it was possible for the communities to live
up to the high pedagogical standards of the Talmud.
Accordingly, an elementary teacher was not permitted to
teach more than twenty-five pupils without an assistant.
With an aide, he was allowed to teach forty pupils. Above
this number, it was necessary for the community to engage
two full-time teachers.[23]

All the circumstances surrounding these emergency measures showed that normally education in the elementary
and secondary grades was the private concern of the parents
and the teachers.[24] Nevertheless, Barfat expounded its
social character when he censured R. Samuel Halav, a
teacher whom he and Duran otherwise esteemed highly,
for imposing unfair terms upon the parents of his pupils:[25]

> In the work of God it is not meet for one who fears
> the Lord to make such terms, for those who would
> educate their sons in the study of the Torah are dis-
> couraged at heart when unjust and oppressive condi-
> tions are imposed upon them.[26]

On the other hand, the dignity of the teacher was asserted
by Ibn Adret when he rejected the plea that the conditions
of labor applied to the work of the teacher. The teaching
of wisdom was not to be classed with other work.[27] Duran,
who championed the cause of the scholar and the teacher,

ruled that no maximum wage scale could be imposed upon
the teacher, because learning was priceless.[28]

Throughout the course of instruction, the motive was
never lost sight of that the study of the Torah was a religious precept for which no sacrifice was too great. This
was the ancient Jewish equivalent of the modern principle
of compulsory universal education, with this vital difference, that the religious conception recognized no exemptions
of age or circumstance. As a noted authority of the fourteenth century pithily expressed it:

> Every Israelite is in duty bound to set apart a period
> every day and evening for study, whether he be poor
> or rich, sound in body or maimed in limb, young or
> old — aye, even the beggar who walks the streets.[30]

The devotion to study which is displayed in the responsa
by persons far past the school age, and long after they had
left the official schools, is often aglow with religious fervor.[31]

Because of the continuous religious obligation connected
with study, vacations were not favored by the Jewish
authorities. The written agreement of the *kahal* of Mazone
(מאזונה), granting the public teacher in its employ an annual
vacation of ten days, stands out as unique in the rabbinical
documents. When this teacher extended his vacation to
three months and demanded his salary, the plea was not
only denied but he was severely censured by Duran for
daring to hold up the study of the Torah and he was told
that he had incurred the guilt of sin for which judgment
would be meted out by Heaven.[32]

In Spain, no less than in France and Germany, the basis
of Jewish education was a knowledge of the Hebrew prayers,
the Bible and the Talmud. The first Hebrew words which

the Jewish child learned to recite in infancy proclaimed:
"Moses commanded us the Law as an inheritance of the
congregation of Jacob. Hear, O Israel: the Lord our God,
the Lord is One."[33] A child's formal educational career
began theoretically at the age of six,[34] but it was more likely
to commence when he was three or four years old.[35] In
the prayer book he learned the decipherment of the Hebrew
characters, and the Pentateuch was his primer. The study
in the classroom was co-ordinated as far as possible with
the services in the synagogue. Thus the biblical selections
which were taught in the school were regularly chosen
from the current *parashah*.[36] The weekly lessons, comprising
at first only a few sentences, were gradually increased until
they corresponded to the Sabbath reading of the synagogue.
Owing to the dearth of books, the teacher was permitted
to write the biblical lessons on a chart and to erase the
sacred text when a new selection was to be studied. Duran
traced this practice back two centuries to the time of Ibn
Migash and Maimonides' father.[37] Importance was attached
to the exercise of the memory.[38]

At about the age of seven, the bright Jewish lad was initi-
ated in the study of the Mishna. In his eighth year, Barfat's
grandson was introduced to the study of halakic subjects
and the intricacies of talmudic dialectics (סוגיא), and he
knew by heart parts of the mishnaic tractates Berakot,
Ta'anit, Megillah, Rosh Hashanah and Yoma.[39] His study
periods were divided equally among Talmudics, Bible and
the intensive study of the *parashah*, which included the
rabbinical commentaries and the Targum translations.[40]
No mention is made in the responsa about grammatical
studies or writing exercises. Obviously, the center of gravity
lay in subjects more directly religious.[41] Thus the musical

recital of the accents of the Bible appears as a distinctive feature of the early training of the Jewish boy.[42] The chanting of the *haftarah* in the synagogal service by tender male debutants years before the age of religious majority was defended as an educational measure and, as rival parents eagerly outbid each other to secure this privilege for their sons, it became incidentally a source of revenue to the synagogue and consequently difficult to abolish, despite the misgivings of the scrupulous.[43]

Pedagogical programs and ideals were discussed in Hebrew and Arabic writings and sometimes were made the subject of independent treatises or special chapters of larger works.[44] The authors of these programs were not professional teachers, but philosophic theorists. Their conceptions of Jewish education presented an amazing picture of educational planning and scope of study. Although these accounts varied in many details, they revealed essential unity of plan and purpose. The function of education was to enlighten the mind, to discipline the character and to prepare the soul for its ultimate union with God. In these curricula, the programs of study invariably included Hebrew and secular subjects. The Hebrew studies comprised the Bible and its rabbinical commentaries; Hebrew grammar and the Targum as an introduction to talmudic Aramaic; the Mishna and the Talmud and ethical and religious classics. The secular subjects were logic which, based on Aristotle's *Organum*, included also his rhetoric and poetics, mathematics (arithmetic and geometry, music and astronomy),[45] physics (i. e., optics, mechanics), medicine (natural sciences) and the crown of all learning — metaphysics.[46] Judah ibn Tibbon (1120–90) laid stress also on Hebrew and Arabic orthography and calligraphy, on style and chronology.[47]

A knowledge of Arabic was presupposed in all the syllabi, and later also a knowledge of Latin, although the hostile character of much of this literature was never forgotten.[48]

These encyclopedic plans reflect the accomplishments of an impressive roll of Jewish savants and the ambition of hosts of Jewish students, when universal knowledge was still considered to be within the grasp of the individual mind. But this broad prospectus cannot seriously be taken as the syllabus of popular Jewish education, even at its zenith in the golden era in Spain. There is no evidence to show that these pedagogic plans were ever discussed at the sessions of the communal councils. Jacob Anatoli's studies of mathematics and philosophy under the guidance of his father-in-law, Samuel ibn Tibbon, were derided as a waste of time by those who expressed the popular point of view.[49] The philosophical writers addressed themselves to self-taught students whose courses of study were to extend over a lifetime. Thus Ibn Abbas' curriculum called for a period of study from the age of three or three and a half years, at the utmost, to the age of forty, "when the student should turn away from all worldly concerns, gird himself with strength of heart, arm with the weapons of soul and mind and enter the Garden of the Lord and go up on the Mount where God said He shall dwell — that is, the science of metaphysics." This, he advised, should be studied in the books of Aristotle with the aid of the commentary of Ibn Roshd.[50] Obviously Ibn Abbas was proposing an ideal program of life rather than an academic curriculum. Indeed, the warning against the alluring study of *hiddushim* and *tosafot* (novellae and glosses to the Talmud), which is sounded in some of these writings and described as a waste of time, was clearly a protest against the educational program of the established institutions of learning, which had popular support and were sanctioned by the great and pious majority of the community.

No scheme of popular education is conceivable without the corresponding instruments of public instruction. One looks in vain, however, for any institutions where these elaborate curricula could have been taught. They were not mentioned in the anti-philosophic controversies of the thirteenth century, although they would have been the primary targets of attack.[51] It may be confidently premised that nowhere in the Middle Ages did the educational system built up by the Jews make room for an extensive training in secular subjects. Jews were not invariably excluded from the Christian and Mohammedan schools;[52] but it is not to be assumed that they flocked or were admitted in appreciable numbers to the mediaeval universities of the Christians or Mohammedans.[53] Jacob b. Makir ibn Tibbon (Don Profiat), famous astronomer and physician, was said to have been professor at the University of Montpellier[54] and regent of its faculty of medicine;[55] but it is difficult to reconcile this fact with the resolution of the synod of Montpellier in 1258 which prohibited the faithful from seeking the aid of Jewish physicians under threat of excommunication, or a similar restriction by the synod of Avignon in 1282.[56] The statute of the University of Lerida, dated 1300, prohibited its students from indulging in unbecoming amusements or from disguising themselves as Jews or Saracens.[75] By special favor of the bishop of Salamanca in the fifteenth century Abraham Zacuto was allowed to attend the university of that city and was later elevated to its teaching staff; but this is not to be generalized.[58] The synod of Salamanca, which held its sessions under the shadow of the famous university of that town, had solemnly declared that Jewish physicians offered their services only to kill as many Christians as possible.[59] The University of Montpellier, where Hillel of Verona and Leon Joseph, the Hebrew translator of Latin medical works (1392 and 1402), received their medical education, forbade by statute the sale of medical books to Jews.[60] Such laws strongly argued for the absence of contact, understanding or sympathy.

In the main, therefore, Jewish students were compelled to draw upon Jewish sources for their secular no less than their religious studies; and, furthermore, their amazing accomplishments in the domains of science and philosophy were attained by private study rather than through a system of formal instruction. The teaching of the secular disciplines, to the extent that it was practiced, was mainly private and individual.[61] Although, in principle, the living word of the teacher was preferred to the written text,[62] these students were compelled by force of circumstances to acquire their knowledge of secular subjects through arduous self-application and the private study of texts and books. This no doubt accounts, in part, for the intensive activity of the Hebrew translators of the standard Arabic-Greek books in all branches of science and philosophy. These works were obviously intended for the earnest student rather than the general reader and they filled an important and ever-increasing demand as the Jewish intellectual centers shifted from Arabic-speaking to Latin countries.[63] Gradually, this literature grew until it included also translations from the Latin, Spanish, French and Italian. Interest in romance literature appeared as a new manifestation on the borderline between the thirteenth and fourteenth centuries.[64] Thus the pen bridged the chasm formed by the corrosions of prejudice.

However important and significant this activity may have been, the encouragement and the sanction of the community were focused on the mastery of talmudic lore in all its branches. It was deemed essential to the spiritual well-being of even moderate communities to provide talmudic instruction of at least a secondary grade. The higher instruction in Talmud and Jewish law was, as a rule, entrusted to the local rabbi, who in this capacity was called by the descriptive epithet מרביץ תורה, "disseminator of sacred learning."[65] Though no student was debarred from the lectures by reason of poverty, the secondary courses in Talmudics, like the elementary, were not generally free.[66] Talmudic schools were established in the private homes of wealthy patrons who constituted themselves eager students and disciples of the men of learning.[67] In this course, the text of the Talmud, its commentaries and super-commentaries and the codes of religious law formed the main subjects of instruction, the student being thus prepared for the advanced studies of the higher academy, the *yeshibah*.

The *yeshibah*, a time-honored institution of post-exilic Judaism and the direct spiritual descendant of the Sanhedrin, formed the pinnacle of the educational structure. It was not distinguished from the lower schools by any external signs. The terms, "elementary," "secondary" and "higher schools," or "academies," are employed here with reluctance, for want of better terminology to designate the Hebrew academic gradations which were essentially of loose, flexible character. The *yeshibah* was entirely dominated by the personality of the teacher who was its head. The standing of a school was directly commensurate with the fame of its rector. He presided over its sessions in the *bet ha-mid-rash*,[68] itself one of the oldest creations of post-biblical Judaism, known by name already to the author of Ecclesiasticus.[69] Not infrequently, the lectures were delivered in the synagogue[70] or in a building adjoining it.[71] The famous academy of Cordova in the tenth century, which is the first *yeshibah* on record in Spain, was housed in the synagogue of the *bet ha-midrash* (בית הכנסת של בית המדרש).[72]

Ibn Daud's account of the scene in the synagogue of Cordova when the learning of R. Moses b. Hanok was dramatically revealed before the academic assembly contained all the essential features of the *yeshibah* of the later centuries.[73] The rector of the academy, Rabbi Nathan, was the judge, or rabbi, of the community. He was described as a great and saintly man. Pressing litigants waited patiently in the corridor or courtyard, while he was delivering his discourse before the students in the hall of the synagogue on a complicated subject in the tractate of Yoma. The atmosphere was charged with heated discussion in which the students asked provocative questions and often challenged the opinions of their master. The presence of mature, bearded students excited no surprise or comment. The head of the academy towered above his hearers not by seniority of age or prestige of office but by superior learning; and when he once unexpectedly found a master in a raggedly attired stranger, he proclaimed him, with saintly self-abnegation, teacher and master. He gave up his honored post and declared himself from that day on the pupil of R. Moses, who was forthwith acclaimed rabbi, judge and teacher. With the accession of R. Moses, the Cordova school rose to fame. From all parts of Spain and North Africa students flocked to the lectures of the famed master. This,

A scene in a synagogue
(see p. xi)

in brief, is the historic description of the prototype of the memorable *yeshibot* in which were to be trained the master-minds of Spanish Jewry.

From Cordova, the torch of learning was carried to Lucena. Through the renowned leadership of Isaac Alfasi and his brilliant pupil and successor Joseph ha-Levi ibn Migash, the academy of Lucena brought world fame to the Spanish schools. In Maimonides, who fled to Egypt, a fugitive from the wrath and intolerance of the Almohades, the learning of the Jews of Mohammedan Spain reached its acme of brilliance and maturity. Arabic-speaking Jewry was never to regain its supremacy on the Iberian Peninsula. The centers of learning were steadily shifted northward to the Christian domains of Spain. R. Jonah Gerundi in Toledo, and his cousin Nahmanides in Gerona, revived the traditions of Cordova and Lucena. With the ascendancy of their joint pupil, R. Solomon ibn Adret, the academy of Barcelona became the spiritual capital of Spanish Jewry and the city retained to the last the proud title of "Mother in Israel." Ibn Adret lived to see a great academy arise in Toledo under the direction of the German talmudist, R. Asher. For a half century the southern capital rivaled and threatened to eclipse the city of the north, where R. Perez ha-Kohen succeeded Ibn Adret. R. Judah honorably filled his father's post, but his illustrious, youthful contemporary, R. Nissim, held the position once made famous by Ibn Adret and restored its prestige. His disciple, R. Isaac Barfat, added to the fame of Barcelona and brought honor successively to the academies of Saragossa and Valencia over which he presided during the course of his checkered career. Thus an almost continuous chain of the leading *yeshibot* extended from the foundation of talmudic

studies in Spain in the tenth century to the persecutions of
1391, which formed the prelude to the final catastrophe.
Academies of lower rank existed in every notable city, among
which those of Seville, Alcalà, Calatayud and Tortosa may
be especially singled out.

The exposition of halakah, in its broadest sense, was the
aim and sole content of the studies pursued in the *yeshibah*.
The interpretation of a difficult passage in the tractate
Yoma and the elucidation of other related questions, as
shown, made the fortune of R. Moses b. Hanok. In the
succeeding *yeshibot*, too, the understanding of the talmudic
text remained the subject of prime concern and the field of
distinction. The immediate goal of even the most advanced
students was the correct understanding and keen analysis
of a particular passage or halakic theory rather than the
comprehensive survey of the entire field of Talmudics.
Mediaeval authors commented on the fact that, even in the
yeshibot of greatest fame, the purpose was no longer to complete the entire cycle of talmudic tractates.[74] Barfat extolled
his teacher, the famed halakist, R. Nissim Gerundi, for his
mastery of three talmudic orders.[75] With the diversification
of talmudic literature and the development of commentaries,
codes, glosses and novellae, the scope of talmudic studies
broadened and there naturally developed a wide latitude
for differentiation of method and viewpoint in halakic
studies.

The lectures of the rector gave unity to the diversified
halakic subjects studied by the disciples in the *yeshibah*.
The basis of the rector's disquisitions was usually the text of
a talmudic tractate. He illumined the text with original
comments and, through dialectic reasoning, derived new
points of law and method. By these contributions the

master lent individuality and distinctiveness to his academy. The reflections and comments of famous rabbis were treasured by the students and were eagerly prized by eminent scholars and teachers.[76] In this manner, the commentaries, glosses and novellae, which surround the printed talmudic text and fill numberless independent volumes, largely originated. Many of them indeed owe their written preservation to the notes of the pupils. Foreign students from distant communities spent years of study in the school of R. Asher at Toledo, writing down his critical comments on the text of the Talmud and, on their homeward journey, displaying their *tosafot*, or glosses, everywhere to admiring scholars.[77] R. Asher's methods and views were expounded in the academy of Toledo by his son, R. Judah, who succeeded him. Thus R. Menahem b. Zerah studied under R. Judah the two talmudic Orders, Zera'im and Toharot, "according to the system of R. Asher." He added also: "And I read before him in review the text of the Orders of Mo'ed and Nezikin and the tractate of Gittin, and I fixed the variant readings according to his text."[78] In the *yeshibah* at Alcalà, the Talmud was studied with the *tosafot* of the French glossator, R. Perez, under R. Joseph ibn al-Aish.[79] In Barfat's academy at Saragossa, the students were engaged in writing exegeses and novellae to the talmudic tractates on which he lectured.[80]

The one-sidedness of the *yeshibah* studies is all the more surprising as many of the famous teachers gained lasting distinction in the non-talmudic branches of Jewish learning and in the secular sciences. Only the authoritative word of the law, however, was taught in the *yeshibah* even by the most liberal academicians. Maimonides' *Guide to the Perplexed* was ostensibly written for the private reading of one

disciple.[81] At the *yeshibah*, Nahmanides evolved *hiddushim*
in his talmudic lectures; in the solitude of the Holy Land,
he poured out his soul in the completion of his immortal
commentary to the Bible.[82] It is significant that Shem Tob
Palquera who, in his philosophic ardor figuratively converted
the metaphysical Greeks into students of rabbinical Judaism,
timidly taught that the reading of Aristotle's metaphysics
might be suggested to the student, but should not be made
the subject of instruction.[83] Hasdai Crescas, it must be
noted, discussed philosophical problems at his academy;[84]
but in the main it was the talmudic subtleties, rather than
the *Light of God*, that were displayed before his students in
Saragossa.[85] More than half of the rabbis whose works form
the basis of this exposition were practicing physicians, some
of them of great fame; nevertheless, in the eulogistic praise
of a rabbi-physician, the distinction was not forgotten that
medicine was "theirs" and the Torah "ours."[86]

From this it is equally evident, however, that the intellectual interests of the students and the teachers of the Spanish
yeshibot—and the same may be said of the schools of the
Provence and Italy — were by no means confined to their
restricted curricula. Some students distinguished themselves
as grammarians, exegetes and poets; while others attained
to fame in the secular sciences of mathematics, astronomy
and medicine. Their works are the gems that give special
luster to the literary history of Spanish Jewry. Even in these
celebrated authors, their extra-rabbinical attainments were
generally regarded not as substituting but as supplementing
rabbinical knowledge, the pursuit of which was the primary
duty of every Israelite.[87] In the religious scale, indeed, an
imperfectly written halakic work outweighed in importance

a finished literary classic whose immediate theme was not the
Law of God.

It is true that poets, scientists and philosophers were not
wanting who rebelled against the strictly halakic ideal.
From the beginnings of the renaissance of the Hebrew
language in Spain, the poets and grammarians quarreled
with the official sponsors of Jewish education for their neglect
of Hebrew linguistic knowledge, which was extolled by
them as the key to the understanding of the Bible, the revealed Word of God. The attack against the methods of
the *yeshibah* was carried further by the extreme exponents
of philosophy. They maintained that all branches of knowledge, including rabbinic learning, were but bypaths which
properly led to the sphere of metaphysics. They openly
advocated the subordination of halakah to religious philosophy. These views, however, never gained social dominance.
They nowhere succeeded in deflecting the course of studies
in the official academies. Under the spell of Maimonides'
influence, the rationalistic tendency came to have an increasingly greater sway on the intellectual classes; but it
finally led to a reaction and crisis which shook the spiritual
foundations of mediaeval Jewry, after which the influence
of the *yeshibah* was enhanced as the sanctum of the Torah
to which all classes paid homage.[88]

The spirit of the *yeshibah* found its truest expression in
the personality of the rector. He was not only a source of
emulation to the students; he was the living embodiment
of their highest ideal. It was the fondest hope of a noble
disciple to approximate his master in learning and religion.
For the rector was no mere schoolman; he was the sage and
the scholar. Outside the walls of the academy, in the community at large, he was the custodian of Judaism and a

regenerating moral and spiritual force among his people. Despite the antagonisms and defeats which a fearless sage necessarily incurred often in the fight against the abuses of evil men, he was a dominating moral figure in the community and he wielded considerable legal powers.[89] Little wonder then that the scholars of the academy saw in their master the idealization of learning and the fountain of inspiration for their self-sacrificing studies.[90]

An account of the prestige and the prerogatives enjoyed by the master will help us to understand the mental outlook of the students as well as the hopes that inspired them during the years of apprenticeship in the *yeshibah*. The status of the rector in the community was not dependent upon his principalship in the academy. While the latter office was elective, or self-assumed when the rector was also the founder and supporter of the *yeshibah*, the main legal privileges which the incumbent enjoyed were determined not by the electorate but by the fixed law of the Talmud. These rights, furthermore, with which ancient authority clothed him were not bestowed upon him as rector, or *rosh yeshibah*, but as sage and scholar, the *talmid hakam*, who was defined legally as a person

> whose vocation is the Torah; who makes the study of the Law his permanent occupation and his work only a temporary engagement;[91] who meditates continually on the Law and does not interrupt his studies to engage in idle matters, excepting to pursue his livelihood for this is his duty, as it is said, "An excellent thing is the study of the Torah combined with some worldly occupation; all study of the Torah without work must in the end be futile and become the cause of sin;" one whose heart is intent upon his studies and who, when finished with his work, immediately

returns to the house of study; who preaches nobly and acts in conformity therewith; and whose reputation among his fellow men is spotless.[93]

Such a person ranks as rabbi; he has submitted his neck to the yoke of the Torah, and it is not right to lay upon him any impost of the king or princes.[94] It is incumbent upon the community to free the *talmid hakam* from all taxes and even to defray from the communal treasury the governmental taxes which are levied upon every person separately. Scholars are likewise under no obligation to contribute to the funds which the community must raise for the building of the town wall, the barring of the gates and other provisions for guarding the city. Even if the scholars are exceedingly rich, the community must defray their taxes, because they are singled out for exemption not by reason of poverty, but in recognition of their learning.[95]

As representative of the majesty of the Torah, the *talmid hakam* commanded personal reverence.[96] He was vested with full authority to defend his honor against abuse and insult by putting the offender under the ban until he pleaded forgiveness.[97] He who offended the dignity of the scholar was not only exposed to the *herem*; he had also to pay the sage a fine of one pound in gold, the equivalent of one hundred and five grains, for each offense.[98] No communal enactment could deprive the *talmid hakam* of these important weapons.[99] While the minor scholars, who freely exercised the power of the *herem*, aroused the resentment of the smaller communities, the distinguished rabbis of the larger cities were strengthened with additional powers by the local authorities.[100] If the scholar himself declined to defend his honor by means of the ban, it was incumbent upon his colleagues to pronounce the *herem* and thus to uphold his dignity.[101] The king, too, supported the *talmid hakam* in this power.[102] Thus Pedro IV warned his officials not to interfere with Isaac Barfat when he exercised this prerogative and not to force him to make peace with those who caused him offense.[103] The archives also reveal this monarch's communication to Rabbi Nissim Gerundi in the same vein, but strangely enough no trace of this incident is to be found in the responsa of either rabbi.[104] It should be recalled that Barfat was Rabbi Nissim's disciple and that he held no rabbinical post in Barcelona at any time, certainly not during his teacher's tenure of office. But it was as a *talmid hakam* that he wielded this dread weapon.

Rabbi Asher granted unqualified approval to a learned scholar who, disregarding the seniority in age of his less learned brother, excommunicated him because of the unfraternal abuse which he had heaped upon him. "For, showing no respect for scholarship, he acteth not in the manner of thy people and his younger brother is nowise bound to honor him."[105] In the eyes of Maimonides, it was not only the part of wisdom but the more ethical procedure for the sage to overlook the rudeness of the ignorant towards him; but he, too, maintained that the scholar was morally obligated to resist public insult. For him to ignore personal attack under these circumstances would be to encourage disrespect of the Torah, and he would bear moral responsibility for the result.[106] More direct and intimate than the dictum of the *Code* was Maimonides' private counsel in a responsum:

> It is best for a rabbi, even if he be an exceedingly great man, to lead his community with gentleness and to forego the honor that is due him; he should protest, but with mildness, against everything that ought

to be opposed; then the people will accept his words with gladness, and he will bring them back to the right path with ties of love.[107]

A local burial custom occasionally revealed the reverence with which the last remains of a *talmid hakam* were treated. Thus in some cemeteries, the remains of the *kohanim* were interred near the wall for reasons arising from the laws of priestly defilement; but the body of a *kohen* who had been a scholar was buried in a plot of central prominence. This tribute was paid to the successor of Ibn Adret, R. Perez ha-Kohen, in Barcelona.[108] More striking still was the tribute paid earlier to the remains of the famous Provençal rabbi, Abraham ben David of Posquières, when *kohanim* were especially selected for the honor of digging his grave.[109]

Although the *talmid hakam* was not required to hold public office either as rector or judge,[110] his rank and prestige did not permit him to lead the retired life of the cloistered scholar. He was irresistibly drawn out of his seclusion to aid in the councils of the *kahal*, to promote learning, to guard the moral and religious condition of the community and to represent his brethren on political missions no less than in religious disputations.[111] Private scholars were chosen together with men of wealth to act as hostages for their brethren and thus frequently paid the penalty of their prominence by periods of torture and incarceration in the prisons of their extortioners.[112] R. Isaac Barfat, who held no office in Barcelona, wrote to R. Solomon Zarfati in explanation of his long delayed reply:

> Thou dwellest in tents and thy work is done through others and there is none to make thee afraid or to terrify thee, whilst I must suffer the burden of earning a livelihood. Furthermore, it is nearly five months

since wicked men arose among us who invented a false charge against our great teacher, R. Nissim, with the result that six honorable men of our community, among whom were included the sage Don Hasdai, my brother and I, were surrendered to the government and we are still kept in hostage innocently. Since then my steps have not crossed the threshold of the house of study.[113]

The name of *talmid hakam*, however, was usually associated with the *yeshibah*, for it was amidst disciples that the sage truly gloried in his divinely appointed task, and he naturally welcomed academic leadership.[114] It was not unusual for scholars of wealth to maintain their own *yeshibot*.[115] In the public academies, the scholar was called to this post by the communal authorities.[116] This position gained for him the title of Elder (זקן) or Sage (חכם), and he became the acknowledged head, or the rabbi of the community.[117] Saragossa, Majorca and other Jewish centers of importance acknowledged more than one spiritual leader and, as their reciprocal relations were ill-defined, there often resulted considerable friction from this arrangement.[118] Originally it was the function of the rabbi to act as judge (דיין) or presiding judicial officer (אב בית דין) in all matters of litigation.[119] This, in the main, continued to be his recognized duty and prerogative.[120] Gradually, however, in the larger cities, the rabbi's direct participation in the affairs of the court was in part withdrawn.[121] Thus the *Bet Din* in Saragossa seems clearly to have been officially independent of Rabbi Isaac Barfat.[122] Nevertheless, morally, the rabbi dominated its proceedings and, in difficult cases, he assumed the right of superior jurisdiction. Barfat urged Rabbi Amram of Valencia personally to supervise all divorce cases

in his community, stating that this had been the practice
of Rabbi Perez ha-Kohen and Rabbi Nissim Gerundi; for
these cases involved such fine technicalities that few rabbis
(חכמים) could claim expert knowledge of them, much less
the mass of dayyanim.[123] Furthermore, because of his
superior knowledge, the rabbi was virtually an appellate
judge, though he is not to be confused with the government
appointee who bore this title (דיין הסלוקין) and whose
decisions, in turn, were dependent upon the opinion of the
learned rabbi.[124] He subjected the decisions of the Bet Din
to a critical examination and did not hesitate to reverse
any of their judgments if they were legally defective. The
courts therefore found it often more expedient to consult
the opinion of the rabbi in advance,[125] precisely as the legislative council sought his legal confirmation of their proposed
enactments.[126] The regulations of the guilds were likewise
subject to rabbinical sanction and confirmation.[127] The
responsibility which weighed upon the talmid hakam in
his judicial capacity was expressed by Barfat in characteristic rabbinic metaphor: "I fear every judgment as it comes
before me. I proceed cautiously and I tremble before it, as
if a serpent and a scorpion were wound around my heel."[128]

The question of remuneration for the rabbi raised a controversy which lasted for centuries. Ostensibly, it was a legal
controversy in which both sides argued points of law and
multiplied precedents,[129] but, beneath the surface of formal argumentation, it represented the struggle of a purely
idealistic conception of learning against the compromises
which life exacted. The conviction was deeply rooted in
Jewish thought that learning was its own reward, that it
must not be made to serve worldly ambition or be tainted

by monetary awards. The exhortations of the sages of the first century of the common era were popularized through the *Ethics of the Fathers*: "Make not of the Torah a crown wherewith to aggrandize thyself nor a spade wherewith to dig. So also used Hillel to say: 'He who makes a worldly use of the crown of the Torah shall waste away.'" "Hence," concluded the author of the Mishna, "thou mayest infer that whoever derives a profit for himself from the words of the Torah promotes his own destruction." More directly binding was the later dictum of the Talmud which purported to express the spirit of Moses' injunction to all succeeding teachers of whom he was the prototype: "As I taught you freely so shall ye teach them without reward." On this authority, it was the accepted norm in the third century that teachers of halakah or haggadah were not permitted to accept tuition fees, the only exception being made in favor of the elementary Bible instructor.[130] Nor was it considered proper for students to depend for their livelihood upon public generosity.[131]

Notwithstanding the inherent difficulties and sacrifices, this ideal was on the whole successfully maintained by the talmudic teachers. They earned a livelihood as artisans, craftsmen and traders. Many of them led a life of penury bordering on starvation rather than invite public support.[132] The only material benefits which were accorded to them were exemption from taxes[133] and a certain priority at the market places,[134] and Maimonides compared these privileges to the biblical tithes and heave offerings for the priests and the levites. In post-talmudic times, however, the great academies of Babylonia could not long be maintained without large public funds. Other passages of the Talmud, of equal authority, were then invoked, lauding the merits of those who supported the study of the Torah.[135] The geonim frankly appealed for the support of their educational institutions to the communities of the diaspora, and the Jews of Spain were prompt and liberal in their response until the rise of talmudical academies in Spain diverted the funds for the maintenance of the local *yeshibot*. It was against this prevalent system of financing the talmudical schools that Maimonides raised his voice in protest.

He was aware, he said, that his words would have no effect upon the majority, not to say upon all, of the great teachers of the Torah. Nevertheless, he would break silence and spare neither predecessors nor contemporaries. He charged that they pervertedly disregarded the plain dictum of the Fathers,[136] that they relied upon passages misunderstood by them and deliberately assessed individuals and communities by leading them into the absurd belief that it was incumbent upon the people to give financial aid to the sages and their disciples and to all who made a vocation of the study of the Torah. All this was an error. They could not possibly advance any proof for their contention either from the Bible or from the dicta of the talmudic sages and they had no leg to stand on. On the contrary, an examination of the talmudic records would not reveal any instance where the rabbis appealed to the public for money. They gathered no contributions for their great academies nor for the exilarchs nor for their judges, teachers or any of the great scholars. Surely, had any one of the numerous scholars who suffered poverty stretched forth his hand, he would have been overwhelmed with rich gifts; but no rabbi would thus demean himself. The acceptance of money would have been a desecration in the eyes of the people. For the study of the Torah would come to be regarded as a secular profession

by which a livelihood was gained and the people would
despise it. Finally, disposing sharply of the characteristic
proofs of the other side which were argued by "confused
madmen,"[137] Maimonides felt satisfied that he had silenced
his opponents even though he had previously despaired of
convincing them.[138]

Maimonides' academic-rabbinic career, untouched by the
slightest material reward, eloquently sustained this doctrine.
With fervent enthusiasm, he impressed these high standards
upon his disciples. Thus, to a beloved pupil, he wrote:
"Better in my eyes is a single *dirhem* gained by you as a
weaver, a tailor, a carpenter than a rich revenue enjoyed
under the auspices of the Head of the Captivity."[139] By
this vigorous stand, Maimonides revived the old standards
of the Talmud. It is true that he did not succeed in rev-
olutionizing the practical administration of the *yeshibot.*
The care and support of the poor students could not be
abandoned; but he set up the ideal for the accomplished
scholar. It became unethical for a rabbi and public teacher
to accept payment for his services and, as a rule, he earned
his livelihood through business investments, loans or the
practice of medicine.[140] To belong to the rabbinical profession in the thirteenth century was equivalent to being a
philanthropist by vocation in our day.[141] Owing, however,
to the fearful economic dislocation of the Jewish communities
in the latter half of the fourteenth century, brought about
by persecution, massacres and the Black Death plague, the
ideal could no longer be maintained, and it became the rule
for the rabbi and public teacher to accept a fixed salary for
his services.[142] Even then, however, the practice was assailed on the authority of Maimonides; and the elaborate
defense of the prevailing custom which was worked out by

its defenders painfully revealed the conscientious scruples of the rabbis as well as the communities.[143] Simon Duran was not "the first Spanish-Jewish rabbi to take pay."[144] But his public apology for the acceptance of a salary, which could not but be humiliating to his pride, is clear proof that even in the early fifteenth century, a rabbi could not enjoy his salary without misgivings.[145]

There are no figures available as to the number of students who were regularly in attendance in the major *yeshibot.*[146] The references to foreign students, who came from France, Germany, Bohemia and Russia to study under Spanish teachers, not only reflect the cosmopolitan character of the *yeshibah* similar to that of the general mediaeval university,[147] but also suggest a considerable enrollment of domestic students. The pilgrim who parted from his wife and home to study at a distant shrine of learning is touchingly represented by a Russian student who traversed a continent to receive instruction from a German teacher in Spanish Toledo. The sad end of his pilgrimage is poignantly revealed in the following meager account given in a legal document:[148]

And this is the deposition of the witness: "When I was in Majorca, I met a student who presented me with an open letter, signed by our teacher R. Asher, which certified that the name of the bearer was Asher. He related that he came from Toledo where he had studied under our teacher, the above mentioned rabbi, and he showed me glosses to various talmudic tractates of which the said rabbi was the author. From his story, which I verified later, I learned that he had left Toledo with the intention of returning to his native country. After this, a young man arrived, Samuel by name. He was a resident of Seville but was traveling through Majorca. Without my questioning him, the conversation turned to the student. He said: 'A certain noteworthy German[149] student who departed from this city and who had studied under R. Asher arrived in Seville where I was residing. He stayed with me a day or two and then took his leave. As I escorted him on his way, I observed that he fell into a fever. I pleaded with him to return, as he was faint, but he declined and continued on his way to another city. A few days later, a messenger brought the news that the student was sick and approaching death. I hired a horse and hastened to visit him. When he saw me, he rallied somewhat, became calm and said, "Now let me die, since I have seen thy face."[150] I did whatever was in my power to encourage him, but it was of no avail, and after a short time he departed this world. I honored his remains, and we buried him.' "

This testimony was, of course, taken to free his wife from the marital tie. Inquiries at the *yeshibot* brought out the fact that Asher had come to Toledo accompanied by another student, Jonathan, and that there was also a Bohemian student, Reuben, in Toledo, who identified Asher as having been a native of Russia.

The foreign students were usually of mature age and ripe attainments. The French and German students in the Spanish academies prided themselves on the dialectic training which they had acquired in their native countries.[151] The display of this typically Franco-German Jewish faculty by the students was not viewed favorably by R. Isaac Barfat[152] who, in general, however, expressed profound appreciation of Franco-German learning.[153]

The countries from which the foreign students in the Spanish *yeshibot* were drawn depended upon the changes which occurred in the political and cultural fortunes of

Spain. In the period of Mohammedan supremacy, when the native Jews spoke only Arabic,[154] and this was also the language of instruction,[155] the Spanish *yeshibot* attracted students almost wholly from Arabic-speaking countries.[156] Arabic was then described as only another, though inferior, form of Hebrew,[157] and halakic works were composed in it.[158] Hanok b. Moses taught the Talmud in Arabic[159] and in that tongue the entire Talmud or Mishna[160] was rendered by Ibn Abitur.[161] With the spiritual devastation wrought in the twelfth century by the advent of the Almohades came the turning point in the cultural history of Spanish Jewry.[162] The Jewish center of gravity shifted northward. Meanwhile, the political mastery of the Iberian Peninsula was passing from the Saracen to the Christian. Spanish was the tongue of the now conquering population and Spanish was the language of the Jews in the ever increasing territory where the rule and civilization of the native Spaniards were being re-established.[163] Castile was in many parts still predominantly Arabic even centuries after the transfer of political mastery to the Christian rulers,[164] and as late as the fourteenth century the Jews spoke and wrote Arabic in Toledo;[165] but Arabic was no longer the medium of halakah there or in any part of Christian Spain. Nor did Spanish ever become the literary vehicle of halakah. Was it, however, the language of instruction in the talmudic academies, and were the French, German, Bohemian and Russian students who now found their way to the Iberian Peninsula compelled to learn the Spanish vernacular in order to understand the lectures of Nahmanides, Ibn Adret, Nissim Gerundi or Isaac Barfat? Undoubtedly, in the confluence of students from the diverse European countries, Hebrew became frequently a medium of speech.[166] Was

Hebrew, however, the official language of the *yeshibot* as
Latin was in the Christian universities?[167]

The sources are bafflingly uncommunicative on this point.
On the one hand, we have the testimony of Moses ibn
Gikatilla of Cordova (d. 1060–70) that the Jews of Catalonia
and the Provence were devoted to the Holy Tongue and were
accustomed to speak it.[168] On the other hand, the Provençal
Mordecai Kimhi, at the end of the thirteenth century,
complained that the younger generation spoke only the
language of the country and that even the majority of male
adults could not speak Hebrew.[169] This was also the burden
of the mystic Abraham Abulafia in the days of Ibn Adret
who deplored that the Jews everywhere spoke the language
of their country. In Sicily, they spoke three languages: the
native tongue, Greek and Arabic. But as for Hebrew, if
it were not for the sacred literature, it would not have
survived as a language.[170] Nevertheless, it is as difficult to
imagine R. Asher lecturing at Toledo in Spanish — he had
no understanding of Arabic, which was the popular language[171]— as it is to conceive his Spanish students struggling
to understand German.

The proverbially paternal affection of the Jewish teacher
for his pupils[172] is especially prominent in the letters of
R. Isaac Barfat. It was with deep gratefulness that he recalled in later years the kindness of his teacher, R. Nissim
Gerundi: "Thou hast carried me in thy arms like a father.
Thy goodly spirit led me into the right path and thy right
hand supported me."[173] Years after his departure from
Barcelona, he mourned for the precious students who died
during the plague which had ravaged the north of Spain:
"They were like children unto me."[174] He was solicitous
about the material as well as the spiritual welfare of the

students, and those who were in want received through him
financial support or were taken into the shelter of his home.[175]
He depended largely upon the secretarial aid of his students
to enable him to carry on his heavy correspondence, but it
was also characteristic of him that he laboriously drafted
and copied his own responsum in order to save the valuable
time of his student-secretary.[176] On joyous occasions and
in moments of sorrow, he spoke and wrote of his students in
terms of endearment.[177]

Amidst the general scarcity of books in the Middle Ages,
the *yeshibot* seem on the whole to have been well supplied
with the necessary texts.[178] Succeeding generations gratefully remembered the Spanish Maecenases, Ibn Shaprut and
Ibn Nagdella who, in addition to other illustrious deeds,
also furnished the academies of Cordova and Malaga with
the required talmudic volumes.[179] In later times, however,
this practice evidently became so general that individual
gifts no longer stood out in bold relief. Indeed, the feeling
was often forcefully manifested that books were objects of
public interest and it was unethical for a private owner to
refuse the loan of his book to a serious applicant. Thus a
student who was denied a book of commentaries by a colleague felt justified in stealing it and vowed not to return
it until he had copied the contents.[180] The action of the
student was even upheld by the local rabbi, though Alfasi
reversed the decision and severely denounced the act.[181]
The Jewish communities prevailed on Alfonso III to declare
their books exempt from liability for debt or from being
taken in pledge for debts incurred by their owners.[182] A
rabbinic judge (*dayyan*) of the early fourteenth century
was prepared to confiscate books which the owners declined
to put into general circulation. He fined a recalcitrant

person ten gold *maravedís* daily until he consented to the loan of his book. R. Asher gave his approval to this measure with the stipulation, however, that the owner was to be indemnified for the depreciation of his books in accordance with the estimate of a board of three experts.[183] The typical Jewish bibliophile, however, needed no coercion. The testament of Judah ibn Tibbon was popular and well remembered beyond the confines of the Provence: "And thou shalt not refuse to lend any of thy books to one who has not the means of buying them, provided that he can be trusted to return them to thee."[184] Scholars freely cooperated and assisted one another with citations from books which were not readily accessible.[185]

The widely scattered bibliographical references that occur in most responsa frequently indicate the size of the author's private library,[186] which was often the most treasured part of his fortune.[187] The manuscripts comprising the Spanish-Jewish libraries are to this day noted for their finish and accuracy, the particular virtue of the Spanish Arabs.[188] Castilian Hebrew manuscripts, in particular, were esteemed highly and held to be superior to the Aragon-Catalonian manuscripts.[189] Books share the fortunes of their owners, and the fate of the Jewish libraries in Spain was correspondingly less turbulent than in other European centers. Even in times of civil war and brigandage, the literary collections were sometimes spared by the marauders.[190] In the fearful summer of 1391, however, the fury of the Christian mobs descended upon man and book alike, and the libraries shared in the fate of the general massacre. The written word, like the living spirit, never revived completely from the holocaust.[191]

CHAPTER XVI

RABBINIC CULTURE

THE rabbis whose writings form the basis of this work reflect more faithfully than any other single group or source the cultural norm of Spanish Jewry — the thoughts and feelings of the masses who did not willingly lose themselves in the clouds of mysticism or the sophistries of rationalism. They were close enough to the people to share, in many instances, the foibles of the age; they also towered above them sufficiently to guide them safely out of the morass of false messianism and dissolving pseudo-philosophies.

The educational program which they sponsored and which was represented by the *talmid hakam* was distinctly religious and even specifically halakic in character. At no time, however, did it preclude the study of subjects outside the domain of religion. The center of mental gravity was the Law, within the very heart of Judaism, but the pursuit of secular knowledge, though not a religious mandate, responded to the natural craving of intellectual beings. While the community officially did not promote secular education, the Spanish-Jewish authorities generally approved its cultivation as long as it was subordinate to the program of religious instruction and did not tend to undermine faith. Duran (1361–1444), who represented in his person the fullest tradition of the Spanish rabbinate, devoted himself assiduously to science and philosophy in order the better to vindicate the Torah against unbelievers.[1]

The Hebrew poets, grammarians and Bible exegetes grew
indignant over the neglect of formal instruction in Hebrew
linguistics and blamed the talmudists.[2] They deplored the
superficial knowledge of Hebrew among the masses, a situation which compelled even the creators of the neo-Hebrew
classics to write many of their works in non-Hebrew tongues.
They decried the fact that Hebrew was no longer the spoken
tongue of the Jews and pleaded passionately for the study
of Hebrew grammar and philology. Even the strictest
halakist, however, did not oppose the study of these subjects
on principle.[3] It was inevitable that, as the Talmud and its
auxiliary studies absorbed the attention of the students,
the other subjects should assume a place of secondary
importance.

Far from opposing philological studies, the Spanish rabbis
and the rabbinically educated laity were themselves men
of linguistic accomplishments. They were not only thoroughly versed in Hebrew and in the colloquial use of the
vernacular; they also mastered the literary usage of the
Romance vernacular and studied the literary, classic language of their country, which was either Arabic or Latin or
both.

The close affinity which existed in the earlier period
between the Arabic language and Jewish learning in all its
manifestations, including the strictly rabbinical, is well
known.[4] For almost three centuries, from the tenth to the
twelfth inclusive, Arabic was the primary vehicle of Hebrew
philology and biblical as well as talmudic exegesis. It was
not only the medium in which Jewish scientists made their
contributions to mathematics, medicine and other sciences;
it was not only the language in which Jewish thinkers
formulated the earliest systems of Jewish philosophy, ethics

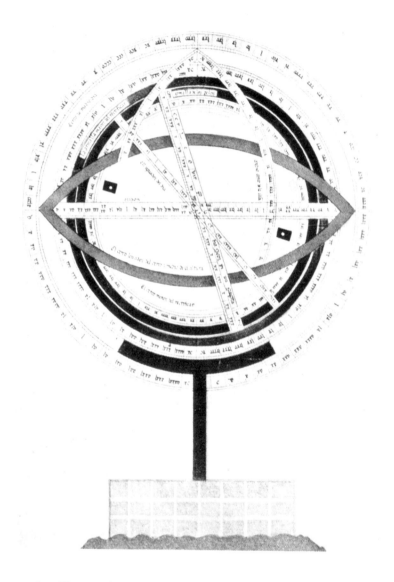

Armillary sphere constructed by a Jewish astronomer for
Alfonso the Wise of Castille, 13th century

(see p. xi)

and theology; it was also the language of halakic literature, including talmudic commentaries, codes of law and rabbinic responsa.[5] When the cultural tide turned with the ebb of the twelfth century and the great Jewish centers were destroyed in Moslem Spain under the Almohades, the knowledge of Arabic was preserved in the northern provinces by the educated classes, rabbis and laymen. It was then that the important school of translators from the Arabic into the Hebrew, Latin and Spanish arose. Isaac ibn Sid, the pious reader in the synagogue of Toledo, was the pride of the court of Alfonso the Wise. He edited the famous astronomical tables which were euphemistically called the Alfonsine Tables. Jewish physicians — Judah Kohen (b. Moses), Abraham and Samuel Levi — were members of the court and were engaged to translate Arabic works on astronomy and astrology into Castilian.[7] It may also be recalled that Spanish and Provençal scholars were invited to the Sicilian court of Emperor Frederick II to interpret the Arabic-Greek classics to the scholarly fraternity with whom the royal patron surrounded himself.[8] Rabbis of the type of Ibn Adret and Barfat, who were, first and foremost, strict talmudists and who lived the greatest part of their lives in non-Arabic communities, understood Arabic and were conversant with its literature. Thus Barfat quoted Arabic medical works and Sa'adia's writings,[9] and Ibn Adret replied to the Arabic polemical writings of Ibn Hazm.[10] As to the rabbi-physicians, a thorough knowledge of Arabic was indispensable for the study of medicine, according to a well qualified witness of the fourteenth century.[11]

Latin never replaced Arabic as a medium of Jewish culture. It was not only linguistically alien; it was spiritually hostile and historically inimical. Nevertheless, the

knowledge of Latin was cultivated among the rabbis and
the laity not alone for the value of its scientific literature,
which increased towards the thirteenth century, but even
more so for its practical value in statesmanship and religious
self-defense.[12] As judges, the rabbis were frequently called
upon to examine the Latin documents of the Christian
notaries.[13] Learned rabbis could not dispense with a knowledge of the Vulgate and the Christian polemical literature
in Latin if they were to defend the cause of Judaism in the
religious disputations which were forced upon them.[14] Simon
Duran, whose responsa illuminate conditions in Spain as
well as North Africa, raided the literary arsenals of church
literature to forge his *Bow and Buckler.*

The Romance languages, on the other hand, were cultivated as native tongues, and were referred to by various
rabbis "as our language."[15] Bahya b. Asher, popular Bible
commentator and one of the best known disciples of Ibn
Adret, frequently quoted Arabic, Spanish and French equiv-
alents of biblical words.[16] Barfat rendered difficult Hebrew
terms into Spanish much in the manner of Rashi's *la'azim.*[17]
He criticized the Spanish translation of the scroll of Esther
which was recited on Purim in the synagogue of Saragossa
for the sake of the women who did not understand Hebrew.[18]
His teacher, Rabbi Nissim in Barcelona, did not understand
Castilian;[19] his native language was obviously Catalan.

The rabbis frequently corresponded with the king, the
bailiffs and other officials concerning juridical cases in which
Jews were involved, in the native languages of the country.[20]
To please Alfonso the Wise, Jewish scholars translated
"the code of rabbinic law" (*toda la ley de los judíos*) into
Castilian.[21] Pedro IV, in 1383, expected the Jews to prepare a Catalan translation of Maimonides' *Code*; other-

wise he threatened the Jewish communities of Barcelona,
Gerona and Perpignan with the forfeiture of his royal
favor.[22] Barfat analyzed points of difference between the
Jewish and the Spanish laws in given instances, referring
to the national codes and revealing, in addition, an understanding of comparative law.[23] Legal terms are frequently
quoted in Spanish, which is referred to as "our tongue."[24]

The religious disputations, too, into which the rabbis
were forced by Christian zealots, show not only their dialectic skill and mastery of Christian as well as Mohammedan
doctrine, but give evidence of the ease with which they
could fence and parry in the language of their opponents,
which was also their native tongue. The famous disputation
of 1263, which Nahmanides conducted against the apostate
Pablo Christiano in the presence of King James I of Aragon
and his court and church prelates, was debated in Catalan,
the language of the country.[25] As Ibn Adret had frequent
discussions with Raymund Martin and other Christian
theologians, whose views he cited for refutation in his
responsa,[26] he must have conversed with them either in the
vernacular or Latin. He taught his correspondent in Lerida
how to combat the arguments of the *Pugio Fidei* and referred
to his own polemical and apologetical compositions.[27]

That so few polemical works of the Jews were written in
Latin or Romance is no doubt due to their dread of the
Church and the Inquisition.[28] Nevertheless, Hasdai Crescas,
at the request of Christian liberals, wrote a Spanish work
(c. 1398) in refutation of Christian dogma,[29] and his pupil,
the philosopher Joseph Albo, followed his example some
decades later.[30] The Jewish preacher and courtier, R. Joseph
ibn Shem Tob, who translated the Spanish polemical work
of Crescas into Hebrew in 1451, frequently debated with

Christian scholars and preachers, undoubtedly in Spanish, which he calls the "language of my country."[31]

The two principal languages of Spain, Catalan and Castilian, both left their traces in the responsa literature. As if prompted by a premonition of their destiny, the Jews of each Iberian province adhered to their beloved language all the more tenaciously as the century of doom and exile advanced upon them. It became increasingly the language in which they formulated the statutes and regulations of their social and communal life. They made it also the literary medium of their lighter vein. Not the least interesting phase of this activity was the ease with which various talented sons of Spanish Jewry linked the two languages by facile translation.[32]

The sciences of the Middle Ages, furthermore, were cultivated by the exponents of the halakic ideal, because these sciences were directly related to Jewish religious life.[33] They were assimilated within the very range of halakah through the calendrical institutions which are based on astronomical calculations, and because of the hygienic regulations and the anatomical basis of many of the dietary laws. Often an halakic decision depended on scientific opinion and the rabbi's verdict waited upon the word of the more expert scientist.[34] A knowledge of mathematics, and especially geometry, was essential to the understanding of various talmudic tractates[35] and the halakot treated therein.[36] The first Hebrew work on geometry curiously bears the name of *mishna* (משנת המדות),[37] and even a translation of Euclid was designated by this classic name.[38] The calculations entering into the laws of usury, the reduction of ancient coinage to contemporary currency and the determination of weights and measures required skill in elementary mathematics.[39] Nevertheless, the study of mathematics received but little attention in comparison with the pursuit of astronomy which was considered the most important branch of the mathematical sciences.[40]

As early as talmudic times, astronomy was called the "Jewish Wisdom,"[41] the study of which was a religious injunction, while its neglect was open to severe censure.[42] Astronomical laws from the halakic standpoint were treated in such well-known early works as the *Baraita of the Mystery of Intercalation* (ברייתא דסוד העבור), the *Baraita of Samuel* (ברייתא דשמואל) and the probably pseudepigraphic *Baraita of Rabbi Ada*.[43] Beginning with the ninth century and the Arabic scientific period, the Jews developed also a general interest in astronomy, and their literature covered all the phases of the science then known. Among the authors are to be counted scientists like Abraham b. Hiyya, grammarian-exegetes like Abraham ibn Ezra, philosophers like Judah ha-Levi or Levi b. Gershon, and also noted talmudists like Isaac b. Baruk Albalia, the rival of Alfasi, Zerahiah ha-Levi of Lunel and the encyclopedic Maimonides.[44] Jewish writers not only contributed to the literary preparation of Arabic, Latin and Spanish translations and editions of the ancient works of the Greek astronomers; they also developed astronomic theories in original works of their own. They prepared independently and in conjunction with others the celebrated astronomical tables of the Middle Ages. They wrote on the astrolabe, quadrant, sphere, sundial and other astronomical instruments which they improved by new inventions and theories.[45] Cartography, for instance, was in the hands of the Jews of Majorca, one of whom was the first to apply the astrolabe to navigation.[46]

What gave this science so prominent a place in Jewish

thought, however, was its relation to the calendar. For the central problem in Jewish calendrical calculation was the adjustment of the solar year with the lunar months, or the proper arrangement of a calendar whose months were lunar while its cycle of festivals was agrarian and necessarily based on the solar seasons. For this reason, in the opinion of Duran, astronomy must have originated with the Jews.[47] The lunisolar cycles had to be regularly compensated by means of intercalation, and a special branch of astronomy was developed known as *hokmat ha-'ibbur*, the science of intercalation, upon which depended the religious calendar of Judaism. Thus it is not surprising to find that the production of the most comprehensive astronomical work in Hebrew literature, *Yesod 'Olam* by Isaac Israeli, was directly stimulated by so zealous and exclusive a halakist as Rabbi Asher of Toledo.[48] In great part, the Alfonsine Tables owe their origin to the *hazzan* of Toledo.[49] Similarly the *dayyan* of Saragossa in 1335 compiled a work of astronomical tables.[50] Abraham Zacuto, rabbinical historian of the fifteenth and sixteenth centuries, was a celebrated astronomer at the time of Columbus and played an important part in his success.[51] Enthusiastic halakists, who deplored the necessity of drinking draughts of "Jewish Wisdom" from Greek fountains, comforted themselves with the fiction that the reputed astronomy of the Greeks was really a full-grown product of the Jewish intellect which the Hellenists had wrung from the sages of vanquished Judea as a prize of war during the time of the Second Commonwealth.[52]

On the other hand, Jewish authorities differed as to the merits of astrology, which was another branch of applied astronomy.[53] This "science," universally credited in ancient and mediaeval times, had its foundation in the theory that the position and the course of the stars reacted upon the sublunar world and influenced the fate of its human inhabitants. The art of observing the position of the stars, and thus forecasting the outcome of events and divining the fate of human beings, had become a profession which was in great demand at the royal courts; Jewish courtiers, astronomers and physicians were obliged to compete in divination and the casting of horoscopes. The unpopularity of this profession among the Jews, however, is sufficiently attested by the paucity of strictly astrological works in Hebrew literature.[54] Nevertheless, with the notable exception of Maimonides who combated astrology both on religious and rational grounds,[55] no voice was raised against its theoretical claims. Rationalists like Abraham b. Hiyya and Abraham ibn Ezra defended the validity of astrology as a science, while the great religious authority, Nahmanides, in a responsum "concerning diviners, sorcerers and astrologers," affirmed his belief in the "decree of the stars." They who feared God, it is true, had no need to be concerned with astrological speculations. Prayer and righteous living would counteract the evil omen. But this protection required God's miraculous intervention and was a special act of grace, whereas one should not rely on miracles. It was therefore wise to heed the warnings of the constellations, to be wary of "unlucky" days and to turn to prayer and penitence when the constellations caused foreboding.[56] God's prescience was likened to the augury of the astrologer, which forecasts but does not compel the future.[57] The custom prevailing in these countries of holding marriages only at the time of the full moon, said Nahmanides, was not to be considered divination. It was rather to be compared to the tradition of anointing a king at a spring so that his government might be prolonged.[58]

For increase, in contrast to decrease, was a good omen.[59] In his medical practice, Nahmanides accepted the view, which medical science adopted from astrology,[60] that the engraving of a lion on a metal sheet, if performed at an auspicious moment, cured diseases of the loin.[61] Such a cure was bitterly assailed by enthusiasts of the Talmud as being not only contrary to reason but opposed to Jewish law.[62] For, they argued, it was forbidden to engrave the image of any of the figures of the *Merkabah*,[63] of which the lion was one. Furthermore, as the cure would be contrary to the laws of nature, it was a heathenish, superstitious practice which is proscribed by the Talmud as an imitation of the "ways of the Amorite."[64] In the Provence, this opposition developed into a great controversy among the native rabbis.[65] To Ibn Adret, however, before whom this question was raised in correspondence, the fact that Nahmanides, "who had no superior in learning, authority and piety," believed in such a cure was sufficient sanction. He skillfully brushed aside the opposition based on talmudic grounds and contended that as the remedy was well known to physicians, there was no doubt that it was based on an empirical truth even though it did not harmonize with the accepted and tabulated laws of natural science.[66] For, otherwise, healing by amulets, too, would have to be banned, and yet the Talmud expressly favored this practice.[67]

It will be noted that the opposition to, rather than the defense of the fantastic notions of astrology was based on biblical and talmudical authority.[68] In the background of general mediaeval superstition and belief, whatever opposition was raised by learned Jews to astrology was based on the conceptions of Jewish law. Characteristically, it was

Maimonides who struck the keynote of antagonism to this as well as other forms of obscurantism:

> Anyone who has faith in these and similar things and believes in his heart that they contain truth and wisdom, but that the Torah has forbidden them, belongs to the fools and the senseless and is to be classed with women and children.[69]

Anyone who acted on the prognostication of the soothsayer and deliberately arranged to do his work at the time set by the astrologers transgressed the biblical command, "And ye shall not practice augury,"[70] and was to be punished by flagellation.[71]

Though the protest of Maimonides was re-echoed in later generations, it was not on philosophical or rational grounds but on the plane of Jewish theology and ethics that astrology met with the most determined opposition.[72] For instinctively it was felt that the exaggerated emphasis upon the influences of the constellations and the belief in the unalterable decrees of the stars and planets were a check upon the omnipotence of God and a denial of free will, which is the cornerstone of Jewish ethics. Rabbi Abraham b. David, the keen and unsparing critic of Maimonides, argued that while God transferred the fate of man to the control of the constellations, He also endowed him with intellect to wrest his own destiny from this blind power.[73] Ibn Adret, a firm believer in astrology, nevertheless contended that to believe in the fatal influence of the spheres on the lives of his fellow Jews was tantamount to the denial of individual Providence.[74] Indeed he did not hesitate to ascribe this attitude toward Providence — an attitude from which he shrank — to those talmudic rabbis who placed Israel under astrological influ-

ences.[75] That God emancipated the Jews from the fatalism
of the spheres by means of the Torah was preached in the
synagogue by R. Judah b. Asher.[76] Duran freely disclaimed
any intimate knowledge of astrology since it had no bearing
on the Torah. Formerly Jewish sages had been masters of
this science, but in his own time little was known except
what was still imperfectly preserved by physicians and
peasants. He advised his correspondent in Bersak, R. Samuel
Halav, not to trouble himself with the study of astrology,
for it did not lead to perfection.[77]

Most characteristic of the Spanish rabbinate was the
practice of medicine.[78] Indeed, among the many Jewish
physicians,[79] who as a class formed the nobility and aristocracy of Spanish Jewry, it is often hard to distinguish
whether in any instance the medical practice was associated
with the rabbinical dignity or not.[80] Aside from their interest in the science — medicine in the Middle Ages was the
equivalent of the present-day natural sciences and formed
part of the curriculum of a liberal education[81] — a considerable number of the rabbis turned to the medical profession for a livelihood because they were opposed to the
acceptance of a salary for the performance of their rabbinical
duties.[82] It was possible to become a physician without the
formality of university studies, as a royal license to practice
medicine could be obtained by passing a prescribed examination under the sponsorship of a recognized physician.[83]

Ethical and religious aspects of the medical profession are
preserved in the responsa which are not expressed in the
medical literature proper.[84] The liability of physicians for
errors in the treatment of their patients was legally defined
and a distinction was drawn between the responsibility
involved in medicinal prescriptions and surgical operations.[85]

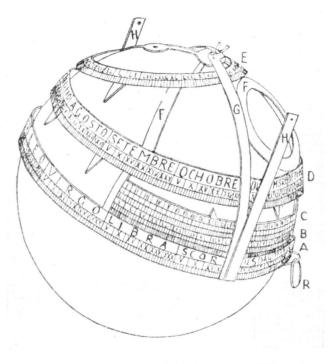

A spherical astrolabe of Alphonso the Wise of
Castille constructed by a Jewish astronomer

(see p. xi)

Medical opinions were sought in halakic decisions,[86] while religious standards in turn influenced medical practice.[87] Thus astrological medicine, which commanded general respect and acceptance, was treated by Jewish physicians from the religious standpoint of Judaism.[88] The efficacy of amulets was upheld by talmudic precedent.[89] Ibn Adret seriously outlined the conditions under which it was permitted to break the Sabbath laws in order to prepare in writing an amulet for a sick person or a woman in labor.[90]

It was not permitted to cure disease by the recital of biblical verses, for this not only savored of magical incantation but constituted a denial of the Torah: "For the words of the Torah are a healing of the soul and not a cure for the body."[91] It was furthermore a religious transgression for physicians to decline to treat patients who required their services, though it was also their right to charge a fee therefor.[92] Ibn Adret emphatically expressed the view that it was the duty of a physician to give professional aid to all who asked for it, Jew or Christian.[93] His teacher Moses b. Nahman had often rendered obstetrical service to Christian women.[94] The learned Saul ha-Kohen Astruc was eulogized by his friend in exile, Rabbi Isaac Barfat, for the unselfish use he had made of his fame and medical skill, extending his services gratis to the poor, even to his enemies, and lavishly distributing his income among the needy, Jews and Moslems alike.[95] Therein he followed the earlier noble example of Maimonides in Egypt, whose writings profoundly influenced the code of ethics as well as the medical practice of Jewish physicians in later centuries. Maimonides' self-revealing letter was long remembered and prized as an ethical testament to the medical profession.[96]

In the ghastly records of human bigotry it would be

difficult to find a more cruel distortion of fact than the wicked accusations against Jewish physicians which, as we shall see, were made the basis of restrictive church legislation.[97] Time and again, Christians were told by their spiritual healers that Jewish physicians practiced their art in order to poison and kill their patients.[98] Suspicion naturally breeds suspicion. Consequently a Hebrew code of the fourteenth century, in the same spirit, warned against entrusting a case of serious illness to the Christian practitioner; the codifier, however, had no objection to a gentile medical expert and furthermore declared that, if the patient was influential at the court, he might trust himself to any Christian physician who was not an avowed enemy.[99]

Religious concessions as well as important social distinctions were granted to the medical profession. Thus, in the city of Calatayud, physicians only were permitted to hold public religious services in their homes.[100] Kings and popes, prelates and princes afforded them special protection[101] and they were frequently exempted from the shame of the Jewish badge.[102] The royal patrons, at times, freed their favored physicians from taxes; but this was usually at the expense of the *aljamas* who jealously resisted these concessions.[103] In the interest of medical science, physicians were exempted or excluded from public office in the *aljama* of Majorca.[104] Jewish and Christian physicians vied for public appointment and in numerous instances superiority of medical skill triumphed over popular prejudice.[105]

As no doubt the duties of all public physicians were similar, the contract between the consuls of Collioure and "Master" Albert del Puig or Dupuy (de Padio), physician, may be taken as a representative arrangement. It is an interesting example of socialized medicine. The physician, on assuming

the duties of his office to which he was generally appointed
for a term of years, made a medical examination of every
person in the territory under his jurisdiction and then gave
everyone advice according to his findings, in the light of his
knowledge of the science of medicine and as God inspired
him. He treated the poor in the public hospital. He was
obliged to visit every sick person three times a month. For
any visit above this number, which he deemed necessary,
he was permitted to charge a fee. During the term of his
contract, he was not permitted to leave the city without the
permission of the consuls, or public authorities. For these
services, he was exempted from every form of public tax,
besides receiving a stipulated annual salary which was
twenty *livres de tern*.[106] Christendom valued the medical
profession higher than Moorish North Africa did in the
fifteenth century, and thus the rabbi-physician who proudly
disdained to be paid for his rabbinical duties in Majorca
was reluctantly compelled to accept an official salary as
rabbi, when he fled to Algiers to escape the massacre of
1391.[107]

Strangely enough, it was in the field of medicine that the
weeds of superstition struck deepest root. For in all mediaeval medicine there was a twilight zone where popular
belief adumbrated scientific observation and favored
remedies savoring of magic and superstition. A mother was
advised by a woman physician (חכמה) to cure her daughter
by taking her to the river bank and washing her with a
compound of oil and salt, which was then to be thrown into
the river. She was warned to be on her guard against gentile
observers who might accuse her of witchcraft.[108] It was
characteristic of superstitious Christians to attribute magical
power to Jews.[109] Sheep's milk suckled directly from the

animal was supposed to have special therapeutic properties.[110] Amulets and talismans were popular and could not
be altogether uprooted.[111] The belief in ghosts and evil
spirits was not as common as in France and Germany, but
was not unknown in Spain.[112] The influence of astrology on
medicine was necessarily pernicious.[113] Unfortunately, the
Talmud, in many instances, countenances superstitious
beliefs and practices.[114] Nahmanides supported them,[115]
and consequently Ibn Adret reluctantly leaned toward them,
while he frankly confessed himself sorely perplexed as to
whether they ought to be permitted or banned as heathenish
superstitions.[116] Because of talmudic support, even so
distinguished a philosopher and rabbi as Hasdai Crescas
would not disown belief in spirits or in the efficacy of in-
cantations and amulets.[117]

The opposition of the rabbis to the extravagances of the
pseudo-Messiahs and their hallucinations, however, was
unequivocal and steadfast. The false prophet was the twin
of the evil spirit. Both left behind them a trail of disaster;
both grew in the same underbrush of ignorance and credulity.
Barfat was informed that a Christian proselyte to Judaism
proposed to bring down the moon. Indeed, he was believed
to have the power to mount the clouds. The story ran that
he saw, in one of the clouds, a devil (שד) carrying off a
victim at terrifying speed, but by the power of incantation,
he stopped the evil spirit in his flight. Barfat replied that
only morons lent credulity to such tales, which were relatively harmless. When, however, after backsliding to
Christianity, the man sought to return to Judaism, the
gates were closed to him and he found shelter in the religion
of Allah and His Prophet.[118]

Less childish and far more confusing to the tortured

spirit was the role of the pseudo-prophets and social re-
deemers who arose periodically from the midst of the
Jewish people in answer to the eternal quest for peace and
salvation. Young and enthusiastic, honestly self-deluded
and carried away by frenzied hallucinations, they called
upon their people to fast and pray, to share their possessions
with the poor and to prepare for a miraculous return to the
Holy Land. They created a profound impression as harbin-
gers of the messianic era. The mass hysteria which they
aroused was politically dangerous in the extreme under
Christian and Moslem rule alike. In his famous *Epistle to
Yemen*, Maimonides, with penetrating insight and an
inimitable array of logic and fact, exposed the false and
dangerous claims of such a pretender who had thrown his
unfortunate, afflicted brethren of the South into a seething
turmoil of doubt and confusion. Messianic impostors were
not a new phenomenon, he pointed out, nor limited to any
age or country. They had appeared again and again under
Moslem rule and also in Christian France, and invariably
death and destruction followed in their wake.[119]

In like manner, too, Ibn Adret resolved the doubts of the
communities that appealed to him concerning the prophetic
claimants that arose in his time. Without the emotional
appeal of Maimonides' letter, but rather in the impersonal
phraseology of a legal analysis, he advised the community
of Avila not to be carried away by the vagaries and exaggera-
tions of a pretender to prophetic inspiration. It was alleged
that an angel regularly appeared before the "prophet," who
was both ignorant and illiterate. With the angel as his
mentor and under his supernatural dictation, he was said
to have composed a marvelous, mystical work, accompanied
by an equally inspired commentary, which surpassed

ordinary human understanding. Witnesses of unimpeachable integrity testified to the "prophet's" lack of education and also to his lack of association with men of learning. Being unable to impeach the testimony, Ibn Adret made feeble attempts to explain the phenomenon in natural terms; but although he was not altogether satisfied with his own explanations, he had no hesitation in rejecting the supernatural claims of the pretender. Like Maimonides before him, he was fortunately able to appeal to the talmudic conception of a true prophet, which was exacting. Prophecy could not descend upon an ignorant soul, nor upon an unworthy generation, nor on soil outside of the Holy Land.[120] It was furthermore inconsistent with the nature of prophecy to express itself in the form of a long dictated volume. The story undoubtedly called for painstaking investigation but under no condition could a claim be set up for the prophet.[121]

The man of Avila was not the only one to be unmasked by Ibn Adret. Prior to him there had arisen the romantic and enigmatical figure of Abraham Abulafia of Saragossa, a mystic and cabalist, whose influence was destined to be more permanent in the development of the esoteric cult.[122] Descended of a well-known and respected family, trained in philosophy and the Talmud, Abulafia lost himself in mystic fantasies and visions which were in part induced by ascetic practices. Among the vagaries of his career was a futile journey in search of the Lost Ten Tribes on the banks of the mythical Sambation River, and an inspired pilgrimage to Rome to convert Pope Nicholas III to Judaism, from which he barely escaped with his life. Undismayed, he continued in his mad course and boldly announced himself a prophet and the messiah incarnate to the bewildered Jews in Sicily. Many fell under his spell and, though the hour of redemption was to strike six years later, in 1290, his adherents were feverishly preparing for the messianic journey to the Holy Land. At this critical juncture, the guidance and authority of Ibn Adret were invoked by the distracted community of Palermo. Adret immediately sensed the danger and in no measured terms denounced the self-constituted messiah as a charlatan, whose fantastic and deceitful notions could parade as wisdom only before imbeciles.[123] Not content with his own effort, he rallied other communities in the attack upon the impostor, until he succeeded in thoroughly discrediting the preposterous claims of the would-be redeemer.[124]

Adret referred to this experience in his public letter concerning the "prophet" of Avila. He recalled also the curious incident of an unlettered boy in Lerida who, in an over-wrought state of mind, recited poetry and other original compositions and finally cured himself by a medical prescription which he composed during his state of ecstasy. Adret heard of many other occult tales reported to him, principally from Germany, but he was confident that an impartial and thorough investigation would explode all these supernatural claims.[125] This, it must be borne in mind, was the attitude of a strict talmudist who was destined to wage war against philosophers and their blind followers.[126] How curious, therefore, that a century later it was a rabbinical philosopher like Hasdai Crescas, author of the *Light of God,* credited by modern scholars with having been the fore-runner of Spinoza, who allegedly supported the messianic claims of another self-constituted prophet, one Moses Botarel.[127]

Undoubtedly the frequency of so many occult phenomena was directly related to the spread of mysticism which developed with such intensity after the public emergence of the cabala in Spain during the latter half of the thirteenth century. But the fact should be emphasized that the authors of our rabbinic responsa, who were the spiritual ballast of their communities, were surprisingly unaffected by the vagaries of the extreme mystics. With the sole exception of Nahmanides, they took little part in the development of cabalistic teachings. It is true that some of Ibn Adret's disciples followed the cabalistic trend. His pupil, Bahya b. Asher, whose fame rests on a commentary to the Pentateuch, filled the volume with cabalistic notions.[128] But the mystic note was not evident in his strictly rabbinic disciples or in his academic successors. As for Ibn Adret himself, aside from a natural reverence for his great master Nahmanides and a leaning toward his naive pietism, he gave no evidence of any interest in theoretical cabala and was an inveterate foe of all its occult and supernatural manifestations. The celebrated Rabbi Nissim Gerundi, successor to the post of Ibn Adret, openly criticized Nahmanides for his connection with the cabala.[129] Barfat, who embodied the spirit and traditions of Ibn Adret a century later, scorned the central teaching of the cabala, the theory of divine emanations in ten gradations; for, as he quoted, "the Christians believe in the Trinity; the cabalists in the Unity of Ten."[130] He furthermore opposed the cabalists' manner of prayer, for he felt that they interposed the divine emanations as a barrier between the worshiper and God.[131]

From the foregoing it would appear that the rabbis were aware of no hostility between religion and the sciences, between faith and empirical knowledge. At the very threshold of the Arabic period, however, metaphysical speculation followed closely in the wake of scientific ratiocination.

Now mediaeval Jewish philosophy was essentially a reconciliation of dissimilar elements. It was avowedly an attempt
to harmonize an apparent disparity between Jewish beliefs
and the wisdom of the Greeks, between the Bible, the
Mishna and the Talmud, on the one hand, and the Aristotelian and the pseudo-Aristotelian works, on the other. The
forced harmonization of Hebrew Revelation and Greek
Reason necessarily transformed the older conception of
talmudic and biblical tradition, even as the mediaeval atmosphere affected the exposition of the ancient Hellene. It
compelled on the part of the Jew a reinterpretation of
tradition, of scripture and even of God. While this mental
operation saved for Judaism those restless intellects who
were troubled by the fundamental problems of existence, the
result was distinctly disconcerting not only to the unlettered
masses who preferred an unquestioning, uncritical faith as
handed down by the fathers, but also to the great majority
of the learned, to whom metaphysical subtleties had no profound meaning. A reaction therefore set in which assumed
violent manifestations; and in the bitterness of the controversy the auxiliaries of philosophy, the sciences, were also
branded as enemies of pure faith.

The controversy can be sketched here only in outline
and mainly in its relation to the rabbis upon whose responsa
this work is based.[132] The wave of rationalism was from the
beginning accompanied by a countercurrent of mysticism.
The people at large showed their distrust of philosophic
innovations passively by keeping aloof from them. As the
Arabic civilization developed, however, with its strong
propensity toward philosophic speculation, the intellectual
horizon of the Jews widened, a new appreciation of the
sciences and literature dawned upon them and, for the first

time, wide Jewish circles evinced real enthusiasm for metaphysical studies. This new interest also strongly affected
the exponents of talmudic and halakic scholarship, so that
whatever opposition still lingered against the metaphysical
transformation of Judaism lay dormant for two centuries,
while philosophical and ethical classics were making their
appearance and the structures of biblical exegesis and
Hebrew philology were being built. What has been said of
Maimonides may well describe the age: it philosophized the
Talmud and talmudized philosophy. Suddenly, however, in
the twelfth century, Moslem civilization collapsed in Spain;
Christian ecclesiasticism, with its system of the Inquisition
and the forcible suppression of heresy, rapidly supplanted it;
and in this atmosphere the popular distrust of the over-
rationalization of religion, which hitherto had been latent,
now came to the surface.[133]

The struggle began in the lifetime of Maimonides and
its center was not Spain but the two centripetal poles of the
Jewish intellectual world: Bagdad, the spiritual capital of
Oriental Jewry, dominated by the Gaon Samuel b. Ali;
and the populous cities of Provence, famed for their talmudic
academies, the tragic home of the Albigenses and the shelter
of Jewish refugees who fled there from the fanaticism of the
Almohades. The writings and the person of Maimonides
were in the main the battlefield on which the opposing
spiritual forces met in combat. But as the controversy raged
on for fully a century, the issues were broadened in scope
and finally the rabbis and the communities of both Spain
and the Provence were drawn in.

Abraham b. David of Posquières, a renowned talmudist,
opened the controversy. His attack was not directed against
Maimonides' metaphysical treatise, which he could not read

because it was written in Arabic, but against the great legal
code in Hebrew which Maimonides introduced by an exposition of his philosophic views.[134] While the criticisms of
the Provençal rabbi were scattered and diffuse,[135] the attack
of the Gaon Samuel was more effectively concentrated on
Maimonides' theological views.[136] Shortly thereafter, about
the year 1202, the torch of opposition was raised in Toledo
by the young, impetuous and aristocratic Meir b. Todros
Abulafia, who addressed a public letter to "the sages of
Lunel," denouncing Maimonides' eschatology and his conception of immortality and calling for vigorous action.[137]
It was a bold move and it was slow in gaining momentum.
Abulafia obtained a hearing in Northern France and won
the support of its leading authority, R. Samson of Sens,[138]
but his letter was treated with contempt in Lunel and he was
ridiculed in rhyme and verse by the poets of Spain.[139] Meanwhile, enthusiastic disciples were rendering the Arabic
works of Maimonides accessible to the people in Hebrew
translation, and the Maimonidean system was being interpreted and popularized in homilies and readable texts.

But the simple, trusting faith of the popular mind was
not to be swept aside. A redoubtable opponent in the person
of the revered talmudist, Solomon b. Abraham of Montpellier, arose to engage the adherents of philosophy in
vigorous combat, and he was blindly followed by two fanatical disciples, David b. Saul and Rabbi Jonah Gerundi.[140]
What he lacked in philosophical training was compensated
by holy zeal. He did not propose a theoretic refutation of
the philosophic school. Nor did he direct his opposition
against any particular philosophic tenet or religious dogma.
From the start, he entered the lists as a prosecutor rather
than as a controversialist. Standing almost alone, except

for the support of two of his disciples, Solomon anathematized the philosophic writings of Maimonides, interdicted the sciences and pronounced the sentence of excommunication against those who engaged in the study of profane literature or who treated the Bible allegorically and dealt too freely with the aggadic portions of the Talmud.[141] It was an unprecedented act in mediaeval Jewry, and one can see in it the unfortunate Christian influence on Judaism. For, only shortly before, the Fourth Lateran Council had similarly interdicted the study of certain philosophic texts and Pope Gregory IX had ordered the University of Paris to eliminate them from its curriculum. Indeed, the entire anti-Maimonidean controversy was but a weak Jewish counterpart of the agitation against Aristotle and Averroes in the Christian camps during the thirteenth century.[142] The cry of heresy which had wrought havoc among the Christian natives of Provence now re-echoed with disastrous, though less bloody, consequences among the Jewish communities. With the aid of his disciple and emissary, R. Jonah Gerundi, Solomon b. Abraham rallied the French rabbis to his cause.[143] But a storm of indignation broke out in the Spanish communities. The opponents of secular learning had sadly blundered. In their antagonism to Maimonidean thought, they had allowed themselves to speak slightingly and even to slander the reputation of the great master who was loved and revered by the lowly masses no less than by the aristocracy of learning and the men of worldly attainments. The champions of science and philosophy were not slow to seize upon this tactical blunder of their opponents. They thundered against those who dared quench the light of the great luminary who rescued Israel from ignorance, error and folly. The authorities of Saragossa, led by the influential aristocratic physician Bahya b. Moses, branded Solomon and his two disciples as "three corrupters and misleaders of the people."[144] The weapons which Solomon had used against his antagonists were turned on his small band, not alone by prominent individuals but by the collective action of important Jewish communities. While in his own city the learned attacked him bitterly, the neighboring communities of Lunel, Beziers and Narbonne excommunicated both him and his disciples. In vain did Nahmanides appeal to the communities of Aragon, Navarre and Castile to withhold judgment until both sides could be heard.[145] Led by Saragossa, the communities of Huesca, Monzon, Lerida and Calatayud followed the example of the Provençal Jewries and pronounced the sentence of excommunication upon Solomon and his two disciples.[146] The *kahal* of Toledo was barely restrained from taking a similar course by the determined opposition of its aged rabbi, Meir Abulafia ha-Levi, and the influential physician Judah ibn Alfakar.[147] Despite this setback, however, victory seemed to crown the efforts of the Maimunists. On all sides, Solomon was being deserted by his followers. Even in France the ban against the study of Maimonides' works was being lifted. Nahmanides again futilely proposed a compromise on which he thought all parties could agree.[148] Realizing his failing strength and blinded by fanatic zeal, Solomon finally resorted to the execrable measure of denouncing the philosophic works of Maimonides to the Inquisition in Montpellier as heretical and dangerous. There was no doubt as to what the attitude of the Dominican heresy-hunters would be. Two decades earlier, they had consigned the physics and metaphysics of Aristotle to flames.[149] They could not be expected to show greater leniency to the Jewish Aristotle. With great ceremony, the priests applied the torch, kindled from the light of the candelabra in the monastery, to the funeral pyre of Maimonides' philosophic works.[150] Consternation filled the hearts of the pious as the words of the sage leaped into flame in the lurid auto-da-fé in Montpellier.[151] The works of the immortal philosopher also fed the fires of hatred, and vengeance followed swiftly. By some unknown method and agency, the followers of Solomon were apprehended, convicted of the crime of informing, which was then a capital offense,[152] and in accordance with the barbarous laws of the time, their tongues were cut out. It would seem that Solomon himself also lost his life.[153]

The controversy continued to rage.[154] Although the exact sequence of events cannot be definitely established, it is fair to assume with Graetz that within less than a decade, in 1242, the Dominicans again made a bonfire of the writings of Maimonides, this time in Paris.[155] But it was no partisan victory, for in forty days the Talmud itself was made to lick the flames of the Inquisition and the whole house of Israel was filled with mourning and despair.[156] No soul was more seared by these strange fires than the saintly Jonah Gerundi, first among Solomon's crusaders. With the abject humiliation of a penitent sinner, he arose dramatically in the synagogue at Paris — and again in Montpellier and in Barcelona — and recanted:

> I am smitten with shame and remorse that I opened my mouth against our holy master, Moses b. Maimon, and his writings. I hereby confess with all my heart that Moses and his teachings are true; that we are the deceivers. I undertake henceforth to visit and prostrate myself over his grave in the company of ten

persons; to visit the grave for seven days and to repeat daily, "I have sinned against the God of Israel and against our master, Moses b. Maimon, for I have spoken perversely against his books."

Death intervened and the vow remained unfulfilled, but the name of Moses ben Maimon trembled on his lips during the final agony of a terrible death.[157]

The antagonists on both sides were now silenced; but the controversy was not yet at an end. Two generations later, about the year 1300, the conflict broke out anew. It revealed that in the interim the views of the "philosophers," as the rationalistic school was called, had gained much headway among the masses. Philosophical homilies and allegorical expositions of the Bible were being expounded from the pulpit which, it must be remembered, was the popular lecture platform of mediaeval Jewry.

In the struggle which was renewed, Maimonides was no longer the center of the controversy. Nor was the attack directed against his philosophic writings or his lofty conception of Judaism, unacceptable as it was to many through its rejection of alleged anthropomorphisms and its denial of miracles.[158] It was the wild extravagances of the younger disciples that struck terror in the hearts of the religious conservatives and drove them to a general opposition of secular learning. It was charged that the new philosophers showed no restraint in their arbitrary treatment of the Bible. They freely allegorized the biblical narratives into philosophic generalities and boldly denied their historical character. By the same method of allegorical interpretation, they tampered with the laws of the Torah and caused their partial abandonment in practice. This alleged danger to the integrity of Judaism, which was largely based on rumor and was grossly exaggerated, alarmed even the rabbis who were trained in philosophic thinking and brought about the new reaction against liberal education.[159]

The moving spirit in the new arraignment of science and philosophy, Abba Mari b. Moses, was a man of culture and high social position.[160] A native of Lunel, but residing in Montpellier, he was known as Abba Mari of Montpellier and also by his aristocratic title Don Astruc de Lunel.[161] He was well versed in the study of philosophy and personally professed profound reverence for Maimonides.[162] Zealous in the cause of faith, Abba Mari was no mystic or blind fanatic. With the same earnestness that he combated the philosophers, he also denounced the superstitious use of various talismans, the astrolabe and other astrological devices, opposing therein not only the opinion of the scientists but also the great authority of Ibn Adret.[163]

In an inflated and obscure style, he described the mournful state to which Judaism had been reduced by the perversions of the philosophers. The burden of his doleful complaint was that there were many who broke the fences of the Law, who destroyed the covenant and who regarded the study of the Torah as secondary to the alien sciences, which were their true delight. They filled volumes with their farfetched philosophic homilies. They were steeped in the study of logic and physics and in the works of Averroes and Aristotle.[164] It was not the study of the philosophic texts of the ancients, however, which was to be condemned, for these books misled no one. The danger of heresy lurked in the Jewish philosophic writings, which were read by the students unsuspectingly on Sabbaths and holidays and were regarded by them as divinely inspired. These works it was a religious duty to burn and completely destroy.[165] Abba Mari's wrath was kindled when he beheld boys in their teens coming from other cities to give vent to their views publicly in the synagogues, preaching not the word of God but their own notions. Abraham and Sarah were treated as symbols of matter and form. David, King of Israel, sweet singer who had gained his place in the Synagogue through numerous songs of prayer, was subordinated to Aristotle and Plato, though they had produced no religious poetry or liturgical composition.[166] Abba Mari was determined to speak boldly and not to spare those who were thus shattering the foundations of faith. He deplored the fact that he could wage war only with tongue and pen. But his figurative speech, which was not free from bombast, is not always to be taken literally. Thus he complained that he had not the power to cut down (the horns of) the destroyers of the Law. He would tear out their hearts and dip in their blood.[167] But what in sober language he really aimed at was to prohibit the study of secular subjects and, in extreme cases, to excommunicate those who defiantly taught doctrines which were destructive of faith and revealed religion. To his honor it must be said that he maintained the controversy on a high plane. The one purpose that inspired his agitation was to rescue the literal sense of the Scriptures from the nebulous transformations of the philosophers and to uphold the historic character of Judaism against the arbitrary and dangerous tendencies of the allegorists. To those who accused him of personal animosity, he justly retorted that in his indictment of the rationalistic school he never attacked any person by name and he did not even single out the communities where these philosophic tendencies were especially rampant.[168]

Abba Mari could not hope, however, personally to impress the age with his theological views. In his own city, there dwelt the famous astronomer and physician, Jacob ibn Tibbon, said to have been regent of the faculty of medicine at the University of Montpellier,[169] and the famous poet, physician and philosopher, Jedaiah b. Abraham, not to mention others of less fame, who were all redoubtable defenders of science and metaphysics. Indeed, the whole of the Provence was a veritable stronghold of the philosophers. Abba Mari therefore addressed an appeal to the sage of Barcelona, "the man in whom dwelt the spirit of God," to rise in defense of God's cause against the rebellious and overbearing generation.[170]

Ibn Adret, though a ready and dexterous master of polemics in the fight against Christian and Mohammedan theologians, was loath to enter the lists in the Jewish controversy, despite his hearty accord with Abba Mari.[171] But the latter was not easily to be dissuaded from his purpose. By sheer persistence, he succeeded in forcing Ibn Adret to assume the leadership of the movement against liberal education and free philosophic inquiry.[172] Urged repeatedly to express his views, Ibn Adret finally advanced beyond the position of Abba Mari. With deeper insight than his correspondent, he argued that Judaism was not safe against the ancient Greek philosophers merely because the latter were known as pagans. Inherently, philosophy was a dangerous rival of the Torah. The fascinations of speculative thought seduced the minds of men from the study of the sacred law. Man, who was part of nature, was drawn to and attracted by natural law and impelled to rebel against divine law. He who succumbed to the philosophic point of view would no longer credit the miracles of the Bible. He became incapacitated for the appreciation of revealed law. Witness the contempt in which the exponents of revealed religion were held by the adherents of philosophy, whereas any fool who prated in philosophic terms was accounted a sage. The paganism of the Greek philosophers did not in the least detract from their influence. On the contrary, Aristotle was a name to conjure with. His authority was sufficient to protect any untruth, however absurd. It was this fatuous blindness which let no verse of the Bible stand unturned. Abraham and Sarah were changed into matter and form. The twelve sons of Jacob were symbols of the twelve constellations. Amalek was represented as the evil spirit in man, and Lot and his wife were but intellect and matter, respectively. With deep scorn, however, Ibn Adret absolved the philosophic preachers of the sin with which Abba Mari charged them, of revealing the secrets of creation against God's will. It was only their madness which these fools revealed.[173]

Revolting as these doctrines appeared to him and dangerous as was their tendency, Ibn Adret would again in nowise commit himself to a program of active hostility against the rationalist school, a program, moreover, which had not been clearly defined by Abba Mari.[174] He addressed, however, letters of exhortation to persons of prominence in the chief Provençal cities and urged them to organize opposition against the new tendency and its representatives.[175] It was from one of these correspondents that the suggestion finally came that Ibn Adret call upon the local authorities everywhere to pronounce the ban of excommunication against the study of Greek and Chaldean works, medical books excepted, by persons under thirty years of age.[176] The ban was to fall both on teacher and pupil. His friends assured Ibn Adret that this moderate measure would find support even among the rationalists. Ibn Adret, in reply, strongly favored the plan that the Jewish youth should be

grounded in the knowledge of the Torah before being permitted to venture upon the study of philosophy. It was
essential that the Jewish sages should have priority over
the Greek philosophers, and no one would rejoice more than
he to see the ban adopted by those Jewries which were
seriously affected by the teachings of the philosophers. But
he questioned the wisdom of making the ban universal. It
was wrong to disturb the blameless communities which had
not even a conception of such abuses. He was especially
concerned over the Spanish Jewries. For both Castile and
Aragon had at one time paid homage to the idol, metaphysics, but were now happily free from all heretical tendencies.
It was with great reluctance and many misgivings that Ibn
Adret finally dispatched a solemn letter to the chief offending
community of Montpellier, which he signed together with
the other rabbis and notables of Barcelona, invoking the
authorities of the Provençal city to forbid the study of
philosophy by students under thirty years of age and offering to countersign any *herem* which would be issued by
them.[177]

But what he had dreaded came to pass. His proclamation
divided the community into two camps. No united action
seemed possible, and Ibn Adret's plea could not be carried
out.[178] The conservatives, having misled Ibn Adret, now
addressed an apologetic letter to him,[179] while the liberals
respectfully but firmly rebuked the authorities of Barcelona
for their hasty judgment and unwarranted interference in
the internal affairs of a sister community.[180]

Ibn Adret and his council completely lost heart. They
were taken aback, they explained, at the resentment which
developed against their action in Montpellier. Their letter
to the *kahal* was not intended to be an admonition, much

A page from Avicenna's *Kanon*, I, dated 1474

(see p. xi)

less an assertion of authority over them. It was an answer
to the urgent plea of Abba Mari, who, they had believed,
represented the general sentiment of the Jews in Montpellier.
Convinced now that they had mistaken the temper of the
community, they would definitely withdraw from the controversy.[181] To Abba Mari, who, undismayed by his reverses,
urged Ibn Adret to further action and pleaded with him
to show his good faith by anathematizing the study of science
and philosophy in Barcelona, Ibn Adret replied that it would
be manifestly unjust to the holy congregation of his city.[182]
And while he offered to negotiate with the individual ring-
leaders of the liberal faction of Montpellier, if these would
be pointed out to him,[183] he pleaded with Abba Mari to
abandon his agitation and seek peace.[184] But Abba Mari
was relentless. Utilizing the presence in Barcelona of Rabbi
Asher, a German refugee and noted foe of all the profane
sciences, he brought additional pressure on Ibn Adret and
virtually forced him into an aggressive course.[185]

For a long time, nevertheless, the controversy lingered.
Letters passed back and forth.[186] Both sides were marshal-
ing their forces. Ibn Adret and Abba Mari set about to
strengthen their cause by seeking new adherents in the
Provençal cities, especially in Perpignan.[187] An attack by
Jacob b. Makir[188] met with a vigorous rejoinder from Ibn
Adret.[189] Adret regretted that his old age prevented him
from making a journey to Montpellier to settle the con-
troversy in person.[190] Meanwhile, letters poured in on Ibn
Adret from Aix, L'Argentière and Beaucaire.[191] Again Abba
Mari pleaded for a *herem* to be issued jointly by Ibn Adret
and Rabbi Asher and their colleagues.[192] Rabbi Asher
proposed instead the convocation of a synod of Spanish and
French rabbis and friends of science to consider ways and

means of reconciling both parties and restoring unity of
faith in Israel.[193] But his voice found no echo. Definite
headway was finally made when Jacob b. Judah, a follower
of the zealous party, on his own initiative, made a five-day
tour through the Provençal cities in behalf of the proposed
herem. He included the most important communities in
his propaganda, and he pleaded with them to ratify the
herem by official communal vote.[194] Promptly the ten representatives of the community of Lunel addressed Adret,
invoking him to vigorous action and assuring him of their
full support.[185] Ibn Adret was heartened by this expression
of confidence and he pledged himself anew to the cause,
vowing to wage war on the liberal faction to the end. But
he feared bearing the brunt of the attack and therefore
exhorted the *kahal* of Lunel to take the leading part in the
suppression of premature philosophic studies.[196] The *Nasi*
of Narbonne, Kalonymos b. Todros, became an ally too.[197]
No official body, however, appeared ready to take the initiative and there was again a lull in the controversy. Ibn Adret
fell into a long sickness. Abba Mari and the zealous *Nasi*
were perplexed by Ibn Adret's silence, until a belated dis-
patch, arriving eight months later, convinced them that Ibn
Adret's heart was still in the fight.[198]

A new impetus was now given to the struggle. Ibn Adret
was reluctantly convinced that it was his duty to lead the
agitation.[199] No other individual or community dared to
assume the initiative.[200] Abba Mari in the Provence, the *Nasi*
at Narbonne and Ibn Adret in Barcelona, through his disciple R. Samson (Sason), moved to bring into line fifty communities to underwrite the proposed *herem*.[201] Much secrecy
attended this new move. Abba Mari's was the guiding

spirit, and he now modified his program somewhat. The minimum age for the study of the proscribed subjects was reduced from thirty years to twenty-five. On the other hand, all public instruction in philosophy was to be prohibited, regardless of the standing and maturity of the lecturer, and henceforth such instruction was to be strictly limited to private classes.[202] In the resolution which Abba Mari and the *Nasi* Kalonymos finally drew up at the request of Ibn Adret for his promulgation,[203] the proscription was narrowed down to include only the works of the non-Jewish philosophers. The works of the Jewish authors were clearly exempted from the *herem* in this tentative draft.[204] This was the basis of Ibn Adret's formula and, accordingly, on the Sabbath of Lamentations (Ab 4th — July 26th) in the year 1305, the Jewish community of Barcelona was assembled and, amidst great solemnity, the reader with the scroll of the Law in his arms proclaimed:

> ... We are servants, servants of the Lord. He hath created us and unto Him we belong. By the power of *herem*, vested in us, we decree for ourselves, our children and all who are associated with us that, for fifty years henceforth, no member of our community under the age of twenty-five years shall study the works of the Greeks on natural science or metaphysics, either in the original language or in [Hebrew] translation. And no one in our community shall teach these branches to the children of Israel under the prescribed age, lest these sciences entice them and draw their hearts away from the Law of Israel, which transcends the wisdom of the Greeks ... We exempt, however, from our decree the study of medicine, for although this too is a natural science, the Torah expressly sanctions the healing craft of the physician.[205]

It was not philosophy in the abstract, however, which the pious feared most. It was rather the allegorical interpretation of the Bible and the symbolic representation of the Law, which the philosophical attitude encouraged, that constituted the real menace to true faith. Another ban, more impassioned in tone, was therefore pronounced specifically against the preachers and exegetes who treated the biblical theme from Creation to Revelation as an allegory. Accursed were to be those who destroyed the authority of the Law, who expounded the Urim and Tummim on the principle of the astrolabe, who denied revelation, who discredited the motives of Moses in prohibiting the eating of swine and who treated the biblical commandment concerning phylacteries as a symbol and figure of speech. These sins would be upon their souls. They would not be forgiven till their bodies would be cast into the unquenchable fire of hell. All Israelites were in duty bound to place them under the ban:

> ... Behold, therefore, by the authority of the Court on High and by the authority of the court on earth, we declare these transgressors and men of presumption accursed and under the ban. They shall sink even deeper until they return thoroughly penitent. Their books are works of heresy and should be consigned to the flames, or the owners thereof will be liable to excommunication. But those that shall turn back and repent, Heaven will be merciful unto them, the Court on High and the court on earth will absolve them, the curse will change to a blessing, their work will prosper and they will be inscribed for life and peace ...[206]

The *herem*, thus announced, was the climax of three years' agitation.[207] It was signed by Ibn Adret, his rabbinical colleagues and the lay heads of the Barcelona community. Barcelona had blazed the way. It now sounded the call to its sister communities similarly to range themselves on the side of God and the Torah.[208] Even in Montpellier it was hoped that the majority, who were holy and untainted, would rally this time round the banner of Abba Mari.[209] But all such expectations were doomed to disappointment.

Before the official report of the *herem* reached the borders of the Provence, its effect was already nullified in Montpellier by a coup of the leaders of the liberal party, which threw the followers of Abba Mari into great discomfiture. For, still controlling the majority vote, the liberals passed a resolution which was binding upon the entire community and which put under the ban anyone who, because of ecclesiastical interdiction, debarred his son from the study of science in any language whatsoever.[210] The honor of Maimonides' name was to be jealously defended, and indeed no author was to be condemned because of his philosophy.[211] He who offended against any of these resolutions was to be excommunicated. To intimidate their opponents, this time the liberals appealed to the governor of the city to aid them; and this Christian official gave them a richly merited rebuke. He informed them that he had no interest in their internal affairs and that his sole motive in opposing educational restrictions in the sciences and metaphysics was to open to the Jewish youth the potential means of conversion to Christianity.[212]

In vain was the protest of Abba Mari and his party. The plea that the Barcelona ban applied only to the works of Greek and Arabic authors went unheeded.[213] The only recourse left to them in self-defense was to broadcast their protest and to seek exemption from the communal

resolutions at the hands of the universally recognized rabbinical authorities.[214] The protest was made as effective as
possible. Seventy signatures were affixed to an official
statement (אדרכה) vigorously repudiating the counter-*herem*
of the liberals.[215] Couriers were dispatched to Barcelona and,
subsequently, to the numerous cities of the Provence,
denouncing the ban as unjust and illegal.[216] A flood of
rabbinic opinion began to pour in from all parts of Spain
and France which emphatically vindicated Abba Mari's
adherents.[217] The agitation stirred the great rabbi of
Perpignan, Menahem Meiri, who had hitherto not committed himself, to declare himself at last; but, alas, there
was scant comfort for Abba Mari in this much sought-
for declaration. For although he dismissed lightly the
counter-ban of the liberals, he was unsparing in condemnation of the would-be inquisitors and their unrighteous cause.
In characteristic fashion, Abba Mari suppressed the letter.[218]
But victory was with the rationalists. The ban against
freedom of thought which had threatened from Barcelona
was definitely averted. Abba Mari could no longer hope
to drive philosophy and science out of Montpellier.

Far more creditable than the tactical victory was the
theoretical defense of the liberal party which was under-
taken by the eloquent Provençal poet, who was himself a
philosopher and scientist, the noted Yedaya b. Abraham
Bedersi. It was not the anathema that stirred the poet to
eloquence. For science needed no defenders; it was invul-
nerable; it could not be uprooted. What fired the poet's
resentment and moved him to speech was the public defamation of a sacred Jewish community. For Ibn Adret and his
colleagues had dispatched a letter to all parts of Spain,

France and Germany in support of the anathema, holding
up the Jews of Montpellier and their allies in thought to
opprobrium and branding them with heresy. It was to
ward off the danger of the moral annihilation of his fellow
citizens by their own people and to seek justice at the hands
of their traducers that led Yedaya to reply to Ibn Adret.

With the utmost reverence for the wisdom and the noble
character of Ibn Adret, Yedaya took Ibn Adret severely
to task for the manner in which he had allowed himself to
be misled by the malicious and exaggerated reports of his
misinformers. The least that the accused might have
expected from Ibn Adret was a fair hearing; yet this was
denied them. What were they guilty of, which was not
sanctioned by the precedent of their illustrious fathers?
Was it not by their philosophic interests and scientific
pursuits that the sages of Provence had always been distinguished from their brethren in Spain and France? The old
issues were being revived for which their fathers had already
been persecuted, and their assailants were renewing the
ancient feud in which the Provençal sages battled as champions of Maimonides in the name of Truth.

Yedaya, however, did not content himself with mere
generalities and counteraccusations. Each count in the
indictment against his party was brought to light and
refuted. It was not true that anyone doubted the historical
character of the patriarchs as portrayed in the Bible. Nor
had he himself ever heard of the twelve tribes being identified
with the twelve constellations. Infidel astrologers pointed
with significance to the coincidence between the number of
Israelitish tribes and that of the constellations. It was proof
to them that Israel, too, like other nations, was subject to

the laws of astrology. Even they, however, did not deny
the historical character of the tribes of Israel; how much
less the Jewish exegetes who proudly cited the history
of the Jewish people and pointed to the common triumphs
and defeats which united them as proof that One God
— and He alone — ruled over all Israel, and that the
various tribes were not subject to the influence of the
divisions of the zodiac! It was fatuous to believe that any
Jew would surrender the historic glory of his people, quite
aside from the fact that traces of the original tribal divisions
were still evident in contemporary Israel through the three-
fold classification of Kohen, Levite and Israelite. Thus
a number of the accusations were based on misunder-
standing and others, which he enumerated, were purely
libelous fabrications. The absurdity of some of those
statements, he stated, ought to have been their own refutation. Thus the Urim and Tummim were to no one more
sacred than to the disciples of Maimonides, whose conception
of prophecy rested on their unique, divinely inspired character.

In short, it was not true that the literal sense of the Bible
was being violated. The Talmud, on the other hand, as
was well known to Ibn Adret, was replete with mystic
truths, hidden in legends, parables and strange homilies.
Surely Ibn Adret must concede the duty of the learned to
penetrate the mysteries of these theosophical truths! In
such expositions, the allegoric method had to be resorted
to freely. At times, the mystic tales were woven round
biblical characters. Thus it was the allegorical interpretation of these haggadic stories which created alarm in the
minds of the uninitiated and caused reports to spread that
Abraham and Sarah were alleged to be only matter and

form. Charge the preacher with the folly of indiscretion, if you will. It certainly was an offense to reveal hidden mysteries to the untrained and immature; but surely it was no heresy. And the offending tactlessness of an individual was certainly not a crime to be laid against a whole city.

Yedaya now called Wisdom, or Philosophy, dramatically to her own defense against Ibn Adret's personal arraignment. For to Ibn Adret all the former charges were only isolated symptoms of a deathly sickness with which philosophy had infected Judaism by means of the alien sciences, rhetoric and metaphysics. Wisdom thereupon arises to protest against her defamation, pleads for her persecuted votaries and demands recognition of her services in establishing truth on a firm basis, by dispelling superstition and freeing Judaism from the inroads of astrology and the pernicious influence of the amulet and other forms of witchcraft.

Thereupon followed a popular presentation of the contributions of philosophy — which to Yedaya meant Maimonidean philosophy — to religious thought, in the course of which he analyzed various philosophic concepts and threw interesting light on the shades of religious and philosophic opinion which were held by his contemporaries. Philosophy proved the existence of God, His unity, His incorporeality, and interpreted His attributes negatively. It established the validity and the true nature of prophecy. It distinguished between the various degrees of prophecy and furnished the criteria with which false claims to divine inspiration could be exposed. Of the most profound importance was its demonstration of the truth of the doctrine of free will. For only this rendered tenable the thesis of reward and punishment, which in turn bore directly on the nature of Divine Providence. Philosophy demolished numerous falsehoods in the minds of men, which weakened their faith in God and His powers. It conceived of the soul as pure spiritual essence and rejected the unethical theory of its transmigration. By its aid, Maimonides had also demonstrated against Aristotle the thesis of *creatio ex nihilo.* Finally, philosophy opened to the rare and chosen spirits the sublimest mysteries of Creation which God vouchsafed to only a few of His prophets.

The alleged attack of the philosophers on the belief in miracles was untrue. Neither Maimonides nor his disciples imposed any check on the omnipotence of God which would render belief in miracles impossible. On the contrary, they affirmed with zeal the power of God to suspend the laws of nature temporarily or permanently. What they denied emphatically was, in the first place, a change in the attribute of God Himself and, secondly, the assumption of an inner contradiction: as, for instance, that a thing was and was not at the same time. These distinctions were vital to true faith. It followed that all the narratives of the Bible were to be taken in a literal sense, save those which referred to the Deity in anthropomorphic terms. Yedaya even applied the same standards to the Talmud, excepting that where there was no definite religious value in the miracles mentioned there, he asked that such be rationally interpreted so as not to render the supernatural commonplace.

Addressing himself directly to his interlocutors, he bade them look into the past and read the verdict of history. In every land of the dispersion Jews had once entertained crude notions of God as a corporeal being until there arose, in Arabic-speaking countries, geonim and men of wisdom who were imbued with a knowledge of Arabic literature and philosophy and utilized the methods of metaphysics gradually to clarify and deepen the popular understanding of the religious truths of Judaism, especially those which related to God's unity and incorporeality. Yedaya marshaled the chief philosophers from Sa'adia to Maimonides, cited their works and gloried in the final triumph of Maimonides in establishing, for all time, the truth of God's incorporeality and making it the accepted belief in all the camps of Israel. This was the crowning achievement of Maimonides' lifework. He attained to it not through divine inspiration, but through the arduous preparation of long sustained study. His knowledge comprehended the philosophy of Aristotle and the commentators, the mathematics and kindred sciences of Euclid and his school, the astronomy of Ptolemy and his disciples, the medicine of Galen, Hippocrates and their followers. The Torah in the fullness of its tradition was known to him, and no one equaled him in originality of understanding and insight into the secrets of the Law and prophetic truth. Much of his life was spent in studying metaphysics and speculative thought. Yet none of his sainted teachers caviled at him or found fault with his studies or methods.

Turning again to the *herem* proper, Yedaya showed that the ban itself lacked consistency. Thus astronomy as a purely physical science was not proscribed; yet astrology, which was an inseparable part of the same science, was unquestionably antagonistic to religion. Even medicine in its experimental branches was often difficult to distinguish from the practices of popular superstition, which were strictly prohibited by the canons of Judaism. Why then should not these sciences, too, be included under the ban because of their possible incompatibility, at times, with the religion of Israel? Surely, mere expediency would not be thought sufficient justification. If the urgency of physical disease justified the physician in the study and practice of medicine despite its "risk," the same standards ought to apply to the speculative sciences which pertained to the health of the soul.

In their philosophy the men of the Provence stood with Maimonides and derived their theories from his works. Could a man be called a heretic or even faltering in faith, who believed implicitly that God created the world out of the void, who believed furthermore in the miracles of the Bible, in the divine inspiration of the prophets and also accepted the records of the rabbinic sages?

With eloquent personal appeal, Yedaya pleaded with Ibn Adret to heal the schism. He pleaded for the honor of Maimonides' name, so famous among the gentile nations and reflecting glory upon the whole house of Israel. Ibn Adret owed this as a duty to himself, the father of his generation, and in justice to the glorious communities of the Provence, which cultivated the Torah and the sciences with sublime indifference to material motives. The report of religious dissension in Judaism was bound to reach gentile ears and would be hailed by them with joy. Was not the fate of the Jewish community precarious enough, in a world which was bent on its destruction, without the further aggravation of inner strife?

Surely it was incumbent upon Ibn Adret, who gave countenance to the controversy, to suppress it now. He must recognize the futility of continuing the feud. "For the heart of this people cannot be turned from the love of science and literature, while their body and soul are kept together. If Joshua himself were to demand it, they would

not obey him. For they feel that they wage war in defense
of Maimonides and his works; and for his holy teaching,
they will sacrifice their fortunes, their future generations
and their very lives." Having left nothing undone to move
them from their purpose and having failed, Ibn Adret
could now with clear conscience work to restore peace and
amity in Israel.[219]

This extraordinary appeal must have created a profound
impression in Barcelona. But Abba Mari did not see fit to
record it in his account of the controversy. The very survival
of this famous epistle is due to its accidental appearance
amidst Ibn Adret's responsa. Though it seems hardly
likely that Ibn Adret should have let so weighty a document
go entirely unheeded, no reply has been preserved. Moreover, Yedaya's letter not being dated, it is difficult to place
it in its proper setting. It appears clear, however, that
shortly after the promulgation of the *herem*, its effect recoiled
upon its authors. They felt alarmed at the bitterness and
inner strife which their action engendered in the sister
community. Above all, they dreaded Christian interference. Three months after the solemn pronouncement of
the *herem*, Ibn Adret and his colleagues, without rescinding
their own action in Barcelona and, while confirming the
legality of the protest of Abba Mari's party against the
counter-*herem* of the liberals, appealed to Abba Mari and
his fellow agitators to abandon the struggle and make
peace.[220]

But there was no peace. Abba Mari continued to fortify
his cause with letters of approbation from spiritual and
lay leaders of Provençal communities. He collected enough
material to fill a volume — a one-sided volume to be sure.[221]
The opposition, it may be assumed, was no less active in

its own way. Thus the Jewish communities were being unceasingly drawn into a war between Reason and
Faith.

The struggle was tragically short-lived, however. While
the Jews were bitterly contending the respective claims of
religion and science, the cynical, unscrupulous king of France,
Philip IV, who had broken with the Church and had
dissolved and looted the Order of the Templars, issued
secret orders on January 21, 1306, for the imprisonment of
the entire Jewish population of France, a command which
was executed to the full on the tenth day of the fatal month
of Ab. The Jews were given one month's time in which to
leave the country or face the alternatives of baptism or
death. Among the hundred thousand Jewish souls of France
who went into exile were the Jewish princes and intellectuals
of Montpellier.[222]   Abba Mari and his followers fled to Arles
and the Tibbonide family, which led the opposition, found
refuge in Perpignan.

In exile, both parties held on even more tenaciously to
their spiritual heritage of which the enemy could not despoil
them. It is a sad commentary on their tragic fate that they
carried the bitterness of the feud with them. Rumors
reached Ibn Adret in Barcelona that the opponents of Abba
Mari instigated the ruler of Perpignan to forbid Abba Mari's
settlement in that city when he was compelled to leave
Arles.[223] Abba Mari did succeed, however, in establishing
himself in Perpignan, and the old controversy flared up
again. This time, the famous college at Toledo, headed by
R. Asher and his colleagues, added fuel to the cause of the
antiliberals.[224] But Abba Mari's records end at this period.
He shot his last bolt at the opposition in a funeral oration

on the death of Ibn Adret, four years later (1310).[225] Beyond
this, nothing further is known of his career. With his dis-
appearance, it would seem, the organized opposition to
liberal studies also came to an abortive end.

True to Meiri's prediction, the *herem* of Ibn Adret and the
counterban of the Montpellier liberals remained dead
letters on the statute books. Boys continued to be trained
in the study of philosophy at an early age. The prolific
philosophic writer, Moses Narboni, born in 1300, was taught
philosophy by his father at the age of thirteen. Only two
decades after the promulgation of the *herem*, R. Levi b.
Gerson, praised as a great talmudic authority and Bible
exegete by strict talmudists, completed one of the boldest
and most daring works of mediaeval Jewish philosophy.[226]
Hasdai Crescas, famed as a talmudist, wrote, at the end of
the fourteenth century, *The Light of God*, a striking land-
mark in the development of Jewish philosophy.[227] A century
after the controversy had raged in the Provence and Spain, a
pious Jew inquired of R. Isaac Barfat whether physics and
metaphysics were forbidden studies. Barfat, in reply, referred to Ibn Adret's letter denouncing the study of metaphysics, but made no allusion to the *herem* proper.[228] The
adherents of philosophy continued to clash with those who
opposed its study as the source of heresy and apostasy, but
there was no vindictive struggle or campaign of persecution.[229] Descendants of those who opposed philosophic
studies most bitterly became ardent devotees of the banned
subjects.[230] Indeed, on the eve of the final expulsion from
Spain, a namesake of Ibn Adret's father, perhaps a direct
descendant, was studying Averroes' *Intermediate De Generatione* in the school of R. Isaac ibn Shem Tob in Aguilar de

Campóo.[231] No authority was formidable enough, no anathema deadly enough, to banish freedom of thought from Judaism.

However, a period of general decline, political, social and intellectual, had set in among the chief Jewries at the end of the thirteenth century. Persecutions were being relentlessly visited upon them with ever increasing regularity, and a series of local and general expulsions followed in the course of the fourteenth and fifteenth centuries which changed the map of Jewish history. Inevitably, there resulted an ever-widening rift in the intellectual communion between the Jews and their environment. The Jews were thrown back more and more upon the mental and spiritual resources of their own traditional lore, and the tendency to mysticism, which began strongly to assert itself in Spain during the thirteenth century, made rapid headway.

The process of decline ran its own course in each country. In Spain, the curve of decline descended very gradually. Rabbinical scholars generally continued to engage in science and metaphysics.[232] Hasdai Crescas, in fact, expounded philosophical dissertations to the disciples of his *yeshibah*;[233] and the chief talmudic authorities in Spain, even in the fourteenth and fifteenth centuries, were distinctly men of secular education. The famous disputation of Tortosa, which was remarkable for the length of its duration and its spectacular display, revealed in a striking manner the extent to which liberal studies were cultivated by Spanish and Provençal Jews a century after the ban on secular learning had been proclaimed.[234] The Jewish delegation of twenty notables, who were chosen from the communities of Aragon to defend their religion before the papal tribunal, were not only learned in Jewish lore, but also thoroughly equipped

by general education, literary ability and philosophic
training and acumen. Don Vidal ibn Labi, the head of
the delegation, spoke Latin fluently no less than the
ex-rabbi and apostate, who posed as the champion of the
pope and of the Christian side in the controversy. R. Joseph
Albo, another member of the Jewish delegation, was one of
the most popular Jewish philosophers of the Middle Ages.
Indeed, from the thirteenth to the fifteenth century, the
missionary zeal of Christian churchmen compelled the Jews,
in self-defense, to become familiar with the religious literature of the rival religions, thus widening the extent of Jewish
studies.[235] In the physical sciences, too, the influence of
the Jews was still very marked in the fourteenth and fifteenth
centuries. It was in this period that the nautical sciences
received their greatest development, in which the role of
the Jews was very significant. The Jewish professor, Zacuto,
taught mathematics, astronomy and medicine to Christian
students at the University of Salamanca to the very last
days of the Expulsion. But the circle of Jewish students
who engaged in these broad studies became more restricted
until the tragedy of the Expulsion brought to an end one
of the most glorious chapters in the history of Jewish culture.

CHAPTER XVII

THE SYNAGOGUE AND ITS AUXILIARY
INSTITUTIONS

THE path of Jewish education and culture led inevitably to the precincts of the synagogue. As the ideals of the academicians, whether philosophic or strictly talmudic, were inconceivable apart from the principles and the problems of the Jewish religion, so physically, too, the schoolhouse was either an adjunct to or a part of the synagogue structure. In the eyes of the schoolmen, the house of study ranked higher than the house of worship in the gradation of holiness,[1] but from the more important social point of view, the synagogue was the mother institution, and on its grounds were erected the schoolhouse, the public assembly hall and the various charitable institutions.[2]

Architecturally, the synagogue was the most imposing structure in the *juderia*, built generally in Moorish design, sometimes also partly Gothic. Some of the synagogues had been originally mosques which the Christian conquerors presented to their Jewish subjects as a sign of favor or gratitude.[3] Every important community had more than one house of worship.[4] Of these, the chief synagogue was prominently located in the center of the *calle* in the heart of the *aljama*. Ready access to the house of God was not merely a matter of convenience. In times of danger, it involved the safety of life and limb.[5]

The sacred edifice towered high above the surrounding residences; but it kept circumspectly within certain prescribed limits, not to vie with the jealous church nearby whose spires reached heavenward on the other side of the gate.[6] The synagogue attracted the eye by its architectural beauty and its broad, noble dimensions. The entrance to it led through the *'azarah*, the open court, where the people used to gather on weekdays and where much of the administrative activity of the community was carried on.[7] Here or in the synagogue proper, one could present his grievances before the city councilors as they met to plan and legislate for the community welfare.[8] Here, too, the tax commissioners kept their ledgers, as every member of the community from fifteen years and upward filed before them.[9] Flanked on one side was the all-important schoolhouse, or *midrash*, where students both young and old were engaged in study.[10] The city fathers, too, frequently reserved a room in this building for their councils.[11] On the other side was a social hall or court, used for festive occasions, or an institution housing the wayfarer and the stranger.[12]

Dim glimpses of the synagogue interior are discernible in the fragmentary records. Allusions are repeatedly made to tall, stately columns and beams; the raised, elevated platform from which the reader's prayers were chanted and the rabbi's exhortations were preached; the carving on the walls and the effusive inscriptions on the shrine — the *hekal* — in which the sacred scrolls were encased.[13] Then there are the octagonal columns, with their curiously carved capitals and the Moorish arches in the old Toledo synagogue, the present Santa María la Blanca; the richly colored façades of the Cordova edifice; and the friezes on the walls of the Samuel ha-Levi synagogue, known as El Transito, with its profuse Hebrew inscriptions perpetuating the memory of the founder's noble life.[14] A synagogue lit up by sunlight was considered conducive to the mood of prayer.[15] The four-teenth-century synagogue of Samuel ha-Levi in Toledo was picturesquely lighted through its narrow windows near the roof. On Sabbaths and holidays, the synagogues were flooded with the illumination of lamps and hundreds of candlelights to induce the spirit of joy and festivity. For "where there was light there was rejoicing, for was it not written, 'The Jews had light and joy and gladness and honor?' "[16] What concerned the average worshiper most, as it touched his pride and social vanity, was the seating arrangement. Fre-quently, feeling ran high on this subject, and the available information accordingly is quite detailed.

Elaborately carved stone benches were built along the walls in some of these edifices.[17] Children did not occupy the seats of the adults, but they sat at the feet of their parents on stone footrests or roamed at will in the unoccupied portion of the interior.[18] Other synagogues were furnished with various types of chairs, semicircular benches and divans, revealing the strong individualism of the worship-ers. This bizarre effect grew out of the strange custom, prevalent for economic reasons in many communities, of allowing the worshipers to construct the seating in the places assigned to them at their own cost and according to their own plan, either by themselves or in association with their neighbors.[19] But even in a house of worship, neigh-borliness is not synonymous with fraternity, and many vexatious disputes arose in consequence.[20]

Upon the completion of a new synagogue, a committee assigned seating space to the members of the *aljama* in accordance with their social standing, and the distribution

Samuel Abulafia's synagogue at Toledo

(see p. xi)

was made a matter of official record.[21] Occasionally, the owner's name was inscribed on the seat.[22] If the division was made according to family grouping, no person could transfer his place to a stranger without the consent of the group.[23] But, as a rule, the authorities made the awards to the individuals outright, with full proprietary title and the privilege of transfer by gift, sale or bequest.[24] Special compartments were built for women.[25]

At times, the traffic in synagogue seats was so active that it was possible to create a quasi-monopoly and an artificial price inflation which the *aljama* had to counteract.[26] Newcomers or those who were not fortunate enough to share in the original partition of the synagogue were barred from setting up temporary chairs or spreading a carpet matting in the center of the auditorium. They had, however, the privilege of renting from the more fortunate members the seats which were not in use; and, if necessary, the communal authorities intervened forcibly in their behalf with stubborn seatholders.[27] The synagogue officials ruled with iron control. Protests were unavailing, and heavy fines were imposed on those who insisted on occupying seats which were assigned to others.[28] It is curious and significant to find the monarch himself, King Pedro IV, intervening in behalf of his jeweler, Guedaliah Avenarama of Saragossa, to secure for him the coveted privilege of erecting two seats in the synagogue of Calatayud.[29]

A utilitarian purpose, combined with a holy zeal to glorify the God of Israel, can therefore be discerned in the building of multiple synagogues which everywhere adorned the typical Jewish quarter.[30] The city of Seville was particularly rich in this regard. Four years after the conquest of the city, in 1248, Alfonso X presented the Jews with three mosques

to be converted into synagogues.[31] Grown to a prosperous
community of six to seven thousand families, this *judería*
had twenty-three synagogues before its destruction in 1391.[32]
The *aljama* of Calatayud boasted of seven synagogues and
chapels of prayer and study, besides private places of worship which drew enough worshipers to threaten the attendance in the public institutions.[33] The destruction of the
eight synagogues of Valladolid was mourned in Samuel
Çarça's tragic recital of the consequences of the fratricidal
war between Pedro the Cruel and Henry de Trastamara
(1366–68).[34] Outstanding among the sacred edifices in
Saragossa were the Great and the Little Synagogue, the
Benveniste edifice and one erected by a benevolent fraternity, the prominent *Bikkur Holim* Society.[35] The poet
Judah al-Harizi spoke with pride of the several magnificent
synagogues in Toledo, which were among the most beautiful
in Spain.[36]

Among the synagogues in Cordova there were at least two
of historic interest. The chief synagogue, completed in 1250,
was of great height and of such magnificence that it aroused
the wrath of the archdeacon and the local chapter. Pope
Innocent IV made it the subject of a papal bull in a vain
effort to interfere with its construction, "as causing a scandal
among faithful Christians, and much harm to the church of
Cordova."[37] The other edifice, reared in the *Calle de los
Judíos* a half century later (1315) by its patron and architect,
Isaac Moheb, had a happier sequel.[38] Fallen from its high
estate after the Expulsion, its origin completely obscured,
it came somehow into the possession of the shoemakers'
guild at least by 1722. Then, in 1884, it was romantically
rediscovered by two lovers of historic antiquities, the
historian D. Fidel Fita and D. Romero y Barrios. As a

result, it stands today restored according to its original design, its façades decorated with colored faience, its walls richly ornamented with Hebrew verses from the Psalms — the west wall containing the only Arabic dedication to be found in any synagogue in Spain — a beautiful architectural gem in Moorish design, adopted by modern Spain as a national monument. An inscription of four Hebrew lines on the east wall poignantly recalls the name of the founder, the year and the mood in which he built and prayed:

מקדש מעט ונוה תעודה שכללו
יצחק מחב בן הגביר אפרים
נבנה שנת שבעים וחמש בנין שעה
נקומו אל וחיש לבנות ירושלים

A miniature sanctuary and a house of testimony
   built by
Isaac Moheb son of the honorable Ephraim
In the year 75 [1315] as a temporary structure.
Arise, O God, haste to rebuild Jerusalem.

Benevolent fraternities and economic guilds vied with individual philanthropists in the zeal to glorify the Divine Name and to perpetuate their own memory. The weavers' guild and the honored benevolent society each had its own synagogue in Calatayud, primarily intended for its own members.[39] Similarly, a charitable fraternity in Saragossa as well as the important burial society in Huesca each built its own house of worship.[40] The building of sanctuaries both of worship and study was a cause which especially kindled the imagination and the enthusiasm of Jewish aristocrats of wealth and public position. Hardly a reference is to be found in any of the responsa to a community tax levied for a synagogue building fund.[41] But in all parts of

Spain there were men of fame who, with princely munificence, dedicated their talent and their wealth to glorify the
Divine Name through the creation of these monuments of
piety and devotion.

A century and a half before Don Samuel ha-Levi dedicated
the shrine which bears his name, Joseph b. Samuel ibn
Shoshan, a fellow townsman, built a synagogue in Toledo
which aroused the wonder of poet and traveler.[42] King
Pedro IV conferred a high privilege upon his Jewish courtiers
when he granted several of them permission to build themselves synagogues in accordance with their wishes and at
their own cost.[43] King Alfonso XI of Castile appealed to
Pope Clement VI in behalf of the synagogue built by Joseph
of Écija in Seville.[44] Samuel, of the noble Benveniste family,
erected a house of worship in the city of Barcelona.[45] There
was also an Abenvenist synagogue in Saragossa.[46] In Calatayud there was the magnificent Ibn Yahya edifice besides
two other chapels of prayer and study that bore the names
of their founders.[47] The building of Jewish shrines of worship continued to the early fifteenth century[48] when, as a
result of two tragic catastrophes following close upon each
other, in 1391 and 1412-15, the synagogue and its votaries fell
before the fury of the mob, inflamed by unbridled religious
fanaticism. The Jewish population of Spain was decimated
in one generation by massacre and wholesale conversion,
and hundreds of synagogues were looted, pillaged and burned
or were annexed to the nearest churches and convents.[49]

Only a deep, passionate love of God could have inspired
the Jews to build these altars of religion with such profusion
and munificence. For from earliest times, the Church looked
with jealous feeling upon the rise of new synagogues under
the shadow of the Cross.[50] Under ecclesiastic sponsorship,

Theodosius II, in 415 and again in 423, interdicted the building of new synagogues or the repair and embellishment of the existing institutions.[51] Justinian not only reinforced these restrictions; he was the first Christian emperor to command the wholesale destruction of synagogues in his newly conquered territory in Africa in 535.[52] Determined upon the subordination of the Synagogue, the ecclesiastic authorities were zealous to the point of naiveté in their extreme efforts to prevent Jewish houses of worship from towering above the neighboring churches or exceeding them in general dimensions. In 1221, Pope Honorius III ordered the archbishop of Bourges to destroy the new synagogues which had been erected in his province contrary to canonical decree.[53] Ecclesiastic wrath was aroused when a synagogue towered in height above a neighboring church. Innocent III deemed such conduct "insolence,"[54] while Innocent IV described it as "a scandal among faithful Christians causing much harm to the Church."[55] Ferdinand Martinez made the growth of the synagogues the object of his inflammatory incitement, as he led the mob in an unholy crusade of pillage and murder.[56] Under Alfonso X, the *aljama* of Toledo built a magnificent synagogue, which was the largest and most beautiful in Spain;[57] but it was this king who crystallized the mediaeval attitude of the State in his code, *Las Siete Partidas:*

> In no part of our dominions may any new synagogue be erected without our permission; but should the existing ones fall into decay, they may rebuild and repair them on the same site and in the same manner as before; but they may not enlarge, elevate or beautify them. The synagogue which is otherwise constructed is to be confiscated and given to the principal church of the place where it is erected.[58]

Having thus both a material interest at stake as well as a religious position to defend, the Church kept a watchful eye upon the Synagogue to frustrate any design to ornament and beautify it or in any way to augment the sanctuary dedicated to the God of Israel.[59] Not only was the king's license requisite for the construction of a synagogue,[60] but also the local bishop's sanction,[61] so that the number as well as the dimensions of the synagogues would be sure to be held down to a rigid minimum. Despite these obstructions, the creative and religious impulse could not always be denied. With the aid of a generous purse and the will of a benevolent monarch, the stumbling blocks were cleared and the Spanish *juderías* were distinguished for the number and magnificence of their institutions of divine worship — at least until the fateful end of the fourteenth century.

Ultimately the Church reaped the harvest of this rich architectural cultivation. In the quarter century which followed the fearful year 1391, as one *judería* after another was wiped out by massacre and wholesale conversion, their synagogues were seized and crosses planted on them.[62] Broken by torture and terrified by visions of devastation and death, thousands of Jews saved themselves at the baptismal font and, in some instances, even sought that their synagogues should share their fate by being converted into churches.[63] For unless they had been looted, destroyed and set on fire, it was only a fitting sequel, to paraphrase the words of Innocent III, that "places divested of the blind Jewish perversion of faith should receive the light of grace under the name of the Christian religion." Indeed, annexing Jewish houses of prayer after a massacre or expulsion was a natural and inevitable part of the mopping up process in the war between the Cross and the Torah.

Against their will, some of the churches were forced subsequently to surrender a small number of these synagogues
to the enfeebled communities which were restored after the
reign of terror was over.[64] As the Jews began to dig themselves out of the ruins, they started anew to build modest
houses of worship under a program severely restricted by
church officials, from the pope down to the local abbot.[65]
But hardly had they begun to adjust themselves to the new
conditions when, in 1415, they were met by a bull of Pope
Benedict XIII which ordered them to close all synagogues
recently built or repaired, and especially those which had
previously been transformed into churches. Furthermore,
only one synagogue, the smallest and the least pretentious,
was to be allowed in each *judería*, regardless of the size of the
community and the number of its former synagogues.[66]
Half a century later this policy was formulated as a state
program in a compromise between Henry IV and the mag-
nates of the realm.[67]

It was under these conditions that the joint conference
of the Castilian *aljamas*, in 1432, called upon the small communities of ten to twenty families to set up places of prayer.
For prayer, the proclamation declared, was an essential
part of the service of God; the verse "to serve Him with all
your heart" was defined by the rabbis and tradition to mean
worship, which was truly service of the heart; and, furthermore, prayer was most acceptable to God when offered in
the synagogue in community worship.[68] With the expulsion
of the Jews at the end of the century, however, these houses
of prayer, too, were doomed.

With the edict of expulsion went the confiscation of all
communal property of the *aljamas* and the Church at last fell
heir to the remaining synagogues.[69] It found the conversion

of stone and mortar less troublesome than that of the human
mind and spirit. Time has taken its toll; and many of these
edifices have fallen into disuse. The old synagogue of Segovia,
dedicated as the Church of Corpus Christi, was burned in
1899.[70] Two of the historic synagogues in Toledo were
closed as churches in 1888 and, together with the restored
synagogue in Cordova, are preserved by modern Spain as
historic national monuments.[71] Others, like the magnificent
S. Bartolomé Church in Seville, stand under the shadow of
the Cross, melancholy witnesses of the departed hosts of
Israel. So strange, however, are the mutations of fate that,
at the present writing, the wrath and fury of Spain's rebellious sons are turned upon the Church with that ferocity
which in former centuries had signalized her triumph over
the fallen Synagogue. During this whirlwind of passion and
violence, a strange fellowship unites the converted synagogues and the native churches as they jointly mourn the
desolation visited upon them.

It was but natural for the Synagogue to share the fate
of its votaries. It was the nerve center of the community
life. The various types of synagogue, from the democratic
community institutions in which, it was argued, all enjoyed
equal rights,[72] to those that grew more narrowly out of
economic guilds, philanthropic societies and the foundations of court grandees,[73] admitted of no variation in ritual,
religious outlook or theological principle. They expressed
those social-economic alignments which at times seriously
divided the *judería* on vital questions of economic and
political importance.[74]

The Synagogue was not alone the altar of religion; it was
the crucible in which all the issues of life were fused — economic, political, religious and social. The courts of justice

met within its precincts.[75] Oaths were administered near
the shrine of the Torah.[76] Bans of excommunication were
solemnly pronounced by the reader with the scroll of the
Law in his arms.[77] Resolutions and ordinances voted by
the communal authorities were submitted to the worshipers
for approval during divine services.[78] The king's demands
were proclaimed in the halls of worship.[79] Tremblingly the
rabbi was forced to hurl curses and imprecations from the
pulpit upon the faithful who would not testify against
their beloved ones and thus betray them to the Inquisition.[80]

In distress, the Jew repaired to the synagogue and sought
God through prayer and fasting.[81] When prolonged drought
threatened to bring famine in its train, the blowing of the
shofar heightened the solemnities of prayer.[82] When the rain
descended at last, the synagogue was the scene of great
rejoicing amidst the chanting of the Psalms of Praise
(*Hallel*).[83] When pestilence broke out in Seville, in 1449, the
Jews marched out of their synagogues into the streets
of the city in solemn procession with the Torah in their
arms, strewing branches as they marched and praying for
the end of the plague. Their Christian townsmen had engaged in similar solemnities. But far from welcoming the
Jewish plea for divine aid, Pope Nicholas V resented it,
curiously, as a reflection upon the efficacy of Christian
prayer and expressed his extreme displeasure with the
church officials who had sanctioned the Jewish processional.
Thus intolerance triumphed and with it came the papal
vindication of the canon of Seville, Antonius Ferrari, who
had been excommunicated and thrown into jail for insub-
ordination by the more liberal curia of the bishop of Seville.[84]

From their synagogues, the worshipers, attired in prayer
shawls (*tallit*), with the Torah in their arms, marched

patriotically to receive the king whenever he passed through
their city.[85] Although the Jews were taxed for this display of patriotism, one of the first acts of Ferdinand and
Isabella was to restrict the religious attire to those who
carried the scrolls of the Law.[86] The same restriction was
made to apply to funeral processions, which the decree
curiously coupled with the king's reception. In the same
edict, the chanting of Hebrew dirges in the public streets
was prohibited.[87]

Within the synagogue, the individual could, by means
of the ban, seek redress from social wrongs and false accusa-
tion.[88] On the other hand, the Jewish authorities were at
times compelled to take drastic measures against the violent
invasion of synagogue premises by personal quarrels and
public resentments which led to fisticuffs and even blood-
shed.[89] Lost articles were restored to their owners through
synagogue proclamations;[90] sales of real property were
similarly published.[91] In a city of many synagogues, like
Saragossa, to establish a clear title it was necessary to make
the announcement of the sale in three houses of worship.[92]
The charities were an integral part of the synagogue. It
was therefore natural for offerings and donations to be
announced during the services.[93] In some communities, the
rite of circumcision was performed in the synagogue.[94]
Special chants and prayers heralded the presence of the
bridegroom among the worshipers.[95] Even an ignorant
bridegroom was trained to read a suitable portion from the
scroll of the Law.[96]

Repeatedly, the Jewish authorities warded off the attempts of the bailiff to convert the synagogue into a house
of detention.[97] On the other hand, the rabbis felt no com-
punction about turning parts of the building into a hostelry

for the stranger or wayfarer and for the more permanent residence of the scholars and their disciples.[98]

Study was an integral part of the Jewish ritual of worship; but synagogues differed in the relative emphasis which they gave this feature. Thus there arose two types of synagogue: the *Bet ha-Keneset*, or synagogue proper, which as its name would indicate, was the popular house of worship and assembly; and the *Bet ha-Midrash*, a smaller chapel devoted to study primarily, in which services too, however, were held in the appointed manner.[99] The one was representative of the entire community; the other appealed to particular groups who emphasized study as an essential feature of the religious life. The atmosphere of the *Bet ha-Midrash* was more intimate than that of the synagogue proper but cold formality was not a feature of Jewish worship in either place of prayer. Despite rabbinical disapproval, the worshipers enjoyed accompanying the cantor's chanting with loud voice and, no doubt, continued to cantillate with gusto even if the censorious Rabbi Asher considered it as bordering on levity.[100] For the public reader to indulge in secular songs was a serious offense in Arabic countries in the days of Alfasi.[101] In general, the position of this official was more important in Mohammedan countries than in Christian territory.[102]

As a religious official, the *hazzan* was highly esteemed, and his office was secondary to that of the rabbi alone. He was required to possess a musical voice, to be endowed with Hebrew learning and to have a pious character.[103] The duties of his office included not only the chanting of the divine service and scriptural reading from the scrolls of the Law, but also the art of scribal writing. The post was elective, salaried and frequently handed down from father

to son for several generations.[104] Christian noblemen, from
the king to the knights, including ladies of the court,
showed surprising interest in the lot of the *hazzan*, sometimes to the chagrin of the congregation.[105]

On the high Holy Days, especially on the Day of Atonement, it was customary for the rabbi to intone the services.[106]
The honor of being called to the Torah on a religious holiday
became a vested interest and, when the holder of the honor
died without issue, was claimed by Pedro IV as his due.
Of course, the king sought it so that he could assign it to a
Jew, his personal physician.[107] Customary usage quickly
congealed into fixed traditions which were adhered to in
minute detail. The order of the prayers and the manner of
their recital in the leading communities were adopted as
precedents in other places and formed the basis of local
rituals, or *minhagim*.[108] The *minhag* of Barcelona in particular was highly esteemed.[109] The attempt to incorporate
the reading of the Ten Commandments as part of the fixed
prayers was defeated in Spain as it had been repeatedly
frustrated in talmudic days.[110]

CHAPTER XVIII

CHARITIES

IN THE daily program of the Jewish religion, prayer and study have been associated from earliest times with the practice of good deeds and the ethical life. As a prologue to the daily morning devotions, the Jewish worshiper has been accustomed to recite from the prayer book the following passage from the Mishna:

> These are the things the fruits of which a man enjoys in this world, while the stock remains for him for the world to come: namely, honoring father and mother, the practice of charity, timely attendance at the house of study morning and evening, hospitality to wayfarers, visiting the sick, dowering the bride, attending the dead to the grave, devotion in prayer, and making peace between man and his fellow; but the study of the Law is equal to them all.[1]

Long before the dawn of Christianity, the synagogue made charity an essential of religious worship. Benevolence and worship formed the pillars upon which human society rested, according to an ethical dictum of Simon the Just of the second century before the Christian era.[2]

Intimately related to the mediaeval synagogue, therefore, were various charitable foundations in which the *juderías*, disciplined in suffering and affliction, expressed their true character. "We have never heard," said Maimonides, "of any Jewish community that did not have a charity chest."[3] Another Jewish author advanced the liberal view that the test of religion was to be found in the conduct of its adherents, and he pointed to philanthropy, or hospitality, as belonging to the virtues of Jewish character that gave Judaism its supreme rank among the religions of mankind.[4] Alfonso the Wise appreciated this characteristic of his Jewish subjects when, as he reorganized the *juderías* in his conquered Moorish provinces, he assigned them not only fields and vineyards, dwellings and places of worship, but also *casas de la merced*.[5] Spanish Jewry could well be proud of the number of its philanthropic institutions and the wide scope of their activities. This fact was sadly manifested after the Expulsion, when the Crown took inventory of the possessions which the exiled communities left behind them.[6]

The philanthropies included educational trust funds, eleemosynary charities, care for the orphaned, the dowering of the poor, hospitals, wayfarers' lodgings and the extremely important societies for visiting the sick and for performing the rites of burial.[7] Special funds, in addition, were created as the need arose. When, for instance, captive Jews were thrown on the slave market, the appeal for their redemption met with quick and generous response.[8] The ransom of an unknown Jewish captive by the Cordova community in the tenth century brought about a new epoch in the history of Spanish Judaism, when the obscure prisoner turned out to be Rabbi Moses b. Hanok.[9] As an unhappy climax, the whole of Spanish Jewry formed potential victims of the slave market when the cruel expulsion of 1492 drove them helplessly upon the shores of the Mediterranean in search of a new abode. All the resources of the Mediterranean Jewries were strained to redeem those who actually fell into the clutches of the corsairs and pirates who infested the seas. One of the noblest heroes in this final tragedy of Spanish Jewry, Don Isaac Abravanel, had previously gained melancholy distinction as an organizer of large-scale funds to redeem his captive brethren.[10]

The basic funds for most of these philanthropies were obtained by taxation, either through special assessments or as part of the general taxes which provided for the budget of the *aljama*.[11] The detailed regulations, described in the Talmud, for the raising of charity funds were substituted in the Spanish *juderías* by a loose system which combined compulsory assessments with voluntary contributions. It was a recognized principle that contributions to charity must be proportioned to the means of the donor.

> In some places, however [said Ibn Adret], every man gives as much as he pleases; in others, he contributes in the same proportion as he pays to the royal taxes; but most blessed of all is he who gives to the utmost of his power.[12]

In his famous *Code*, Maimonides established the principle of the tithe as a proper standard of giving for the average Jew.[13] Rabbi Asher b. Yehiel, during his rabbinate in Germany, induced the members of his community formally to adopt this principle, and this ratio remained a personal and family tradition of the Asherides long after they settled in Spain.[14] In order to make this tradition more binding, Rabbi Asher and his sons formulated it as a family vow and, in turn, this resolution was adopted by his grandsons.

An accurate record of these family proceedings was preserved in the last will and testament of Judah, the son of R. Asher, dated in the year 1346:

> We, the undersigned, have stood by a certain ordinance which we have in the handwriting of our grand-

father, R. Asher of blessed memory, of which this is
the text: " 'Hear my son the instruction of thy father
and forsake not the teaching of thy mother.' Seeing
that in the country whence we migrated, our fathers
and our fathers' fathers were wont to set aside to
God, as charity for religious purposes, one part in ten
of all business profits — as our rabbis said in their
comment on the text: 'Thou shalt surely tithe all the
increase of thy seed,' which text they applied to
traders overseas who devoted one tenth of their gains
to those laboring in the Law — therefore we have
continued in the footsteps of our fathers, and have
taken on ourselves the obligation to set aside a tithe
of all our profits in business, whether interest on investments or trade transactions. Three-fourths of
that tithe we will deposit in a chest, controlled by two
treasurers, by whose authorization all grants shall
be made to the necessitous. And this undertaking
we have assumed for ourselves and our offspring to
observe, to do and to maintain it. The treasurers
whom we have elected are the brothers R. Jacob and
R. Judah (whom may God preserve!). These obligations we have duly signed on the ninth day of the
month Marheshvan, in the year 75 (in the abbrevi-
ated reckoning) anno mundi [1315]. Asher b. Yehiel,
Solomon b. Asher, Jacob b. Asher, Judah b. Asher.
Eliakim b. Asher."

And close to these signatures [continued the will and
testament] is a document to the following effect:

"We, the undersigned have agreed that included
in the terms of the ordinance written above shall be
whatever is or shall be in the hand of any of us,
whether it consist of money, legacies, gifts, marriage
settlements, or any other property. Each of us shall
be bound to set aside the proper amount and place
it in the hands of the trustees within eight days of the

same becoming due." So far the form of the second document. The signatories are: Solomon b. Asher, Jacob b. Asher, Judah b. Asher, Simeon b. Asher.

A third document is appended in conclusion:

"We, the undersigned, take upon ourselves all the ordinances relating to the tithe, inscribed above, even as our lord, our father, did, and (we contract) that each of us shall pay the contributions named, as is mentioned above. In attestation of this we have here signed our names on the New Moon of Elul, in the year 5106, anno mundi [1346]." [And the will adds:] So far the third document, which bears the signatures of Solomon b. Judah, Yehiel b. Judah.

The reason for appending these ordinances to his will was explained by the testator, "so that with God's help my younger children also will sign it." Also, "Perchance another (not of my family) seeing it, may be prompted to assume the same obligation."[15]

From this will, it is apparent that the tithe was a voluntary, self-imposed tax. This is also borne out by another testament of a certain Solomon, son of the "holy" martyr R. Isaac, son of Zadok, a Provençal or Spanish Jew of the fourteenth or fifteenth century. In a remarkable program of self-taxation, which included a tax on every pleasurable occasion in life, he added:

And in addition to this, between New Year and the Day of Atonement in each year, I shall calculate my profit-balance, and give a tithe of it. Should I be unable to make an exact calculation, I will give approximately according to my impression of the proper sum. And I will include this tithe together with all the money accumulated as above, and the total shall be set aside for religious purposes, to dispose of as

I deem best. I also retain the liberty to employ the money in any speculation which promises gain, in order to augment the fund for charitable purposes.[16]

Voluntary gifts and private endowments always formed important features of the communal philanthropies.[17] In the course of time, every community accumulated possessions of money, landed estates, rentals and liens from bequests and gifts that sprang from religious devotion.[18] The synagogues, too, were the recipients of special trusts for religious and philanthropic activities, and their endowments paralleled the communal holdings.[19] Extremely important adjuncts were the *confrarias*, or benevolent brotherhoods, which were founded and chartered in the more advanced communities for specialized activities in community welfare.[20] So closely knit were these organizations that frequently they built their own synagogues and chapels of study.[21]

Charity estates were tax-exempt.[22] Their liquid funds were invested in commercial enterprises or lent on interest,[23] unless the purchase of land was stipulated in the gift.[24] Rabbinic interpretation dealt leniently with public trusts and allowed their investment on terms which would have been forbidden to private capital as trespassing on usury.[25] A cautious donor stipulated that his funds were not to be invested in loans at a rate of interest in excess of what the law allowed.[26] Houses belonging to the charities were rented; fields, gardens and vineyards were cultivated and the produce was sold or distributed in kind to the poor.[27] To administer these trusts, special officers, known as *berurim*, *gizbarim* or *gabbaim*, were appointed by the communal and synagogue authorities or, more generally, were elected annually by popular vote.[28] The Crown recognized

these trustees as part of the official administration of the
aljamas.[29] In one instance, a royal edict guaranteed the
independence of these officers from interference by the other
communal officials.[30] They were sworn to perform the
duties of their office with integrity and impartiality, and
were expected periodically to present an account of their
stewardship.[31]

Gifts and bequests to charity were made freely and
generously, with the frequent stipulation to conserve the
capital and to expend the income only.[32] It was not unusual
to will the whole or the major part of one's possessions for
philanthropic purposes — "dedicated to holiness" was the
favorite Hebrew expression.[33] The legacies were deeded in
trusteeship either to the *aljama* or the synagogue, or were
set up as independent trusts with special provisions for
their administration. Strict laws — somewhat archaic and
akin to the regulations which pertained to ancient Temple
property — safeguarded the management of these foundations.[34] The trusts were sacredly kept; no diversion of
charity funds was permitted even for urgent community
needs; and the courts were restricted in their right to sanction the interchange of philanthropic funds or even to confirm the advantageous sale of property which had been
"dedicated to holy purposes."[35]

The favorite objects of philanthropy, private and public,
were to make education freely accessible and to provide
the poor with food, clothing and other necessities of life
according to their accustomed station.[36] Judicial rulings
and private sentiment favored generous outlays for teachers
and pupils, "so that the Torah would not be forgotten in
Israel."[37] Numerous legacies and donations, therefore,
supplemented the educational budget of the *juderías*, usually

styled *Talmud Torah*. In many communities, associations known as *Talmud Torah* fraternities or *confrarias* were formed to promote study within their own ranks and to support the public institutions of learning.[38] Occasionally, a patron of learning set up an independent educational foundation. One of the most interesting endowments of this description was a trust established by the celebrated founder of the Seville synagogue, Joseph ha-Levi of Écija.[38a] Fortunately, the trust agreement has been preserved, both in the original Hebrew as well as in the official Spanish transcript.[39]

This foundation dedicated to the service of God was a perpetual trust for the Jewish people throughout the world. It consisted of an estate of vineyards, houses, gardens and currency in the amount of five thousand gold *maravedís*. The trust was to be under the joint control of the *aljama* and the founder and, after his death, his successor in the family. They were to select a *mayordomo* and with his aid to administer the estate, the money to be invested for profit and the landed property to be leased annually, with the exception of the two mansions and the storehouse of the garden. From the total income, there were to be deducted the necessary expenses for the maintenance of the estate in good order and repair. A certain amount was also to be set aside for the purchase of additional land. Out of the surplus a stipend of four hundred gold *maravedís* was to be paid annually to the resident rabbi of the community of Ecija, Rabbi Yoçafia, who conducted the talmudic academy, or to his successor; an additional sum, three hundred *maravedís*, was to be expended upon the students who were enrolled in the local *yeshibah*. These subventions were in lieu of the seven hundred *maravedís* for which the estate of the founder was then liable annually to the rabbi and his pupils. In addition, fifty *maravedís* were to be spent every year on textbooks at the direction of the head of the academy.

It was furthermore stipulated that during the lifetime of the founder, one doubloon was to be paid the reader of the Joseph ha-Levi synagogue on the day following Yom Kippur if he recited the blessing upon the founder's name during the service on the previous day. The same arrangement was to be in effect after the death of Joseph ha-Levi, if a prayer for the repose of his soul was pronounced on the Day of Atonement.

After these payments were made, the remainder of the accrued income was to be added to the liquid capital until it mounted to eight thousand *maravedís*. Out of the increased income, an additional subvention of four hundred *maravedís* was to be paid to Rabbi Yoçafia or his successor in place of the like amount which he was then receiving from the *kahal* of Écija, and a sum of one hundred *maravedís* was to be spent upon the students, making a total of four hundred *maravedís* for the latter. Whatever surplus remained was to be spent at the discretion of the *aljama* with the advice of the founder or his successor. These stipulations were to be adhered to in perpetuity.

As for the two mansions and the garden referred to above, they were reserved as a residence for Rabbi Yoçafia or his successor, free of rental. If the rabbi chose to dwell elsewhere, however, the property could be leased and the proceeds added to his allowance.

The founder reserved for himself or his successor the right to alter any of the above stipulations, save the right to withdraw any part of the funds for his own use or that of his children. Provision was made, however, for the possible contingency of utilizing the funds to relieve the financial distress of more distant relatives of the family.[39a]

In the communal program the duty to the poor was secondary only to the demands of education. Romantically ideal in theory, the practical standards for the relief of poverty were also humane in the extreme. The noble views of Maimonides, in particular strongly affected social thinking and practice.[40] Out of scattered talmudic precepts, he constructed an ethical ladder of eight successive rungs. The first and highest level was helping the poor man to sustain himself. Then in descending order there followed: he who gave to charity without knowing who was the recipient and without the recipient's knowing the donor; he who gave secretly, knowing the beneficiary but without the latter's knowing his benefactor; he who gave not knowing the recipient, but with the recipient's knowledge of the donor; he who gave (both knowing) without solicitation; he who gave after he was asked; he who gave insufficiently but with good grace; and lowest on the ladder was he who gave with bad grace.[41]

Great stress was laid not only on generosity but on delicacy in giving. Above all, the poor were to be spared the blush of humiliation. They were not treated as a class but as individuals, and help was extended to the needy in accordance with their station in life and their previous standards of living.[42] Occasionally, the Christian poor, too, were aided by Jewish charities to promote "the ways of peace."[43] Families in distress, who were too proud to make their needs known, were sought out and help was given them surreptitiously under the guise of gifts or loans, if necessary.[44]

Dowering the marriageable daughters of the poor was prominently featured in the scheme of Jewish charity.[45]

The cost of this entire program was, in the main, supported by a levy on wealth and was, therefore, borne chiefly
by the powerful upper class.[46] As a rule, this method was
accepted as sound in theory and fair in practice. But
occasionally the richer class rebelled against the excessive
burden. In a time of economic distress, when the poor
increased in number and the cost of living rose to exorbitant
heights, a heartless attempt was made by a rich coterie to
send the poor begging from house to house as an ingenious
measure to distribute and equalize the burden of their
support among all classes in the community. But the
proposal met with indignant and emphatic rejection as being
contrary to law and decency. "Nay, in their homes they
shall stay and not as beggers knock at the doors," cried the
men of the middle class, "for they are our brethren and our
flesh. Their support rests on the community and we will
all pay our share according to our means, and let the court
use its power of enforcement."[47]

Ibn Adret lost no time in upholding the contention of
the middle class on every count. For talmudic precedent
was clear that an individual's obligation to support charity
was in direct proportion to his wealth; that every poor
person must be supported; that even if he declined aid, he
must be assisted through the subterfuge of a loan or gift;
and that, furthermore, the amount given any person must
be measured by his station in life so that more should be
given to him who came of good family on account of the
honor of his position. How totally repugnant, therefore,
was the idea of sending poor people to beg at the doors!

Not without a touch of irony he concluded: "Even though the present generation is indeed poor — in ideas no less than in money — it is, nevertheless, the universal practice to support the poor from the community chest which is raised by assessment on the wealth of the inhabitants." The principle rejecting house-to-house begging was later incorporated in the standard code, the *Shulhan 'Aruk*.[48]

In the inventories of Jewish communal property which were prepared for Ferdinand and Isabella after the Expulsion of 1492, there were included a number of community hospitals.[49] Visiting the sick was a time-honored religious commandment.[50] Under the name of *Bikkur Holim* the faithful united in benevolent fraternities the better to carry out this precept of love.[51] These *confrarias* no doubt fostered and helped to establish the institutions for the sick. They were popular and influential — the *confraria* in Saragossa was well known for its important synagogue.[52] There is merit in the suggestion that, because the duty of visiting the sick was performed so faithfully, there was little occasion for parish visiting by the rabbis as a ministerial function.[53] As the Spanish rabbis in particular, however, were in so many instances also practicing physicians, they naturally attended the sick in the course of their medical practice. Needless to say, they attended the poor freely and made no distinction of race or creed.[54]

Strangely enough, the most aristocratic and exclusive brotherhood was the burial society, which not only attended to the loving services of the last rites, but also undertook to regulate the moral and religious conduct of its members. Known in Hebrew as כת הקברים, referred to in the vernacular sources as *confraria delos cavafuessas*, also *de fodiendis sepulturis*, this lugubriously named society played a cheerful

and important part in the social life of the community.[55]
Fortunately, the statutes of the *confraria* of Lerida have
been preserved, together with the confirmation of the
Infante Alfonso in 1323 and King Pedro IV twenty-five
years later, so that one can view the inner workings of this
socially important organization of mediaeval Jewry.[56]

The *confraria* was a closed corporation. Its membership
was restricted; admissions were voted upon by carefully
planned balloting. The organization was governed by an
elected board, the *adelantados*, who exercised strict control
over the conduct of its members by means of the ban,
monetary penalties and the threat of expulsion. The king's
sanction was required for the organization of this society
and kindred fraternities. The right to establish these *confrarias* was usually conferred as a privilege upon individual
aljamas. The *takkanot*, or statutes, by which the brotherhoods were ruled were formulated by the *adelantados*,
adopted by the membership and then submitted to the ruler
for confirmation. At times, the proposed statutes concentrated power and authority in the fraternities which tres-
passed on the rights of the sovereign. In the case of the
Huesca society, the Infante Alfonso unceremoniously struck
out the offending clauses and confirmed the main body of
the statutes.

The primary purpose of the burial league was naturally
centered in the preparations and rites surrounding death
and burial. Members of the fraternity were covenanted to
perform these solemn duties for one another, to participate
as mourners in the funeral procession and in the attendant
religious services. In order not to burden the entire membership, the society was grouped into numbered divisions
which rotated semiannually, and each member's responsi-

bility was limited to his own division. From seven groups in 1323, the Lerida society grew to eight divisions in 1348.

No one under sixty years of age could evade personal service except in case of sickness, imprisonment, travel or preoccupation with matters of public interest. Night duties could not be imposed except by a majority vote of the division. There were fixed rates of payment for grave-digging, and the terms of payment were outlined in the statutes to avoid embarrassment at the time of emotional strain.

The *confrades* were also to share with one another the happier celebrations of life. They prayed on the Sabbath with the bridegroom and with the father of a newborn child. They attended the weddings of a brother's children, and those who were officially delegated brought six tapers in honor of the bride and groom. They also paid Sabbath sickcalls on the *confrades*.

The election of the *adelantados* — one for each division — was approximately semiannual or every seven months; and a period of two years had to elapse before one attained eligibility for re-election. Acceptance of the office was mandatory under penalty of the ban for a month's duration. The usual oath of office was required within three days of the election. At the end of their term, the *adelantados*, who had full power of administration over the real property and mobile possessions of the *confraria*, rendered an account of their stewardship to their successors; and the new incumbents were responsible for the repayment of any advances or loans which the outgoing officers had made for the brotherhood.

The penalty for sowing discord in the society was expulsion. Civic honesty and exemplary religious and moral

conduct were required of every member. Gambling was
forbidden under threat of the ban, and a persistent offender
was dropped from the ranks. Severe punishment leading to
expulsion was prescribed for any member who entertained
loose Christian women or notorious gamblers at his home.
The *confrades* were required to attend daily morning services
at the synagogue before starting their work. On Fridays,
they were to show due regard for the Sabbath by cessation
from work at an early hour. Punctilious observance of the
religious regulations regarding food, drink and dress was
mandatory. Resistance to the authorities of the *confraria*
was strictly forbidden.

Every member was obligated three times a year to donate
three *dineros* or more to the *confraria*. The society also
received gifts and bequests. Its possessions included real
property, mobiles and liquid funds. The *confraria* of
Huesca maintained its own *casas del almidras*, chapels of
prayer and study, and a rabbi, or *hakam*, to instruct the
members and to lecture to them on subjects of Jewish study.

The *confrarias*, or leagues of various types, played an
increasingly important role in the fourteenth and fifteenth
centuries. Originally adjuncts to the communal charities,
they expanded their functions and became self-governing
units, held together by rigid disciplinary authority. Had the
aljamas been permitted to develop normally during these
centuries, the *confrarias* would gradually have become
integrated in the political structure of the *kahal*. As it was,
their evolution was arrested and they remained to the end
social agencies which implemented in many important
directions the educational and charitable program of the
aljama.

The various types of benevolent leagues, no less than the

individual philanthropic institutions, grew out of definite
social needs. The romantic love of Zion, which found such
poignant expression in the prayer and poetry of the Hebrew
bards in Spain, failed to create any organized institution
on the Iberian peninsula, such as flourished later in Rome.
The Palestine leagues which we find in the capital of
Christendom under the names of *Hebrat Yerushalayim* or
Hebrat Erez Yisrael, had no counterpart in any Spanish
center during the thirteenth and fourteenth centuries, the
period which is reflected most fully in the responsa of the
Spanish rabbis.[57] Evidently Palestine did not seek support
at this time and sent no emissaries to Spain. This was the
period when the Holy Land attracted in all the countries
of Christendom adventurous Jewish spirits, who wearied of
endless persecution and longed for the spiritual peace and
freedom which was romantically associated with the land
of their fathers.[58]

Although, during the greater part of this period, the lot of
the Jews of Spain was happy in comparison with that of
their French and German brethren, many of them found the
religious and ecstatic appeal of Zion irresistible. In small
family groups rather than en masse, they set out for the
Holy Land.[59] To steel their courage — for it required
heroism to cross so many hostile barriers of state, language
and religion — many took the vow to carry out their holy
resolves.[60] Some faltered and prayed for absolution,[61] but
others remained undaunted in the face of cruel fate and
tragedy and bravely persisted in the pursuit of their goal
in fulfillment of the vow.[62]

Thus we read the story of two rabbis, Hezekiah and Jacob
by name, who vowed and entered into a mutual covenant
in Cordova, in November 1317, to set out with their wives

and children for the Holy Land.[63] The terms of the covenant and the circumstances surrounding it invest the story with unusual interest and pathos, which even the dry language of a legal compact cannot altogether conceal. The text of the oath follows:

In honor of the God of Israel who chose Jerusalem as the seat of His eternal habitation and in honor of the Torah, in all its perfection, which went forth from Zion, we, the undersigned, have taken upon ourselves as a religious duty and have vowed before the Mighty One of Jacob that we will go up to the land of Israel, the land of life, to dwell in Jerusalem or in a place near it, as we may agree. There we will do the will of God and serve Him with a perfect heart. There is the house of our God and the gate of Heaven; and we will find acceptance as we fulfill His commandments and take upon us the yoke of the Divine Kingdom and His service.

We, therefore, vow each to the other with the scroll of the Law in our arms, with the permission of God and with the assent of the community, that we shall be associated together as partners for a period of seven years, during which time we will not separate from each other. If it be the will of the Creator that we have enough to support ourselves and our families, we shall both devote ourselves wholly to the study of the Torah. If, God forbid, we prove unworthy of this grace and the income does not suffice for both our families, then let one continue his studies and the other engage in worldly occupation to support his associate and his dependents, contenting himself with such time as may be left him for study. After a fixed period, he may call upon his partner to alternate with him and to engage in work while he will devote himself to study. All the profit shall be divided between us and used in accordance with our needs and the necessities of our families. If, Heaven forfend, the efforts of one do not prove sufficient to support the two families, then both of us shall engage in work and we will share the earnings equally as partners, regardless of the amount that each of us shall contribute.

The terms of the agreement shall go into effect immediately after we set out upon our journey from the city of Cordova. If, God forbid, an accident prevents one of us from going to Palestine, the other shall be absolved from this covenant and vow until the hindrance is removed; for the vow and the oath are taken expressly on the condition that both of us shall be associated as partners. These conditions apply equally before and after we reach Palestine.

As part of the oath, we solemnly agree not to resort to legal nullification and not to allow ourselves to be dissuaded jointly or singly from our enterprise. And even if the king should oppose us, we shall strive with all our power to continue to the land of life. But if, God forbid, we should be prevented from leaving at the time set for our departure either by reason of human compulsion or sickness or for want of a sailing vessel, or if there break out war or famine,[64] then we shall wait until the obstacle is removed and afterwards continue on our journey. For the vow is not annulled by postponement; it is binding upon us as long as we live, provided that we act together in partnership.

Furthermore, upon our arrival in Jerusalem, we shall devote one fifth of the money in our possession, whether in gold or silver, for a religious purpose for the glory of God and His Law. Should we unfortunately need any part of it subsequently for our sustenance, we may each of us draw upon the fund in accordance with our due — for it is upon this condition that we dedicate the fund.

We likewise agree to live at least the first year in Jerusalem, afterwards it shall be optional. The time set for our departure shall be no later than two years from this date in the month of Marheshwan in the year 78, anno mundi (November 1317).

The events which followed the sealing of the covenant of Rabbis Jacob and Hezekiah reveal the hardships which beset those who undertook such a perilous pilgrimage. For when the date set for their departure in 1319 arrived and they had sold all their possessions in preparation for the journey, the news reached them, as they were about to engage passage from Cordova to Seville, that the Portuguese fleet, acting upon the command of the pope, had orders to plunder and seize every Jew and Moor on the Mediterranean Sea. Determined to ascertain the true facts, the two rabbis proceeded to Seville, leaving their wives, their children and all their possessions in Cordova. They found, however, that the blockade was completely effective and that no vessel could sail for Malaga, Barcelona or any other port from which one could set out for Palestine. Seeing this, R. Hezekiah persuaded his friend to return to Cordova, while he remained in Seville, ready to report and to take advantage of any change in the naval situation. Thus much time elapsed. Hezekiah transported his family and his books to Seville and established residence in the city.

In the meantime, a series of misfortunes befell his friend, R. Jacob, in Cordova. In a short period, four of his children died — a sure sign to the trembling father of God's wrath for the nonfulfillment of the vow. One only son remained,

and daily Jacob feared that he, too, might be snatched from
him by the dreaded angel. He implored his friend to hasten
the preparations and to send him word about proceeding to
Palestine. Finally, the hoped-for news arrived. He was to
hasten to Seville and Hezekiah would have all preparations
made for their passage to the Holy Land. Quickly, Jacob
sent word confirming the arrangements. But, suddenly,
intensive warfare broke out between Cordova and Seville;
the roads were closed; and, although Jacob was anxious to
take the risk, his family and friends detained him against
his will. Hezekiah, in the meantime, relying on his friend's
assurance, had hired a vessel and put all his belongings
upon it. He tarried as long as he could and, when Jacob
failed to appear, he left without him. But misfortune
pursued him, and he was forced to return to Seville, this
time determined, however, not to set sail for Palestine
with his friend, as he, too, felt that he was the victim of
God's displeasure. For, as he now explained to the dismay
of his friend, R. Jacob, the vow to go to the Holy Land
conflicted with another oath which he had previously taken
and which no longer left him free to leave the country for
a prolonged period.

The despair of R. Jacob broke forth in elegiac terms as
he pleaded with the great and revered rabbi of Toledo,
Asher b. Yehiel, for wisdom, guidance and moral help. The
denouement is left to the imagination. Rabbi Asher readily
brushed aside Jacob's legal scruples and easily proved that,
in the light of Hezekiah's latest revelation, the vow to go
to Jerusalem never had any validity. Nevertheless, he
held out to him the thought of proceeding to Palestine
alone. Whether Jacob did so and found peace for his tortured soul we shall never know. But it is otherwise abun-

dantly clear that many Spanish Jews from all walks of life found their way there in increasing numbers during the century that elapsed between Nahmanides' flight to the Holy Land as a lone fugitive[65] and the time when Barfat exclaimed that "everybody goes to Palestine."[66]

CHAPTER XIX

SOCIAL RELATIONS BETWEEN JEWS
AND CHRISTIANS

PERSONAL conduct and human relationships cannot be wholly constricted by canons of law nor held perpetually in the vise of institutional authority. An element of spontaneity in human nature will inevitably break through elaborate, unnatural barriers erected by man's devices and build a channel for human good will and an outlet for free social contacts. Notwithstanding the stringent program of church and state laws which aimed strictly at segregating the Jewish community from the Christian population, the numerous instances of happy, reciprocal relationships between them show the healthy resistance of human nature to an artificial policy of division and separation. The good will generated was not sufficient to change the current of history; nevertheless, its existence was a hopeful and happy symbol.

Except for the shameful badge, which the Church was determined to fasten upon every Jew and Jewess from the age of adolescence upwards and which the Jews were equally determined to resist,[1] it was difficult outwardly to distinguish the Spanish Jew from his Christian countryman. They both spoke the same language;[2] they bore similar names;[3] they wore the same clothes;[4] and, in the upper social ranks, Jewish aristocrats vied with Spanish noblemen in personal splendor and luxury. Retinues of Moorish slaves

attended them and their families.[5] Jewels and ornaments,
silks and furs adorned their persons.[6] They rode costly
mounts, owned villas and hunting grounds.[7] Indeed, the
ostentation of the small rich coterie caused the communal
authorities grave concern. They deplored its inevitable
effect in rousing the envy and cupidity of the hostile population; and, without waiting upon the unfriendly legislation
of the Cortes, the *kahal* in many communities passed various
sumptuary regulations to suppress the flaunting of wealth
and rich possessions.[8]

The social gradations within the *judería* were neither so
steep nor so rigid as in feudal society. At one end, there
was no military caste or hereditary nobility; at the other
end, there was no class of serfs or slaves. It was a resourceful,
many-sided people that had much to contribute to the life
of the surrounding population. Here wealth and learning,
public service and personal piety were the basis of social
preferment.[9] Education was widespread.[10] Personal talent
and initiative met with reward; but so swiftly and precari-
ously did the wheel of fortune spin, only the most agile
and quick-witted could even temporarily maintain their
position.[11] From this population, Spanish kings drafted
their financiers and diplomats. Jewish statesmen proved
wise counselors and diplomats and discreet confidants of
their royal masters.[12] The tax collectors and the bailiffs
were doomed to personal unpopularity; but normally they
were recognized as necessary agencies of government. The
nation's most noted scientists and physicians were drawn
from the *judería*.[13] While the men of science and the literary
personages mingled chiefly in court circles, the medical
experts reached out to all classes of the population, many
of them being noted for their noble service to the poor

without distinction of race or creed. Jewish physicians were
familiar court figures.[14] In an age when royalty was idealized as a divine institution, and court life appeared as
national romance to the starved imagination of the lower
classes, these physicians were regarded with awe and admiration, as kings and noblemen entrusted their lives and the
health of their families to their ministrations. In many
ways, therefore, the varied activities of the Jews led to
friendly, social contacts between them and the dominant
population.

In the commercial sphere, no visible barriers separated
Jewish, Christian and Saracen merchants during the major
period of Jewish life in Spain.[15] They freely engaged in
business transactions with one another and formed numerous
partnerships.[16] Christian contractors built Jewish homes and
Jewish craftsmen worked for Christian employers.[17] Jewish
advocates represented gentile clients in the secular courts.[18]
Jewish brokers acted as intermediaries between Christian
and Moorish principals.[19] As a by-product, such continuous daily contacts inevitably fostered tolerance and
friendly relationships, despite the irritations kept alive in
the name of religion.[20] Notwithstanding numerous ecclesiastical bans, Jews, Saracens and Christians interchanged
gifts on holidays and at family celebrations,[21] and a benevolent king — on rare occasions, it is true — made a friendly
gift to a synagogue building fund.[22]

That the Jews in all the important cities of Spain found
it expedient and necessary to live in their own quarter
under high walls and barricaded gates, even under normal
conditions, is sufficient proof that they were living perpetually under a cloud of hostility and danger. Nevertheless,
so long as the *judería* was a "voluntary" institution, erected

by the Jewish residents for their own protection, there was
no opprobrium attached to it.[23] It had imposing residences,
magnificent synagogues, and mansions surrounded with gardens, orchards and vineyards.[24] Sanitation in the *judería* was
superior to that in the corresponding non-Jewish section.[25]
Although every important city had its own Jewish quarter,
many Jews had their dwellings in the outer city adjoining
those of their Christian neighbors[26] — indeed, at times,
under the very shadow of the church.[27] On the other hand,
it was not unusual for Christians to live in the *judería*
proper,[28] and even a bailiff had his official residence there.[29]

Despite the excesses of fanatical priests, whom the authorities could not control and, notwithstanding the agitation
of the more responsible Inquisition, the Church of Rome
does not bear the onus of having advocated the expulsion
or the physical extermination of Jewry in any Christian
state. There were many other elements that conspired with
the religious forces to create the unhappy conditions which
led to the degradation, torture and final expulsion of so
cultured and valuable an element as the Jewish population
in Spain. The political and economic forces naturally thrust
themselves into the foreground. The low state of culture
in which crude religious beliefs and superstition had their
roots, the credulity of the masses, so easily deluded by
miracles and swayed by sorcery, formed fertile soil for the
weeds of suspicion, bigotry and primitive savagery — the
underbrush which, once ignited, could not be stamped out
until the work of destruction was complete. Nevertheless,
it is fair to say that a totally different outcome would have
eventuated for Spain and the Jews were it not for the
genius of the Church militant that never wearied, faltered
or retreated in the course of a thousand years in the set

goal to unify the faith of Christendom and to annihilate or reduce to impotence and ignominy those who denied her supreme claim to rule in heaven and on earth.

The issues which divided the Church and the Jews were both material and theological. The former were capable of compromise and adjustment; in the latter domain, the Church brooked no compromise and yielded no ground. Of a material nature, the chief object of contention was the tithe on the products of the soil and the income from real property and also the first fruit offering.[30] The Church claimed these dues from Jews and Saracens no less than from Christians.[31] The Jews, on the other hand, strenuously opposed this demand not only as an economic burden, but also as an unwarranted ecclesiastic imposition.[32] Fortunately for the Jews, the interests of the secular rulers lay in supporting the Jewish contention.

The controversy lingered for centuries.[33] The issue was never settled definitely. The exemption of the Jews was not conceded by the Church at any time, nor did the latter succeed in gaining the assent of the Jews in regard to this tribute. The question arose intermittently, and whatever side to the dispute had the support of the ruler gained its objective for the time being.[34] The Church stressed the claim that when Jewish ownership of land was of recent origin and was derived from Christian title, to deny the tithe was to deprive the churches and the monasteries of the income upon which their existence depended. At the same time, the Church did not surrender its asserted rights in Jewish property of original Moorish title.[35] As the extent of Jewish ownership of landed property increased, the grievance of the Church was correspondingly accentuated.[36]

The secular rulers who arbitrated these cases were in a dilemma. Their sympathies presumably lay with the Church, but their own temporal interests coincided with the Jewish viewpoint. With pious resolution, James I of Aragon conceded the tithe to the Church but made the important distinction that it was applicable only to lands of recent Christian ownership, not to patrimonial estates.[37] Alfonso VIII of Castile, on the other hand, risked the thunder of Innocent III by upholding his Jewish subjects in their refusal to pay the tribute.[38] Nor were Innocent's successors, Honorius III and Gregory IX, more successful with Ferdinand III.[39] The archbishop of Toledo, treating directly with the Jews of his diocese, effected a compromise by commuting the tithe for a fixed annual payment, but the concordat was not of long duration.[40] Alfonso the Wise heeded the admonition of Innocent IV, in 1254,[41] but about thirty years later, in 1285, it was necessary for Sancho IV to order his Jewish subjects to pay the tithe[42] and, in 1313, it was still the object of legislation by the Council of Zamora.[43]

What is most astonishing is the paradoxical action of prelates who continued to farm the tithes and other ecclesiastical revenues to Jewish and Moorish financiers as late as the fifteenth century. Little wonder that the Cortes at Ocaña, in 1469, cried out indignantly to King Henry:

> But even worse is done in your kingdoms; for many prelates and other ecclesiasts farm to Jews and Moors the revenues and tithes that belong to them; and they enter churches to apportion the tithe among the contributors, to the great offense and injury of the Church.[44]

Not the material but the theological issues, however, stirred the Church to unremitting, relentless warfare. One of the most unhappy chapters in the history of European civilization was inaugurated and motivated by a passionate desire to promote a religion whose gospel was love, and to force eternal happiness upon a people which refused to believe that it belonged to an unregenerated mankind. With the weird contrariness which often affects human nature, the vision of the millennial era and the desire to hasten its coming led the votaries of religion to use weapons dipped in venom — a method calculated to infect with its poison all who engaged in the unholy combat.

The earnest objective of the Church was to make Christianity coextensive with humanity. In this missionary program the hoped-for conversion of the Jews was peculiarly desirable and urgent. "We cherish converts from Judaism with even greater affection," Gregory IX wrote to two Jewish converts in 1236, "because we hope that if a branch of a naturally wild olive tree ... brings forth delightful fruit, all the more so will branches broken off a sacred root."[45] But more important still, the conversion of "the remnant" was a necessary prelude to the second coming of the Christ.[46] Almost any means seemed justified to bring about this end.

What seemed so impelling and self-evident to the churchman, however, was vigorously combated by the Jew, whose faith in the One God was supreme and led him to accept death and martyrdom joyously as a means of sanctifying the Holy Name. To meet this defiance, the Church utilized every means within its power: on the one hand, polemics and propaganda, promises of salvation in heaven and temporal blessings on earth; and, on the other hand, threats, instigations and violence. Naturally, voluntary

conversion was the ideal aim of the Church. Pope Gregory I
had given emphatic utterance to this principle in 591:
"Conversions wrought by force are seldom sincere and such
as are thus converted seldom fail to return to their vomit
when the force is removed."[47] Baptism "should be a voluntary offering, not a forced one," Innocent IV wrote to the
King of Navarre.[48] This sentiment became the law of the
Church.[49] But there were many impetuous zealots, within
and without the hierarchy, with but little regard for law,
who had no patience with Utopian attitudes and who set
about to force the coming of salvation with savage brutality.
When these attacks were sporadic and unorganized, the
resultant conversions were temporary and, in the end,
negligible in quantity.[50] Under the Visigothic kings, during
the pre-Mohammedan period, the Jews of early Spain
(587–711) were subjected to a thoroughgoing experiment
of repressive legislation by Church and State, in order to
drive them forcibly into the Christian fold.[51] But the experiment could not be pronounced a success even before
the extinction of Visigothic rule. For no sooner did a wave
of active persecution pass over, when the forced converts
returned to the old faith en masse, notwithstanding severe
penalties which the laws decreed for backsliders.[52] During
the reconquest and the establishment of the native Spanish
kingdoms when broad toleration prevailed, conversions
were few in number, and this state continued through the
thirteenth and into the fourteenth century when the persecutions began on a large scale.[53] Moreover, Christian
conversion was, in a measure, counterbalanced by Jewish
proselytism, although this was carried on under the grave
and imminent peril of death.[54]

With all the encomiums and the indulgence heaped upon

the convert by pious Christians, his lot was not an enviable one. He cut himself off from his past. Usually he was not followed by his family into the new faith. The children dropped his name.[55] If he died, there was no religious mourning for him.[56] He was regarded as a blot upon the family. The disgrace of one convert in a family was enough cause to warrant the disruption of the wedding engagement of an innocent relative.[57] His former brethren regarded him as a renegade and ostracized him. The converts smarted under the opprobrium and took special offense at the epithets which were hurled at them, such as renegade, apostate and similar names, whether in Hebrew or in the vernacular.[58] Quarrels, leading to fisticuffs and more violent fighting, followed.[59] Paradoxically, the Christian rulers generally encouraged the loyal Jews to disinherit the converts according to Jewish law[60] and, where this was not done, they themselves confiscated the property of the converts to the *fiscus*.[61]

The clergy and the local officials naturally came to the rescue of the neophytes.[62] The Third Lateran Council, in 1179, proclaimed for all Christendom that no convert to Christianity should under any condition be deprived of his property rights, "for converts ought to be in better circumstances than they had been before accepting the Faith."[63] It became quite customary in European countries outside of Spain for ecclesiastical establishments to support and maintain the converts indefinitely on the theory that "a new plant should be strengthened not alone by the dew of doctrine, but nourished also by temporal benefits."[64] In Spain, the first important measure to implement the church viewpoint was the act of renunciation on the part of James I of Aragon in 1242,[65] which Innocent IV praised in glowing terms.[66] Fired with missionary zeal, James swept

aside all earlier provisions, statutes and customs tending
to hinder or to discourage those who desired "the orthodox
faith and the font of baptismal salvation." Henceforth,
no convert was to lose any of his property rights nor could
he be deprived of his inheritance: "For even as they merit
the grace of God, so shall they be known to have ours, whose
duty it is to imitate His good will and favor." Furthermore,
he prohibited the taunting of a convert by such names as
"renegade," *tornadizo* or the like. In the same act, he
also inaugurated the policy of forcing Jews to listen to missionary preachers in the churches and in their own synagogues.[67] This led to so many attacks and outbursts by the
mobs who accompanied the preachers that he later regretted
the act and annulled it, though he subsequently revived it
with the important restriction that the band escorting the
preachers be limited to ten in number.[68]

But it was hardly to be expected that this monarch's
zeal and self-denial would remain a permanent policy.
James II found it expedient to renew the decree in 1297,[69]
and then to reaffirm the policy of James I at the Cortes of
Barcelona, in 1311, probably under the influence of the
Council of Vienne.[70] But as late as 1389, John I regarded
the older conception of the automatic lapsing of the convert's
wealth to the *fiscus* as the prevailing law of the land, which
he was willing graciously to waive in favor of a particular
candidate for baptism.[71] Likewise in Castile, Alfonso X
decreed in *Las Siete Partidas* that Jews who turned Christian
should retain their property and also their rights of inheritance, "the same as if they were Jews,"[72] but the Council
of Valladolid, in 1322, still found it necessary to protect the
converts in their customary rights of inheritance[73] and, in
1380, John I solemnly announced at the Cortes of Soria

that he who abused a Jewish-Christian by calling him
Marrano, *tornadizo* or a similar name was to be fined three
hundred *maravedís* or jailed for fifteen days.[74]

Not only did the converts arouse the deep antipathy of
their former coreligionists, who felt that they and all that
was holy to them were betrayed by the apostasy, but they
did not always find great favor among their new brethren
in faith. Despite the laudation of professional theologians,
the character of the average "voluntary" convert was
generally not one to inspire trust or admiration. Without
hazarding any generalization, it is interesting to note that
in the various cases of converts whose personal antecedents
are known, conversion was a means of escape from the
penalties of crime, murder, adultery or blasphemy.[75] King
James II felt that he acted "for the glory of God and the
holy Catholic faith" when he extended pardon to a criminal
who had been "divinely inspired to embrace the Faith" after
he had committed murder.[76] Such converts often showed
their true colors by turning vindictively upon their people,
inciting the clergy to boycott the Jews, until they, as well as
the priests, were bribed into silence.[77] Their vituperation
of the old faith, the abuse which they heaped upon their
former brethren,[78] the unrestrained manner in which they
broke into the synagogues to carry on religious disputations
and to force their preachments upon the unwilling worshipers caused even James I and some discriminating
churchmen to doubt their sincerity and good faith.[79]

It would seem, moreover, that the more learned and
gifted the converts, the more keenly did they smart under
the reproach and contempt of their former friends and
colleagues.[80] Consequently, either out of revenge or in self-
vindication, they were determined to force their adversaries

out into open verbal battle in a tournament in which the odds were heavily on their side. Amidst the plaudits of the Christian audiences and with the loud acclaim of the high dignitaries of Church and State, they hoped to bring low their enemies and thus to regain their self-esteem. Some who entered the Church and sought ecclesiastical rank and promotion were driven by their ambition to crusade for the destruction of the old faith and the burning of the Talmud.[81] In 1240, Nicholas Donin dragged the leading rabbis of France before a Dominican tribunal in Paris to debate with him the right of the Talmud to live; and the celebrated Nahmanides was summoned to the palace of James I in Barcelona, in 1263, to engage with Pablo Christiani in a religious tournament in the dazzling presence of the royal family and a brilliant assemblage of nobles, knights, burghers and princes of the Church.[82] As tournaments, they were among the most unchivalrous spectacles in Christendom. The rules of the battle were one-sided. Often the debate degenerated into an inquisition of the Jewish contestants, or "information." Neither side truly convinced the other, though both sides claimed victory. Whoever won in the abstract, the Jew was made to pay the penalty of defeat.[83] Thus, even though Nahmanides' brilliant defense of his faith against the baptized Jew won the sincere admiration of so zealous a Christian as King James I,[84] he suffered banishment from Spain — a severe blow for the aged rabbi, and yet a mild punishment in comparison with the penalty which the Dominican confreres of Pablo Christiani had planned for him.[85] Not until the zeal of the Preaching Brothers was reinforced by the terror of undisciplined bands, who spread death and devastation among the *juderías* in the succeeding century in mounting crescendo, was the grace of the new faith "revealed" to thousands who fled to the baptismal font to be "saved."[86] Raymond Martini, writing the *Pugio Fidei* (The Dagger of the Faith) in 1278, had to console himself with the belief that when Jesus promised salvation to the Jews it was only to "one of a city and two of a family" (Jer. 3.14), or even, following talmudic analogy, to "two out of six hundred thousand."[87]

All the more aggravating, therefore, must have been the reports that reached the church authorities of active proselytism on the part of the Jews. For although Judaism had long ago abandoned all missionary ambitions,[88] pagans and Christians, in individual cases, pressed for admission to the Jewish fold and submitted to the rites of Jewish baptism and circumcision.[89] It was the fear of proselytism that led the Church to object so strenuously to the holding of slaves by Jews, especially Christian slaves.[90] But the converts to Judaism were not drawn from the class of slaves alone. A glimpse at the records of the Inquisition reveals the amazing fact that free Christians sought out distant Jewish communities, there to be taken under the wings of the God of Israel.[91] How great the ranks of proselytes were numerically must forever remain problematical. The retribution visited upon the proselytes and all who participated directly or most remotely in the conversion rites was so swift and terrifying that every effort was bent upon destroying all incriminating evidence. Nevertheless, it is quite apparent that it was no unusual phenomenon for proselytes to be drawn to Judaism from the ranks of pagans, Moors and Christians, even at the risk of confiscation, slavery and death.[92] Ibn Adret described the order of the blessings which were recited at the initiation of a proselyte. That this was not a theoretical discussion is shown by his concluding remark: "And this, I have observed, is the practice which is followed here."[93] Not only ritual questions, but practical considerations affecting the proselytes and their heirs are discussed in the responsa literature.[94]

From early times, the Church was apprehensive of the appeal and contagious influence of Judaism. It sought to counteract the danger of Jewish proselytism by severity of punishment as well as by extreme preventive measures of an antisocial character.[95] Not only did the Church view with alarm the proselytism of Christians, but it set its face hard against the conversion of Moors to Judaism, or Jews to Mohammedanism. However fainthearted or openly rebellious some Spanish kings might have been in regard to other aspects of the anti-Jewish legislation of the Church, they could not help but share fully in the ecclesiastical viewpoint in regard to Jewish proselytism.

Acting in concert with the Church Council of Tarragona, James I, in 1235, strictly forbade Jews and Moors to convert one another "under penalty of the loss of their person."[96] Alfonso X proclaimed a similar decree at the Cortes of Seville, in 1252.[97] The *Fuero Real* decreed that a Christian who turned Jew or Moor was to die by fire; the Jew who induced the Christian to turn from his religion or who circumcised him was to die for the act and his property was to be confiscated to the king.[98] Alfonso X wrote somewhat more circumstantially in *Las Siete Partidas*:

> Such evil results from Christians turning Jews, that we order that any Christian who does shall suffer death, the same as if he had become a heretic. We furthermore ordain that his property is to be treated in the same manner as we have ordained that of heretics to be treated.[99]

In another section dealing with the manner in which Jews must live among Christians, death and confiscation were meted out to the Jew who converted a Christian.[100]

In the reign of James II, the Inquisition was particularly active in ferreting out and punishing all who were implicated in proselytism, the monarch in every instance moderating the severe sentence of the ecclesiastical tribunal. Indicted by the inquisitor, Fray Juan Llotger, on the charge of aiding and abetting relapsed Jewish converts as well as others who had come from foreign parts, the *aljamas* of Barcelona, Tarragona, Montblanch and Villafranca saved themselves from civil and criminal prosecution by the payment of 10,000 *sueldos* to the king on October 10, 1311.[101] Ten Jews of Tarragona being involved in the conversion at Toledo of two German Christians, their property was confiscated, they were banished to exile and, in addition, the entire *aljama* was condemned to pay a fine of 35,000 *sueldos*.[102] Four years later, the *aljama* of Majorca was indicted by the Inquisition and similarly dealt with on account of the circumcision of two Christians in that city.[103] In 1326, Solomon de Quatorçe and his daughter Hora were sentenced by the heresy-inquisitor and the bishop of Tarazona to the confiscation of their property for the conversion of a French girl to Judaism.[104] Within a year, in 1327, the *aljama* of Calatayud and all its members individually were penalized by the same tribunal with the total confiscation of their property because of the proselytism of two Christians and the reversion of a baptized Jew to his former faith.[105] In the hour of deepest gloom, on the very eve of the final expulsion, there were Christian souls ready to embrace martyrdom as Jews together with the communities that heroically dared to accept them.[106] What food for reflection

A street in Old Toledo
(see p. xi)

is afforded by the contrast between the Jewish proselyte, who could only face hardship, deprivation and death for his act of faith, and the Christian convert whose change of religion, however motivated, gained for him not only the approbation of the whole Christian world, but the material and active support of the greatest ally in mediaeval Christendom, the Church of Rome!

The sweeping gains in the pagan world could not compensate the Church for the frustration of its aims in regard to the Jews. Indeed, the greater the other accessions to the Christian ranks, the more obstinate and unreasoning seemed to be the persistence of the Jew in his own faith. Under the circumstances, it was difficult for the proud church prelates to be tolerant or understanding of the Jewish state of mind. Drawing upon the richly vituperative vocabulary of the older saints and Church Fathers, they spoke of the Jewish religion as "Jewish blindness." Judaism was not a *religio* but a *perfidia*. The Synagogue was a castoff woman, like Hagar, "a rejected and despised wife." The Jews were "slaves rejected by God."

But the church attitude was not wholly one of baffled rage and contempt. A strange element of mysticism was associated with the anomalous survival of the Jew. Even Innocent III, with all his intolerance and bitter invective, conceded that "they were the custodians of the Law."[107] For Gregory IX, "the proof for the Christian faith comes, as it were, from their [Jewish] archives."[108] Although the pious churchmen pointed with horror to the guilt of the crucifixion, they also spoke with awe of Israel's divine past and the glorious promise that was bound up with the saving of the remnant.[109] Furthermore, the haughty arrogance of the Church stood psychologically contradicted by its own besetting fear of the effect which Jews and Judaism were bound to have upon the Christians who were even indirectly exposed to their influence.[110]

The net result of this emotional complex was a combined program of doctrine and law which deliberately drove a wedge between the Jews and their Christian countrymen and hopelessly disrupted the possibilities of a normal social relationship between them.[111] The right of the Jew to life — and to the pursuit of unhappiness[112] — was based on the appalling dogma that he was the eternal witness of the crucifixion and bore its guilt upon his soul.[113] For this he was to be shunned by the faithful. His very presence on the streets during religious processions and on the solemn days of the Christian religion was considered an offense and was repeatedly prohibited.[114] In every way, he was to be made to feel his inferiority and degradation. He was to be denied any position of authority. He was not to serve his king or the state as counselor or diplomat, as bailiff or financier.[115] He was not to be trusted as physician or apothecary.[116] Not even the innocent ties of friendship were to be tolerated between neighbors of different faiths. They were not to break bread together nor share each other's family joys and sorrows.[117] They were not to bathe together,[118] nor was a Christian to live in the house of a Jewish master as servant or nurse.[119] Marriage between Jews and Christians was interdicted.[120] Cohabitation between them was punishable by death for the Jew and by a less severe penalty for the Christian partner.[121] The extreme penalty was also decreed for proselytism[122] and for Jewish ownership of Christian slaves.[123] To make the moral segregation complete and absolute, the idea of a distinguishing sign or badge on the garment of the Jew was appropriated from Moham-

medan practice by the Fourth Lateran Council with the
determination to fasten this symbol of shame upon every
Jewish man and woman in Christendom.[124] The logic of
these laws led inevitably to the subsequent herding of the
Jewish population into compulsory physical segregation
within their *juderías.*

It would be unprofitable to trace the course of this in-
human program in all its details. Only the main features
will be dealt with here. As a rule, the laws were first promulgated by the popes and the councils, local and ecumenical.
The national legislative assemblies fell readily into line and
then the combined pressure of the ecclesiastical and the
national forces was brought to bear on the kings and the
feudal lords to adopt them and to clothe them with their
authority. For, theoretically, the Church had no direct
jurisdiction over the Jews where it did not enjoy temporal
authority. It had no direct means of enforcing any of the
ecclesiastical laws regarding them.[125] Its sole threat of
punishment was the invocation of complete social ostracism,
including the economic boycott, by the faithful against
the Jews. It was the Christians, not the Jews, who were
threatened with ecclesiastical discipline, principally excommunication, if they failed to observe the boycott declared
by the Church. The more direct and far more effective
means of enforcing the ecclesiastical will upon the Jews
was to appeal and, if necessary, to compel the secular
agencies to adopt the policies of the Church with full responsibility for their enforcement.[126] Thus the laws of the Church
came to be incorporated bodily into the legal framework
of the European states from the early Theodosian and
Justinian codes down to the legislative output of king and
Cortes in Aragon and Castile.

That the Jews succeeded in resisting for centuries this crushing program is an intriguing commentary on mediaeval social history. Prolonged resistance by the Jews would have been utterly impossible without the sympathy and cooperation of friendly Christian forces.[127] The strength of these ties can be measured by the vehemence displayed by the Church in its determination to break asunder all the bonds that held together the diverse population.

The sorrowful attempt to humiliate a religious group by fastening a badge of degradation upon its individuals was avowedly based on the existence of such intimate personal relationships between Jews and Christians that there was grave and imminent danger of carnal relations between them. It is curious to note, incidentally, that what seemed so grievous in the eyes of the Church was not the danger of loose morals but of sexual union between a Christian and one not of the true faith. The offenders were threatened with dire punishment — death by fire was the prescribed penalty[128] — although more frequently the confiscation of property was deemed sufficient expiation.[129] Nevertheless, even such severity did not seem a sufficient deterrent to those who bore the responsibility for the salvation of Christian souls. It was imperative, they argued, to place a prominent, distinguishing mark on the outer garments of the non-Christian population to prevent a "wicked mingling on the part of the Jews with Christian women, or on the part of Christians with Jewish women."[130] This was the ostensible reason, solemnly proclaimed by pope and council, for fastening upon "each and every Jew of both sexes a sign, viz., one round patch of yellow cloth or linen, to be worn on the uppermost garment, stitched over the heart and another behind it ... The full size of this sign shall be four digits in circumference."[131]

It is difficult to believe that this reason was more than a pretext or that the badge was intended for any other purpose than to visit humiliation upon the nonbeliever and subtly to warn off the faithful from too close an association with those who were so visibly damned. Even those popes who were ready to believe and to repeat the most revolting libels[132] never urged this particular legislation because of alleged acts of immorality, but solely as a preventive measure. Certainly the sources yield no indication of any widespread laxity in morals between men and women of different faiths. To be sure, isolated cases of illicit relationships occurred,[133] and they caused the Jewish authorities grave concern because, in all such instances, the sin of the individual Jew — unlike that of his Christian mate — was visited upon the whole community.[134] But not by the widest stretch of the imagination could the condition be described as sufficiently widespread to call for united action by all the powers of Christendom.

The crusading spirit with which the Church agitated for the enforcement of the badge is not to be accounted for by the occasional lapses from the moral code. On the contrary, the badge was aimed and designed to break the Jewish morale. It was the honor and prestige commanded by influential Jews that led the teachers of Christianity to seize upon this degrading invention of the Mosque as a means of destroying Jewish influence. This ulterior motive betrayed itself unconsciously when, for instance, the measure to differentiate the Jews by a mark upon their clothing was coupled with the rebuke that they assumed aristocratic airs, that they were accustomed "to wear round and wide capes after the manner of clerics and of members of the holy orders. As a result, it often happens that sacerdotal honor and undeserved reverence is paid them by travelers and strangers."[135] The costly garments of brilliant cloths and silks and furs, the flowing robes, the striking hose, the jewels and ornaments worn by Jews and Jewesses, were cited as provocations that called for corrective laws and especially the imposition of a special sign upon their clothes.[136]

The first clear demand for differentiating Jews and Saracens from the Christian population by their apparel was made at the Fourth Lateran Council on November 11, 1215:

> ... we decree that these people (Jews and Saracens) of either sex, and in all Christian lands, and at all times, shall easily be distinguishable from the rest of the populations by the quality of their clothes.

While the preamble states the above-cited reason concerning possible promiscuity between the sexes, a curious explanation is appended at the conclusion of the decree, viz., "especially since such legislation is imposed upon them also by Moses."[137] No allusion is made to the fact that the idea as well as the practice of stigmatizing the nonbeliever by such means was purely Mohammedan, and that from the days of Omar it had been applied impartially throughout Mohammedan territory to Christians as well as to Jews and Magi.[138] The conciliar decree did not at this time specifically mention the badge, but there was evidently no doubt as to its meaning. Twenty years later, the Council of Arles, urging obedience to the legislation of the Roman pontiffs and the statutes of the Fourth Lateran Council, decreed specifically:

... that all male Jews from the age of thirteen and up, when outside their homes, except when on a journey, must wear upon the outer garment, upon the breast, a round badge of three or four fingers in width. Jewish women from the age of twelve and up shall wear veils when outside their homes.[139]

From the first, the decree struck consternation in the hearts of all European Jewries, but nowhere was the resentment felt so deeply as in the *juderías* of Aragon and Castile. The same Council had seriously attacked the Jews economically, curbing their moneylending activities, demanding tithes and other offerings from their landed property and reviving the old ban against their holding public office. The Council had also forbidden them to appear in the streets during Holy Week and Easter Sunday, and had otherwise interfered with their personal freedom.[140] But nothing, it seems, wounded the sensibilities of Spanish Jewry so deeply as the attempt to stigmatize them by an outward sign. Rather than be branded, they prepared to migrate from the country, and the exodus which started from Castile assumed such proportion as to threaten the welfare of the state.

This situation was graphically described by Pope Honorius III, who had received the account from the king of Castile and the archbishop of Toledo:

> On behalf of our dearest son in Christ, Ferdinand [III], the illustrious King of Castile, as well as on behalf of yourself, we have been informed that the Jews who reside in the Kingdom of Castile are so seriously wrought up over that which was decided with regard to them in the General Council in the matter of wearing a sign, that some of them choose rather to flee to the Moors than to be burdened with such a sign. Others conspire because of this, and

make secret agreements. As a result, the King, whose
income in large measure derives from these very Jews,
can hardly raise his expenses, and serious misfortune
may befall the Kingdom. Wherefore we have been
humbly petitioned both on behalf of this King as well
as yourself, that our permission be given you to set
aside the execution of this edict, since you cannot proceed to its enforcement without great trouble.[141]

A somewhat different note was struck in the appeal of
James I of Aragon. In his kingdom a special sign or badge
was not needed, he claimed. Differences of clothes had
"from ancient times" set apart and distinguished Jews from
Christians. The new sign ordered in the name of the recent
Council was used as a scheme of extortion by the members
of the clergy. In protest, the Jews were leaving his country,
"much to his loss and that of his kingdom."[142]

Under this pressure, the pope was compelled to yield
ground. With the archbishop of Toledo he temporized:

... since in our paternal solicitude we desire to
assure the peace of this King and his Kingdom, we,
by these letters give you authority to suspend the
execution of the said decree for as long as you may
think fit, unless you receive a special Apostolic
mandate with regard to it in the future.[143]

But it did not take much more than two years for the
pope to change his mind and, utterly ignoring the above
suspension, to order the archbishop to enforce every detail
of the conciliar legislation with special emphasis on the
sartorial statute.[144] In regard to the situation in Aragon, he
curiously left the decision to the offending clergy. For while
the report of clerical extortion drew a severe rebuke from
His Holiness, the archbishop of Tarragona and his suffragans
(some of whom were charged with the offense) were told to

use their own judgment as to whether a special sign was really necessary in Aragon to assure the separation of the Jewish and Christian populations.[145]

However, no church decree could be effectively enforced against the Jews without the royal assent. In Aragon, James I proved more pliant to the papal will than his fellow ruler, Ferdinand III of Castile. Although posthumously Ferdinand was found to possess sufficient holiness to deserve canonization, his lifelong policy in regard to the Jews aroused the wrath of his pontiff. "In contempt of the decrees passed in the General Council about Jews," Gregory IX complained, "and upon his own authority, he annulled the regulation that required the Jews to wear signs by which they might be distinguished from the faithful."[146] The king of Navarre, Sancho VII, and his successor, Thibaut I, were similarly admonished by Gregory with equally barren results.[147] Innocent IV still complained in the above vein to the bishop of Cordova twenty years later.[148] James I, on the other hand, acted as a more dutiful son of the Church. As early as 1228, he ordered the Jews of his kingdom to wear distinctive signs upon their clothing.[149]

But neither in Aragon nor in Castile nor in any other of the Spanish provinces was there consistent observance of this law, which was so deeply resented. The Council of Tarragona, in 1238, and again in 1282, vainly pleaded for its enforcement.[150] As late as 1325, the Jewry of Castellon de Ampurias dared to defy the bishop of Gerona on the ground that the jurisdiction over their clothing as well as their persons and their homes rested solely with the temporal authority.[151]

In Aragon, the process of nullification was largely one of individual exemption. Physicians, influential courtiers

and men of finance were generally excluded from the
law. Prosperous communities with a generous purse were
able to purchase complete immunity or, at least, the privilege to reduce the offensive badge to an innocuous size.[152]
The badge of shame was thus turned into lucrative traffic.[153] Barcelona Jews enjoyed special favor.[154] Valencia
seems to have escaped the *capa rotunda* until it was decreed
by Pedro III in 1283.[155] In Castile, Jewish resistance was
even more successful. Although, in *Las Siete Partidas*,
Alfonso X recapitulated all the statutes of canon law regarding Jews and Moors, including the provision for a distinctive
sign upon their clothing,[156] the code, as is well known, had
no recognized legal standing for at least a century after its
promulgation.[157] When the Council of Zamora, in 1313,
decreed that the Jews were to be compelled to wear a special
mark, they pointed as a precedent to the practice of "other
states."[158] Five months later at the Cortes of Palencia, the
church decree was enacted for the first time as the law of
the state during the minority of Alfonso XI, and the Jews
of Castile were in the future to wear a badge "as in France."[159]
But whether the law was enforced at this time is more than
doubtful.[160] In 1369, the Castilian city Molina capitulated
to Pedro IV of Aragon and, under the terms of capitulation,
Pedro IV recognized the right of the *aljama* in the future
to retain the same freedom from the badge which it had
heretofore enjoyed under Castilian sovereignty.[161] Henry II
reluctantly yielded to the pressure of the Cortes of Toro in
1371 and ordered Jews and Moors thereafter to wear a
distinctive mark — a red circle on the left shoulder. But
this was avowedly a revolutionary measure, a break with
the past, and was not easy to enforce.[162] It was in 1405, at
the Cortes of Madrid, that Henry III decreed that Jews

and Moors were to be forbidden the luxurious dress of flowing robes and slashed hose and were strictly to be enjoined to display a sign or badge on their outer garment.[163]

Older than the device of the badge and supplementary to it was a series of canonical prohibitions, all of which had the same unfortunate objective — to set up in the Christian mentality a sinister attitude of suspicion and distrust in regard to the Jews which would destroy the possibility of intimate and cordial relationship with them. The Church was no more successful in forcing immediate obedience to these regulations than to the wearing of the badge. The monotonous reiteration of these prohibitions by pope and council, the reinforcement of these antisocial laws by repeated enactments of the various Cortes only reveal the fact that the prolonged resistance of the Jews was aided and abetted by the mass of the Christian population as well as by the rulers of the country.

With great severity, the Church set its face against permitting Christians to live in Jewish homes as domestic servants or nurses[164] and, at times, it was also added "that no Christian midwives shall assist at a Jewish childbirth."[165] Not only was the fear expressed that such close contacts might lead to proselytism[166] but, either directly or by innuendo, more sinister motives were suggested. Thus Innocent III wrote to the king of France:

> ... they [the Jews] work such abominations [with them] as are more fitting that you [the king] should punish than proper that we should specify.[167]

Gregory IX was more blunt:

> They have, moreover, Christian nurses and maid-servants in their homes, and they commit among

these servants enormities which are an abomination and a horror to hear.[168]

Innocent IV not only harped on the same theme, but regarded the association of a Jewish master and a Christian servant as "an insult to the Christian faith."[169]

The Spanish legate of Gregory IX successfully impressed these teachings upon James I of Aragon early in his reign.[170] The ecclesiastical laws and exhortations were loudly echoed in the assemblies of the Cortes.[171] The *Fuero Real*, issued by Alfonso X as a standard charter to a number of the prominent cities of the realm, contained also a section, *De los judíos*, in which it was specifically prohibited for a Jewess to nurse a Christian child or for a Christian woman to act in this capacity to a Jewish infant.[172] Judging by the context, the purpose of the royal legislator was to prevent religious heresy and proselytism. There was no suggestion of the fear of immorality. According to the *fuero* of Sepulveda, confirmed by Ferdinand IV in 1309, a Christian woman who nursed a Jewish or Moorish child was to be publicly whipped and driven out of the city.[173] Even kings who were noted for their zeal in protecting the interests of their Jewish subjects yielded in this regard to the demands of the popular assemblies, probably because it did not seem to be a restriction of great consequence.[174] Nevertheless, simple Christian women, unconscious of any depravity, continued to live and to serve in Jewish homes and to nurse Jewish infants, despite all the enactments of pope and council, king and Cortes; for the question was still a living issue through the fourteenth and even in the fifteenth century.[175]

The hardships which Jewish families encountered in engaging servants for their domestic needs on account of these repeated enactments were mitigated in part through the use of slaves. The constant wars with the Moors and Mediterranean piracy supplied the markets of both Christian and Saracen countries with an abundant supply of captives who were lucratively converted into slaves.[176] To this traffic, whether carried on by Christians or Jews, the Church interposed no objection until the thirteenth century.[177] As international traders, the Jews, no doubt, helped to supply both the Christian and the Saracen markets with slaves drawn from opposite camps.[178] They also purchased slaves for their own use: Moors and pagans in Christian countries, and European or Christian slaves in Mohammedan territory.[179] On the whole, it would appear that the use of slaves was more extensive among the Jews in earlier Mohammedan Spain and the surrounding countries than in the later Christian kingdoms.[180] Nevertheless, in these countries, too, and particularly in Castile, slaves were quite common in the homes of wealthy Jews, and the relation between them and their masters appeared singularly free of harshness or cruelty.[181] On the contrary, the few personal incidents which come to light in the sources show the solicitude of the owners for the welfare of their slaves.[182] In a number of instances, the love of the master for his beautiful slave, although not pleasing to the strict moralist, led to her liberation, to the acceptance of his religion and to their marriage or quasi marriage.[183]

The slave was a member of the Jewish household and was not permitted to labor on the Sabbath day.[184] Whether it was necessary to semi-proselytize the slave by circumcision or by the Jewish ritual of baptism in the case of a female was a question on which rabbinic opinion differed and custom varied.[185] Talmudic law required the rite.[186] Without it, the slave could not be domestically useful.[187] But as the

practice became dangerous in Christian countries, where it
was interpreted as proselytism, law and custom were gradually modified to follow the trend of the changed conditions.[188]
Although eunuchs were in great demand in Eastern harems,
rabbinic law remained opposed to castration, and Jewish
traders were to this extent at a disadvantage in competition
with Christian slave dealers.[189]

The attitude of the Church toward the Jewish ownership
of slaves was neither friendly nor altogether inimical. The
formulation of its policy on this moot question dated
back to the days of Constantine and the adoption of Christianity as the religion of the Roman Empire.[190] The Theodosian and Justinian codes contain sections of legislation in
regard to it, and the letters of Pope Gregory I show his
deep concern with the question.[191] From the beginning,
a broad distinction was drawn between Christian and
pagan slaves. The ownership of Christian slaves by Jews
was interdicted; pagan slaves were generally allowed.[192]
This remained the basic law of mediaeval Christendom,
with the startling addition of the death penalty for a
Jew who kept a Christian slave in his possession.[193] It
must be remembered that Christian teaching during the
Middle Ages did not condemn the institution of slavery
as such — not even Christian slavery.[194] The objection
to Jewish ownership of Christian slaves merely lay in
the doctrinal repugnance to the thought that the "son of a
slave" should rule over the "son of a free woman."

Even in regard to pagan slaves, however, complications
were bound to arise. For was it not likely that Jewish
owners would seek to proselytize their slaves?[195] The
Church could hardly be indifferent to such a contingency.
Even more vexing was the question as to what was to become

of the pagan slave who sought and received Christian baptism. As a Christian, he could no longer continue to serve the Jewish master. Was he then to go free and was his former owner to lose all equity in this human cargo? Would this not be an invitation to all such slaves to gain their freedom at the baptismal font? Much as this would accord with church policy, the king could not look with equanimity upon the wholesale confiscation of property in which he had a strong, potential proprietary interest.

The Church early attempted to meet this problem by fixing an arbitrary price, twelve *solidi*, for the head of every baptized slave of Jewish ownership, and by making the church where the baptism was celebrated liable to the owner for this amount.[196] This came to be established in canon law. Innocent III appealed to its authority and Gregory IX included the provision among his decretals.[197] But the price was evidently confiscatory and was so recognized by the secular rulers. Demanding full compensation for their baptized slaves, the owners were able surprisingly to force the churches to pay the full market value of the emancipated slaves. In vain were the threats of Innocent III.[198] On this subject, he met resistance not only in Castile, but even in the northern kingdom of James I of Aragon. Various expedients to discourage the flight of slaves through the door of the Church were tried. A ransom of twelve *morabatins* was placed on the head of every such slave, which he himself was to pay to the crown representative[199] or, as later modified, to his old master.[200] By another royal decree, the boon of freedom as a reward for baptism was withdrawn and the neophyte remained a slave and belonged to the king.[201]

Whatever the deterrent may have been, it is a striking

fact that the Jewish masters were not deserted on any large
scale by their slaves through the appeal of the Christian
faith. Some, indeed, found freedom by adopting the religion
of Judaism, but this was a dangerous course both for master
and slave.[202] In the latter half of the fourteenth century,
Jews of Barcelona were encouraged to purchase Turkish and
Tartar slaves, in which their Castilian brethren also joined.[203]
They must have performed the rite of circumcision upon
their slaves because, in 1380, King John I of Castile, who
was otherwise incensed against his Jewish subjects, denounced them for this practice and threatened them with
dire punishment. They were said to have admitted to their
fold Tartars, Mohammedans and other foreigners.[201] Three
years later, the same monarch defended the Jews' right to
keep their slaves, against the fanatical Fernando Martinez,
who preached murder against them and herded their
slaves forcibly to the baptismal font.[205] After the holocaust
of 1391 and the annihilation of the *aljamas* that followed a
generation later, it is difficult to see how any Jews could
have retained their slaves. Nevertheless, in 1465, at Medina
del Campo, it was found necessary solemnly to reiterate that
no Jew was to keep Christian slaves and that he who did so
knowingly would meet death.[206]

The dietary laws of Judaism, which fostered social separation and, for this reason, might have been welcomed by the
Church, aroused the ire of its representatives and provoked
them to acts of bitter retaliation. It is difficult to believe
that the popes and other high dignitaries of the Church were
so uninformed about the rudiments of the Jewish religion
and that it was ignorance which led them so grossly to mis-
interpret the purposes of these laws.[207] Dark motives were
attributed to the Jews who sold food which they would not

eat themselves.[208] These were offered as reasons for retalia-
tory measures to prevent Christians from dealing freely with
Jews in foodstuffs, milk, meats and wine.[209] Although in
Spain the laws were honored in the breach and no serious
attempt was made to put them into practice,[210] they accomplished their object in nursing insidiously the seeds of
popular distrust.[211]

In this unholy program of promoting religious "purity"
by deliberately fomenting suspicion and distrust in the
popular mind against the adherents of other faiths, a mortal
blow was aimed at Jewish and Moorish physicians.[212] A
series of church councils, held in France and the Provence
during the thirteenth century, warned the faithful against
taking any drink or medicine from Jews. The clergy was
admonished so to instruct all under their control, and the
lords of the land were ordered to compel their Jews, under
threat of punishment, not to occupy themselves with medicine. Christians who entrusted themselves to the healing
care of the Jews were to be excommunicated.[213] This became
part of canon law.[214]

Spain was not fertile soil for such teachings in the thirteenth century. *Las Siete Partidas*, which otherwise faithfully
reflected the regulations of canon law, echoed the sentiment
to the extent of prohibiting to Christians all medications
prepared by Jews, but permitted the consultation of Jewish
physicians on the sinister condition that the prescriptions
were to be compounded by Christians who knew and understood the ingredients.[215] It was early in the fourteenth
century that the Church of Spain took up the battle. In
1313, the Council of Zamora banned Jewish physicians "notwithstanding their learning and reputation."[216] Nine years
later, the Council of Valladolid repeated the prohibition in

the interest of the faithful to save them "from the danger of death."[217] At Salamanca, in 1335, the ecclesiastical attitude was "that under the pretext of surgery and medicine, they craftily insinuated themselves with the people, to the injury of the faithful."[218] Finally, the condemnation of the Holy See was pronounced in the bulls of Benedict XIII, in 1415,[219] and Eugene IV, in 1442, addressed especially to the bishops of Castile and Leon.[220]

A more unfortunate target for the arrows of bigotry could hardly have been selected. Jewish physicians, as a rule, were more than skilled practitioners. They ranked among the intellectual and cultural aristocracy of Spain. They counted among them men of worldly affairs and many outstanding literary personalities: poets, scientists, exegetes, philosophers. Their knowledge of both Arabic and Latin made them an important link between the culture of the East and the rising civilization of the West.[221]

As physicians, many attained international fame. Royal personages from distant countries pressed for their services in times of critical illness, when the mask of bigotry and prejudice is torn away.[222] Frequently, they were the object of diplomatic correspondence.[223] There was hardly a Spanish king, queen or nobleman who did not have in his retinue one or more Jewish physicians in attendance upon him and members of his family.[224] The gratitude of these patients and their boundless trust and confidence are all well documented in the sources. In many instances, these physicians possessed versatile talents. They combined insight and innate tact with worldly knowledge and rich linguistic ability. Above all, they were noted for great mental resourcefulness and fidelity of soul. Despite the barriers of ingrained prejudice, therefore, they wielded great influence over the hearts of kings and princes and became important personages at the court, honored with public office and entrusted with delicate political missions of great importance to their sovereign and the state.[225] Nor was the popularity of the Jewish physicians limited to the court grandees. Their high esteem among the populace is best attested by the fact that although the municipal councils, as a rule, bristled with hostility to Jewish interests,[226] some of them employed Jewish physicians as salaried officials in charge of the public health.[227]

It was the prestige and honor of this class that the Church aimed to destroy, and the effort met with signal failure both in Aragon and in Castile. Hundreds of Jewish physicians are cited by name casually, en passant, in the Spanish sources down to the reign of Ferdinand and Isabella.[228] Isaac Benveniste was only one of a group of Jewish physicians who waited upon James I of Aragon;[229] but he was so endeared to his royal patron that Pope Honorius III, in 1220, granted him a special letter of protection upon the solicitation of the archbishop of Tarragona and the bishops of Lerida and Tortosa.[230] Samuel Benveniste, of the same family, was the most distinguished physician in Barcelona at the beginning of the fourteenth century, and the good offices of the queen and the king were solicited to restrain him from moving his residence from the city.[231] Pedro III extended grants of favor and protection not only to Jewish physicians in Aragon and Catalonia, but also in Sicily which was under his dominion.[232] The physician who attended Pedro IV before he was king was gratefully remembered after the king's death, not only for the services rendered to him but also to his father, Alfonso III.[233] James II was particularly grateful to Abraham des Castlars, an important literary figure, for his attendance on the Infante Don Pedro during a grave illness.[234] During his own illness, Jewish physicians were summoned from Huesca and Saragossa to his bedside.[235]

Pedro IV surrounded himself and the royal family with a veritable staff of Jewish physicians.[236] Several of these he drew into the diplomatic service and sent them on secret political and military missions.[237] Magister Menahem was not only his physician but also his astrologer and alchemist whose experiments he encouraged and followed with keen interest.[238] Pedro interested himself in the case of the Jewish physician who had been condemned by the Inquisition for allegedly resorting to magic[239] and, on the other hand, he interceded with the *aljama* of Majorca to exempt Aaron Abdalhac from holding public office so as not to interfere with his medical duties.[240] He conferred the right to practice medicine upon Shem Tob Shaprut, well-known author of the apologetic work *Eben Bohan*, famous for his religious disputation with Cardinal Pedro de Luna, later the antipope Benedict XIII.[241]

Jewish physicians were prominent at the court of John I, even after the massacres of 1391, and were counted among his *familiares*.[242] In 1397, while King Martin was on an expedition to Sicily, Queen María took advantage of the absence of her royal consort to forbid Jews to practice medicine among Christians because, forsooth, they were enemies of the Christians and desired their death. But upon his return, King Martin countermanded the decree.[243] It is interesting to note that of the fourteen Jewish physicians whom he exempted from the prescribed medical examinations, eight were from the city of Calatayud.[244] Following upon the bull of Benedict XIII in 1415, Ferdinand I, several months later, repeated the proscription of Jewish physicians,[245] but Alfonso V annulled this and other harsh provisions in 1419.[246] We therefore find Jews in the practice of medicine throughout the fifteenth century down to the very period of the Expulsion.[247] Indeed, the Spanish annalist Zurita relates how in 1468 the aged monarch, John II, was saved from blindness by the skillful operation of a Jewish ophthalmologist whom he indentifies as the rabbi of Lerida.[248] There was not a noble or prelate in the land who did not keep a Jewish physician — a Jewish devil, in the venomous phrase of Alphonso de Spina, General of the Franciscans and author of the vindictive *Fortress of the Faith* (1459).[249] Despite the Franciscan monk's dark warnings and misgivings, the rival Dominican Order was not deterred from seeking and obtaining the permission of Innocent VIII, in 1489, to continue to employ Jewish physicians.[250]

In Castile, too, there is a continuous and brilliant record of Jewish medical service at the royal courts and among the nobility, the clergy and the nation at large.[251] Serving Alfonso VI, conqueror of Toledo, was the physician Amram b. Isaac ibn Shalbib, who was his private secretary and acted for him in many important affairs of state.[252] Another physician at his court was the famous *Nasi*, Joseph Cidellus, who also enjoyed his confidence and trust.[253] Those were critical days in the period of the Reconquest, and these physician-diplomatists and other Jewish statesmen were invaluable to Alfonso in his diplomatic maneuvers. Their extraordinary influence and importance in affairs of state gained for Alfonso the stinging rebuke of Pope Gregory VII, but the reproach went unheeded.[254]

The course of Jewish physicians in Castile paralleled the careers of their Aragon confreres. One may single out Judah ibn Wakar, physician to Don Juan Manuel while the latter

was regent for Alfonso XI, who appears in the responsa of
Rabbi Asher as the avenger of Jewish morals.[255] Rabbi
Hayyim stands out as the private physician of the archbishop of Toledo, who in gratitude appointed him to the
post of chief rabbi and judge over the Jews in his archbishopric in 1388.[256] Jewish physicians made regular calls
at the monasteries to attend the nuns in sickness. This
scandalized the legate of the archbishop of Toledo, but all
that he requested was that in the future a Christian escort
should accompany the attending physician.[257] Henry II
waived political considerations when, in 1367, he refused to
grant the petition of the Cortes of Burgos to dismiss among
others the Jewish physicians of the royal household. "We
consider it right to grant what is asked in reason, but such a
request was never made to any other king of Castile." He
maintained this position during the critical period of the
civil war when he was in desperate need of all the popular
support he could rally.[258]

Among the medical attendants at the court of Henry III,
two figures stand out prominently: Don Moses Çarçal,
gifted in composing Spanish verse,[259] and the more famous
Meir Alguades, who had already served in the court of
John I, and who, by royal appointment, was the chief rabbi
of all the Castilian communities.[260] He was independently
distinguished as an astronomer and philosopher and as the
translator of Aristotle's *Ethics*.[261] To his people, he was the
"prince of princes, a light and a savior," during the lifetime
of the patron king.[262] Little did they then foresee his tragic
end; his arrest on the farcical charge of conspiring to dese-
crate the host; the torture on the rack, the forced confession
of "guilt" and, to boot, also the "confession" of administer-
ing poison to the late king; and finally the barbarous execu-

tion, when he was torn limb from limb.[263] Practicing medicine was at best a precarious occupation when the *physicus* was held responsible for the patient's death.[264] It was perilous in the extreme when there were enemies at court and one of them was an apostate of the stripe of Paul de Santa María.

The hour of gravest danger to the existence of Jewish physicians in Castile loomed early in the fifteenth century during the minority of John II, through the combined attack of the fanatically inspired queen mother and Pope Benedict XIII in their proclamations of 1412.[265] But the clouds passed.[266] Their edicts were unenforced, and when the monarch grew to maturity he completely reversed their policies. It was during his reign that the ban of Pope Eugene IV fell on the Jewish medical profession, but within eight months of its issuance John II whittled away much of its harshness by a liberal interpretation of the decree which was definitely contrary to the pope's intent.[267] Certainly the ban did not affect his own attachments. For both he and his successor, Henry IV, surrounded themselves with Jewish physicians who, like so many of their predecessors, often combined the medical and diplomatic services at court with rabbinic juridical duties as well as with the tax administration of the Castilian *aljamas*.[268]

Joseph ben Shem Tob, physician in ordinary to Henry IV, was a worthy successor to Don Meir Alguades. He valiantly defended his faith against the attacks of Christian theologians. He enjoyed the confidence of his king, who entrusted him with a highly delicate mission to the king of Portugal. In his later years, he lost favor and finally died a martyr's death.[269] A happier fate was the lot of his fellow physician at the court, Samaya Lubel, who suffered at the hands of the rebellious and short-lived King Alfonso, but who was reinstated after the victory of Henry IV in 1469.[270] King Ferdinand and Queen Isabella confirmed, in 1488, the privileges granted by Henry IV, in 1465, to Isaac Aboacar, the physician of the marquis of Santillana. Despite her fanaticism, Queen Isabella did not dispense with her Jewish physicians, whom she valued and upon whom she conferred important privileges.[271] One of these, it appears, accepted baptism rather than face exile in 1492.[272] Undoubtedly, Marranos filled the numerous medical posts left vacant by the braver spirits who wandered with their people into exile. But it is a fitting sequel to find, twenty years later, in 1512, one of their spiritual successors, in the role of ambassador of the king of Tlemcen, summoned to Spain to heal the ailing Spanish monarch. As if to create a dramatic climax, it happened that the ambassador stayed at the home of a Marrano physician, Juan Serrano, giving the Inquisition grounds to hail the unfortunate host before the dreaded tribunal after the ambassador returned in peace to his country.[273]

CHAPTER XX

IN THE SERVICE OF THE KING
AND THE STATE

FAR more virulent than the attack upon physicians was the agitation fomented against the host of Jewish officials at the Spanish courts whose influence, at times, was paramount in the affairs of state. Whatever his personal attitude toward his Jewish subjects may have been, no Spanish ruler apparently was able to dispense with the services of Jewish financiers, administrators and diplomats. In the unremitting warfare with the Saracens and the mutinous nobles, the Jews were a great source of strength to the sovereign of the state. He was able to rely implicitly on their wholehearted allegiance and to utilize their intelligence, statecraft and their great material resources. From the beginning of the Reconquest till the capitulation of the last Moorish fortress on the Peninsula in 1492, Jews were to be found in the Spanish states, especially in Castile, in key positions as ministers, royal counselors, farmers of state revenue, financiers of military enterprises and as major-domos of the estates of the Crown and the higher nobility.[1]

The careers of these Jewish statesmen form an integral part of the economic, political and diplomatic history of the Iberian states. To be properly evaluated, their activities must be studied in relation to the growth and development of the Spanish kingdoms from the chaotic, impoverished

221

condition of the earlier Middle Ages to the later period of consolidation and world power. However fascinating such a study may be, a detailed analysis of this character does not come within the scope of the present treatment. Here it will suffice to point out the general trend and character of the services rendered by the Jewish grandees.

An office which seemed virtually to have been created for the Jewish courtier was that of *alfaquim*. This was a loose title, derived from the Arabic, which literally meant learned in the law but actually covered a wide range of functions: physician to the royal family, literary scribe or personal secretary to the king, official interpreter and translator, emissary to foreign courts, traveling companion and counselor of the king, the queen or the infante. The cultural and scientific attainments of these courtiers and especially their literary skill and knowledge of Arabic were of the greatest aid to the Christian rulers in their political negotiations with the Moorish kings. The courtiers were indispensable in the formulation of treaties and they were an important link in the rapidly shifting political alliances. They entertained foreign ambassadors and, in turn, traveled to foreign courts on diplomatic missions for their sovereign.[2]

In addition to the office of *alfaquim*, Jewish notables occupied prominent positions in the central administration of the country as the king's representatives. Frequently they also represented the nobility and even the feudal prelates of the Church.[3] In Aragon and Catalonia, down to the end of the thirteenth century, they were most prominently identified with the office of bailiff, a royal official whose duty it was to collect the revenue, administer the *patrimonio real* and to exercise limited governing authority in the name of the king. There were numerous gradations in the order of bailiffs and the Jewish officials were to be found in all classes.[4] Some were confined to limited fiscal duties in the management of crown property. Others were empowered with ruling authority as the king's representatives in the government of important cities. Highest in rank during the reign of James I was the bailiff Judah de Cavalleria, who is said to have been also chancellor of the realm.[5]

In Castile the public offices occupied by Jews covered a still wider range.[6] Surrounded by court intrigue and always uncertain of the ambitions of their truculent vassals, the Castilian kings leaned heavily on their Jewish counselors whose fidelity was not marred by conflicting loyalties. They admitted their Jewish favorites to the intimacies of court life, appointing some as royal porters and standard-bearers and elevating others to membership in the royal council. Here, too, the *alfaquim* was a popular figure at the court. Among this class were to be found the royal physicians, astrologers and scientists. As in the court of Aragon, so in Castile, Jews proved to be shrewd diplomats and indispensable to the king and the council in their dealings with the Moorish and North African states. The administration of taxes was largely in Jewish hands. As the prevailing system of taxation in Castile was that of farming the anticipated revenue to the highest bidder, one required large funds of ready capital to compete for this important branch of government service. Consequently, the office of *almoxarife* often fell to the Jewish bidder by default of Christian competition. Thus it happened, too, that even the church prelates appointed Jews to these posts in their own feudal territories.[7] Indeed, so completely was the office of *almoxarife* identified with the Jews that, to appease popular wrath, the title was changed to *tesorero*[8] but, needless to say, the change of name did not alter the character of the office nor the officeholder.[8]

In addition to those who held official court appointments, there were numerous persons who because of their wealth or learning were welcome at the king's court and were singled out by their sovereign as "faithful" and "dear" subjects. Many of them were the recipients of royal grants and concessions, no doubt in consideration of important services.[9] The leading rabbis of the realm were personally known to the rulers and were generally treated with the deference due to their office.[10] Indeed, the mutual friendship and confidence that grew out of this relationship were later idealized in popular tales which were a blending of history and romance.[11]

With the Jewish courtiers, public service was generally a life career in which the son usually succeeded the father, caught by the glamour and the adventure of princely association. The favor of princes is notoriously fickle; but as long as the satellites basked in the royal sun, they gathered honors and special privileges which set them apart from their coreligionists. They were freed from the disgrace of the badge even in the periods when its enforcement was general. Their delight in personal splendor and colorful, luxurious dress was indulged in despite the communal enactments which frowned upon such frivolity as vain and socially dangerous. As these and other more important constitutional privileges were bestowed upon the court favorites and their families, there grew up within the *aljama* oligarchical groups that constituted its worldly aristocracy—the Nasi, Profet, Cavalleria, Ravalya, Bonafos, Portella families — each in the possession of patents, rights and privileges which not only conferred upon them valuable holdings, lands and revenues, but a special status in law, particularly in relation to taxes and to the courts of justice.

Walking with princes and standing before kings, these favored sons were the natural champions of their people's cause. All their influence and the weight of their wealth were needed to retain for the *aljamas* the good will and the protection of the sovereign. Their position, despite its outward splendor, was by no means enviable. Their very prominence made them a ready target and their riches a tempting prey. Surrounded by court intrigue and religious hostility, their life was in constant peril. When they were victimized, the fall was precipitous, the end tragic. Nevertheless, to the honor of their class be it said that, in the main, they not only fought valiantly in self-defense, but they also stood guard over their communities, on the alert to counteract the machinations and evil designs of the enemy from whatever direction the attack came.

The unique position and the strategic value of this political vanguard were well understood in the *aljamas*. Honors and grants of favor, which were within the power of the *kahal* to bestow, were showered upon the privileged individuals who proved their worth. What is more striking, liberal interpretations of the sacrosanct ritual law were permitted in their favor to render it possible for them to meet the social demands of their exalted position.[12] Nevertheless, a privileged class is doomed to vainglory and other more venal vices. It will inevitably produce men addicted to selfish, ignoble motives as well as those inspired by a lofty sense of duty. The court grandees were therefore alternately the hope and the despair of their communities. Within their ranks were the noblemen who arose as public saviors in the hour of need. But in the midst of them were also

traitors who exploited the needs of their brethren to their
own selfish advantage, court sycophants who used their
power to thwart the true leaders of their communities.
Needless to say, in the darkest hour of persecution they
were the first to desert their people. Bitter were the reproaches of the moralists and historians as they recalled
how the pomp and ostentation of this group aroused the
envy and hatred of the populace, how their misdeeds recoiled
upon the heads of their innocent people.[13]

The influence and the power of the Jewish notables
aroused widespread antagonism. Mediaeval courts were
hotbeds of intrigue and bitter jealousy. Every important
post held by a Jew was deeply resented by the many dis-
gruntled noblemen who coveted the office. Furthermore,
as the Jews were conspicuously identified with the collection
of the royal revenue and the people groaned under the
burden of taxes, the Jewish officials were hated by the
populace as the tools of oppression. But the most determined opposition came from the Church. Its theological
arrows proved more fatal than the rapier of the jealous
courtier or the blow of the economic foe.

In its divinely appointed role as defender and champion
of the people as well as the faith, the Church could right-
eously cry out against the numerous iniquities which were
inherent in the system of feudal tyranny. But the Church
used its enormous powers not to destroy the source of the
evil but to divert the popular revolt into a blind attack
upon the Jews in public office. In thus damming the torrent
of popular discontent and channeling its overflow into the
current of an anti-Jewish crusade, the Church forfeited a
great moral opportunity. For, obviously, it was not the
flaming passion for justice but calculating ecclesiastic

policy that swayed the heart and the mind of the mediaeval churchmen.

The attitude of the Church toward Jewish officeholding had no relation to the character of the individual office-holder nor to the needs or the social conditions of the country. It was based on the general conception that the degradation of the Jew was necessary for the greater glory of the Christian religion. As early as 438, the Church crys-tallized this attitude into law through the Theodosian Code. It was revitalized in the Visigothic legislation. It was made the theme of papal bulls and conciliar decrees. Thus for over a thousand years, the Church labored to make this unhappy theological concept the public law in all Christian countries. That this attitude of discrimination was not a spontaneous expression of popular sentiment is evident from the manner in which the Church proceeded to rally the populace to its own point of view. Both the subtle power of flattery and the more dangerous appeal of dark innuendo and vague inflammatory denunciation were in-voked. It flattered the native population to believe that for Jewish officials to exercise authority over them was a moral perversion of the divine order, an exaltation of Satan, an insult to the Faith, an elevation of the slave over the freeman. At the same time, they were repeatedly told on the most solemn authority that Jewish officials were con-spirators against the State, that treason and death lurked in their hearts.

In this vein Gregory VII wrote to Alfonso VI, conqueror of Toledo, in the year 1081:

> We admonish your Highness that you must cease to suffer the Jews to rule over the Christians and exercise authority over them. For to allow the Christians to

be subordinate to the Jews, and to subject them to
their judgment, is the same as oppressing God's
Church and exalting Satan's Synagogue.[14]

Without a scintilla of proof and in the face of all contrary
evidence, Innocent III and Honorius III solemnly proclaimed that Jewish statesmen were traitors. Thus Honorius
III wrote "to the illustrious King of Aragon," in 1220, when
James I was a lad of twelve years:[15]

> Know that we have heard that much loss has come
> to Christians from the fact that whenever you have to
> send your messengers to the noble Miramoline or to
> his subjects, never, or rarely, do you send others than
> Jews, who expose to him the plans and the state of the
> Christians and reveal their secrets. Therefore we have
> thought that your caution ought to be aroused and
> warned that, when you have to send such messengers,
> you should rather send Christians, since you ought
> not to hope for faithfulness from the unfaithful. Nor
> does it seem plausible that those who impiously deny
> Christ Himself should be faithful to Christians.

Similar letters were dispatched to the kings of Navarre,
Leon and Castile.[16] Anticipating the flat rejection of this
unsolicited advice, Honorius III simultaneously addressed
admonishing letters to the archbishop of Toledo, the
apostolic legate, the bishops of Leon, Zamora, Burgos,
Palencia and other officials of the Church, ordering them to
exert effective pressure on the rulers in regard to this matter.[17] What the Spanish prelates did, we do not know. It
is clear that the ecclesiastic warnings and threats were of
no avail.

Fortunately for Spain, at least during the heroic twelfth
and thirteenth centuries, no part of the Spanish population,
not even the native clergy, it would appear, allowed such

preachments utterly to destroy the happy state of tolerance
which the Mohammedans had brought to the Iberian
Peninsula. Thus a glorious period was made possible for
Spain and its diverse population of Christians, Jews and
Moors. It was during these golden centuries that Jewish
talents were drawn upon most freely in the administration
of the Spanish kingdoms. The state treasuries were largely
in their hands. They administered the revenues and organized the supplies which were essential for the military
successes of the heroes of the Reconquest.

Even prior to the founding of the Aragon-Catalonian
kingdom, Sheshet Perfecto in Barcelona, bearing the Hebrew
title of *Nasi*, or prince, signed official documents in behalf
of the reigning Count Ramon Berenguer III who was one
of the creators of the territorial greatness of Catalonia.[18]
Jewish bailiffs served under Ramon Berenguer IV, in whose
reign the union of Aragon and Catalonia was effected in
1137.[19] One of these officials was the son of the above-
mentioned Sheshet Perfecto.[20] The important office of
repositarius was filled by Alazar, a Jew.[21] Whether Alfonso II
granted concessions to the Order of St. John or issued
privileges to the inhabitants of Torre-Miro or fixed the
boundaries of the city of Lerida, the charters were stamped
with the *signum* of the Jew Jafia, the royal bailiff.[22] It was
he who stood surety for the king before the Order of the
Templars.[23] He was bailiff of Barcelona[24] and also of Lerida.[25]
He or his namesake also filled the same post in Tarragona,
besides acting as bailiff of the bishop of Tortosa.[26] As a
reward for his valuable services, King Alfonso presented him
in perpetuity with a house and a workshop near the royal
palace in Lerida[27] and, in characteristic mediaeval manner,
also granted him an order on the Saracen meat market of

the city for a daily gift of two pounds of lamb as long as he lived.[28]

Again, a member of the prominent Sheshet, or Profet, family appears as a royal bailiff, physician in ordinary and traveling companion of King Alfonso II and also of Pedro II. This was none other than the *Nasi*, or Prince, Sheshet b. Benveniste, well known in the world of Hebrew letters, who is scarcely recognizable in the dry legal records which bear his signature in Hebrew characters.[29] He was the recipient of favors and gifts at the hands of three successive rulers, Ramon Berenguer IV, Alfonso II and Pedro II, whom he served as *alfaquim* and bailiff. These grants were shared by other members of the family who were also close to the royal personages as physicians, interpreters and literary secretaries.[30]

So highly were the services of the Jewish officials regarded that they were generally continued in office by succeeding monarchs through several generations. It was therefore characteristic of Pedro II to retain his father's aides in addition to younger men whom he himself appointed and who passed on to the reign of James I.[31] He assigned the bailieries of Barcelona,[32] Saragossa,[33] Lerida[34] and Tarragona[35] to Jewish appointees, while the office of *repositarius* of Aragon was held successively by Alazar[36] and Bondia.[37]

Undoubtedly, Jewish power and influence at the court reached their zenith in the brilliant reign of James I, which was also the period of greatest expansion for the kingdom of Aragon-Catalonia. Throughout his long reign, this great sovereign — a contemporary, be it recalled, of Emperor Frederick II, Louis IX of France and Edward I of England— utilized to the full the financial genius and administrative skill of a host of Jewish officials in the consolidation and reorganization of the kingdom which his extensive conquests made necessary. In his *Chronicle*, James speaks intimately of the Jewish secretaries and interpreters who accompanied him on his journeys.[38] Among those whom he singled out especially were En Astruc and the brothers Don Bahiel and Don Solomon whom he styled *alfaquim* and whose tact and judgment he greatly admired.[39] Not only James I, but later his son and grandson, too, Pedro III and Alfonso III, retained a Jewish staff who accompanied them on their travels and military expeditions and served as their secretaries, interpreters and ambassadors to foreign potentates.[40] Indeed, this became an established practice with Spanish royalty.

Although early in his reign, at the Cortes held in 1228, he himself decreed that no Jew was to hold public office or exercise any authority over Christians, he consistently ignored this ecclesiastically inspired interdiction.[41] His wise statesmanship impelled him to entrust the finances of the country to those who had the talent and the capacity for this all important work, regardless of race or creed. As a result, he commanded the services of able Jewish financiers who reorganized the fiscal administration and placed the country's finances on a sound basis. Through skillful manipulation and with hazardous financing out of their own resources, they continued to ease the strain upon the royal treasury, which was chronically depleted. With great success they floated public loans, personally underwriting them in great measure and thus enabling James to prosecute to a happy conclusion the expensive expeditions in the Balearics and Valencia. They converted the potential riches of the country into productive wealth. They administered the extensive and far-flung royal monopolies,

the salt marshes and silver mines, the duties and excises of
the domestic markets and the customs and tariffs of foreign
imports and exports. Above all, they played an important
role in the collection of the enormously complicated taxes
characteristic of mediaeval society. To perform these
functions effectively, they were of necessity clothed with
royal authority. Thus we find an astonishing number of
Jews who were royal bailiffs over the cities and over the
country at large, exercising broad jurisdiction over the
person and the property of the Christian inhabitants of
these territories.

The important bailieries of Barcelona,[42] Gerona,[43] Besalu,[44]
Saragossa,[45] Tarazona,[46] Tortosa,[47] Huesca,[48] Lerida,[49] Valencia,[50] Murviedro[51] and other minor places[52] were filled by
Jewish incumbents. Among those who figured most prominently in the state transactions were Samuel Bonafos, who
was bailiff of Catalonia as well as Barcelona,[53] Astrugo
Jacob Xixon,[54] Benveniste de Porta, the brother of Nahmanides[55] and, most important of all, Judah de Cavalleria,
the "Rothschild of Aragon."[56]

A man of immense wealth and great ability, Judah served
James in the dual capacity of public administrator and
private financier. Out of his own fortune he supplied James
with the money to build a fleet in the campaign against the
Moors in 1263, and he repeatedly helped with the supplies
of soldiers and munitions.[57] Perhaps it afforded the financier
amusing reflection when he advanced the loan of ten thousand *sueldos* to enable his king to appear in style befitting
his rank at the church council convoked at Lyons by
Gregory X in the cause of a holy crusade.[58] But it was as
controller-general of the revenues of the realm that Judah
was most important.[59] At first bailiff of Saragossa,[60] later

also bailiff and governor of the city and the kingdom of
Valencia,[61] his duties were not confined to those localities
alone. The entire fiscal administration of the country was
under his absolute control and, although it is not clear that
he bore the title of chancellor, he undoubtedly played a
decisive role in the consolidation of the kingdom.[62]

The ascendancy of Jewish officials under royal favor and
protection continued in the reign of Pedro III after his
father's death in 1276. Pedro was emphatic in his desire to
have Jewish counselors and aides at his side. Samuel b.
Abraffim Abinnaxim was in constant attendance upon the
king as his *alfaquim* and Arabic scribe.[63] Judah de Cavalleria, Muça de Portella, Aaron Abinafia and various members of their families continued to be prominently associated
with the public service as royal bailiffs.[64] But the central
position of importance was now held by the Ravaya family.
Joseph Ravaya, formerly bailiff of Gerona, was promoted
to the rank of *thesaurar*, treasurer of the realm, and in this
capacity accompanied his king to Sicily, where he died in
1282.[65] In the latter years, Moses Ravaya, his brother,
received authorization at his own discretion to dispose by
lease of the bailieries of any or all cities of the entire kingdom of Catalonia, Valencia and Aragon.[66] Moses (Alcos-
tantin) *alfaquim* was royal bailiff of Saragossa,[67] and Bel-
shom Levi was the bailiff in the city of Besalu.[68] Likewise,
the bailieries of the cities Jativa and Segorbe were manned
by Jews and the superintendence of the royal works in
Valencia entrusted to them.[69] Jewish emissaries were dispatched to Granada, Barbary, Sicily and to stations within
the kingdom.[70] In any internal conflict, Jewish notables
defended the king's cause. Thus, when a revolt of the nobles
broke out in Catalonia, the Ravayas supplied the king

with ammunition and pay for the soldiers at the siege of Balaguer.[71]

By this time, however, the high tide of Jewish influence had been reached. The reaction came curiously as part of a constitutional battle between the Estates and the Crown. The nobles and the cities sensed danger to the nation's liberties in the growing absolutism of the monarchy and especially in the concentration of enormous powers in the king's hand-picked council. The expansion of the kingdom through conquest, especially Pedro's adventures overseas in Sicily, were draining the man power and the economic resources of the country. The tax burden upon the cities was crushing. Worse still, new forms of taxes were devised for which there was no precedent in established custom. Constitutional privileges were flouted, so it was claimed. Convictions without due process of law, arbitrary and unjust confiscations were charged against the king's officials. Resentment grew high. A rebellion of the nobles and the cities was in the making. The Union, or League of the Nation, created in the reign of James I, was revived once again to save the old privileges and liberties which were so dear to the heart of the Spaniard. The cry was raised that it was essential to curb the king's power, to banish his evil counselors and to purge the palace and the government of Jewish officialdom.[72]

The grievances and demands were voiced at the Cortes, in September, 1283. After some hesitation and change of venue, Pedro III capitulated. He issued the famous General Privilege, which has been likened to the Magna Charta. Under the same pressure, he confirmed the resolution of the Cortes that henceforth no Jew was to hold a public office which entailed jurisdiction over any Christian subject.[73] That no drastic change in the status of the Jewish communities ensued immediately is not surprising. No concession drawn from a king under duress was likely to be followed by prompt enforcement. In any event, an untimely death soon cut short the rule of Pedro III. But the changed conditions were more evident in the reign of his son and successor, Alfonso III.

In the six years of his rule, Alfonso, indeed, attached to his person a considerable number of Jewish aides, or *alfaquims*,[74] especially in the roles of physicians,[75] interpreters, secretaries and diplomatic agents.[76] Jewish emissaries were sent on public missions not only to Moorish Morocco and Granada,[77] but also to Christian Castile and Sicily.[78] When the sons of Judah de Cavalleria enjoyed royal favor, it was, no doubt, for services rendered.[79] Jewish financiers, too, apparently continued to be active in the service of the Crown. Early in the reign, the veteran Muça de Portella, who had been royal bailiff under James[80] and Pedro,[81] dominated the scene as the central figure in the fiscal administration of the realm;[82] but this fact aroused violent resentment in the ranks of the nobles. Hardly had Alfonso ascended the throne, when the members of the Union, taking advantage of his youth and the critical political situation, presented new grievances for redress[83] and clamored for the banishment of the king's counselors, Muça de Portella among them.[84] In one regard, at least, Alfonso was spared making a painful decision; for Muça died conveniently shortly thereafter.[85] But Alfonso's complete surrender to the Union is well known. With this fact, therefore, is to be associated his proclamation, in 1289, against Jews holding public office. How difficult it was totally to eliminate Jews from the fiscal administration is shown by the subsequent career

of Ismael de Portella, who filled his brother's place and continued to be an important factor both under Alfonso III
and James II and, in addition, was the *dispensator* of the
Infante Don Pedro.[86]

But while the demand for Jewish services persisted and
the kings continued to avail themselves of the fiscal and
administrative capacity their Jewish subjects so often
demonstrated, it would seem that these functions were now
of private character. They no longer carried with them the
prestige of official positions. The Jews ceased to be appointed
royal bailiffs in the cities. The process of political liquidation
had begun in earnest.[87]

Thus, in the longer reign of James II, there was to be seen,
on the one hand, a close attachment of the Jews to the
Crown and to the personal service of the king and, on the
other, their virtual elimination from the governing machin-
ery of the country. The Portella family, despite its flight
after the death of Muça, was restored to grace and continued
to play a prominent part in public affairs.[88] To Ismael de
Portella was entrusted the negotiation of peace terms between the kingdoms of Aragon and Castile in 1304, and his
skill gained for him the friendship and the admiration of the
queen of Castile as well as that of the Greek princess, who
espoused the interests of her royal cousin James II.[89] James
gratefully acknowledged his valued services to the Crown,[90]
and honored him, a member of the royal household, with
the appointment as appellate judge in all litigations arising
in the Jewish courts of Aragon.[91]

The Infanta María, James' pious daughter, a nun in the
convent of Sigena, was glad to have Jewish major-domos
manage her worldly estates.[92] The Infantes Pedro and
Alfonso had even greater reason for gratitude to their

physicians and *alfaquims*.[93] Jewish courtiers attached to the royal household served the king as secretaries, counselors on foreign affairs and emissaries to the courts of Granada, Morocco and Tlemcen.[94] On a voyage to Sardinia, the Infante Don Alfonso was accompanied by two Jewish physicians. He was also joined by Solomon Scapa, whose services he required.[95] Isolated instances of Jewish tax collectors, farmers of the royal revenue and holders of minor governmental posts are found occasionally.[96] But with rare exception,[97] Jews were conspicuously absent in the bailieries of the kingdom.

Under Pedro IV, the scope of Jewish activities broadened again. In his personal associations Pedro included a number of Jews as *familiares*.[98] Maçat Avengenes is frequently mentioned as the king's banker.[99] Jahuda Alatzar stands out as one of the important figures in the financial transactions of the royal household. He helped to finance the war against Castile, provided funds for the queen's needs and equipped a fleet of ten vessels which the royal couple placed at the disposal of the pope in his passage from Rome to Avignon.[100] For a time, the royal mint was controlled by a Jewish company.[101] Jews appear as farmers of taxes and tolls, as assistants to the royal treasury, as high officers armed with the authority of the state.[102] Once more a scion of the De Cavalleria family, Benvenist, stands out as royal commissioner, *commissari per lo senyor rey*.[103] True it was that the king's moods were unaccountable. His suspicions were easily aroused, his temper flared up dangerously. Upon the instigation of corrupt informers, he was ready to throw his most trusted Jewish confidants into jail, threatening them with death and torture, while the entire *aljama* trembled in fear of expulsion.[104] But these

volcanic eruptions were characteristic of mediaeval kings
in general and of the country and the period in particular.
On the whole, Pedro's relationship with outstanding Jewish
personalities was marked by cordial esteem and especially
by an appreciation of their literary and scientific talents
even more than of their fiscal value.[105] Indeed, the Jewish
contributions to the culture and science of Spain during the
latter half of the fourteenth century helped to render the
period of Pedro's reign a brilliant chapter in the history of
Spanish civilization.[106]

Nevertheless, Pedro the Ceremonious did not permanently
interrupt the downward spiral of Jewish influence in the
public life of the kingdom. The imprecations and the incite-
ments of the rebellious priest of Écija near Seville were
destined soon to take effect and to cross like a hurricane over
the boundaries that divided the kingdoms of Castile and
Aragon.[107] When this catastrophe overtook the *aljamas* in
the following reign in 1391, it undermined their economic
existence and permanently disorganized Jewish life on the
Iberian Peninsula.[108] Among the tens of thousands who
found illusory safety in baptism during the succeeding
decades were to be found many of the leading financiers and
courtiers who now filled the highest posts in the government
as Marranos.[108] Their brilliant and hectic careers form a
lurid chapter in Spanish history, which does not, however,
come within the framework of the present treatment. Even
among the unhappy remnant that survived the terrible
destruction there were, indeed, still to be found individuals
who rose to eminence in the courts of John I and Martin I.[110]
Nevertheless, the sun had set long ago upon Jewish officialdom in the courts of Aragon and Catalonia at the end of
the thirteenth century.

More dramatic and intensely adventurous was the career of the Jewish grandees in the palaces of the Castilian kings. The line of succession of Jewish statesmen and financiers in the service of Castile extends to the last days of the Expulsion and draws fittingly to a close with the heroic figure of Don Isaac Abravanel. Economically less developed than the eastern kingdom and politically more disturbed and unsettled, the circumstances in Castile were highly favorable to the nurturing of that remarkable talent for government and finance which distinguished the Spanish Jew. Amidst the crude Castilian population, Jews attained positions of eminence unequaled in any other Christian country; but the degree of danger and insecurity was commensurate with the height of their elevation.

While Gregory VII thundered against Alfonso VI for placing Jews in positions of trust and authority,[111] Alfonso's ambassador at the court of Al-Mu'tamid, Amram b. Isaac ibn Shalbib, was facing death by crucifixion because of the fidelity with which he defended his sovereign's interests.[112] Another Jewish courtier in Alfonso's palace was Joseph Cidellus, famed as a Spanish statesman and also praised as a redeemer of his people. Judah ha-Levi sang his praises in flowing Hebrew verse; and Archbishop Rodrigo of Toledo recorded in the Latin annals his service to the king and to his daughter, Queen Urraca.[113] The gifts showered upon him by his royal masters were characteristically withdrawn after his death and were distributed among various churches; but he at least escaped falling a victim in the massacre of Toledo.[114] His kinsman, Solomon (ibn Farusal) Çidello was not so fortunate. Returning in triumph from a foreign political mission, he met death at the hands of an assassin, and Judah ha-Levi's song of welcome turned into a mournful dirge.[115]

Although canon law and papal admonition were thus ignored, church precept was not entirely forgotten and hypocritical lip service was given it on important occasions. After the insurrection in Toledo which followed upon the death of Alfonso VI in 1109, his royal son-in-law granted a series of privileges to the mixed population of the city, Mozarabs, Castilians and Franks, in which, with pious language, he promised that no Jew or recent convert was to hold public office in the city and its environs.[116] This clause in the charter of Toledo became a stereotyped provision in the constitutions of the important cities later to be annexed to Castile, although they usually carried the nullifying clause which excepted the *almoxarife*.[117] In 1130, the inhabitants of Escalona obtained a concession from Alfonso VII that no Jew or Moor would be appointed judge over Christians.[118] But neither Alfonso VII nor the later kings of the thirteenth and fourteenth centuries allowed themselves to be handicapped by these restrictive provisions. Thus Alfonso VII placed the entire royal revenue in the hands of his Jewish *almoxarife*, Judah ibn Ezra.[119] Moreover, he conferred signal military honor upon this scion of the family of literary fame, by appointing him governor of Calatrava, placing him in command of an important fortress on the frontier.[120] Judah's helpfulness to the refugees who fled from the oppression of the Almohades and his less benevolent acts in suppressing the Karaitic sect, activities which his official position rendered possible, were gratefully recorded by a contemporary Hebrew annalist. In simple biblical style, the Jewish historian ascribed to God's mercy the favor which Judah found in the eyes of his king.[121]

Alfonso VIII's pro-Jewish policy evoked Innocent III's severe rebuke.[122] Although he needed Innocent's crusading support in his war against the Moors, nevertheless, in his choice of counselors and officers of state, he was undeterred by the pope's expressed displeasure. In diplomatic negotiations and in the fiscal administration, he placed great reliance upon his Jewish courtiers, entrusted them with duties of utmost importance and raised them to positions of eminence in which they received the homage of proud Castilian hidalgos.[123]

In vain proved the interdiction of the Fourth Lateran Council then under the sway of the greatest potentate that ever occupied the throne of Peter.[124] Unheeded went the warning of Honorius III.[125] Although Ferdinand III, known to history as St. Ferdinand, did include in the charters of some of the reconquered cities a clause disqualifying Jews from holding public office,[126] his contrary practice was the despair of Pope Gregory IX, if the violence of the language reflected the true intensity of the latter's feeling:

> ... and although it had been decreed in the Council of Toledo[127] as well as renewed in the General Council[128] that Jews should not be placed in public office, since under such a pretext they are very dangerous to Christians, and since it is absurd that one who blasphemes against Christ should exercise power over Christians, nevertheless, secular dignities and public offices are entrusted to them, by the use of which they rage against the Christians and cause some to observe their rites.[129]

Alfonso X, in general, presented the strange paradox of a brilliant prince and an inept ruler; a pathetic figure lost in the intrigues of the palace and in the fog of diplomacy, who, nevertheless, even in his lifetime enjoyed world fame as the wise scholar-king. In his relations with the Jews, similarly, a note of contradiction obtrudes itself. The famous code which he fathered, *Las Siete Partidas,* incorporated almost wholly the canonical conception of the Jewish status. Its legal provisions in regard to the Jews might have been culled from any of the existing collections of conciliar acts. In regard to state positions it specified that no Jew should hold any public office or post empowering him to pass sentence on Christians.[130] But aside from the fact that the code was not officially promulgated for almost another century, its spirit was wholly contradicted by Alfonso's continuous and many-sided associations with his court Jews in the sciences, in finance and in government. It is precisely the reign of Alfonso X which was illumined by the remarkable achievements of the Jewish group which shed luster upon his name and which in turn reflected brilliantly the high social and cultural position of Castilian Jewry. Isaac ibn Cid, the pious precentor of the Toledo synagogue, who, together with Don Judah b. Moses ha-Kohen, drew up the celebrated astronomical tables, the so-called Alfonsine Tables, and whom the king admiringly styled "my sage";[131] Isaac's collaborator, Don Judah, the learned court physician, who not only ministered to the king's physical ailments but also stood in close personal relationship to the royal patron as astrologer and astronomer;[132] the *alfaquim* Xosse or Yuçaf who collaborated in astronomical works with his royal patron;[133] Samuel ha-Levi, the inventor of an ingenious waterclock, who worked on the invention at the king's bidding;[134] and the school of Jewish scholars and translators whom Alfonso commissioned to translate Arabic scientific works — all figure prominently in the history of

Spanish literature.[135] Their accomplishments undoubtedly afforded the scholar-king deep satisfaction and created a bond of personal sympathy between him and these gifted Jewish subjects. Moreover, Queen Violante apparently shared her consort's predilections for noble Jewish personalities. A cabalist rabbi, Don Todros Halevi Abulafia, was one of her *familiares*.[136] His contemplative mind, the intuitive mystic strain of his personality, his kindly wisdom stirred the imagination of the royal household and they sought his companionship. He accompanied the royal court on the journey to Beaucaire, in 1275, and remained with the queen in Perpignan while Alfonso was with Gregory X in Beaucaire, vainly pleading for his right to the imperial title over the Holy Roman Empire.[137] To the king, Don Todros was "the Rabbi;" to the Hebrew poet he was "the head of the exile of Spain."

The Jews whom Alfonso appointed over the exchequer as *almoxarifes* made their power felt to the remotest ends of the kingdom. They farmed and therefore controlled — frequently with Christian associates — the royal taxes, fines and imposts. They collected the tolls on the highways, the customs at the ports and the charges (*servicios*) laid upon the cattle as they were herded seasonally to the pasture lands.[138] As *recabdadores de las rentas del rey*, collectors of the public revenue and controllers of the treasury, their sway extended over the nobles and the clergy as well as the third estate. A letter from the *almoxarife* Çulema to King James I promptly won for his cousin in Aragon immunity from royal taxes.[139] Proud of mien and carriage, cultured and refined in manner, dressed in knightly attire and surrounded with courtly pomp and ceremony, the Jewish grandees held their own with the highest ranks of the Spanish aristocracy. Under

Alfonso's drastic program to curtail every form of luxury and extravagance in the interest of national economy, it fell to Zag de la Maleha to prescribe the diet and supervise the attire of the proudest hidalgo and to grant or deny him the coveted privilege of mounting a steed.[140] Jewish courtiers were intimates of the royal family and were at times drawn into the unhappy domestic quarrels which disgraced Castilian royalty, as Don Zag de Maleha discovered to his undoing.[141]

The influence of the Jewish *almoxarifes* was particularly important in the period of economic experimentation under Alfonso X.[142] Don Çulema (Solomon), whom he appointed to the high treasury post early in his reign, had been one of the elder statesmen in his father's government, and his influence was potent even in the court of Aragon.[143] Upon Çulema's death, Alfonso possessed himself of his fortune.[144] Nevertheless, Çulema's son, Zag de la Maleha, later entered the king's service, gained the post of *almoxarife* and became one of the most important, but ultimately a most tragic personage in the royal court.[145] His life was celebrated by contemporary Hebrew poets and his fateful death stirred their muse to deep mourning.[146] They relate in detail, as do also the Spanish court chroniclers, how he fell a victim to the court intrigues which ultimately sent Sancho to war against his father. Under duress or by error, Zag turned over to Sancho the imperial fund that Alfonso had set aside for the army at Algeciras. In revenge, Alfonso ordered his erstwhile favorite dragged in chains through the city streets before the eyes of the infante and savagely put to death.[147] Other Jewish "princes," too, were thrown into jail. One courtier saved his life through baptism and another, though innocent, was dragged to a traitor's death. The property of the victims was automatically confiscated.[148]

Notwithstanding the cruel fate of these victims of Alfonso's unhappy old age and family discord, his rule, on the whole, was distinguished by tolerance and friendship toward the Jews of his court, whom he raised to positions of eminence and authority. Among these were the *almoxarife* Don Meir who was praised for his learning by Nahmanides; his equally influential sons, Zag (who is generally confused with the son of Çulema, Zag de Maleha) and Joseph; also his son-in-law Abraham aben Xugen.[149] To these may be added the *almoxarife*, Ihuda Abenxabal, who built his own synagogue in Seville; likewise, the royal secretary, or *escrivano*, Yuzef Barchilo; the *alfaquims*, Yuçaf and Zac Zuheyel (Çuchiel) of Jerez; and also Don Yuçaf Pimetiella, the *alfaquim* of Talavera, who signed a treaty with the city of Burgos in behalf of the king, in 1279.[150] It is little wonder, therefore, that Alfonso's policy stirred the anger of the Church. The threat of evil days was held over his head by Pope Nicholas III, because in the conduct of the government he gave preference to Jews over Christians.[151]

Sancho IV, who was the principal cause of his father's "evil days," was not inclined to be influenced by the papacy which had supported the father against the rebellious son. Conscious that he was indirectly responsible for the *almoxarife* Zag's execution, Sancho appointed the son to fill the father's post.[152] Early in his reign, in 1287, Sancho entered into an amazing agreement with Abraham el Barchilon by which he surrendered to him, for two years, the most extensive rights over the revenues of the kingdom. These included, among other privileges, the concession to mint all the

coinage in the realm, the right to take possession of all
estates left without heirs, the collection of various classes of
fines, penalties, imposts and taxes; the right to the income
of the royal chancellory; the import and export duties; the
income from the iron works and salt marshes; and, most
significant of all, because of the position in which it placed
Abraham in relation to the powerful nobles and prelates,
the restoration of all the royal property that had been
lavishly and improvidently squandered upon the nobility
and the churches.[153] A more glaring opportunity to amass
riches and to reap ill will can hardly be imagined.

The perils and adventures to which this type of Jewish
courtier was exposed, the constant tension under which he
lived, the manner in which he reacted to the triumphs and
defeats which checkered his career are revealingly portrayed
in a poetic *divan* penned by an associate of Abraham the
Barcelonian, Todros el Levi, who was not only a gifted
poet but also a resourceful financier, who served as a high
treasury official under three royal patrons.[154] Todros el Levi
began his official career in the service of Alfonso X. Associated with the *almoxarife* Zag de Maleha, he was thrown
into prison with him but escaped the death sentence. With
the ascendancy of Sancho to the throne, he was restored to
power and influence at the court, and he joined Abraham the
Barcelonian in ambitious transactions connected with the
royal revenue. Despair engulfed him when he was hurled
into prison a second time, but once again he was vindicated
and his spirits soared high. His poems reveal how he exulted
in the triumph which he thought would soon be his. It would
be for him to command, and the fallen would rise and the
proud would be brought low.[155]

The archives of the period contain records of other Jews

in high positions as financiers of the king's military needs, tax farmers, collectors of the revenue and *almoxarifes* in the service of the king, the queen and the infante.[156] Meanwhile, resentment was mounting in the cities against the inherently vicious system of farming out the public revenues for private profit. At the Cortes of Valladolid, in 1293, a demand was made upon the king not to entrust the collection or farming of taxes to knights, *alcaldes*, *merinos* and Jews and, furthermore, to abolish altogether the practice of farming the taxes.[157] Receiving the royal assent, the resolutions became law, but their enforcement seemed impossible under the existent circumstances.

The reigns of Ferdinand IV (1295–1312) and Alfonso XI (1312–50) began as minority reigns with all the acute disturbances which attend such periods. Ferdinand became king at nine; Alfonso was only a year-old child when his father died suddenly at the age of twenty-six. Queen María de Molina was regent during her son Ferdinand's minority and was also the controlling person in the regency of her grandson Alfonso. With the infantes at hand angling for power and preferment, especially during the minority of Alfonso XI, the royal court was a breeding place of cabal and intrigue. Fearing misrule and despotism, the cities organized themselves into a voluntary brotherhood, or *hermandad*, "for the honor and security of the king and his successor and for the honor and safety of the land."[158]

The new forces were in full command at the Cortes of Valladolid in the opening year of Ferdinand's reign in 1295. Nothing less than the dismissal of all the officers of the palace was demanded of the new government, their successors to be drawn from the ranks of the *omes bonos de las villas*. No Jews were to be included in the new official family.[159] At this stage, the resentment was directed not merely against the Jews at the palace, but equally against clerics and nobles who were associated in the popular mind with the tyranny of the central government. At the Cortes of Burgos held in May, 1301, Ferdinand proclaimed that the taxes voted by the Cortes (*servicios*) would not be farmed nor would their collection be entrusted to nobles, clerics or Jews.[160] The resolution failed of enforcement for, twice within the following year, similar petitions were addressed to the throne at the Cortes of Zamora and at Medina del Campo, these petitions meeting with a more equivocal response from the king.[161] In 1305, at the Cortes of Medina del Campo and again at the Cortes of Valladolid, in 1307, Ferdinand declared that Jews would be eliminated in the future as collectors or farmers of taxes,[162] but one can hardly discern in practice any animus toward Jewish officials during this reign. Queen María, the regent during Ferdinand's minority, appointed Don Çag Abenayes as her *almoxarife*.[163] Subsequently, Don Moses was her treasurer.[164] Ferdinand's *almoxarife* was Don Yuda Abravaniel.[165] Another Jew, Don Samuel, was the confidant upon whom he relied to such an extent as to arouse the jealousy of the queen-mother and, perhaps, also to inspire an assassin's attack upon the life of his favorite.[166]

During the long minority of Alfonso XI, when the country as a whole suffered from the many crosscurrents of political agitation, the Spanish Church took the lead at the Council of Zamora, in 1313, to agitate for the complete exclusion of the Jews from the life of the Spanish people.[167] The ecclesiastical conclave, stirred by the General Council of Vienne, which had been held in 1311, enacted the entire devastating program for the suppression and humiliation of the Jewish population. The decree against the appointment of Jews to positions of authority and honor was now part of a thorough-going program which included the imposition of the badge, the social segregation of the Jews from the Christian popula-tion, the ban against Jewish physicians, the prohibition against the employment of Christian servants and nurses and other baleful provisions of canon law. The effect was immediate. Within five months, the Cortes of Palencia adopted these resolutions in their entirety, obtaining first the confirmation of the Regent Don Juan and, ten days later, the sanction of the co-regents Queen María and the Infante Don Pedro.[168] They severally pledged themselves henceforth not to appoint for the king or for themselves any Jew to the post of *almoxarife*, collector or sub-collector of taxes, controller of accounts, royal inspector, secretary or other officer of state. This action, however, was taken under intensive ecclesiastical pressure. The true sentiment of the Cortes was opposed to clerics in the government as well as Jews. The same Cortes very significantly incor-porated first the demand of the earlier national assemblies which had found no echo in the Council of Zamora, namely that no noble, cleric or Jew should be allowed to collect or farm the taxes.[169] This demand was even narrowed down, two years later at the Cortes of Burgos, to embrace only clerics and Jews and it had the confirmation of all three co-regents.[170] The combined influence of the cities organized in the *hermandad*, or brotherhood, was again exerted at the Cortes of Carrion, in 1317, to procure the adoption of the earlier resolution that no nobles, clerics or Jews be allowed to farm the taxes.[171] The municipal representatives did not hide or disguise their distrust of clerical influence at the royal court. At the Cortes of Valladolid, in 1322, it was decreed at the insistence of the *hermandad* that all clerics as well as Jews be removed from any office connected with the royal chancellory and, in addition, it was provided that clerics, Jews and Moors be not allowed to farm the taxes.[172] As if to shake off this unwelcome association, a church council was convened in the same city three months later, which again promulgated the entire series of anti-Jewish laws, among them the prohibition against the appointment of Jews to public office.[173] This time, however, the secular powers showed no haste to follow the ecclesiastical lead.

It is doubtful whether the legislation of the Cortes had any immediate practical effect. The frequent repetition of its enactments tend to cast doubt upon their effectiveness. The *hermandad* itself treated with Rabbi Don Moses, the receiver-general, as the king's representative, and Queen María acknowledged him as her steward (*mio despensero*).[174] Don Juan Manuel, who succeeded to the regency in 1319 after the death of the Infantes Pedro and Juan, showed great partiality to his physician, Judah b. Wakar, and evidenced a strong desire to respect the privileges of the *aljamas* and to restore their constitutional rights.[175] He was so utterly devoted to Don Solomon, his physician, that he commended him to his wife and his sons in a glowing tribute in his last will and testament.[176] It is even asserted with plausibility that his friendship for Don Solomon was the inspiration of parts of the infante's beautiful work, *De las maneras del amor*.[177]

Whatever doubts or fears the Jews entertained regarding their status during the weak and timid rule of the regents were dispelled when Alfonso XI took the reins of government. Although only thirteen years of age when his majority was formally declared by the Cortes, he was king in fact

as well as in name. Upon the advice of his uncle, the Infante
Don Felipe, he selected the Jew, Joseph of Écija, as trusted
counselor. He made him a member of the royal council
and appointed him *almoxarife mayor* over the finances of
the realm. Joseph's magnetic personality and his great
wealth made him a commanding figure in the palace. An
accomplished musician and a lavish host, his home was
noted for the brilliance of its social gatherings. Of artistic
temperament, he was endowed with a vivid imagination and
a taste for brilliant display which he was in a position to
gratify. He drove to the palace in his state carriage and,
on his travels, an escort of knights accompanied him. He
captivated the heart of the young king, and was honored
with important and dangerous missions.[178]

Whoever swayed the heart of a king was suspect with
the people; Joseph, therefore, became the object of popular hostility. Sent on a delicate mission to the infanta
at Valladolid, he was besieged at the palace by the populace
who clamored for his surrender. Only the most energetic
action of the king saved Joseph's life.[179] But the Cortes
now took up the fight and, in 1328, Alfonso was compelled
to discharge his favorite minister.[180] It was a mere gesture,
however, for shortly afterwards he reinstated him.[181] Consequently, when the Cortes met again, in 1329, a petition was
addressed to the king to bar Jews from the palace and to
deprive them from holding any public post. This time
Alfonso temporized with the Cortes and left Joseph un-
disturbed in his position.[182] Joseph's continued influence
upon Alfonso was recognized even in the court of Aragon,
as can be seen from a curiously personal letter which the
king there addressed to the Jewish "*almoxarife mayor* of
the most noble king of Castile." In this letter the king

told Joseph how he had recovered from an attack of fever and desired the services of two Castilian players who were in Tarazona, and stated that he would appreciate Joseph's intercession with the king of Castile in his behalf.[183]

Alfonso's favor was extended to another Jewish courtier, Don Samuel Aben Huacar (Ibn Wakar), who stood in intimate relationship to him as his physician and astrologer.[184] He granted him a valuable concession which was connected with the collection of import duties, but which conflicted with the interests of the *almoxarife*. An unhappy rivalry ensued between Don Samuel and the *almoxarife* which undermined the power and prestige of both.[185] Far more dangerous was the concession of the mint which Don Samuel obtained from the king with the express purpose of debasing the coinage. The artificial rise in the cost of living which followed was attributed not to Samuel individually, but to all the Jews. It was widely heralded that Jews enriched themselves at the expense of the nation. An unscrupulous demagogue, Gonzalo Martinez de Oviedo, originally a protégé of Don Joseph, the Jewish minister, suddenly rose to power. Holding out the bait of enormous confiscations to the Crown, he was given the authority to imprison the two most important Jews at the court, together with many members of their families. Their doom was sealed. Don Joseph died wretchedly in prison and Don Samuel met death under torture. The confiscation of their property was a matter of routine.[186]

Had Gonzalo Martinez continued his triumphant career to the end, he might have succeeded in his avowed purpose of destroying the Jews. But he died a traitor's death.[187] Meanwhile, Alfonso XI, as if unmoved by the tragic fate to which he had condemned his erstwhile favorites, continued to retain Jews in important posts as *almoxarifes*, collectors of taxes, secretaries and members of the royal chancellory.[188]

The course of Jewish officialdom under Pedro strangely paralleled the experience in the previous reign. There was a Jewish physician and astrologer at the court, Abraham ibn Zarzal, who exercised great influence upon the king.[189] Don Samuel el Levi filled the role of Joseph of Écija. He was the confidant of the king, a member of the royal council (*privado*) and chief treasurer (*tesorero mayor*) of the realm.[190] He was, likewise, the king's diplomatic emissary. Thus, in 1358, he was entrusted with a mission to negotiate a treaty of peace between Castile and Portugal.[191] Like his prototype Joseph, Don Samuel was a protector of his people and a builder of synagogues. Among these the famous shrine in Toledo, which bears his name, still stands.[192] Again, like his predecessor, he is described as handsome and noble, as one who found favor in the eyes of the king and was raised "above the mighty and invested with almost royal honors."[193] His power was great;[194] he dispensed royal patronage and filled state offices with members of his family and with personal followers.[195] He lived in a palace, and eighty black slaves waited upon him.[196]

The physician and astrologer Abraham ibn Zarzal likewise was high in the king's favor and wielded great influence. To quote the envious court chronicler: "Don Abraham and Don Samuel, with lips as sweet as honey, obtain from the king whatever they ask."[197] While the country was torn with strife, the courtiers amassed great riches. In the hysteria engendered by the cruel and unnatural war waged between Pedro the King and his half brother Henry of Trastamara, the accumulation of so much wealth by the Jewish grandees aroused envy and hatred. "They suck the

blood of the afflicted people; they lap up their possessions
with their tax-farming"— thus wrote Don Pedro Lopez de
Ayala, the chronicler more noted for his style than his
veracity.[198]   Agitation like that fomented by Gonzalo
Martinez brought the parallel to a close. Arrest, confiscation, torture, death on the rack — such was the fate of the
richest and most powerful court grandee, Don Samuel el
Levi. The reports of the confiscated wealth included fabu-
lous quantities of gold and silver, reaching legendary proportions.[199]

Violent injustice and rapacious ingratitude were part of
the code of kings. The cruel fate of Don Samuel affected the
relations of the Jews to the king as little as Alfonso's earlier
treatment of his court favorites. Throughout Pedro's disturbed rule, Jews continued as important members of his
government in the royal chancellory, in the fiscal administration, in the stewardship of royal property and in the
dangerous, provocative offices connected with taxation.[200]

Indeed, Pedro's partiality toward the Jews and their
reciprocal attachment to him were distorted into a scandalous war issue. A grave menace to the existence of the
Jews in Castile was thus created when the tide of battle
turned in favor of the contender for the throne. Because
they loyally supported the legitimate king with their fortunes
and their lives, in striking contrast to the Church which,
through the pope, renounced and excommunicated him, they
were marked victims for attack and vilification. All the
latent hostility against them was lashed into bitter fury.
Not only did thousands of Jews die in battle, but many
more were butchered in massacre; the strength of the
aljamas was utterly crushed by the ruinous fines and the
annulments of Jewish loans that followed in the wake of

Henry's triumphs. Above all, Jews became a symbol and an object of popular detestation. The dream of Innocent III was coming true at last.[201] Pedro's final defeat and death seemed like a signal for the humiliation and extermination of the Jews. Thus, when the news of Pedro's end was relayed to Pope Urban, he exclaimed: "The Church must rejoice at the death of such a tyrant, a rebel against the Church and a favorer of the Jews and Saracens. The righteous exult in retribution."[202]

But Henry II revealed true statesmanship when he came into power. While as a war measure he raged against the Jews during the evil conflict and fanned the flames of national hatred against them, he gallantly acknowledged their valor and loyalty when the fratricidal duel was over. "Such subjects a king must love and reward," he acknowledged, "because they maintained proper loyalty to their conquered king unto death and did not surrender to the victor."[203] During the heat of the conflict, the Cortes of Burgos, under the hysteria of war passion, represented to him that "all cities, towns and places of the kingdom consider that all the evils, misfortunes, murders and banishments that have happened in past times" were due to the malevolent advice of Jewish officers and court favorites. They petitioned Henry to exclude Jews from all public offices and from any post, even that of physician, in the palace of the king, the queen or the infantes. Henry demurred at the "unreasonableness" of the request. With studied evasiveness he replied: "Although there are some Jews employed in our court, we shall not appoint them to our council nor give such power to them from which any injury might result to the country." More revealing still was his reply to the petition for the exclusion of the Jews from the farming of taxes: "I would have farmed them for less to Christians, but there were no applicants."[204]

It is little to be wondered at, therefore, that at the conclusion of the war, when Henry found himself king over a land economically prostrate, with a treasury virtually bankrupt, he summoned Jews to his aid and entrusted them with high offices of state in order to bring about the effective rehabilitation of the country. Don Joseph Pichon had been one of Henry's trusted aides before he became king, and he grew steadily in power until he became one of the most important figures in the court of Henry II. His signature appeared on official documents as early as 1366.[205] In the following year, he was on an important mission to the king of Aragon.[206] In 1369 his title was "chief treasurer and manager of the revenues of the realm."[207] He was the controller general (*contador mayor*) in 1371.[208] The range of his activities brought him into official relationship with the municipalities, the churches, the monasteries and the religious-military Order of Santiago.[209]

Unfortunate, however, were Pichon's relations with the Jewish community. He was strangely unpopular with his own coreligionists, for many among them suspected the probity of his dealings with the court and feared his disloyalty. Charges of embezzlement of the treasury were preferred against him by other Jewish courtiers, and his imprisonment followed. Pichon miraculously escaped with a heavy fine and was apparently restored sufficiently to court favor to plot the downfall of his enemies. This, as we have seen elsewhere, led inadvertently, after the death of Henry II, to a disastrous end — his secret trial as informer by a Jewish tribunal — the hasty, furtive execution, the swift retribution upon all who were involved in the judicial

murder, and the withdrawal of criminal jurisdiction from
the *aljamas*.[210]

Of different moral caliber was the younger official, Don
Samuel Abravanel, beloved of his people and retained in the
confidence of his royal masters for three generations. His
public career commenced under Henry II; in 1397 he was
the controller general of Henry III, and the queen's treasurer. At this stage, however, he bore the baptized name of
Juan Sanchez de Sevilla. It is generally assumed that he
was a Marrano and had accepted baptism during the persecutions of 1391.[211]

The prominence of these high Jewish officials and of
many others who filled important posts in the government
led to loud protest at the Cortes of Tor in 1371.[212] The cry
was raised that Jews held high offices and honors in all
parts of the kingdom, in the royal palace as well as in the
territories of the nobles, and that Christians were subservient
to them and were compelled to show them fear and respect.
In the program which the Cortes then formulated, the
first two items were demands for the imposition of the
hateful badge and the elimination of Jews from court
honors and offices of the state. There were further re-
quests for fixing the texture and style of their clothes and
prohibiting them from riding on mules or using Christian
names. The reply of the king was cunningly calculated to
conciliate the sentiment of the populace without injury to the
royal interests or to the state. Thus he showed no scruples
in ordering the Jews and Moors henceforth to put on the
hated badge and to discard the use of Christian names.
But he rejected the proposal to remove the Jews from the
key posts in the government and considered it right to
continue in the course followed by his royal predecessors,

especially his father, Don Alfonso.[213] Indeed, the very tax
which this Cortes voted him, the *moneda*, Henry promptly
farmed to his Jewish *arrendadores*.[214] On the other hand,
when six years later the Cortes at Burgos appealed for the
abolition of Jewish officials on the estates of the nobles,
Henry, who was not averse to weakening the enormous
powers of his baronial magistrates, agreed "that in the
future, no Jew could be their *almoxarifes*, major-domos or
hold any offices under them."[215] Despite its portentous
beginning and notwithstanding the mass hysteria generated
in the cruel civil war, the reign of Henry II still pointed to
the indispensable usefuless of Jewish personnel to the
Spanish kings and the state economy.

The reign of John I (1379–90) illustrated the same
dilemma. The animosity toward the Jewish people was
mounting steadily, John himself showing this feeling to a
greater degree than any of his predecessors, not excluding his
father, Henry II.[216] He was but a year on the throne when,
in addition to supporting other crippling anti-Jewish laws,
he declared himself strongly in favor of the exclusion of
Jews from public office, especially the post of *almoxarife*
of the king, the queen, the infantes or any other noble in
the royal household.[217] Five years later, at the Cortes of
Valladolid, he repeated the decree with the additional penal-
izing clause that any Jew who, contrary to law, would hold
a position of public trust should suffer the confiscation of all
his property.[218] The law was, moreover, set into a legal
framework which featured public whipping as a punishment
for Christians who presumed to live with Jews, especially
nursing women who suckled Jewish infants.[219] Nevertheless,
this monarch entered into close relations with Jewish
grandees in the court of Portugal when he formed an alliance

with Queen Leonora and laid claim to the throne of Portugal.[220] Indeed, according to a Portuguese chronicle, his life
was saved by the timely warning given him by one of these
Jewish counselors.[221] Furthermore, after his plans were
frustrated, King John invited David Negro, the *almoxarife*
of the deceased Portuguese king, to Castile, appointed him
chief rabbi of the Jewries of his kingdom and invested him,
no doubt, with more worldly functions at the court, according to the customary practice.[222] In addition, throughout
his reign we meet, as formerly, Jews in the familiar posts of
receivers, collectors and farmers of taxes.[223]

More amazing still is the illustration afforded by the
succeeding reign, that of Henry III, the Invalid (1390–
1406), another king to ascend the throne during his minority, when he was eleven years old. This was the dolorous
period in which occurred the terrible massacres of 1391,
the greatest calamity which had ever befallen the *aljamas*
of Castile, Valencia, Majorca and Catalonia. Great was the
destruction of life as thousands died and glorified the inef-
fable Name. More fearful was the moral collapse as greater
multitudes fled in panic to save themselves, their wives and
children from the frenzied butchery. The community organizations were demoralized, shattered, in many instances completely abandoned; the synagogues converted into churches
and the community property divided among the predatory
classes. The population that survived the persecutions and
remained in the Jewish fold was impoverished and reduced
to a fraction of its former size.[224] The loss in numbers was
undoubtedly greatest among the wealthy groups and sophis-
ticated worldlings, among whom were the courtiers, grandees
and high officials.[225] Nevertheless, from the depleted, broken
ranks of loyal Jews, the king and his counselors summoned

distinguished men and confided to them positions of trust
and responsibility in the administration of the government.

Early in the reign, before the fearful summer of 1391,
Abraham, son of Don Moses, had been an exalted personage
at the court;[226] but he was not spared the common affliction.
He witnessed the massacre of those dearest to him, only
one son escaping; in addition, he was robbed of his fortune
and reduced to beggary.[227] But the famous physician Meir
Alguades continued his ministrations at the court to the
end of the reign and, as we may assume from the king's
sobriquet, the Invalid, the royal patient must have given
him much concern. His tragic end and the weird circumstances under which his death was encompassed were
eloquent testimonial, in the dark language of mediaeval
conspirators, of his great influence upon the king and the
important place he occupied in court circles.[228]

Among those more directly concerned with the functions
of the government proper were Jews who held positions in
the treasury, playing an important role in the collection and
control of the diversified revenues of the central administration. Joseph ibn Verga (Yuçef Abenverga) was treasurer-
in-chief of the province of Toledo and Estremadura.[229] Don
Zulemna aben Arroyo, whose function as the king's fiscal
officer in the province of Galicia began under John I, continued through the reign of Henry III into the period of
John II.[230] Besides these, there were many other Jews
whom the invalid king appointed as collectors, farmers and
administrators of the taxes.[231] Jewish officials were utilized
by the archbishop of Toledo in the fiscal administration of
his archbishopric.[232] The Cortes of Madrid, assembled in
1405, therefore, no longer spoke of Jewish exclusion from
public offices, but demanded that they be subjected to the

humiliation of the badge, from which Jews at the court had always been exempt.[233]

The premature death of Henry III, which plunged the country again into a prolonged minority rule by two mutually antagonistic co-regents, proved to be a misfortune to the Jews even more than to the country at large. John II was barely two years old when he became king, with the Queen-Mother Catalina and his uncle, the Infante Don Ferdinand, ruling in his name. "Woe to the land whose king is a child," the Jews were soon to learn through bitter experience. The execution of Meir Alguades and the other innocent victims with him was a foreboding augury of the terrible events to come. What prompted the regents in the midst of all their serious perplexities to direct their attention to the Jewish courtiers, it is impossible to say. It is natural to suspect the apostate rabbi, Paul de Santa María, member of the royal council, as instigator of the attack;[234] but the supposition is pure surmise and has no evidence to support it.[235] In any event, on October 25, 1408, a long and solemn proclamation, ostensibly based on the *Partidas*, was issued in the name of the child-king declaring that:

> It is my pleasure that henceforth no Jew of whatever station or rank shall presume to farm any toll, tax or duty which the subjects of my kingdom have to pay within a year from the date hereof, or hereafter annually, whether it be the revenue of excises, *monedas*, tithes, tolls or any other tax; neither shall they be inspectors, collectors or receivers of the same; nor shall they be security, publicly or privately, for any person connected therewith; nor shall they themselves farm any tithes or other temporal or spiritual dues, belonging to archbishops, bishops or masters of the military orders or any other lords

who receive dues from their vassals or subjects. Nor shall they be pledgers, collectors or receivers of those dues and revenues.

Any Jew performing these functions contrary to law was to be penalized by twice the sum of the revenue he received; and if he did not possess the amount, his property was to be confiscated and he was to receive fifty lashes. To put more teeth into the law, two innovations were introduced. The appointing Christian power was to be fined; and the informer as well as the court that passed sentence were to share equally with the Crown in the proceeds of the fines.[236]

This decree, however, was but a preliminary to the savage ordinance of Valladolid, promulgated January 2, 1412. Not since the days of the Visigoths was there such a sinister combination of what passed as religion and statecraft bent upon the degradation and destruction of well over half a million human beings. Jews and Moors were ordered into barred enclosures from which Christians even of the lowest social dregs were rigidly excluded. The ancient privileges of self-jurisdiction and taxation were rescinded. Like serfs, they were now forbidden to change their domicile, and the nobles were warned against sheltering those who fled for refuge. Not only was the practice of medicine and surgery or the compounding of drugs and food preparation denied them, but they were forbidden altogether to trade with Christians or to work for them as artisans and craftsmen or to employ Christians in their homes or to engage them as nurses for their children or as herdsmen, gardeners or shepherds. Every human tie that bound Jews and Moors to their Christian fellows was torn asunder. Members of one group were forbidden to visit the other in sickness, to send them gifts or to engage them in friendly conversation or to attend one another's weddings, funerals or *honras*.[237]

Needless to say, the decree also denied to Jews and Moors all public offices connected with the state treasury or the revenues of the royal family, the nobles or church prelates; the exercise by them of any kind of authority it forbade under heavy penalty. New measures were passed, aimed particularly at the grandees and courtiers who were accustomed to the honors and privileges of their superior station. They were henceforth not allowed to be addressed as Don or Donna either in writing or in speech. In addition to the red badge, a style of dress and an inferior, coarse texture of cloth was prescribed, both for men and women, in order to set them apart from the rest of the population. As the crowning indignity, they were forbidden to cut or shave their beards or to trim their hair. Lashes, fines and confiscations were liberally prescribed as penalties in all these laws.[238] Six months later, the decree was revised in some important particulars, but the chief degrading features remained in the statute.[239]

The edict was timed to produce its most devastating effect. The *aljamas* were still suffering from the consequences of the massacres of the preceding generation. Discouragement and despair were sapping the vitality of Jewish resistance. Desertions to the Church were taking place at an accelerated pace.[240] More latterly the ascetic Dominican priest, Vincent Ferrer, with all the elemental magnetism of a devout fanatic, stormed the country with inflaming oratory. Accompanied by bands of flagellants and spearmen, he invaded the synagogues, a crucifix in one arm and a Torah in the other, and thundered for the immediate conversion of the Jews.[241] It was he who, according to the court chronicler, inspired the infamous edict, and his influence now bore down with crushing weight for the enforcement of the decree in all its harshness.[242] The effect was overwhelming. In his *Letter of Admonition* a contemporary moralist describes the tragedy:

> They forced strange clothing upon us. They kept us from trade, farming and the crafts. They compelled us to grow our beards and our hair long. Inmates of palaces were driven into wretched nooks and dark, low huts. Instead of silken apparel, we were obliged to wear wretched clothes which drew contempt upon us. Unshaved, we appeared like mourners. Starvation stared everyone in the face. Children died on their mother's knees from hunger and exposure.[243]

Few could stand up under the affliction and, least of all, the men of wealth, the rich tax farmers, the Jewish grandees at the court.[244] Many among them lost heart and led the procession to the font. The number of converts in the years immediately following mounted to many thousands. Great communities were reduced to a shadowy existence; the smaller ones, in many instances, disappeared entirely.[245] The finances of the country were seriously disrupted. While the royal revenue suffered most, the nobles and the churches also felt the effect keenly. The grotesque plight of the churches was plaintively described by one of the prelates as "spiritual triumph and temporal bankruptcy." Needless to say, the churches pressed for and obtained from the government other assignments of revenue.[246] That there was to be no retreat of the church forces in the war against Judaism was emphatically indicated in the bull of the anti-pope Benedict XIII, in 1415.[247]

The dominance of the church influence in the affairs of the state, however, ended with the passing of the regency. When John II took the reins of government in his own hands — or rather entrusted them to the more capable and energetic hands of Alvaro de Luna — a more realistic view of the economic and political conditions of the state began to prevail. Alvaro was too astute a statesman not to see the economic folly of the anti-Jewish legislation. His own bitter experience taught him that the gravest need of the hour was to curb the willful baronage that was sapping the strength of the monarchy and driving the country to a state of anarchy. The essential weapon for such a campaign was a full treasury and, consequently, it became a matter of urgent state policy to restore the economic productivity of the aljamas and to utilize once more the experience and resourcefulness of Jewish financiers.

The resultant change was startling. Without rescinding the previous legislation, the revenues of the government were now entrusted to Jewish entrepreneurs on a larger scale than ever. During the years 1427 to 1430, Joseph the Prince (Yuçaf el Naci) controlled the national customs duties.[248] A man of great opulence and culture, a talented linguist and scientist, he was at home in the royal palace and was recognized there as the spokesman of his people and the pleader of their cause.[249] His associate at the court was Abraham Benveniste.[250] They were partners in many important transactions and they jointly supplied the army with money and provisions.[251] The petition of the Cortes of Burgos, in 1430, for the enforcement of the laws forbidding Jews and Moors to hold public office was mild in tone and met with the king's evasive reply: "I will order an examination to be made as to what has been ordained by my father and my pleasure and the papal bulls; and whatever is for the service of God, His divine law, my service and the welfare of my kingdom shall be observed and will not be revoked or modified."[252] Benveniste, who appears to have been Joseph's junior, became one of the most important figures in the reign of John II. He and the all-powerful constable, Don Alvaro de Luna, and the chief steward of the court (*mayordomo mayor*), Don Juan Furtado, formed a triumvirate that governed the country in the name of the king.[253] His memory was gratefully preserved in Hebrew literature as one who revived the spiritual life of Castilian Jewry and turned back the tide of apostasy.[254] In recognition of his services and in accord with popular Jewish sentiment, he was appointed *rab de la corte*, or court rabbi and chief judge of the Jews of Castile.[255]

The ledgers of the royal accountants of this period reveal a network of Jewish tax farmers and collectors of the public revenue and the vital part which they had in the fiscal system of the state government.[256] Abraham Benveniste appears as royal treasurer and in many other major offices connected with the revenues and taxes of the kingdom.[257] His son Joseph was associated with him in many of the financial transactions.[258] Another Joseph Benveniste, of Briviesca, was also an important figure as chief collector of the royal taxes in Old Castile, as controller of the salt mines and as financier of many public enterprises.[259] Samuel Benveniste not only acted as the treasurer of the queen of Castile but for a time he was also in the service of the king and queen of Aragon.[260]

The list of Jewish officials at this time is too long to enumerate here, but one may single out Joseph ibn Shem Tob, who held the major post of director of the royal accounts and whose career richly illustrates the interests and the character of many who appear as bare names on the roster of government officials.[261] Besides being the fiscal administrator of Prince Henry, later Henry IV, Joseph was the physician of the royal family, for which he received an annual salary of 40,000 *maravedís* in 1453.[262] He stood high in the esteem of the palace and was encouraged freely to debate religious and philosophical questions with Christian laymen and priests in the presence of the king and the court grandees. The disputations were often of a sharply polemical character, but he never failed to command respect for his views.[263] When fanatical conspirators raised false religious charges against the Jewry of Segovia, in 1452, he was commissioned by the infante to hurry to the scene with written instructions to the governor and the council of the city and with a reassuring message to the Jewish community. He arrived in Segovia on a Friday with the prince's mandate and the following day, on the Sabbath, he stirred the worshiping congregation with a fervent sermon which fired their hearts with renewed courage.[264]

Wherever he traveled, people flocked to hear his sermons. As a preacher, he combined philosophical reflection and religious fervor. Like many another courtier, he suffered periods of temporary eclipse in royal favor and was then compelled to wander from place to place. During those intervals, he found solace in writing and in preaching.[265] His literary activities covered many fields. As a young man, he wrote a small treatise on economics based on Aristotelian principles; but his major interests were philosophical and he wrote extensively on philosophy, theology and ethics.[266] With unusual clarity and force, he expounded the relations between religion and philosophy, their common ground, their

varying modes of approach to truth and the inescapable
conflict between them. While stressing the cultural value of
philosophy and science, he attached greater importance to
religion both as a means of preserving the integrity of the
Jewish people and as an aid to individual salvation and the
immortality of the soul. Not philosophy in the abstract
but the religion of Judaism alone could save the Jewish
people from spiritual annihilation. With equal fervor, he
set himself the literary task of refuting the more vulgar
attacks upon Judaism made by apostates and missionary
zealots.[267] Such was the man who negotiated the financial
accounts of his prince and king; who with four other notables
represented all the *aljamas* of the kingdom in 1450; who was
sent on a delicate mission abroad to negotiate for the hand
of a Portuguese princess; and who in the reign of Henry IV
finally met the fate of so many other courtiers, the death
of martyrdom.[268]

The favor which Jewish notables enjoyed at the court of
John II and their prominence in his state administration
did not this time meet with any determined opposition on
the part of the Cortes. But the Church was not so com-
placent. High prelates of the Spanish Church pressed Pope
Eugene IV for action while he was still under strong pressure
from the Council of Basel. Thus he was led, in 1442, to
issue an apostolic bull, addressed primarily to the bishops
of Castile and Leon, in which he repeated the harsh provisions of the law of 1412, adding a few more restrictions taken
from canon law and demanding the rigorous enforcement
of the decree in all its features.[269] The danger of a repetition
of the evils of the earlier years of the regency was great.
But John II or, more likely, Alvaro de Luna was equal to the
occasion. Without attempting open defiance of the pope, he

adroitly circumvented the decree by softening through interpretation its harshest features and showing an unmistakable
determination to protect his Jewish subjects.[270] As to the
ban on Jewish officials, even John could not deny its place in
the law; but what he admitted in theory, he could and did
find it expedient to ignore in practice, so that Jewish officials
continued in his service to the end of his reign and several —
among them Joseph ibn Shem Tob — continued to serve
under his son Henry IV.[271]

The twenty years of Henry's rule were visited by all the
evils invited by a weak monarch — anarchy, rebellion and
civil war. During the years 1465–68, a rival throne was set
up for Henry's half brother, Alfonso, and two kings ruled
over the distracted country. City fought against city, and
armies under rival standards were arrayed against each
other in combat till the death of the contender put an end
to the national misery and humiliation. Although the Jews
were not made a political issue between the contending
forces, they were not forgotten by the hostile elements in
the Cortes. In 1465, a commission which had been appointed to adjust the differences between the king and the
nobles who had risen in discontent included in a long series
of recommendations many of the old anti-Jewish restrictions,
among them the provision that Jews were not to be administrators, *almoxarifes*, tax collectors, auditors or major-domos
of the king, the queen, the princes, the nobles, lay and
ecclesiastical.[272]

But Henry IV had no intention to abide by any of the
recommendations of the commission. He operated the
royal finances through Jewish officials not out of favoritism,
but out of economic necessity. It was freely admitted that
Christian candidates were unable to meet the terms of the

competition. The Cortes of Ocaña, in 1469, therefore frankly stated that the king ought to forego the advantages of the superior management of Jewish financiers and farm the revenues to Christians on terms less advantageous to the Crown. The complaint of the Cortes was even more sensationally directed against the rich church prelates. For the vast ecclesiastic properties were also widely administered by Jews and Moors for the same reason of their superior economic ability. In the performance of their duties, so the Cortes charged, "they [Jews and Moors] enter churches to apportion the tithes among the contributors, to the great offense and injury of the Church."[273]

To have followed the course advocated by the Cortes would have revolutionized the entire fiscal administration of the kingdom. Henry IV had neither the energy nor the desire to undertake such an adventure. Although, for the sake of expediency, he gave his assent to the request of the national assembly, neither he nor the more dynamic Catholic Majesties, Ferdinand and Isabella, his immediate successors, made the slightest attempt to translate this law into actual performance. On the contrary, as we approach the tragic end of Jewish history in Spain, the records reveal an ever increasing number of Jews in the service of the government, which was all the more remarkable if one bears in mind the position of the Marranos who filled the highest posts in every branch of the public life of Spain.[274]

Besides Joseph ibn Shem Tob, who served Henry as crown prince and then as king, we find among the prominent tax gatherers a coterie of Palencia Jews, Don Gaon de Vitoria, Joseph and Moses Cales, Samuel Pachon and Joseph Abenataf (ibn Ataf). They, and numerous other Jews who are cited in the records, farmed the taxes, tolls, imposts, duties and excises of the districts into which the country was divided for these purposes. Bishoprics and nobles' estates were also included in their operations.[275]

The outstanding Jewish figure in the court of Henry IV after the death of Joseph ibn Shem Tob was Abraham Seneor. In appreciation of his great "personal merits, his fidelity and the valued services he was rendering the king every day," Henry appointed him, for life, judge of the Jewry of Segovia and, in addition, endowed him with material gifts and privileges.[276] His role as government financier grew to be one of great significance. But his importance extended beyond the realm of finance. Through his personal magnetism and the trust which he inspired in the highest court circles, he became the confidant of kings and princes and was admitted into the intimacies and secrets of court romance. The fate of Spain and the course of its future development centered around the matrimonial prospects of Isabella. Among the many suitors who pressed for her hand, the principal rivals were Ferdinand of Aragon and Alfonso the African of Portugal. The Castilian nobles, fearing domination by Aragon, strongly favored the Portuguese marriage. Isabella, with feminine intuition, was attracted to her Aragon cousin. In this delicate situation, fraught with such consequence for the future, Abraham Seneor became an important factor. Devoted to the infanta, and moved perhaps by the reported friendliness of the Aragon prince and his alleged Jewish descent, he became a strong partisan of Ferdinand's courtship. He pleaded his cause with the grandees at the court and, notwithstanding violent opposition, arranged to bring Ferdinand secretly to his home and then led him quietly to the princess. The fateful marriage followed a few days later with a simple wedding ceremony for which the bride and groom had to borrow money to cover the expenses.[277] Jaime Ram, the distinguished jurist and the son of a rabbi, was repaid, in 1474, the sum of 20,000 *sueldos* which he had advanced to Ferdinand at the critical juncture.[278]

The news of the marriage was distressing to Henry IV, who still entertained hopes of seeing his daughter's legitimacy recognized and her succession to the throne confirmed. Abraham Seneor undertook the task of mediator for the royal couple and succeeded several years later, in 1473, to effect at least a temporary reconciliation between Isabella and her half brother, the reigning monarch.[279] It is not surprising, therefore, that when Henry IV died a year later, in 1474, and Isabella and Ferdinand succeeded to the throne of Castile, Abraham Seneor's influence reached its zenith.

One of the early acts of the king and queen was to appoint Don Abraham Seneor supreme judge and chief rabbi of all the Jewish *aljamas* of the kingdom and to invest him with the authority to apportion the taxes among the communities.[280] This post he retained to the very end of Jewish subsistence in Spain. The queen also endowed him with a life-pension of 150,000 *maravedís*, which included the gift of 50,000 *maravedís* voted him by the Cortes of Toledo in 1480.[281]

We find him actively participating with numerous Jews in the farming and collecting of the royal revenue.[282] The royal couple never wearied of expressing their appreciation of the great services which he rendered them when they ascended the throne, and more recently since the time when, by the grace of God, they came to reign as sovereigns. Thus moved by gratitude, they appointed him, in 1488, to the singularly

נכתב הספר הזה שיש בו ארבעה ועשרים

ספרי הקדש על יד המשכיל ר' המשכיל ר' אברהם באליה נע

במדינת טוליטלה אשר בספרד ונשלם ביריד ניסן

שנת חמשת אלפים ומאתים וחמשים ושתים

לבריאת עולם להוכם השלמר ...

נרו בן החבר הנכבד כר' ... זל הא-ל יזכרהו

להנותבו הוא וזרעו וזרע זרעו עד עולם ובשבעה

בקרן אבמרה שנה הנזכרת יצאי מבוזהלימו נורושים

ברבר המלך נלות ירושלם אשר בספרד וסימניך

בוא יבא ברנה נשא אלומותיו ואני חיים ן חיים

כתמתי בוקיצה המסורת והפליגתית שנת נזר אלהיו

על ראשו לפרט במדינת קוסטנטינה ישעי יקרב

Colophon of a Bible manuscript begun in Toledo in 1492,
four months before the Expulsion

(see p. xi)

important post of treasurer of the *hermandad* with all the
rights and privileges accruing to the office.[283]

True to the noblest traditions of the Jewish courtier, he
utilized his wealth and his prestige to protect his brethren
in the particularly perilous conditions created by the establishment of the Inquisition and the prosecution of a holy war
against the Mohammedan kingdom of Granada.[284] When
the city of Malaga was captured by the Christian forces
and the Jewish population — men, women and children —
were made captive, a huge sum was raised for their ransom
under his leadership and authority.[285] When the *alcalde* of
a city arbitrarily denied the Jews their elementary rights,
or when a Dominican preacher incited the populace and
directed an attack upon the *judería*, Abraham's influence
at the court brought prompt redress.[286] He was indeed the
Head of the Exile, as he was aptly described in an allusion
made to him in a remarkable address of the Jewry of Castile
to their brethren in Rome and Lombardy in 1487.[287]

Seneor revealed the true generosity of his nature in the
support he rendered the famous refugee statesman, scholar
and financier who sought shelter in Toledo, Don Isaac
Abravanel. Although Don Isaac's reputation undoubtedly
preceded him in his flight from Portugal, it is fair to assume
that Seneor sponsored him at the court of Ferdinand and
Isabella. He invited him to participate with him in the
work of the fiscal administration and, before long, Abravanel's extraordinary talent in government financing and
administration brought him to the front ranks as one of the
leading financiers of the royal treasury.[288] Not a shadow of
suspicion or envy marred the relations of the two grandees
who bring to a close the illustrious record of the Jewish

courtiers in Spain. Together they worked with brilliant success to support the final war of the Cross against the Crescent on the Iberian Peninsula.[289] When the war was successfully concluded and the exile of the Jews was decreed on March 31, 1492, Abravanel's outstanding credits amounted to one and a half million *maravedís*, which Ferdinand and Isabella ordered to be paid to him so as to enable the financier, on the eve of exile, to settle his accounts with the royal treasury. Indeed, as a sign of special grace he was permitted by royal grant to take an appreciable amount of gold and silver with him.[290]

Legend unites Seneor and Abravanel, the two foremost courtiers, in the final dramatic scene when they stood manfully before Ferdinand and implored him to save their people by recalling the cruel edict of banishment.[291] But when the king remained obdurate and Torquemada's will triumphed, the two friends parted: Seneor to the font of baptism and Abravanel, like Jeremiah of old, to exile with his people.[292]

NOTES

ABBREVIATIONS

Adret	*Solomon ben Abraham ibn Adret, She'elot u-teshubot. Vols. I-VIII*
AHR	*American Historical Review*
Alfasi	*Isaac ben Jacob Alfasi, Sefer she'elot u-teshubot*
Asher	*Asher ben Yehiel, She'elot u-teshubot*
BAE	*Biblioteca de autores españoles*
Baer I, II	*Fritz Baer, Die Juden im christlichen Spanien: Urkunden und Regesten. I. Aragonien und Navarra; II. Kastilien; Inkquisitions-akten*
Baer, Studien	*Fritz Baer, Studien zur Geschichte der Juden im Königreich Aragonien während des 13. und 14. Jahrhunderts*
BAH	*Boletin de la real academia de la historia*
Barfat	*Isaac ben Sheshet, Sefer she'elot u-teshubot*
Barfat II,	*Sefer She'elot u-teshubot ha-RIBaSH ha-hadashot*
CDIA	*Colección de documentos inéditos del archivo general de la Corona de Aragon*
Cod. Just.	*Justinian Code*
Cod. Theod.	*Theodosian Code*
Duran	*Simeon ben Zemah Duran, Sefer ha-tashbaz*
Greg. Ep.	*Gregorii I Epistolae, in Monumenta Germaniae historica*
HUCA	*Hebrew Union College Annual*
JQR	*The Jewish Quarterly Review, Old Series and New Series*
Jacobs	*Joseph Jacobs, Sources of Spanish-Jewish History*
Maim.	*Kobez teshubot ha-RaMBaM we-iggerotav*
MGH	*Monumenta Germaniae historica*
MGWJ	*Monatsschrift für Geschichte und Wissenschaft des Judentums*
Migash	*Joseph b. Meir ha-Levi ibn Migash, She'elot u-teshubot*
MJC	*Medieval Jewish Chronicles and Chronological Notes by Ad. Neubauer*
MT	*Maimonides, Mishneh Torah*
MWJ	*Magazin für die Wissenschaft des Judenthums*
Nissim	*Nissim ben Reuben Gerondi, She'elot u-teshubot*
RaMaH	*Responsa of R. Meir ha-Levi Abulafia*
REJ	*Revue des études juives*
Régné	*Jean Régné, Catalogue des actes ... concernants les juifs. REJ, LX (1906)–LXX (1920)*
SeMaG	*Sefer mizvot gadol, by Moses ben Jacob of Coucy*
ZDMG	*Zeitschrift der deutschen morgenländischen Gesellschaft*
ZHB	*Zeitschrift für hebräische Bibliographie*
ZJ	*Zikron Yehudah, ve-hu sefer she'elot u-teshubot, by Judah ben Asher ben Yehiel*
ZL	*Zedah la-derek, by Menahem ben Aaron ibn Zerak*

NOTES TO CHAPTER XI

MORAL CONDITIONS

[1] See Joseph Kimhi's dialogue between a Jew and an apostate in his *Sefer ha-Berit* (*Book of the Covenant*); in *Milhemet Hobah*, Constantinople, 1710.

[2] Adret, IV, 314.

[3] Ibid., I, 557; II, 87; IV, 323. Abrahams, *Jewish Life in the Middle Ages*, 87: "Fidelity was expected from the husband as well as from the wife." This statement should be qualified with the reservation that the man's infidelity was far less serious than that of the woman. In the case of the woman, infidelity was adultery, which in theory at least was punishable by death and always necessitated the dissolution of the family. In the man, infidelity constituted a violation of a biblical prohibition, the utmost punishment for which was flagellation, and it in no way disturbed the family relationship legally. This difference is, of course, due to the fact that polygamy has legal countenance in the Bible and is not to be confused with the cynical spirit that accords the man greater license than the woman. Thus, when the man was guilty of adultery, i. e., through carnal relations with a married woman, he shared her fate, regardless of his own status in marriage.

[4] Adret, I, 1193, 1210; Nissim, 30.

[5] Adret, VI, 3; Asher, XXXII, 1.

[6] Adret, I, 596; II, 77; IV, 257. Cf. Asher, XXXII, 12, 15; RaMaH, 255.

[7] Adret, I, 557; IV, 323; Asher, XXXII, 10, 17.

[8] Adret, I, 1187.

[9] Ibid., V, 241; Asher; XXXII, 14.

[10] Adret, V, 241; cf. I, 1251.

[11] Ibid., I, 1187.

[12] *ZJ*, 80, end; Asher, XXXII, 11.

[13] *ZJ*, 80. Cf. Adret, V, 241.

[14] Ibid., I, 1187. See Barfat, 395.

[15] Adret, I, 386.

[16] Ibid., I, 855.

[17] This seems to belong to a group of responsa of R. Meir of Rothenburg, and therefore comes from Germany proper. It was, however, universal in its application.

[18] Burke, *History of Spain*, II, Appendix.

[19] *Quarterly Review*, LXI, 119–20.

[20] Burke, op. cit., II, Appendix.

[21] Cf. Asher, CI, 1.

[22] The following classified data are based exclusively on the responsa of Ibn Adret, R. Asher and R. Judah. There occur at least twenty-one cases where the validity of the marriage was questioned: Adret, I, 551, 773 = 1227, 1179, 1193, 1209, 1210, 1223, 1236, 1241 = VIII, 144; IV, 286, 322; VI, 2; VII, 258 (theoretical?); VIII, 126, 130, 132, 137, 140. Asher, XXXII, 1; LVIII, 4; ZJ, 81. In at least fifteen instances, the legality of the bill of divorce was disputed. Adret, I, 549, 573 (Germany); II, 276; IV, 24 (theoretical?), 186, 201 (theoretical?), 257; VII, 438 (theoretical?); VIII, 129, 143, 146; Asher, XVII, 6; XLIII, 9, 12, 13.

There occur eighty cases bearing on conjugal relations, which may be subdivided as follows:

A) Breaking up of the home because of ill treatment of the wife, twenty-one cases: Adret, I, 571, 693 (theoretical?), 1219, 1237 = VIII, 133; II, 25, 241, 298; IV, 40, 72, 113, 154, 168, 256; V, 264; VII, 477 (family desertion); VIII, 102–4; Asher, XXXII, 11; XXXVIII, 7; XLIII, 7; LXXXII, 2; ZJ, 71.

B) Rebellious wives (נשים מורדות), women who refused to live with their husbands and demanded a divorce, nineteen cases: Adret, I, 572, 628, 859–60 (Germany); 1192, 1235, 1255; II, 112; IV, 52–3; V, 95; VI, 72; VII, 414; VIII, 134, 138, 139; Asher, XXXII, 10; XLIII, 1, 6, 8; ZJ, 73.

C) Women under suspicion of infidelity, ten cases: Adret, I, 557, 596, 832 (Germany); IV, 323; V, 241; Asher, XXXII, 7, 9, 12, 17; ZJ, 80 (in two of these instances, a gentile was suspected).

D) Cases of adultery and fornication, twenty-nine. Between Jewish men and women: Adret, I, 1249; IV, 204; V, 239, 240; Asher, XXXII, 11, 14, 16; LIII, 7. Between gentiles and Jewish women: Adret, I, 1187, 1250 (theoretical?); IV, 257; Asher, VIII, 10(?), XVIII, 13. Master and servant or slave: Adret, I, 610, 628, 1205; IV, 314; Asher, XXXII, 13, 15. Concubines: Adret, II, 363; V, 242; Asher, XXXII, 1, 13; XXXV, 10. Cases of illegitimate children: Adret, II, 219; VII, 55, 180; Asher, XVII, 7; XXXII, 16; LXXXII, 1.

There occur also four cases of theft: Adret, III, 110; IV, 2; V, 173, 243; and fourteen cases of gambling: ibid., I, 755; II, 286 = VII, 501; III, 305; VII, 244, 270, 445; VIII, 252, 281; Asher, XI, 8, 10; XII, 5, 6; LXXII, 1; LXXXII, 2.

The total number of responsa from which the above data were drawn is about 4,500.

[23] Asher, XLIII, 6.

[24] Ibid., XLIII, 8.

[25] ZJ, 72, p. 23b.

[26] Adret, I, 1209.

[27] Ibid., I, 1210.

[28] Ibid., I, 1219.

[29] Ibn Adret could not find an expert in Arabic in the city of Barcelona and its surroundings (Adret, III, 427). In Toledo, literary Arabic was current among Jews (Asher, LV, 9).

[30] Cf. tabulated list in note 22 above. Of the ten cases in class C, five were taken from Ibn Adret's responsa and five from those of R. Asher and his son Judah. As

Ibn Adret's responsa total more than three times the number of the responsa of R. Asher and R. Judah combined, the equal division reflects severely on the communities represented by the latter two rabbis. Furthermore, of the five cases occurring in Adret's responsa, one case (I, 832) did not belong to Ibn Adret but to R. Meir of Rothenburg, another (V, 241) came from Toledo, a third, (I, 596) cannot be considered seriously, so that there remain only two cases which reflect the environs of Ibn Adret. Of the cases in the works of R. Asher and his son, only one can be traced to foreign origin: Asher, XXXII, 9.

Compare also class D, which includes the cases that reflect most seriously upon the morals of the people concerned. Of the twenty-nine cases under this heading, sixteen belong to the responsa of Ibn Adret and thirteen to R. Asher. Of the former, four questions (I, 610; V, 239, 240, 242) came from Toledo, the country of R. Asher, and two from a city which was obviously under Mohammedan influence (I, 1205; IV, 314). Of the remaining ten, one came from Ancosa (IV, 204), two (I, 1249, 1250) belonged to Perpignan, and two questions were apparently hypothetical (VII, 55, 180), so that there remain only five cases which may properly be attributed to Ibn Adret's immediate territory. Over against these stand the thirteen cases of R. Asher (beside Ibn Adret's four questions which came from Toledo) and two from Mohammedan provinces.

[31] *ZJ*, 91, p. 44a: גם ענין השפחות אשר הם תקלה לישראל אשר הם לובשות רקמה ויזנו אחריהם... ושיחרימו חרם גדול בשופרות על כל מי שיבעול בת אל נכר והנמצא שיענש עונש גדול כי כבר ידעתם שקנאין פוגעין בו ודתו מסור בידכם להסיר מכשול גדול כזה כי בעונותינו הרבים כמה בנים ילדו שפחות מישראל. Cf. Baer, I, 164 § 6.

[32] Adret, I, 1219.

[33] Régné, 200, 206, 510, 1029, 1074, 2065, 2517; Baer, I, 171, p. 442. Cf. ibid., I, 179 §29; Adret, I, 1187; IV, 257; Asher, VIII, 10; XXXII, 7; *ZJ*, 80, end.

[34] *SeMaG*, Prohib. 112, no. 3, end.

[35] Baer, II, 125 §72; Asher, VIII, 10; Baer, I, 456; pp. 1037–8. See *Las Siete Partidas*, VII, 25, 10; Baer, II, 63 p. 48; Lindo, 101.

[36] Cf. Régné, 510, 515, 2517.

[37] Ibid., 200, 206, 510, 515.

[38] Cf. ibid., 200, 1029, 1053, 2517; Barfat, 425.

[39] Cf. *ZJ*, 91.

[40] Cf. Asher, XVIII, 13; *ZJ*, 80, end.

[41] Régné, 674.

[42] Barfat, 425; *ZL*, II, 3, 11 p. 107a; *REJ*, XII, 86. On complaint of the Jewish courtier Muça de Portella, Alfonso III ordered the *aljama* officials to expel the Jewish prostitutes from the *judería* (Regne, 1053).

[43] Ibid., 64, 585, 877.

[44] Baer, I, 134; Régné, 2455.

[45] See above, I, p. 130 ff.

[46] Asher, XIII, 4. The injured person in this instance declined to accept the fine and directed that it be paid to the educational fund of the community.

[47] *ZJ*, 36.

[48] Régné, 2261; cf. 1304, 1308, 2098, 2105–6.

[49] See above, I, ch. VII.

[50] Régné, 877, 1007–8, 1099, 1136, 1139, 1149–50; 1192, 1224 and 1234–5; 1238, 1414, 1737.

[51] Ibid., 174, 268, 307, 585, 644, 653.

[52] There are only a few instances of serious charges against a woman: poisoning of husband (ibid., 1902), and infanticide (ibid., 2497, 2506–7).

[53] Ibid., 1099 and 1149–50; 1192, 1224 and 1234–5; 1118–9, 1128, and 1143–4. Extremely notorious was the case developed in Régné, 1242–3, 1265, 1316, 1319, 1328–31 and 1358. Cf. 2455; Baer, I, 134.

[54] Régné, 2399, 2411.

[55] Ibid., 2399.

[56] Cf. Asher, XIX, 1: הוראה זו דומה לחוכא וטלולא בפני המון עם לומר רוב גנבי ישראל נינהו ודבר ידוע ומפורסם לכל שאינו כן . . . ודאי בימי חכמי הגמ' היו עיירות גדולות של ישראל ושכיח גנבי ביניהם הרבה, אבל האידנא לא.

[57] Such cases are few in number and not proved. Régné, 1873, 2518–20; Baer, I, pp. 207, 210.

[58] Adret, V, 243. קוצים מן הכרם . . .

[59] Asher, XLV, 3.

[60] Adret, VII, 445; Asher, LXVI, 8; LXXII, 1.

[61] Adret, II, 286 = VII, 501.

[62] Adret, II, 35; Asher, LXXXII, 2.

[63] Thus Adret, VII, 244: . . . האסור תקנת ותיקין ודאי חטא היתה ומי שבא להתיר פורץ גדר ועושה דמן של בחורים שחוק. כמה קרעים הלביש כמה ריחות הבאיש כמה כוכים יוצאים במחול משחקים ותמה אני האיך פשטה הוראה להתיר בכענין זה אפי' הסכימו כל הקהל בהיתר זה מעצמו נאסר.

[64] Asher, LXVI, 8.

[65] Adret, VII, 445.

[66] Ibid., VII, 244, 270. Cf. Barfat, 266 p. 144a; Baer, I, 179 §28, 304, 325.

[67] Adret, VII, 244, 270.

[68] Ibid., I, 755; III, 305; VII, 4; VIII, 252, 281; Asher, XI, 8, 10; Barfat, 281, 407, 432.

[69] Cf. Adret, IV, 120.

[70] Barfat, 281, 407.

[71] Ibid.

[72] Adret, VIII, 281.

[73] Asher, XI, 8. Cf. Régné, 634.

[74] Baer, I, 325.

[75] Adret, III, 305; VII, 445.

[76] Asher, XII, 6.

[77] Ibid., CI, 6.

[78] Baer, I, 179 §29.

[79] Ibid., I, p. 414, no. 594; p. 975.

[80] See above, I, 125; Barfat, 348; Baer, I, 137.

[81] See above, I, 138 ff.

[82] Cf. אביו שליח: אין אדם חצוף לשים אביו שליח: Adret, I, 1236 and Ḳid. 45a.

[83] Adret, IV, 56.

[84] Asher, XV, 5.

NOTES TO CHAPTER XII

COURTSHIP AND MARRIAGE

[1] Cf. below, pp. 24 ff.

[2] Alami, *Iggeret Musar*, 9, 11. Cf. Maim., *Responsa*, ed. Freimann, Jerusalem, 1934, 370.

[3] Adret, I, 549, 1219; III, 211 = VII, 502; cf. IV, 174, and below, pp. 25 f. Cf. ZJ, 81 p. 31a, where it is recorded that a man stated: "This marriage pleases me and what is good in my eyes appears good to my daughter," and the daughter, silent, stretched forth her hand and accepted the marriage token.

[4] Asher, XXXV, 1.

[5] Cf. below, pp. 22 f.

[6] Adret, I, 1219.

[7] Ibid., I, 549. See, however, Barfat, 193, for a more modern view of a mother's rights.

[8] Abot 5.21; cf. Ḳid. 29b–30a.

[9] Abot 5.21.

[10] Ḳid. 30b; Ket. 52b.

[11] Ḳid. 41a; also Maimonides, *M. T.*, *Hilkot Ishut*, IV, 19, to which might be added the emphatic statement of Rab Judah in the name of Abba Arika: "He who takes a wife for his son while he is under age, to him the words in Deut. 29.18 apply: למען ספות הרוה את הצמאה לא יאבה ד' סלוח לו," translated by Rashi in this connection to mean: "The father joining the moist and the dry, God will not pardon him." Sanh. 76b.

[12] Adret, IV, 174; similarly, Barfat, 198.

[13] Cf. note 44. Sanh. 76a: The verse "Profane not thy daughter to make her a harlot" (Lev. 19.29), according to R. Akiba, applies to one who delays the marriage of his marriageable daughter (המשהא בתו בוגרת) and this statement was amplified by Rab Kahana and motivated by Abaye to read: "What poor man is subtly wicked? He who delays the marriage of his marriageable daughter." איזהו עני רשע ערום זה המשהא בתו בוגרת. Cf. Pes. 113a. בתך בגרה שחרר עבדך ותן לה "Has thy daughter become of age? Set thy slave free and give him to her in marriage." Cf. also Ḳid. 29b–30a.

[14] Ḳid. 29b.

[15] Cf. Harkavy, *Zikron la-Rishonim, Responsen der Geonim*, no. 65; also *Hemdah Genuzah*, no. 162; cf. Abrahams, 166, note 1.

[16] Migash, 115; Adret, I, 789, 803 = 1181, 1147, 1203, 1219, 1236; IV, 169, 174, 207, 324; V, 246; VI, 69; VII, 258, 502; VIII, 14–5; Asher, XXXV, 5, 6, etc.; Nissim, 8; Barfat, 193. See *REJ*, XII, 86.

[17] See Barfat, 193.

[18] Adret, I, 803, 1181. See IV, 207: ומעשה היה בארצנו ונתחי להם בקולי ולולי שכבר עשו היו נמנעין "Such a case occurred in our country and I raised my voice in protest; and had they not already done so, they would have been prevented."

[19] Cf. Asher, XXXV, 5, 6; also Nissim, 8; *REJ*, XII, 86.

[20] Tosafot Ḳid. 41a, s. v. אסור לאדם שיקדש את בתו כשהיא קטנה.

[21] Cf. Isserles in *Shulḥan 'Aruk, Eben ha-'Ezer*, XXXVII, 8.

[22] Ḳid. 29b–30a.

[23] Tosefta Ḳid. 1.11; Ḳid. 29a.

[24] Ibid.

[25] Adret, I, 803.

[26] Barfat, 15.

[27] Asher, VIII, 8.

[28] Nissim, 32.

[29] Adret, I, 1219; III, 211.

[30] Ibid., I, 550, 1206; IV, 314; Asher, XXXV, 1.

[31] Ibid., XXXV, 4.

[32] Adret, I, 550, 1206.

[33] Ibid., I, 549; IV, 314; Asher, XXXV, 1. In Adret, I, 549, the validity of the marriage of a fatherless girl, twenty-five years old, was temporarily held up in court, although she had the sanction of her mother and brothers, only because there were a few opposing relatives. Ibn Adret's decision was that she had to respect the wishes of only those relatives upon whom she was dependent for support and who therefore were her guardians.

[34] Ibid., I, 1219.

[35] Talmudic etiquette is emphatic on this point. Ḳid. 12b: דרב מנגיד על דמקדש בשוקא... ועל דמקדש בלא שידוכי. The force of this statement was weakened considerably by another version which was current in Nehardea: בכולהו לא מנגיד רב אלא על דמקדש בביאה בלא שידוכי. About these two views mediaeval opinion ranged. Maimonides, *M.T.*, *Hilkot Ishut*, III, 22, and *Hilkot Issure Bi'ah*, XXI, 14, and Joseph Caro in *Shulḥan 'Aruk, Eben ha-'Ezer*, XXVI, 7, regarded a precipitate marriage without due preliminary arrangements as an offense punishable by the lash; Asher b. Jehiel, *Halakot*, Ḳid. 12b, and his son Jacob b. Asher, *Tur, Eben ha-'Ezer*, XXVI, 7, regarded it as an offense not corporally punishable. The division of legal opinion was purely academic; in practice the lash was not invoked. Cf. Isserles' glosses to *Shulḥan 'Aruk, Eben ha-'Ezer*, XXVI, 4: "I have never seen a person corporally punished for having betrothed a maiden without preliminary negotiations."

[36] This subject is treated fully in the works of Güdemann, Berliner and Abrahams.

[37] Thus Adret, I, 550, 1180 and 1236=VIII, 131; II, 35; III, 96, 210, 211=VII, 502; IV, 57, 108, 157, 294, 324; V, 246, 237=VIII, 135=VIII, 278; VI, 1; VII, 402; VIII, 273; Asher, XXXV, 2. The name *shadkan* appears in Barfat, 193, but this responsum deals with a German community.

[38] The responsa cited in the note above include all the cases where the *shadkan* might have been a factor, but his existence is not mentioned in any of them.

Thus Adret, II, 35; IV, 57, 108, 324, and VI, 1, are cases where disputes arose when one party withdrew from the marriage agreement. The *shadkan's* brokerage fee would surely have been mentioned under such circumstances. Only one responsum in our collection brings to light a typical marriage agreement through a person who performed the function of a *shadkan*, but this was an exceptional arrangement for which the precedents were not at all clear. But see ibid., II, 79, which deals with a brokerage firm consisting of four partners formally registered by the bailiff to perform the functions of brokers of commerce and matrimony, but it is not stated in the responsum that the partners were actually engaged as matrimonial brokers. Possibly, too, the question may have come from a foreign country. The name *shadkan* does not occur in any of the Spanish responsa, although it was current in the Hebrew literature of the German Jews as early as the twelfth century (cf. Abrahams, p. 170). Cf. R. Meir of Rothenburg, *Responsa*, ed. Prague, 498, 706, 952; ed. Lemberg, 308.

[39] Cf. Adret, IV, 57.

[40] Ibid., I, 1236=VIII, 131.

[41] Ibid., I, 1180. See Barfat, 260.

[42] Maimonides, 127; Duran, II, 39. The liturgy in the synagogue was modified on the Sabbaths preceding and following a wedding.

[43] Adret, III, 291.

[44] Ibid., II, 35; III, 210, 211; IV, 57, 157, etc.

[45] Ibid., II, 2; III, 212; V, 237.

[46] Ibid., III, 96, 212; V, 237; Asher, XXXV, 8, etc.

[47] Adret, II, 194.

[48] Ibid., III, 206, 210.

[49] Ibid., V, 237.

[50] Ḳid. 2b; Nid. 31b.

[51] Adret, V, 237.

[52] Ibid., I, 1180.

[53] Ibid., III, 210.

[54] Ibid., III, 212.

[55] Ibid., IV, 57, passim.

[56] Asher, XXXIV, 2, 3, 4. The following document is a typical engagement contract, though the bride, being fatherless, was represented by her brother and took a more active part in the proceedings than the woman was usually called upon to do.

We, the undersigned, testify that in our presence Reuben agreed with Simeon that Leah, the sister of the aforementioned Reuben, should be wedded to her fiancé, the said Simeon, according to the conditions enumerated below: the said Leah will present as dowry to her fiancé, Simeon, the house which will be hers together with the garden whose boundaries are described and the aforementioned Reuben, in the presence of us the witnesses and in the presence of his honored relatives and those of the affianced

Simeon, followed the legal formality of symbolical delivery (קנין) and declared his complete alienation of the aforementioned garden, which he transferred unreservedly to Simeon, his brother-in-law, and to his sister Leah, affianced to the latter. Then did Leah transfer by the method of acquisition, or symbolical delivery, to her fiancé the entire house and the garden, the boundaries of which were specified above as was customary in real estate gifts given in dowry, investing him with full authority to sell the garden at his pleasure, to take effect at once, without reserving for herself the right of protest at such times. She also pledged and bound herself to the aforementioned Simeon, her fiancé, to be wedded unto him according to the law of Moses and of Israel, without protest or hindrance on the Sabbath *Nahamu* to come.

Simeon, the fiancé, likewise consented and agreed to all the conditions enumerated above and, as is the custom, pledged himself to betroth and wed the aforementioned Leah at the time specified above according to the Law of Moses and of Israel, and to deliver unto her a marriage contract (*ketubah*) and the additional presents according to the custom that prevails here and to register the aforementioned house as part of his dowry to her. He also took a solemn oath, swearing that he would spend of his own capital 200 *sueldos* at the time of their wedding for the bride's necessary purchases.

And in our presence and with our understanding, the bride and the bridegroom swore that they would fulfill their promise and that neither of them should have the right to protest against or revoke any clause stipulated above and that either one should have the right to call upon and compel the other to fulfill the conditions of the agreement. Leah pledged herself in addition by legal symbol for two hundred *maravedís* (to be forfeited to Simeon, if she should break the agreement). It was furthermore agreed that the deeds were to be placed in the hands of a trustee who would deliver them to one party if the other defaulted.

Adret, III, 210.

[57] Ibid., I, 1180.
[58] Ibid., IV, 205.
[59] Ibid., III, 211.
[60] Ibid., IV, 57.
[61] Asher, XXXV, 2b.
[62] Adret, I, 1180; II, 35; III, 211; VII, 502; VIII, 135, etc.
[63] Ibid., II, 35; V, 237; Asher, XXXIV, 1.
[64] Adret, II, 35; III, 96; VIII, 135, etc.
[65] Ibid., I, 550; II, 89; III, 96, 210; IV, 267; Asher, XXXV, 8.
[66] Adret, I, 558, 1180, 1223; VIII, 135; Asher, XXXV, 2, 6, 7, 12.
[67] Adret, I, 1189, 1236; Asher, XXXV, 8.
[68] Adret, III, 96; cf. Asher, XXXV, 8.
[69] Ibid.

NOTES TO CHAPTER XIII

MARRIAGE CUSTOMS AND CEREMONIES

[1] Barfat, 260.

[2] Asher, CI, 5.

[3] Adret, II, 214; IV, 1; Barfat, 301.

[4] Adret, VIII, 283.

[5] Ibid., VII, 517.

[6] Ibid., III, 210.

[7] Ḳid. 12b; Maimonides, *M. T., Hilkot Ishut*, III, 21.

[8] Ḳid. 65a; Maimonides, *M. T., Hilkot Ishut*, IV, 6.

[9] Mishna Ḳid. 2. 1.

[10] Maimonides, *M. T., Hilkot Ishut*, X, 6.

[11] Mishna Ket. 4. 7; Ḳid. 6a; Maimonides, *M. T., Hilkot Ishut*, III, 6.

[12] Cf. Adret, I, 1186, 1241; IV, 273. According to I. H. Weiss, the ring was adopted as a specific symbol of betrothal during geonic times in opposition to the Karaites who insisted literally on the *mohar* mentioned in the Bible: *Dor Dor ve-Dorshav*, IV, 108.

[13] Adret, VIII, 126.

[14] Ibid., I, 551.

[15] Asher, LVIII, 4.

[16] Adret, VIII, 131.

[17] Asher, XXXV, 11.

[18] Adret, I, 1103.

[19] Ibid., I, 1234; VIII, 130; cf. ibid., I, 550, 774; IV, 322.

[20] Ibid., I, 773, 1227, 1241; Asher, LVIII, 4. Cf. Adret, I, 1193, 1210; IV, 286; Asher, XXXV, 11; *ZJ*, 82.

[21] Ibn Adret thus sums up a case where the parents wished to dissolve their daughter's marriage on technical grounds: "No leniency whatsoever can be shown in such cases. He who guardeth his soul should keep aloof from them. It is as dangerous as tampering with the pupil of one's eye."

[22] Ibid., I, 1234; VIII, 130–1: "Although there really was no legal marriage, it is best to be cautious, and therefore the woman ought to have a divorce. If, in the meantime, she was actually betrothed to another man, he too should give her a divorce. She may then remarry the second man, but not the first." Cf. Adret, I, 774. See Barfat, 232.

[23] Cf. Adret, I, 1209, 1210, end.

[24] Asher, LVIII, 4.

[25] Ibid., XXXV, 11; cf. Adret, IV, 322.

[26] Ibid., I, 550.

[27] Cf. above, I, 129.

[28] Adret, I, 551, 602. Such protective vows occur in Nissim, 27, 32.

[29] Adret, IV, 314. See ibid., I, 549: "A *takkanah* exists in all the communities

from Narbonne to Arles, Avignon and Alais, forbidding any man to betroth a
woman who has no parents, without the consent of her brothers and relatives."

[30] Ibid., I, 550; IV, 314; Barfat, 399.

[31] Adret, I, 1206; see Asher, XXXV, 1.

[32] Ibid.

[33] Adret, I, 550; Barfat, 399.

[34] Rabbi Menahem ha-Aruk of Salamanca caused the arrest of a man who
fooled a girl into a mock betrothal ceremony, on the ground that he had violated
the communal statute requiring the presence of ten persons at the marriage
ceremony. The man was given his freedom when he granted the "bride" a divorce.
But the story had an unhappy sequel, for he succeeded in annulling the divorce
and he fled without leaving any trace behind him. Sympathy for the tragic
plight of the innocent woman did not influence Barfat's strict interpretation of
the law. As a result she remained in the pitiful state of a deserted wife. Barfat, 232;
cf. Migash, 122.

[35] Adret, IV, 174; V, 237; Asher, XXXIV, 1, 3, 4. See Barfat, 82, where it is
stated that even when the *erusin* ceremony had been performed previously through
proxy, the rite is repeated, with benediction, at the wedding service under the
canopy, because the two ceremonies are always celebrated together. This was the
custom in Valencia and also in Barcelona: שהיו אומרים שכיון שנהגו לעולם
לקדש בשעת הנשואין וכו'.

[36] Cf. Asher, XXXVII, 1.

[37] This is indicated in two ways: first, by numerous cases involving the validity
of the marriage in which betrothal alone is clearly intended: viz., Adret, I, 551,
558, 565, 602, 706, 773, 774, 1179, 1180, 1186, 1193, 1226 (theoretical), 1227, 1234,
1236, 1241; IV, 273; VI, 1, 2, 3; Asher, XXXV, 2, 8, 11, 12, 13, 14; secondly, by
the cases reporting specific instances of persons who were married to one another
in betrothal but not conjugally: Alfasi, 234; Migash, 53, 122; Adret, I, 567, 568,
549, 789, 802, 808, 867, 1109, 1164, 1189, 1214, 1253; II, 108; IV, 205, 244, 304;
VI, 1; VII, 258; VIII, 120 (VIII, 137 = I, 1164), VIII, 140; Asher, XXXV, 4, 6;
XXXVII, 1; Nissim, 58; Barfat, 82, 260, 266; RaMaH, 255, 257. See Asher,
VIII, 7: ראובן ששהה עם אשתו יותר מעשרים שנה ולא ילדה והוא כדי לידע אם העכבה ממנו
לקח אשה אחרת בקידושין כמנהג הארץ הזאת ונתעברה ממנו ושוב נשאה והכניסה לחופה.

[33] See note 35, above.

[39] Cf. *REJ*, XII, 86.

[40] Migash, 53; Adret, IV, 244; Barfat, 82, 260, 266, 408.

[41] Lea's monumental work, *History of Sacerdotal Celibacy*, treats mainly of clerical
concubinage. The tolerant attitude of the Church is significantly reflected in the
case of the Abbot S. Pelayo de Antealtaria who in the year 1130 was convicted
of having kept no less than seventy concubines. He was deposed from office,
but a benefice in the abbey lands was considerately assigned for his support.
Lea, op. cit. (second edition), 308.

[42] The Council of Toledo in 400 expressed the early church attitude: "But if a
man has no wife, but a concubine instead of a wife, let him not be refused com-

munion; only let him be content to be united with one woman, whether wife or concubine." (Mansi, III, col. 1001, dist. XXXIV, *Is qui*). See Coulton, *Encyclopaedia Britannica*, s. v. Concubinage.

[43] Lea, op. cit., 319.

[44] Yer. Ket. 29d.

[45] Sanh. 21a.

[46] Barfat, 395, speaks of חשוקה in contrast to פלגש, the former being the mistress, who was ב''י קדושין ובלי כתובה.

[47] Asher, XXXII, 13; cf. Maimonides, 130. The Jewish court compelled the owner of a Moorish slave, who was his concubine, either to send her away or to free her and make her his wife. Similarly, Adret, V, 242.

[48] Asher, XXXII, 1; Barfat, 217.

[49] Asher, XXXII, 1.

[50] Ibid., XXXVII, 1.

[51] Ibid., XXXV, 10.

[52] Adret, V, 242.

[53] Ibid., IV, 314, etc.

[54] Maimonides, *M. T., Hilkot Melakim*, IV, 4.

[55] Adret, VIII, 284.

[56] Cf. ibid., I, 1205; IV, 314; Asher, XXXVII, 1; Barfat, 395.

[57] *ZL*, III, 1.2, p. 122b, end.

[58] Cf. Adret, I, 610, 1205; V, 242; Barfat, 395.

[59] Cf. note 57, above.

[60] Adret, IV, 314.

[61] Asher, VIII, 7; cf. Adret, IV, 314.

[62] Cf. Abrahams, op. cit., 207, note 2: "Reading the *ketubah* aloud to the bride was at first an Eastern Jewish custom," for which a fifteenth century authority is cited. Adret (I, 629), however, indicates that the custom was earlier and existed in Spain.

[63] Cf. Tobit, VII, 14. Its early Jewish origin is indicated in Tosefta Ket. 11. 9; B. M. 104a; also Ket. 10a and 82b, where the *ketubah* is referred to as existing long before Simeon b. Shetah. For striking resemblance, see Kaufmann, "Zur Geschichte der Ketubah," in *MGWJ*, LXI (1897), 213–21.

[64] R. Simeon b. Gamaliel regarded the *ketubah* of a virgin as being of biblical origin (Ket. 10a). Cf. standard text of a *ketubah* in Maimonides, *M. T., Hilkot Yib. ve-Hal.*, IV, 33: ... ויהיבנא ליכי מוהר בתוליכי כסף זוזי מאתן דחזו ליכי מדאוריתא Cf. Tosafot Ket. 10a; Tosafot Yeb. 89a.

[65] Mishna Ket. 5. 1.

[66] Adret, II, 330.

[67] B. M. 104b. In Tosefta Ket. 6 these items were included in the *ketubah*. They were properly the dowry and not to be confused with the *ketubah* itself. Maimonides, *M. T., Hilkot Ishut*, XXIII, 11.

[68] B. M. 104b.

[69] Adret, II, 330.

[70] Ibid., II, 149, 330.

[71] Ibid., I, 662; III, 443.

[72] Cf. ibid., I, 629.

[73] Mishna Ket. 7.6; Ket. 72. Maimonides, *M.T.*, *Hilkot Ishut*, XXIV, 11–2.

[74] Mishna Ket. 5. 1; Ket. 57a; Maimonides, *M. T.*, *Hilkot Ishut*, X, 7, 10.

[75] Mishna Ket. 5. 1.

[76] Adret, I, 634. The reason was that all documents had presumably been lost in the tumult or had been destroyed by the looting mobs. Cf. Adret, VII, 542, for an earlier responsum of Sherira in a similar case.

[77] Cf. ibid., IV, 46, where a man paid his wife the full amount of the *ketubah* in order to have her pay her own medical expenses but, when she recovered, he was not permitted to live with her unless he gave her a new *ketubah*. Cf. ibid., II, 58.

NOTES TO CHAPTER XIV

DOMESTIC LIFE

[1] Cf. above, pp. 20 ff.

[2] Adret, VIII, 14–15, 102–3 ff.

[3] Several of the more serious cases are indicated in Adret, I, 571 (Germany), 573, 1237.

[4] Ibid., IV, 72, 186; Nissim, 15.

[5] Cf. Adret, IV, 40.

[6] Cf. RaMaH, 267, also 253, 254; Adret, V, 264; Duran, II, 8.

[7] Alfasi, 235. This responsum may refer to Egypt rather than Spain. From Adret, V, 264, it appears that this was the established procedure during geonic times.

[8] Migash, 101; Adret, IV, 168; VIII, 102–3.

[9] Ibid., I, 692; cf. IV, 72.

[10] Ibid., I, 693.

[11] Ibid., VIII, 102; cf. IV, 168; Duran, II, 8; *ZJ*, 71.

[12] Cf. Alfasi, 119, 214, 217; Adret, I, 634; V, 162; Asher, XLV, 3, 4, 12, 15.

[13] Alfasi, 120, 185; Asher, XXXII, 11; XLIII, 6b; Nissim, 33, 42–3. Barfat, 314; ibid., II, 20, 26; Baer, I, 406.

[14] Adret, I, 597, 1252; Asher, XLV, 25; LI, 1, 4, 6; Barfat, 377–80.

[15] Alfasi, 118.

[16] Cf. ibid., 96, 131, 217, 228.

[17] Asher, XLIII, 13.

[18] Ibid., XLV, 28; XLVI, 2; Barfat, II, 10. The question was raised whether a *kohen* was permitted to live with his wife under a conditional divorce. Rabbi Asher replied in the affirmative (XLV, 23).

[19] Adret, VIII, 254.

[20] Ibid., V, 68; VIII, 272; cf. ibid., III, 313; *ZJ*, 71.

[21] Alfasi, 120.

[22] Ibid. Cf. Maimonides, 123.

[23] Nissim, 38. Compare, on the other hand, the heroic and pathetic story in Asher, VIII, 13. Contrast also Maimonides, *M.T.*, *Hilk. Ishut*, XIII, 19.

[24] Alfasi, 214. See Baer, I, 406.

[25] Ibid., 216.

[26] Ibid., 176.

[27] Jacobs, 148, 946, 1226, 1227; Régné, 113, 359; Baer, I, 249, 406, 452, also p. 414, n. 1.

[28] Ibn Adret pointed out the influence of Islamic custom on Maimonides' theoretical sanction of polygamy: אלא שהרמב'ם ז'ל מראה פנים להיתר שישא נשים רבות כמנהג ישמעאלים שעושין כן. Adret, IV, 314. Cf. ibid., I, 886; Asher, VIII, 7; XLIII, 6b; Nissim, 48; Barfat, 199, 208; also ibid., 15, end.

[29] Cf. Alfasi, 120, 151, 185, 188.

[30] Ibid., 188.

[31] Maimonides, *M. T.*, *Hilk. Ishut*, X, 13; cf. ibid., *Hilk. Melakim*, IV, 4. See Adret, IV, 314.

[32] See above, notes 13 and 28.

[33] Adret, I, 1205.

[34] Ibid., IV, 314.

[35] Thus Abba Mari wrote: ובהיותי בברצלונה לפני הרב מרי ר' שלמה בן אדרת זצ'ל נתלנלו הדברים ..., *REJ*, XII, 88.

[36] Adret, I, 1205.

[37] Barfat, 509–10.

[38] James I defied Jewish law and public opinion when he authorized Joseph de Grasse to marry a second wife in Montpellier and ordered the Jewish community not to interfere in the matter (Régné, 113).

[39] Migash, 129; Adret, I, 812; IV, 267, 280; Asher, VIII, 8; Barfat, II, 20, 26. Cf. Duran, I, 94.

[40] Maimonides, *Responsa* (ed. Freimann), no. 155.

[41] Ḳid. 12b.

[42] Adret, III, 446. See ibid., I, 886; Barfat, 199, 208.

[43] Asher, VIII, 7.

[44] *ZJ*, 89.

[45] Baer, I, 452.

[46] Ibid., I, pp. 343, 653, 712. See above, note 27.

[47] Barfat, I, 509.

[48] The second marriage was treated at times as a trial marriage. The woman was betrothed as a concubine and was married with full legal status only after she became pregnant. Asher, VIII, 7. See also Adret, IV, 314. Not so, ibid., I, 886; Barfat, 199, 208. Cf. Migash, 149–50.

[49] Maimonides, *M. T.*, *Hilk. Ishut*, XIV, 3.

[50] Adret, IV, 256.

[51] Asher, XXV, 7–10.

[52] Bek. 1.7. The change of attitude is recorded by Rami b. Hama in Yeb. 39b. Cf. statement of Abba Saul: "He who marries his brother's widow for the sake of her beauty or out of desire to have her as wife or for any ulterior motive (other than the duty to his brother) is regarded as one who committed incest, and I am almost ready to declare the child of such a union illegitimate" (ibid.). Cf. a similar opinion of Bar Kappara in Yeb. 109a. See comments of Rashi and Tosafot on the statement of Rab, אין כופין, Yeb. 39b.

[53] Migash, 45 (theoretical), 139; Adret, I, 812, 886, 1165, 1202, 1240; IV, 36, 38, 267, 280; Duran, II, 158, 270. Cf. Alfasi, 137; Asher, LII, 1, 8; Barfat, 209, 474; II, 4; Duran, I, 34; III, 25, 285–6.

[54] See the array of authorities cited in Barfat, 209, by a fifteen-year-old youth in defense of his right to marry the nineteen-year-old widow of his brother. He quoted the following authorities: *She'eltot* of R. Ahai, geonic responsa, Alfasi, Maimonides, R. Isaac b. Abraham, R. Samuel, R. Abraham b. David, various Tosafists, R. Meir ha-Levi and "all sages of the Provence and Catalonia." These, he thought, could be depended upon to outweigh the authority of Rashi, R. Tam, R. Moses of Coucy: Barfat, 209; cf. Ibn Migash, 139; cf. also Barfat, 1.

[55] Adret, I, 1169, 1240; IV, 36, VII, 439. Asher, LII, 1, 8; Nissim, 60; Barfat, 1, 209; cf. Adret, I, 802; Nissim, 21.

[56] This feeling of distrust was expressed in an early Mishna, Bek. 1. 7, and it colored the entire discussion of the subject in the codes as well as the responsa. Cf. Barfat, 209. See note 52, above.

[57] Yebamot 4.4; Maimonides, *M. T. Hilk. Nahalot*, III, 7.

[58] Adret, I, 1165, is typical.

[59] See note 55, above.

[60] Adret, I, 1165; VII, 421; Nissim, 61.

[61] Barfat, 209.

[62] Tosafot, Yeb. 39b; Ket. 64a.

[63] Barfat, 1. On the question of *Yibbum* vs. *halizah*, see responsum in Poznanski, *Babyl. Geonim im nachgaonäischen Zeitalter*, 54.

[64] Adret, IV, 36.

[65] Ibid.; Asher, LII, 1.

[66] This procedure was well known in talmudic times and was followed in the later Middle Ages also. Cf. Adret, I, 731, 1242; VII, 438, etc.

[67] Alfasi, 103.

[68] Adret, IV, 257; similarly in Avignon, ibid., IV, 186.

[69] Nissim, 38.

[70] Adret, I, 1237; VIII, 133.

[71] Nissim, 38.

[72] Ned. 11.12; Ket. 5. 6, 9; 7. 2–5, 9; Ket. 77a.

[73] Ibid. See Duran, II, 8. Cf. Adret, I, 693.

[74] Ket. 5.7. Fine distinctions in theory and legal consequences were drawn between the woman who rebelled out of willful stubbornness (בעינא ליה ומצערנא ליה) and one whose attitude was caused by an uncontrollable revulsion (מאוס עלי).

See Adret, I, 1192; VI, 72–3; VIII, 138; Asher, XLVIII, 8; Epstein, op. cit., 145–8.

[75] Adret, VI, 72.

[76] For the literature, see Epstein, 147 n. 16. Cf. Adret, I, 1235; VI, 72.

[77] Alfasi to Ket., 63–4; Adret, I, 1235; V, 95–6.

[78] Maimonides, *M. T.*, *Hilk. Ishut*, XIV, 8.

[79] Adret, I, 1235.

[80] Asher, XLIII, 8.

[81] Idem, Halakot, Ket. 5. 35.

[82] Asher, XVII, 6; XLIII, 9.

[83] Ibid. Cf. Adret, V, 95–6. Cf. Rabbenu Tam, *Sefer ha-Yashar*, no. 24.

[84] Asher, XLIII, 6.

[85] In the responsa of R. Nissim Gerundi, the question occurs once, but his decision is entirely in harmony with Ibn Adret's views and is, in fact, based on them (Nissim, 13).

[86] Giṭ. 90b.

[87] Nissim, 17.

[88] Cf. above, pp. 4 ff.

[89] Adret, II, 382; IV, 46, 72; VII, 519; Asher, VIII, 7.

[90] Adret, IV, 154. See ibid., II, 286; IV, 214.

[91] Ibid., VII, 57, 415. See also *Tur, Eben ha-'Ezer*, 66–89.

[92] Ket. 47b.

[93] Ibid. The old talmudic distinction which divided the wife's property into two categories was adhered to: I. נכסי צאן ברזל "The property of iron sheep" referring to the property which she brought with her as dowry, which was therefore itemized in the *ketubah*, and for which the husband declared himself responsible (hence the name: indestructible as iron and profit-yielding to the husband like sheep that grow wool); II. נכסי מלוג "The property of plucking" referring to property acquired by the wife subsequent to the betrothal, from which the husband "plucked" the fruit without being responsible for the principal. Ned. 88a. Cf. Adret, II, 390, 395; V, 83; VIII, 106.

[94] Ibid., II, 390.

[95] Ibid., I, 760. Cf. ibid., II, 395.

[96] Alfasi, 248.

[97] Adret, V, 57; Asher, XIII, 11; XXXIX, 8.

[98] Barfat, 107. Cf. Adret, I, 11; II, 395; Asher, CVI, 4; ZJ, 72. The question was therefore seriously raised: "What right have Jewish women to give money to charity without the knowledge of their husbands?" (Adret, V, 57).

[99] Alfasi, 52.

[100] Adret, I, 1103; V, 77.

[101] Ibid., I, 923.

[102] Ket. 48a. See Adret, VII, 57.

NOTES TO CHAPTER XV

SCHOOLS, CURRICULA AND EDUCATIONAL IDEALS

[1] Kayserling, "Das Castilianische Gemeinde-Statut," in *Jahrbuch für die Geschichte der Juden und des Judenthums*, IV, 265–334; Fernandez y Gonzalez, *Ordenamiento formado por los procuradores des las aljamas hebreas . . . en Valladolid, el año 1432.* See *REJ*, XIII, 187 ff.; Baer, II, 287; Finkelstein, op. cit., 348 ff.

[2] Ps. 118.20.

[3] Abot 1.2.

[4] Cf. Pe'ah 1. 1; Soṭah 22a; Ḳid. 30a; Sanh. 17b; 'Ab. Zarah 19a–b. See Barfat, 285; *ZL*, 73; Duran, III, 153.

[5] Cf. Sanh. 17b; Shab. 119b; B. B. 21a. When the Jews of Toledo were aroused by the proposal of their authorities to sell a scroll of the Law in order to repair the synagogue, R. Isaac Barfat, upholding the local rabbi, declared that even with the sanction of the entire community a scroll of the Law could not be sold unless the proceeds were needed for the support of students or for the marriage settlements of poor orphans: Barfat, 285; see also Adret, III, 291.

[6] *ZL*, 73a: מושיבין מלמדי תינוקות בכל עיר ועיר שאין מצוה גדולה כמותה. Duran, III, 153: הצבור חייבים להושיב מלמדי תנוקות ביניהם, מתקנת יהושע בן נמלא. Cf. Sanh. 17b; Soṭah 22a; Ḳid. 30a.

[7] Yer. Ket. 8, end; B. B. 21a.

[8] Adret, II, 1, 111; III, 399; VIII, 245; Asher, III, 12; XXXVI, 1. Cf. Barfat, 37, 204.

[9] Margoliouth, in *JQR*, XI (1899), 539, with facsimile facing p. 533; Maim., 384.

[10] Ibid., 182.

[11] Adret, III, 291.

[12] RaMaH, 241.

[13] See below p. 68. Cf. Benjamin of Tudela, *Itinerary*, ed. Asher, 4.

[14] See Duran, I, 64; cf. Ḳid. 29a; Ber. 21b; B. B. 21a.

[15] Adret, I, 873, 1042; VIII, 1; cf. ibid., I, 1157. The father was liable for the payment of his son's tuition even if the teacher did not obtain his consent in advance: thus, David ibn Yahyah quoting Ibn Adret. See Marx, in *HUCA*, I, 623. Cf. Adret, VII, 516.

[16] Ibid., I, 645, 873; V, 229; Asher, CIV, 4.

[17] Adret, I, 386, 669, 1157; III, 291; V, 249; Duran, I, 142. See also letter of David Kimhi to Judah Alfakar: ביתנו פתוח לרוחה, לכל עובר אורח מבקש מנוחה, יניעים בתורה בימים ובלילות, מפרנסי עניים בצנעה, עושי צדקה בכל עת ובכל שעה, גם יש בינינו מקדישי ספרים, לבני עניים החכרים, ונותני שכר הלימוד, במקרא ובתלמוד. *Kobez*, III, 3d. Cf. Benjamin of Tudela, op. cit., 4.

[18] Adret, I, 1157.

[19] Ibid., I, 386; see *He-Haluz*, II, 61.

[20] Nissim, I, 75. The *kahal* of Monzon had a *Hebrat Talmud Torah* as well as

a *Hebrat Kebarim*. The possessions of both societies, together with the synagogue, were converted to the use of the Church in 1414, when the wholesale conversion of the Jewish inhabitants of the city took place. Baer, *Studien*, 149; idem, I, 824.

[21] Nissim, 75: והנה בעיר חמש חבורות רשומות ואלו הן: תלמוד תורה, וחולים, ומאור, וצדקה, וקברים.

[22] Baer, II, 287, p. 282: Kayserling, loc. cit., 294–5; Finkelstein, op. cit., 350–1.

[23] Cf. B. B. 21a. See Finkelstein, 354, n. 2.

[24] In the North African communities, where the Spanish refugees fled for shelter, the community school prevailed. The teacher was the employee of the *kahal* at a fixed salary and had no concern with the tuition fees of the pupils, which were collected by the communal officials. Duran, I, 64; III, 109.

[25] Shortly before Sukkot, Halav threatened to leave the community of Bersak, where he served as teacher and cantor, if the debt of eight doubloons, which some persons owed him in connection with his duties, were not paid by the end of the holiday season. Later, he was persuaded to grant his debtors one month's grace, but he stipulated that he was to receive his full salary and reserve the right to exclude from the class the students whose fees were in arrears: Barfat, 175; Duran, I, 64.

[26] Barfat, 175. This responsum belongs to the period of Barfat's activity in North Africa, but the principle which he thus enunciated is general in its application. Duran disagreed with Barfat and in an independent responsum upheld Halav's action and strongly censured the parents of Halav's pupils: Duran, I, 64.

[27] Adret, I, 1042; VIII, 1: כי למוד החכמה אינה כשאר מלאכות.

[28] Duran, I, 145. He applied the same reasoning to medical fees.

[29] Shab. 119b; Ḳid. 29–30; cf. Duran, I, 2; III, 109, 153. See the eloquent plea in *ZL*, 73a–b: בדורות הללו רפו ידינו מדברי תורה ואין משגיח על כי אבדה חכמת חכמינו ובינת נבונינו. ומי שנותן ללמד את בנו בשבוע זהב אחד כסבור הוא שהרבה מתנות והוציא הוצאות ולא ידעו ולא יבינו מעלות התורה.

[30] Cf. Alfasi, 223; note 31, below.

[31] An interesting illustration is afforded in Adret, III, 319. Two men entered into an agreement that one was to teach the other three times a week and was in turn to be supplied by him with all his wants. They vowed that whoever failed to keep the agreement was to abstain from meat and wine. The studies proved too arduous, however, for the eager student and, rather than continue under the mental strain, he parted from his teacher and followed the ascetic course prescribed in the vow. But this undermined his health, and the local rabbi insisted on the absolution of the vow. Much against his will, he submitted to the rabbi's dictation, but he could not regain peace of mind until he engaged to fast twice weekly for a period of six months. Another, more poignant case, is cited in Asher, VIII, 13. See below, pp. 176 ff. Cf. Duran, II, 52: ובכל זאת עלי דעתי לא זחה ועל פני שמש הכניעה זרחה ומבית ספר לא משתי ואם מצאתי לי רב עדין אותו ששתי. That asceticism was opposed to the spirit and law of Judaism was also the contention of Ibn Migash, 186. See also Jacob Anatoli, *Malmad ha-Talmidim*, 127.

[32] Duran, III, 109. Cf. *ZL*, 74a.

[33] Ibid., 73a: כשמתחיל בנו לדבר מלמדו תורה צוה לנו משה וגו' ופסוק ראשון של קריאת שמע.

[34] Ibid., 73a–b: וכשהוא כבן שש מוליכו אצל מלמדי תינוקות.

[35] Cf. Barfat, 309. Also below, n. 39.

[36] Duran, I, 2.

[37] Ibid.

[38] Barfat, 309; cf. Profiat Duran, *Ma'aseh Efod* (ed. Friedlander and Kohn), 20.

[39] Barfat, 309. At the age of twelve (according to Ibn Daud) or fourteen (according to Meiri) Joseph ibn Migash joined the academy in Lucena which was then established by Alfasi (Neubauer, *M.J.C.*, I, 76; II, 228). Yedaya Bedersi (see below, pp. 134 ff.) entered the academy of Rabbi Meshullam of Béziers at fifteen years of age (*JQR*, VIII (1896), 415).

[40] Barfat, 309.

[41] Compare the lines of the well-known wedding poem which Joseph Ezobi (Perpignan, 13th century) wrote in honor of his son: "But askest thou in what to set thy lore? In grammar much, but in Talmud more, Alfasi, Maimonides, Midrash now and then" (tr. by Friedman in *JQR*, VIII (1896), 537). The popularity of this poem is attested by its double translation into Latin by Reuchlin (Tübingen, 1512–14) and by Mercier (Paris, 1561).

[42] Barfat, 35, 326.

[43] Ibid.

[44] This subject forms the theme of M. Güdemann, *Das jüdische Unterrichtswesen während der spanisch-arabischen Periode.*

[45] See H. Wolfson in *Hebrew Union College Jubilee Volume*, 263 ff.

[46] Güdemann, op. cit., 147 ff.

[47] Ibid., 30. Abrahams, *Hebrew Ethical Wills*, I, 59, 68, ff. Cf. Joseph Ezobi, *Ka'arat Kesef*, tr. by Friedman, in *JQR*, VIII (1896), 537: "For in his penmanship man stands revealed."

[48] "Latin was dreaded and feared as the language of those who destroyed the Temple, who brought low God's nation and dragged them into slavery and contempt, who treated them as the murderers of God; the language in which the Vulgate, fitted to Christian dogma, was aligned against Jewish tradition and its conception of the Bible; a language in which the most atrocious decrees were issued." It was variously designated as Roman, Christian, ecclesiastic and unholy: לשון רומי, לשון נוצרי, לשון גלחות, לשון טומאה. Steinschneider, *Hebr. Uebersetzungen*, 461–2.

[49] Anatoli, op. cit., Introduction.

[50] Güdemann, op. cit., 147 ff.; *MGWJ*, XXXVII, 364.

[51] See below, pp. 118 ff.

[52] Hillel of Verona (1220–95) who pursued talmudic studies at the academy of R. Jonah Gerundi in Spain also studied medicine at the University of Montpellier. Leon Joseph, end of the fourteenth century, likewise studied at the same University (Steinschneider, op. cit., 795). Abraham Zacuto, latter half of fifteenth century,

attended the University of Salamanca. See Francisco Cantera Burgos, *Abraham Zacut* (Madrid).

[53] In "An Introduction to the Arabic Literature of the Jews," *JQR*, XIII (1900–01), 93 ff., Steinschneider stated: "...we find Jews as pupils and teachers in public institutions and lectures [in Mohammedan countries]. Certainly it was but an exception caused by personal fanaticism, when Jews and Christians were not admitted to [such] lectures." Nevertheless, he strangely proceeded to prove the exception rather than the rule. Moreover, he practically withdrew half his statement when in a later work he wrote categorically: *Unter den mir bekannten arabischen Juden findet sich kein officieller Schullehrer.* Idem, *A.L.J.*, p. xvii.

[54] Idem, *Jewish Lit.*, 185.

[55] Jean Astruc, *Mémoires pour servir à l'Histoire de la Faculté de Médecine de Montpellier*, 168.

[56] See Gross, *Gallia Judaica*, 332.

[57] Villanueva, *Viage literario á las Iglesias de España*, XVI, appendix VI, 231, ... *vel ludos facere inhonestos, vel alias velati incedere cum habitu Judearum vel Sarracenarum in magnum opprobrium eorundem*... For similar provision of the University of Perpignan, see R. S. Rait, *Life in Mediaeval Universities*, 38.

[58] M. Kayserling, *Christopher Columbus*, 46–7 and notes.

[59] Döllinger, "Die Juden in Europa," in *Akademische Vorträge*, Nördlingen, 1890, I.

[60] See above, note 52; Steinschneider, *Hebr. Uebersetzungen*, 795.

[61] This was classically illustrated in Maimonides' teaching of mathematics, astronomy, philosophy and theology to his favored and famed pupil, Joseph ibn Aknin: Maimon., *Guide to the Perplexed*, ed. Friedlander, Introd.; Munk, *Notice sur Jos. b. Jehouda*, 36. See Graetz (Hebrew tr.), IV, 373, n. 1. Jacob Anatoli studied mathematics and philosophy under the guidance of his father-in-law, Samuel ibn Tibbon: *Malmad ha-Talmidim*, Introd.

[62] Steinschneider, *JQR*, XIII (1901), 296; Joseph Ezobi, loc. cit.: בחר פי סופרים, לא פי ספרים: "To teachers, not to books, entrust thy mind. Thy soul with living words, not dead e'er bind." Cf. Ket. 111a: אף על פי שהכם גדול אתה אינו דומה לומד מעצמו ללומד מרבו.

[63] This was the reason assigned for the Hebrew translation of Hasdai Crescas' Spanish polemical work. See Graetz, VIII, 164, n. 3.

[64] Steinschneider, *Hebr. Uebersetzungen*, p. xx.

[65] Cf. Barfat, 334, 358.

[66] Adret, I, 1042; VIII, 1; Barfat, 175, 287. Cf. ZL, 73b.

[67] Adret, I, 386. Cf. Neubauer, *M. J. C.*, I, 68.

[68] Adret, II, 314.

[69] Schechter and Taylor, *Ben Sirah*, LI, 23, 32.

[70] Asher, V, 1. This responsum also describes a school building (*bet ha-midrash*) which was constructed from public funds. It consisted of two stories, one used as a lecture hall and the other for classrooms.

[71] Adret, V, 222: עליה הסמוכה לבה'כ שקורין לה מדרש.

[72] Neubauer, *M. J. C.*, I, 68.

[73] Ibn Daud did not apply the term *yeshibah* to the school of Cordova. He reserved this name for the official academies of Babylonia.

[74] See Meiri, *Bet ha-Behirah*. This suggested to Meiri his fanciful explanation of the title גאון, which numerically equals sixty and represents symbolically the sixty tractates of the Talmud which used to be completed in a cycle only in the geonic academies. According to an old responsum, quoted by R. Judah b. Barzilai (11th to 12th century), the popular tractate Nedarim had not been studied in the academy (of Barcelona?) for a hundred years (ibid.).

[75] Barfat, 375: לולי ד' צבאות הותיר לנו שריד דָבָר אחד לדור הוא מורנו הרב הנדול ר' נסים נ'ר היה כאחד מהם לדעת טוב טעם ודעת בקי בשלשה סדרים ודמו ליה כמאן דמנחי בכיסתיה. Immediately preceding this passage, Barfat described, with unreserved praise, the erudition of his teachers, whose wide learning he contrasted evidently with the more limited knowledge of his rabbinical contemporaries. אבל למדוני מנעורי גאוני עולם מגדילי תורה עמם עז ותושיה מלכים ימלוכו קטנם עבה מסתני כל יודעי דת ודין השרים והסגנים והפחוות נקראו רבנים לא מפני עיון הלכה בתוספות ובקיאות במסכת אחת או בשתים לבד ... ומן או חדלו נאספו ממנו בחטאינו נשאר העולם שומם ונלמוד ... Cf. Migash, 114; Barfat, 44. Cf. citations from Judah b. Samuel b. Abbas' *Ya'ir Netib* in Güdemann, op. cit., 147.

[76] Hasdai Solomon, rabbi in Tudela, asked Barfat to send him his novellae on the treatise which he was teaching that season. Barfat, 373.

[77] Asher, LI, 2b; Neubauer, *M. J. C.*, I, 106.

[78] *ZL*, 16.

[79] Ibid.

[80] Barfat, 262. See ibid., 375–6. Rabbi Isaac de Leon's method of study was described by his pupil, Samuel Sedillo, in his methodology, *Kelale Shemuel*, fol. 3a–d, cited by Marx, in *JQR*, XX (1908), 260, n. 15.

[81] *Kobez*, III, 30c. In his letter to Aknin, Maimonides writes: ואפילו לא יהיה לי בזמני זה זולתך די לי. See Introduction to *Moreh Nebukim*, Hebrew translation: ועוררתני פרידתך לחבר המאמר הזה אשר חברתיו לך ולדומים לך ואם הם מעט ...

[82] Nahmanides' *Commentary on Pent.*, Appendix; cf. ibid., Gen. 35.20.

[83] Palquera, *Ha-Mebakesh*, ed. Amsterdam, 47b; Güdemann, op. cit., 157. Cf. Solomon Gandz, "Studies in Hebrew Mathematics and Astronomy," *Proceedings of the American Academy for Jewish Research*, IX, 5–7.

[84] See Introduction to *Or Adonai*.

[85] Barfat, 290. Cf. ibid., 372, 374, 380, 395. Cf. Wolfson, *Crescas' Critique*, 17, 29.

[86] Ibid., 297; cf. 447.

[87] Cf. Duran's characterization of Abraham ibn Ezra: ואף על פי שהחכם ז'ל לא היה רב בקי בדינין אבל כשר היה לעדות ומעדותו למדנו ..., Duran, I, 51. Shem Tob Shaprut (see Graetz, VIII, 21 f., n. 3), author of *Eben Bohen*, an important book on Christianity, and also author of various manuscript commentaries on Ibn Ezra's works, was addressed by Barfat simply as החבר הנבון, החבר or without any title: Barfat, 210, 226, 515.

[88] See below, pp. 118 ff.

[89] See Barfat, 297, 371, 373, 425.

[90] Schechter's "Jewish Boswell," in *Studies in Judaism*, I, 142–6, had many kindred spirits in Spain. Cf. Barfat, 375, 376, 377.

[91] Cf. Abot 1.15; Ber. 35b.

[92] Abot 2.2.

[93] Asher, XV, 8.

[94] Ibid. Cf., Abot 3.5.

[95] Asher, XV, 8. See Duran, II, 142–6. The scholar's exemption from taxes was ostensibly based on the instruction of Artaxerxes: "It shall not be lawful to impose tribute, impost or toll upon them" (Ezra 7.24. See B. B. 8a. Cf. also ibid., 22a). Maimonides cited a decision of Ibn Migash, exempting the owner of vast estates from taxes amounting to thousands of gold *sueldos*, because of his rank as *talmid hakam*, Commentary to Abot 4.5, end. Jonathan b. Jacob claimed exemption from taxes as a *talmid hakam* and was sustained: RaMaH, 248.

[96] Ḳid. 32b. Cf. Adret, II, 291.

[97] M. Ḳ. 17a. The ban was the lighter form of *niddui*, as distinguished from the more drastic *herem*. (Cf. above, I, 56; Barfat, 212). This right was not conferred upon the men whom the king appointed as rabbis if they did not have the personal qualifications of a *talmid hakam*.

[98] Yer. B. Ḳ. 7.6; Adret, II, 291; Barfat, 220.

[99] Adret, I, 460.

[100] Cf. ibid., II, 291; Asher, XV, 9; Barfat, 216, 220.

[101] Ibid.

[102] Baer, I, 288, 378.

[103] Ibid., I, 288 §1.

[104] Ibid., §2.

[105] Asher, XV, 7.

[106] Maimonides, M. T., Hilk. Talmud Torah, VII, 13.

[107] Maim., 7. Similarly, Adret, II, 291.

[108] Barfat, 124.

[109] Solomon ibn Verga, *Shevet Yehudah*, ed. Wiener, 113; Abraham Zacuto, *Sefer Yuhasin*, ed. Filipowski, 220b; Graetz, VI, 323.

[110] Adret, II, 291.

[111] Barfat, 374.

[112] Ibid., 376, 380. See Graetz, VIII, 400–1. To escape this fate was the motive of Rabbi Asher b. Jehiel's flight from Germany, which had such important consequence in the subsequent history of Spanish Jewry.

[113] Barfat, 376. See also ibid., 380.

[114] Adret, VIII, 1. Cf. Barfat, 287. For early classic opinion, see Abot 4.5; Suk. 49a. Abba Mari eloquently expressed this sentiment when he learned of the death of Ibn Adret and paid him this tribute: "Not of thy free will hast thou withdrawn on high. For well do we know how thy precious soul delighted in bringing light to the eyes of the disciples. And for this end, thou didst toil and labor." *Israel. Letterbode*, IV, 75.

[115] Thus Joseph ibn Nagdela was not only patron of learning, but rector of the academy (*He-Haluz*, II, 61).

[116] Cf. Barfat, 192, 252, 287, 378, 445.

[117] Barfat, 377, 378, 379. Even as a transient, the *talmid hakam* exercised influence. Thus, when Hasdai Crescas tarried in Fraga on his way to Castile, he proposed certain changes in the liturgical customs of the community. This time his advice was not heeded. Thereupon, Crescas resolved שבשום מקום שלא מנהגם לבטל יתעצם שלא מוסרם מצד אלא עליהם הקפה ידו תהיה. Ibid., 37. Cf. Meiri, *Magen Abot* (ed. Last, London, 1909), Introduction, especially p. 11.

[118] Thus Barfat and R. Joseph b. David: Barfat, 396–7; R. Solomon Zarfati and En Vidal Ephraim, ibid., 375. Cf. ibid., 179.

[119] Cf. Neubauer, *M. J. C.*, I, 68.

[120] Cf. Barfat's recommendation of a candidate for the rabbinate of Calatayud: יש בו די ורב לדון ולהורות וללמד לתלמידים ולדרוש ולדבר צחות בין בכתב בין במבטא. Barfat, 287. Cf. ibid., 377; also *ZL*, 74b.

[121] See Adret, I, 551; II, 119; III, 3; V, 150. Cf. Barfat, 392, end: ומשרבו הדיינין שאינן מומחין. See Duran, I, 158–62.

[122] Barfat, 508. This was not, however, general even in the time of Barfat.

[123] Ibid., 389. Cf. Migash, 114; Barfat, 44, 202.

[124] See ibid., 227, 381, 393, 494. At times, when the government withheld civil jurisdiction from the Jewish courts, the rabbis instructed the municipal judges in matters of Jewish law. והרב ר' ישראל כתב בפירוש אבות כנגד דברי הרמב"ם דברים נכונים מורים התר למקבלי פרס להורות לשופטי העיירות דרך ילכו במשפטים ולהורות את בני ישראל באיסור והתר :*ZL*, 74b.

[125] Cf. Barfat, 506, 508.

[126] Cf. above, I, 49. Ibn Adret, R. Asher and Isaac Barfat warned their colleagues not to render a written opinion in any case which did not appear before them officially, because shrewd litigants would use the rabbi's opinion to impress the local *Bet Din* in their favor. Adret, III, 98; V, 183 end; VI, 69; Nissim, 75; Barfat 5, 209, 228 end, 370.

[127] Ibid., 399.

[128] Ibid., 382.

[129] Compare Maimonides' commentary to Abot 4.5 and Duran, I, 142–6.

[130] See Nedarim 36b-37a. Cf. also *Mek.*, Wayassa, III: ר' יהושע אומר שונה אדם שתי הלכות בשחרית ושתי הלכות בערבית ועוסק במלאכתו כל היום מעלין עליו כאלו קיים כל התורה כולה.

[131] Cf. Ber. 35b: אמר ליה רבא לרבנן במטותא מיניכו ביומי ניסן וביומי תשרי לא תתחזו קמאי כי היכי דלא תטרדו במזונייכו כולא שתא.

[132] See Yoma 35b; Ber. 17b, 35b; Ket. 105a; B. B. 22a. Cf. Abot 2.2; 4.10; 5. 23.

[133] See above, I, 102.

[134] B. B. 22a.

[135] Ber. 34b; Pes. 53b.

[136] Abot 4.5.

[137] המשונעים המבוהלים.

[138] Maimonides, commentary to Abot 4.5.

[139] Abrahams and Yellin, *Maimonides*, 144–5. See ibid., pp. 216–7.

[140] Güdemann, op. cit., 47. Cf. *Testament of Judah b. Asher*, ed. Schechter, (Pressburg, 1885), 13, 16; Abrahams, *Hebrew Ethical Wills*, II, 180 ff. The other famous son of R. Asher, Jacob, endured poverty all his life: *Tur Orah Hayyim*, §242. See his epitaph in Luzzatto, *Abne Zikaron*, no. 7. Barfat, 376.

[141] Schechter, *Studies in Judaism*, First Series, 192.

[142] Cf. *ZL*, 73b: אע״פ שתורה שבעל פה אין מלמדין אותה בשכר, טרוב הצרות ועול המס. Again, ibid., 74b: כי לדעתי לא היה היום והעבורות נהגו ללמדה בשכר כדי להתפרנס. מרביץ תורה ומורה הוראה לרבים ובפרט בכל ארץ ספרד.

[143] Rabbi Menahem ibn Zerah quotes with approval a commentary on Abot by R. Israel which opposed Maimonides' views on this subject (*ZL*, 74b). Duran, I, 142–6 is a carefully prepared reply to Maimonides' contentions of two and a half centuries earlier. Duran, *Magen Abot* (ed. Jellinek), 64, is a defense of his own practice.

[144] Contrast Graetz, *Geschichte*, VIII, 101. Cf. Schechter, op. cit., 12–3. See Barfat, 192, 252 end, 287.

[145] A more modern example of the same inner conflict is revealed in the life of Moses Sofer. See *Hatam Sofer, Hoshen Mishpat*, 164.

[146] The phrase והעמיד תלמידים הרבה (cf. Abot 1.1) was applied to almost every teacher of fame in the mediaeval Hebrew chronicles. Cf. Neubauer, *M. J. C.*, I, 74, 75, 77, 107; II, 228, 232, 240 (*Bet ha-Behirah*); *ZL*, 242, 243. In Monosque (מניאשקה, or מנואשקה) the rabbi presided over an assembly of twenty-two senior students; but it was a school of no special account. Adret, I, 460.

[147] Cf. Neubauer, *M. J. C.*, I, 68; Adret, I, 395; Asher, LI, 2b; *ZL*, 16; Barfat, 290, 375–6; Abraham b. Solomon, *Sefer ha-Kabbalah*, in *M. J. C.*, I, 106. Of course, Spanish students also migrated to French and German *yeshibot*. Cf. *Ma'aseh Efod*, Introduction; Meiri, *Magen Abot*, 11, 14.

[148] Asher, LI, 2b.

[149] Though a native of Russia, he is designated אשכנזי.

[150] Gen. 46.30.

[151] Barfat, 375, 376.

[152] Ibid. Cf. 373: כי שערי התירוצין לבעלי השכל לא נעלו וכו'.

[153] Ibid., 376: כי מצרפת תצא תורה ודבר ד' מאשכנז... ומבעלדיהם היה תלמוד כדברי הספר החתום. Cf. Adret, I, 724; III, 105.

[154] Bahya ibn Pakudah, *Hobot ha-Lebabot*, ed. Stern, Introd., p. 20: ושאינני בקי. See also בצחות לשון ערבי אשר בה חברתי אותו מפני שהיא קרובה להבין לרוב אנשי דורנו Judah ibn Tibbon's Introd. to the Hebrew translation: ואחריהם היו רוב הגאונים בגלות מלכות ישמעאל בבבל ובארץ ישראל ובפרס ומדברים בלשון ערבית וכל קהלות ישראל אשר היו במקומות ההם מדברים בלשון ההיא, פירשו רוב מה שפירשו מספרי המקרא וסדרי Solomon המשנה והתלמוד בלשון ערבית... מפני שכל העם היו סבינים בלשון ההיא b. Joseph ibn Jacob's preface to his translation of Maimonides' *Commentary on the Mishna*, Order Nezikin; Dukes, *Ehrensäulen*, 23; Parhon, Introd., xxii. Cf.

Dukes, *Mittheilungen*, 181, n. 1; Migash, 53; Barfat, 382: חתם בכתיבה נסה ביותר. כמועאלק כמו שחותמין קצת הספרדים. See Güdemann, op. cit., 20. Steinschneider: *A. L. J.*, **xv–xvi** § 22; *JQR*, XII (1900), 484.

[155] Judah ibn Tibbon admonished his son to read the Bible with the Arabic translation (Abrahams, 65–66). Similarly, Judah b. Samuel b. Abbas, in Güdmann, op. cit., 147.

[156] Neubauer, *M. J. C.*, I, 68–9.

[157] For the mediaeval Jewish conception of the relation between Hebrew and Arabic, see *JQR*, XIII (1901), 306–10; Steinschneider, *A. L. J.*, Introduction, sect. XI. Idem, *Heb. Uebersetz.*, 417, n. 346.

[158] Idem, *A. L. J.*, xxix–xxx; *JQR*, XIII (1901), 455–9.

[159] Solomon b. Joseph ibn Jacob, translator of Maimonides' *Commentary on the Mishna*, Preface to Fourth Order. Steinschneider, *A. L. J.*, § 76, suggests that this report may have confused Hanok with Joseph ibn Abitur.

[160] Graetz, V³, 327, n. 1. Steinschneider, in *JQR*, XIII, 456; idem, *A. L. J.*, § 73.

[161] Ibid.; Abr. ibn Daud, in Neubauer, *M. J. C.*, I, 69: פירש כל הש"ס למלך.

[162] Steinschneider, *A. L. J.*, Introd. xxvi; idem, *Hebr. Uebersetz.*, Introd., §VIII.

[163] Cf. Barfat, 392: הנקרא בלשונו חא'ק. See Steinschneider, *Hebr. Uebersetz.*, xv–xvi. In his autobiography, the mystic, Abraham Abulafia, whose messianic extravagances Ibn Adret combatted, described how the Jews everywhere gave up Hebrew as a spoken tongue and adopted the language of the country in which they lived. In Sicily, they spoke three languages, of which Arabic was one, but not Hebrew. וזה בעוונותינו אנחנו עם כמעט קרה לנו מפני התפזרותינו בין האומות הרבות ובין הלשונות המשונים ששכחנו כל לשוננו וצחותה ודקדוקה ונעדרה כטעם מפני רוב אומתנו ולולי כתיבת ספרינו היה הכל בלתי נמצא. וראה איך היהודים הדרים בין הישמעאלים מדברים בלשון ערבי כהם, והדרים בארץ יון מדברים יוונית, והדרים בארצות הלועזים מדברים לועזות, והאשכנזים אשכנזית והתוגרמים תוגרמית וכן השאר כלם. ואמנם הפלא הגדול הוא מה שקרה ליהודים בכל איסקיליאה שהם אינם מדברים בלשון עז ובלשון יון לבד כלשונות הלועזים והיונים שדרים עמהם אבל שברו לשון ערבי שלמדוהו סימים קדמונים בעת היות הישמעאלים דרים שם. See below, pp. 100 ff. *REJ*, IX, 148–9; XII, 82. Hebrew translations of Latin works made their first appearance in the twelfth century; but the full impetus for the work of translating into Hebrew the writings from the Latin, Spanish, French and Italian came a century later. Steinschneider, *Hebr. Uebersetz.*, §8.

[164] Cf. *Chronicle of James I of Aragon* (tr. Gayangos), 496–7; Barfat, 382, 424–450.

[165] Asher, LV, 9: לשון ערב שנעשית בו תקנת הנישואין ושהורגלו סופרי ארצנו לכתוב בה. שטרי הודאות והלואות ומקח וממכר וכל מיני חיזוקין וקיומין אינה הלשון שמדברים בה ההמון . . . לשון ערב האמיתית היא הנקראת מערבה שנכתבו בו ספרי החכמות החיצוניות . . . ולשון ההמון נקרא הוליא. On vernacular Arabic spoken by Jews, see Steinschneider, *A. L. J.*, xxxi, ff. Arabic was spoken by the rabbi in בלשיט at the end of the fourteenth century. Barfat, 450; cf. also 424. For the identification of this city see *REJ*, XVI, 191; Baer, *Studien*, 146. Cf. Barfat, 382; Duran I, 8; *JQR*, XIII, 303, n. 3.

[166] Cf. Solomon Parhon, *Maḥberet he-'Aruk*, end: והמקומות של ארץ ישמעאל לשון אחת יש להן, וכל האכסנאין הבאין אליהן יקירו את לשונן: לפיכך לא הוצרכו להשתמש

בלשון הקדש להיות רגילין בו. אבל כל ארץ אדום משונים לשונותיהן זו מזו, וכשיבואו אכסנאין See .אליהם לא יקירו דבריהם, הוצרכו לדבר להם בלשון הקדש; לפיכך רגילין בו יותר Steinschneider, *Hebr. Uebersetz.*, xv. Cf. *Zeitschrift für Mathematik*, XII, 8. Cf. Sarton, *Introd. to the History of Science*, II, 352: The University of Montpellier "was partly a Jewish creation and it is said that the earliest teaching was in Arabic and Hebrew; at any rate, Latin was the language used in the twelfth century."

[167] For Latin as the official language of the European universities, see H. Rashdall, *Universities of Europe in the Middle Ages*, Oxford, 1936, I, 516; II, 47, 233; III, 341 f. In Oxford, at Jesus College, Greek and Hebrew were also permitted as conversational languages (Rait, *Life in Med. Univ.*). For speaking English in the classroom undergraduates were promptly flogged (ibid., 67).

[168] Quoted in Dukes, *Mittheilungen*, 181, n. 1: אנשי צרפת היושבים בגבול אחינו בני עשו אין רובם מכיר בלשון ערב והרבה מחבבים את לשון הקודש ורגילין לדבר בה. From the reference to Arabic, it is apparent that Catalonia or the Provence, rather than France, is intended by צרפת.

[169] *REJ*, XII, 82. From a ms. collection of responsa entitled, שו"ת מהרשב"א ורבנים אחרים ז"ל: אבל בזמן הזה שבעונותינו רוב בנינו ובנותינו מדברים אדומי וערבי ויוני וכלשון עם ועם ואפי' רוב האנשים אינם מבינים לדבר יהודית היאך נאמר שהנשים יבינו אותם לשונות האמורים בגמרא: no. 59.

[170] See note 163, above.

[171] Asher, LV, 9. His son Judah's reference to his own early experience when he left Germany for France is obscure, as he probably referred to methods of study rather than to languages: ומשגות למוד אשכנז יצאתי ולשגות צפת לא באתי. (Abrahams, op. cit., 166).

[172] Cf. Abot 4.12; 'Er. 54b.

[173] Barfat, 388.

[174] Ibid., 393.

[175] Ibid., 290.

[176] Ibid., 262. Cf. ibid., 308, end. It was difficult to secure the services of a scribe for this purpose. Barfat once waited two months before he could find a scribe to make a duplicate of a responsum he had written. וזה לי ב' חדשים כתבתי את זה זה ואני יגע ורפה ידים להעתיקו ולכתבו שנית ולא מצאתי או סופר יעתיקנו עד עתה (ibid., 393, end). From his deathbed, Ibn Adret dictated his last responsum to his pupil R. Abraham b. Moses (Adret, VIII, 148): ומרוב חולשת מורי הרב לא יכול לחתום אך אלה הדברים יצאו מפיו . . . הכותב במצות מורי הרב. אברהם בר' משה.

[177] Cf. Barfat, 308, 393. See above, note 114.

[178] In the elementary grades the pupils brought their own books to school (Adret, V, 166). How the lack of textbooks for children was sometimes overcome is shown in Duran, I, 2. See above, p. 70.

[179] Graetz, V, note 21, end; VI, 18.

[180] Alfasi, 133.

[181] Ibid. Gaster, *Ma'aseh Book*, II, 656, no. 254. Cf. S. Gandz, "The Dawn of Literature," in *Osiris*, VII (1939), 463 f.

[182] Régné, 2147, 2308.

[183] Asher, XCIII, 3. When as a result of a foreign invasion, the books of the Jews of Gerona and Besalu were seized and scattered throughout the country, Pedro III ordered that they should be faithfully restored to the original owners upon the payment of their cost to the present holders of the books. Régné 1470.

[184] Ed. Edelman, *Derek Tobim*, 12. Abrahams, *Hebrew Ethical Wills*, I, 81-2.

[185] En Vidal Ephraim, one of Barfat's correspondents in Majorca, copied for him a passage from the *Tur Yoreh De'ah*, which Barfat, strangely enough, did not possess, though it is evident that he was the owner of a valuable library (Barfat, 293). Barfat rendered a similar service to another rabbi in Majorca, R. Moses Gabbai, who did not have the books of the commentators. Ibid., 305.

[186] Besides quotations from numerous tractates of the Talmud, the following authors and works are mentioned or quoted verbatim in Barfat, 394: Geonic responsa, Saadia Gaon, *She'eltot, Halakot Gedolot*, Commentary of Rabbenu Hananel, Rashi, Isaac ibn Giat, Alfasi, 'Aruk, Rabbenu Tam, Responsum of Isaac b. Samuel ha-Zaken, Tosafot of Sens, Maimonides, Abraham b. David of Posquières, Samson's (b. Abraham of Sens) Commentary on the Mishna, *Sefer ha-Terumah* (Baruch b. Isaac of Worms), *Sefer ha-Mizvot* by Moses of Coucy, Nahmanides, Solomon ibn Adret, Asher b. Yehiel, Yom Tob (b. Abraham Ishbili), and finally his own teacher, R. Nissim Gerundi. Barfat's library also contained the following works of R. Isaac ibn Latif: *Zurat 'Olam* in twenty-seven chapters, *Zeror ha-Mor* in eleven chapters, *Rab Pe'alim*, one hundred pages, or eighty-eight paragraphs; commentary on Ecclesiastes, and *Sha'ar ha-Shamayim* (Barfat, 157). When Barfat temporarily moved into a small house, he was compelled to divide his library and to store his books in several houses (ibid., 11; cf. 192). This incident took place after his flight from Spain and is therefore doubly significant, as Hebrew books were strangely scarce in the North African communities (see ibid., 1, 5). Also in Majorca (ibid., 305). A Jewish-Egyptian physician, Ephraim b. al-Zafan, left a library of over twenty thousand volumes (*JQR*, XIII (1900), 102). Cf. Barfat, 1, 5, 192. R. Nissim Gerundi copied for his own use a scroll of the Torah (Duran, I, 51). On libraries and love of books among Spanish Jews, see Steinschneider, *A. L. J.*, xxvii, n. 1; also Abrahams, op. cit., 352-3. A Jewish patron of learning, Don Samuel Sulami, was praised not only for his generosity and hospitality to men of scholarship, but for his indefatigable effort in collecting a great library: *Minhat Kenaot*, 47.

[187] Isaac Campanton, one of the last among the noted talmudic authors of Spain (d. 1463) concludes his ספר דרכי הגמרא, *Introduction to the Talmud*, with this paragraph: אין חכמת האדם מגעת אלא עד מקום שספריו מגיעין ולכן יסכור אדם כל מה שיש לו ויקנה ספרים כי מי שאין לו ספרי התלמוד אי אפשר להיות בקי . . . וכ'כ מי שאין לו ספרי ההגיון או החכמה לא יהיה חכם בה . . . והקורא בספרים שאולים הוא בכלל והיו חייך תלואים לך מנגד. Judah Asheri estimated his library to be worth over 3,000 golden *maravedís* (Abrahams, op. cit., 197; cf. ibid., 170).

[188] See Freimann, in *ZHB*, XIV, 105–12; XV, 26–7.   Cf. Rappaport, *Teshubot Geonim Kadmoniyim*, Introduction, sect. 7.

[189] Dukes, *Mittheilungen*, Introd., v, n. 1, cites Menahem Louzano, Introduction to *Or Torah* as follows: ובכל מקום שתמצא ס'ס הם ספרי ספרד שהם המהוגים הנאמנים. ואעידה לי עדים נאמנים. כתב הראב'ד בהשגותיו על ס' המאור סוף פ'ק דברכות וז'ל ואם נראה בנירסא זו מעט דוחק טוב להעמיד אותה כי נוסחא ספרדית היא עכ'ל.   גם הרמב'ן בס' המלחמות סוף פרק הרואה כתב ז'ל אבל ספרי ספרד יותר נאמנים מספרינו עכ'ל.   Cf. Elias Levita, *Mesorat ha-Massorah*, end.

[190] Menahem ibn Zerah related that during the civil war in Castile, he was robbed of all his possessions and was left with only his books, house and grounds: *ZL*, Introduction, 16b; cf. Régné, 1470.

[191] Before the persecution, the community of Majorca possessed more than sixty scrolls of the Law; afterward, the greater part of the community disappeared and with them their sacred possessions: Duran, I, 51.

NOTES TO CHAPTER XVI

RABBINIC CULTURE

[1] His secular studies comprised the חכמות חצוניות: הקישיות מופתיות, עיוניות שכליות טבעיות, רפואיות הניוניות למודיות (Duran, II, 52). For reference to his early studies in mathematics, see ibid., I, 163.

[2] See above, p. 81. Cf. Jacob Anatoli, *Malmad ha-Talmidim*, Introd.

[3] It was Ibn Adret, the leading rabbinic authority of his age, who rebuked the philosophers for their corruption of Hebrew with the jargon of philosophic terminology. He accused them of unlearning their own Hebrew language, while cultivating all foreign tongues. Abba Mari, *Minhat Kenaot, 48*.

[4] The classic treatment of this subject is Steinschneider's *Die arabische Literatur der Juden.*

[5] Cf. Steinschneider's classification of Jewish-Arabic authors under the following categories: A. Poetry;   B. Linguistics (grammar, lexicography);   C. Exegesis; D. Religious philosophy;   E. Halakah;   F. Mathematics;   G. Medicine (*A.L.J.*, pp. xxviii–xxx). For Spanish halakists in Arabic, see *JQR*, XIII (1901), 455–8.

[6] Rios, I, 447–50; Graetz, VII, 115. See *The Legacy of Israel*, ed. by E. R. Bevan and Charles Singer, Oxford, 1927, 202 ff.

[7] Ibid. Steinschneider, *Hebr. Uebersetz.*, § 370.   Cf. *The Legacy of Israel*, 222–5; see below, 104.

[8] Güdemann, *Geschichte des Erziehungswesens und der Cultur der Juden in Italien*, 105 ff.

[9] Barfat, 35, 442, 452.

[10] See *ZDMG*, XLVIII, 39; Perles, *R. Salomo ben Abraham ben Adereth*, Heb. supplement, Breslau, 1863, 1–24. For Crescas see Wolfson, op. cit., 7 f.

[11] Asher, LV, 9. For Nahmanides' Arabic knowledge see his novellae on Ḥulin 29a (Warsaw, 1859); cf. Perles in *MGWJ*, VII, 87; IX, 176.

[12] Adret, IV, 31, 187; VIII, 77. See "The Jewish Factor in Medieval Thought," in *The Legacy of Israel*, 173 ff.

[13] Adret, VIII, 77.

[14] See below pp. 193 ff.

[15] Barfat, 392. At the request of Don Luis de Guzman, grandmaster of the Order of Calatrava, Rabbi Moses Arragel translated the entire Hebrew Bible into Castilian. This work, which took eight years to complete (1422-30), reveals not only the vast erudition of the rabbinical translator but also his fine literary taste and mastery of the idiom of his country as well as of the classical Hebrew and Latin. Fortunately, the correspondence between Don Luis and Arragel was preserved together with the translation. We may cite the opening letter of Don Luis: "We, Master of Calatrava, send many salutations to you, Raby Moses Arragel, our vassal in our city of Maqueda. Know, O Raby Moses, that we desire to possess a Bible with glosses and comments; and we are told that you can do the work well." See S. Berger, in *Bulletin des Antiquaires*, 1898, 239-44; *REJ*, XXXVIII, 309-11; *Legacy of Israel*, 309-12.

[16] See Bernstein, *Magazin für die Wissenschaft d. Judenthums*, XVIII, 114-8.

[17] Cf. Barfat, 442: (*alcaparras*) פירוש צלף הוא אילן הקפרסין שקורין בלע'ז אלקפארש (*tapares*) או מאפרי'ש. He explained the term פרנין as קורין וקורין רמון כמו עשוי קטנית מין לו בערבי כשכ'ש והוא סלא זרע כמו שומשמין כך מפרש בעדוך ורש'י ז'ל פירש שהוא מין ק'פ. קטנית ובלע'ו מ'ק. He defined עורדין as a fruit which in this country (Valencia?) is called זערודיש and "in our country" שירביש (*serbas*). אונקלי, a loose, informal dress, worn under the cloak, in the house or in the street, is defined as *almejia*, מלבוש רחב שקורין אלטמחשיא'ה. Cf. ibid., 420, where Barfat informs his correspondent that the Spanish פניצ'ו (*panizo*) was דוחן in Hebrew and was therefore permissible food on Passover.

[18] The target of his criticism was the translation of אחשתרנים בני רמכים, Esther 8.10, by לוש פוטרוש פינוש דלאש אינואש, *los potros fijos* (=*hijos*) *de las yeguas*: Barfat, 388.

[19] Ibid., 390.

[20] Adret, I, 551; II, 119; Barfat, 490, 510. Cf. ibid., 387, 515.

[21] Rios, I, 450.

[22] Rubió y Lluch, *Documents per l'historia de la cultura catalana*, I, 309, 338, quoted by Baer, *Studien*, 41, n. 108.

[23] Barfat, 299, 305. Cf. Adret, II, 119.

[24] Barfat, 392.

[25] Cf. Kayserling, *Biblioteca Española-Portugueza-Judaica*, Strasbourg, 1890, Introduction, ix; *REJ*, XV, 6, n. 2. See above note 11.

[26] Adret, IV, 31, 187. See Graetz, VII, 151, notes 1, 2.

[27] Ibid.

[28] For Jewish polemics against Islam in Hebrew and Arabic, see Steinschneider, *Polemische und apologetische Literatur in arabischer Sprache, zwischen Muslimen, Christen und Juden*, Anhang VII, "Jüdische Polemik gegen den Islam," 244-380. The polemical works of Jewish apostates in Spanish and Portuguese were collected

with other anti-Jewish works in these languages in Kayserling's *Biblioteca Española-Portugueza-Judaica*, 114–8. Simon Duran wrote a criticism of the Koran (Steinschneider, *A.L.J.*, xix, n. 1). Isaac Israeli debated with an apostate in 1330: *Yesod 'Olam*, ed. Cassel, Introd.

[29] Only the Hebrew translation by Joseph ibn Shem Tob has survived, the very title of the original being lost. The Hebrew version with commentary was completed by Joseph ibn Shem Tob, in 1451, at Alcalá de Henares, under the title *Bittul 'Ikkere ha-Nozerim*. It was published anonymously at Salonica (?) in 1860, and reprinted by Deinard (Kearny, N. J., 1934). See Steinschneider, *Hebr. Uebersetz.*, 462.

[30] Zacuto, *Sefer Yuhasin*, ed. Zolkiew, 71b: הר' יוסף אלבו בעל העקרים חבר ספרו וחבר ספר אחד בלשון לע"ז. This passage is missing in Filipowski's edition, as was noted by Graetz, VIII, 162, n. 1.

[31] See the citations from Joseph's manuscript works in Graetz, VIII, Appendix, note 4, II. Isaac Pulgar, whose literary activity dates from the first half of the 14th century and who wrote a Hebrew work, *'Ezer ha-Dat* (In Support of the Faith), against astrology, also wrote a special treatise on the same subject in Spanish which is extant in a Vatican manuscript. Cf. Marx, in *HUCA*, III, 324.

[32] Thus the Grand Master of the Military Order of Santiago commissioned his Jewish physician, Don Jacob Çadique de Ucles, to translate into Castilian the Catalan, *Libro de dichos de sabios e filosofos e de otros exemplos e doctrinas muy buenas*, which Jacob completed in Ucles, July 28, 1402. Rodriquez de Castro, *Biblioteca española*, Madrid, 1781, 263 ff., cited in Baer, I, 475.

[33] Cf. Abot 3.18: פרפראות לחכמה, קופות ונמטריאות, and commentary of Yom Tob Lipmann Heller, ad loc.

[34] Cf. heading of responsum, Duran, I, 163: טיורקא, זה שלחתי אל אנבלשים אפרים. Contrast the modest preface, להזכירני מטה ששכחתי. לפי שהיה בקי בחכמת התשבורת בתלמודי מחמת אונס הטלטולים בידיעת דרך חכמי השיעורים בתשבורת נשם כדורי בכללו, with the sharp tone in which he refutes the opinions of his correspondent whose views differed from his own. Cf. ibid., III, 272. On En Blasom Ephraim, see Kayserling, *Die Juden in Navarra*, 170; *Hadoar*, IX, 22–3, 41, 54–5, 71–3.

[35] Viz., Middot, 'Arakin, 'Erubin, Kelim, Ohalot, etc. Cf. Zuckermann, *MGWJ*, IV, 146–56.

[36] Cf. Maim., *M.T.*, *Hilk. Kil.*, IV, 15–6: וכל אלו העניניס מבוארים למי שיש לו חלק בחכמת המידות; Duran, I, 163–6, 172; Steinschneider, *Jewish Lit.*, §21, n. 90.

[37] Ed. Steinschneider, Berlin, 1864; German tr., H. Schapira. S. Gandz, "The Mishnat ha-Middot," in *Quellen u. Studien zur Geschichte der Mathematik*, II, Berlin, 1932; idem, "Studies in the History of Mathematics from Hebrew and Arabic Sources," in *HUCA*, VI (1929), 263–76.

[38] Steinschneider, *Jewish Lit.*, §21 n. 89. A descriptive and bibliographic account of Hebrew and Hebrew-Arabic mathematical literature was prepared by Steinschneider in a series of articles in the *Bibliotheca Mathematica*, 1893–1901, and in the *Abhandlungen zur Geschichte der Mathematik*, 1899, collected and indexed under the general title, *Die jüdischen Mathematiker*, Frankfurt, 1901.

[39] Zunz, *Zur Geschichte*, 535–57.

[40] Cf. Duran, I, 163. Mathematics was treated as an introduction to astronomy by Isaac Israeli. It was quite common for astronomers to write monographs on mathematics.

[41] Deut. 4.6.

[42] Shab. 75a, Suk. 28a. Cf. Duran, I, 104, 106; III, 214–6. See the impressive list of Jewish astronomers in Spain compiled by Steinschneider, *Jewish Lit.*, 183 ff.

[43] Duran, I, 108, compares the merits of the two systems associated with the names of Samuel and Ada, respectively. See Marx, in *Essays and Studies in Memory of Linda R. Miller*, N. Y., 1933, 121–2.

[44] Steinschneider, *Jewish Lit.*, §21. Duran's familiarity with astronomy and its literature is clearly shown in his responsa where he discourses on the subject, not without a touch of pride; I, 104–5, 107–9; III, 214–6.

[45] Steinschneider, *Jewish Lit.*, § 21. Cf. *The Legacy of Israel*, 222–5.

[46] Kayserling, *Christopher Columbus* (tr. Gross), 6. The astrolabe, an ancient metallic instrument used for astronomic observation and for astrological divination, figured in many heated discussions: theologically, because it was identified by some rationalists with the Urim and Thummim on the High Priest's breastplate (Ex. 28.30) and, halakically, in connection with its use on the Sabbath. Ibn Ezra, *Commentary*, Ex. 28.6, Gen. 31.19. Adret, I, 772; *Minhat Kenaot*, 105–7, 111, 119. See Gandz, "The Astrolabe in Jewish Literature," in *HUCA*, IV (1927), 469 ff. Cf. *The Legacy of Israel*, 226–8.

[47] Duran, I, 104: ואולי הגיעו אליהם (אל היונים) ספרינו בבית שני כשנברה ידם עלינו וקראו אותם החכמת על שמם אע"פ שהם הכמתנו באמת וצריכים להורתנו לדעת ענין קביעות החדשים והמועדים אשר תלויים בהם הרבה מצות חמורות כחיוב כרת וזולתם.

[48] Isaac Israeli, *Yesod 'Olam*. See author's prefatory remarks; also Abraham b. Hiyya's *Zurat ha-Arez*, one of the earliest astronomical works in Hebrew, was written at the request of the author's rabbinic teacher. See preface, ed. Offenbach, 1720: וכשבאו לידי שורות יקרות ווטורים יקרים יוצאים מלפני קציני הדור ונבירו—שמש המדע ומאורו—והוד השכל והדרו הנקרא בשם אלהים ובחירו יסנא מאוד שלומו ולפני שמש ינון שמו ויועץ אתי לחבר בחכמת הכככים חבור שיהיה מבאר את ענינה ומפרש כהונן דרכיה ופניה ועמדתי על דבריו הנעימים ומצותיו ומצותי להשלים ראויה ולהתמים מיד השתדלתי לשמוע לעצתו כפי כבודו עלי וחיברתה וכן הוא הדין על כל אוהביו וידידיו וכ"ש על תלמידיו הנתונים על ידי.

[49] See above, p. 99.

[50] Graetz, VIII, 23, n. 1.

[51] Kayserling, *Christopher Columbus*, 13, 14, 46–51.

[52] Duran, 1, 104. See *MGWJ*, XLV, 453–9; Steinschneider, *Jewish Lit.*, §5, n. 25.

[53] See *Kerem Hemed*, VIII, 58–9. Cf. Adret, I, 413; VIII, 283. See A. Marx, "The Correspondence between the Rabbis of Southern France and Maimonides about Astrology," in *HUCA*, III, 311–58. For the general literature on astrology among the Jews, see ibid., 312, n. 3.

[54] See Steinschneider, *Jewish Lit.*, §21, p. 191.

[55] Cf. Maim., *M. T.*, *Hilk. 'Ab. Kokabim*, XI; *Kobez*, II, 24–6. See Maimonides' letter on astrology: Marx in *HUCA*, III, 349–58. The Karaite, Judah

Hadassi, preceded Maimonides in denying the validity of astrology: ibid., 319, n. 14a.

[56] Adret, VIII, 283. See "Iggeret Rabbi Abraham bar Hiyya ha-Nasi..." (on the question of the Chaldaeans), in *Festschrift Adolf Schwarz*, Hebrew section, 23–36; Rosin, in *MGWJ*, XLII (1898), 247–52; 305–15, 345–82, 394–402.

[57] This view was expressed by R. Abraham b. David, Maimonides' critic (see *Hasagot* to *Hilk. Teshubah*, V, 5). Barfat contrasted it with the metaphysical theories of R. Levi b. Gerson (Barfat, 118). In this passage, correct הלכות תשובה for הלכות דעות.

[58] Hor. 12a.

[59] Adret, VIII, 283.

[60] Ibid., I, 825: לפי שנמצא לראשונים בספרי הרפואות שזה מועיל לחולי המתנים, והוא שיעשה בשעה ידועה. Cf. also ibid., I, 167.

[61] Ibid., I, 167, 413, 825.

[62] *Minhat Kenaot*, 1, 3, 5, 7, 17, 36. Adret, I, 413.

[63] 'Ab. Zarah 43b. The *Merkabah* is the divine Throne-Chariot, based on Ezek. 1 and 10. The four faces of the *Merkabah* were the lion, the ox, the eagle and man. See Ḥag. 13b.

[64] The Amorite is the rabbinic designation for the Canaanites in whose statutes Israelites are not to walk: Lev. 18.3. Concerning their superstitious practices, see Deut. 18.9–14. On the rabbinic views concerning astrology, see A. Marx, "The Correspondence between the Rabbis of Southern France and Maimonides about Astrology," *HUCA*, III (1926), 311 ff. Cf. Syriac Apocalypse of Baruch, 60, in Charles' *Apocrypha*, II, 514. Two chapters are devoted to the "Ways of the Amorites" in Tosefta Shab. 6 f., ed. Zuckermandel, to which the Babylon. Talmud, Shab. 67a, refers as פרק אמוראי.

[65] See above, note 62.

[66] Adret, I, 167, 825.

[67] Shab. 115b, etc. On the general subject of amulets in the Talmud, see Ludwig Blau, *Das Altjüdische Zauberwesen*, 86–96.

[68] The talmudic passages usually quoted against astrology were Pes. 113b; Sanh. 66a, 75b; Ḥul. 7b. Among the Jewish opponents of astrology many did not doubt its veracity, but considered it divinely prohibited (Ex. 22.17; Lev. 19.26; Deut. 18.10, 14). For, they argued, the Bible would not prohibit mere nonsense. A correspondent from Montpellier wrote to Ibn Adret in this vein: שהתורה לא אסרה אלא דבר שיש בו קצת עיקר שיש בו כדי למעות (Adret, I, 413). With this attitude, however, Maimonides had no patience.

[69] Maim., *M. T., Hilk. 'Ab. Kokabim*, XI, 16.

[70] Lev. 19.26.

[71] See Maim., *M. T., Hilk. 'Ab. Kokabim*, XI, 9. In his letter to the Provençal scholars Maimonides expressed the view that "our Kingdom perished and our Temple was destroyed" because our forebears spent their time learning astrology instead of perfecting themselves in the art of war and conquest: Marx, op. cit., 320, 350 § 7.

[72] The later Maimunists freely used the notions of astrology in their extravagant Bible interpretations. Thus God kept Israel in the wilderness for forty years to allow the evil star to change its position. Moses ordered Joshua to the front against Amalek because his own star was impotent against Amalek's star: *Jubelschrift zum neunzigsten Geburtstag des Dr. L. Zunz*, 160.

[73] Abraham b. David, *Hasagot* to Maimonides' *M. T., Hilk. Teshubah*, V, 5. See above, note 57.

[74] Adret, I, 148; cf. ibid., 409; also V, 48, end: והוא ענין עמוק מאד. לא שמעה אזני: רק כנקודה מן הגלגל הגדול ולא קבלתי מאבותי כטפה מן הים, ולא אוכל לפרש.

[75] Ibid.

[76] *ZJ*, 43–4.

[77] Duran, I, 106.

[78] Among the rabbis whose writings figure conspicuously in the present work the following were physicians: Maimonides, Nahmanides, Nissim Gerundi, Menahem b. Zerah, Simon Duran. Cf. also Asher, LV, 9; Barfat, 71, 297; Baer, I, 459, 460, 539. For the early literature on Jewish medical knowledge, see Steinschneider, *Jewish Lit.*, §5, n. 26. On Jews in medicine, see I. Münz, *Ueber die jüdischen Aerzte im Mittelalter*, Frankfort a/M, 1922; Scherbel, *Jüdische Ärzte*; Carmoly, *Hist. des Médecins Juifs*, Bruxelles, 1842. A. Rubió y Lluch, in *Estudios Universitaris Catalans, Barcelona*, III (1909): "Notes sobre la ciencia oriental a Catalunia en el XIVen siglo," Appendix, *Metjes y cirurgians juhens*, by Jordi Rubió y Balaguer. S. Krauss, *Geschichte der jüdischen Ärzte vom frühesten Mittelalter bis zur Gleichberechtigung*, Vienna, 1930.

[79] See Baer, I and II, index, s. v. Ärzte. Note especially I, 149, 186, 190, 204, 206, 209, 219, 224, 254, 258, 350, 356, 542, 380, 400, 459, 460, 527 §5, 539, 558, 580, 605; II, 67, 98 p. 89 n. 1, 241, 289 §4, 294, 309, 340.

[80] Cf. Adret, I, 395; Asher, LV, 9; Barfat, 71, 371; ibid., II; 1; *REJ*, LVII, 268 ff; Baer, I, 206, 209, 382, 460, 558.

[81] Barfat possessed medical knowledge without converting it to professional use (Barfat, 35, 338).

[82] Cf. above, I, 115 and II, 87 ff.

[83] Baer, I, 380, 459, 539. David Bonet Bonjorn was examined as physician at the University of Perpignan, June 8, 1390 (ibid., I, 190, end).

[84] Cf. Adret, IV, 122; VIII, 127. See ZL, pt. I, sect. 3, chs. 1–20; cf. Isaac Israeli's *Manhig ha-Rofe'im* or *Musar ha-Rofe'im*; D. Kaufmann, "Propädeutik für Ärzte," in Berliner's *Magazin*, XI, 97–112.

[85] Duran, III, 82.

[86] Cf. Adret, I, 731; Barfat, 251. Cf. Duran, III, 271.

[87] Adret, I, 120 (ed. Venice); VIII, 127; Nahmanides, *Torat ha-Adam*, 7d; Duran, I, 145; III, 82; ZL, 112a.

[88] Cf. above, p. 106. For a physician who combined ophthalmological surgery and astrology, see Baer, I, 539. Don Menahem served Pedro IV as physician, astrologer and alchemist. Rios, II, 299; Baer, I, 224, end.

[89] Adret, I, 167.

⁹⁰ Ibid., II, 281; IV, 245; cf. V, 119.

⁹¹ ZL, 112a. Cf. Adret, V, 119, where Shebu. 15b is quoted: אמר רי'ב'ל אסור
להתרפאות בדברי תורה. See also Maimonides, M. T., Hilk. 'Ab. Kokabim, XI, 12.

⁹² Nahmanides, op. cit.; Duran, I, 145.

⁹³ Adret, I, 120 (ed. Venice). This responsum, curiously enough, was excised by
the censor from the later editions.

⁹⁴ Ibid.

⁹⁵ Barfat, 60.

⁹⁶ The letter dated 1199 (Tishri, 8), was addressed to Samuel ibn Tibbon in
Lunel: Marx, HUCA, III (1926), 335; Kobez, II, 26. He was engaged in translating
Maimonides' chief philosophic work into Hebrew and, discouraged by the difficulties of his task, wanted to visit the sage to obtain his help. Maimonides penned
this famous letter in reply, advising him not to undertake the long arduous journey.
S. Zeitlin, Maimonides, 100–1. See also the earlier letter to Ibn Aknin, dated 1191,
in which he describes the taxing nature of his medical duties at the court of Al-Fadil
as well as his private practice. He had no time for research, and the study of the
Torah was reserved for the Sabbaths only. Cf. MGWJ, LXXIX (1935), 81 ff.

⁹⁷ See below, pp. 213 ff.

⁹⁸ See Grayzel, p. 74, n. 147; Baer, I, 464, §3.

⁹⁹ ZL, 110a.

¹⁰⁰ Barfat, 331.

¹⁰¹ Grayzel, 74–5, 152–7 (nos. 41, 42, 43). Cf. Shebet Yehudah, 88; Baer, I,
252, 580.

¹⁰² REJ, VI, 93 ff.; XVI, 170 ff.; LVII, 268 ff. See preceding note (101); Baer,
I, 219 end.

¹⁰³ Ibid., I, 186, 356, 539; p. 542. Cf. ibid., I, 400. Cf. Kehunat 'Olam (Responsa), 33.

¹⁰⁴ Fita-Llabrés, Los Judíos Mallorquines, 71; Baer, Studien, 113, n. 55. See
ibid., I, 350.

¹⁰⁵ REJ, XVI, 170 ff.; Rios, III, 229; Graetz, VIII, 226, n. 2.

¹⁰⁶ Ibid. Cf. Kehunat 'Olam, 33. See also a much later document in the minutes
of the communal ledger (פנקס) of Posen, describing the election of a Jewish public
physician, his duties to the poor, his relation to the apothecary and other interesting
items. REJ, XX, 285–6.

¹⁰⁷ Duran, Magen Abot, Commentary on Abot 4. 7, ed. Schlossberg, p. 62.

¹⁰⁸ Adret, III, 318.

¹⁰⁹ Grayzel, 73–4.

¹¹⁰ Adret, VIII, 206; cf. IV, 122.

¹¹¹ Maim., 7.

¹¹² Adret, I, 413; VIII, 283; Barfat, 93. Maimonides was impelled to disprove
their existence: Guide, III, 46. Samuel Saporta, in his Maimonidean apologia,
maintained that Maimonides did not deny the existence of demons (Ginze Nistarot,
IV, 62). In the main, however, the rationalist school categorically rejected the
belief in demonology because it was not manifest to the senses or the intellect, nor
was it dictated by tradition. Cf. Zunz Jubelschrift, 154 f.

[113] See above, p. 106.

[114] Cf. above, notes 64, 67, 68.

[115] Adret, VIII, 285.

[116] Ibid., I, 413.

[117] Crescas, *Bittul ʿIkre ha-Nozrim*, Deinard ed., 88.

[118] Barfat, 93.

[119] *Iggeret Teman*, ed. Holub, Vienna, 1873; see Steinschneider, *Hebr. Uebersetz.*, 929–30; Graetz, VI, 277 f. See Baer, in *MGWJ*, LXXIX (1926); Mann, in *Hatekufah*, XXIII–XXIV; Marx, in *HUCA*, III, 349 § 29, 356 § 27.

[120] Cf. Mekilta, ed. Lauterbach, sec. tractate *Pisha*, I, 14–5.

[121] Adret, I, 548.

[122] See Graetz, VII, 19.

[123] For Abulafia's reply, see Jellinek, *Auswahl kabbalist. Mystik*, 13, וזאת ליהודה.

[124] Adret, I, 548.

[125] Ibid.

[126] See below, pp. 126 ff.

[127] Graetz, VIII, 404. See *MGWJ*, 1879, 80 ff.

[128] See Bela Bernstein, *Die Schrifterklärung des Bachya b. Ascher*, 5 ff.

[129] Barfat, 157.

[130] Ibid., הנוצרים מאמיני השלוש, והמקובלים מאמיני העשיריות.

[131] Ibid.

[132] See Joseph Sarachek, *Faith and Reason: The Conflict over the Rationalism of Maimonides*, Williamsport, 1935.

[133] For an excellent summary of the intellectual background of mediaeval Europe for this Jewish struggle between Reason and Faith, see Henry D. Sedgwick, *Italy in the Thirteenth Century*, 2 vols., Boston, 1912.

[134] See Sarachek, *Faith and Reason*, 66–72.

[135] They are generally published in all standard editions of the Code, at the side of the text, under the title "strictures" (*hasagot*).

[136] Cf. *Kobez*, II, 8–9, 31. See Sarachek, *The Doctrine of the Messiah in Med. Jewish Literature*, New York, 1932, 153–7.

[137] Abulafia's letters were collected by Brüll under the title *Kitab al Rasail*, Paris, 1871. See pp. 8, 15. Cf. *Kobez*, II, 34.

[138] Brüll, op. cit., pp. 4, 136–7; *Kobez*, III, 16.

[139] Brüll, 30–7; *Kobez*, III, 7, 11; *Taʿam Zekenim*, 70; Graetz, *Blumenlese*, 149. See A. Marx, *JQR*, XXV (1935), 406–28. *Tahkemoni*, 352; Steinschneider, *Moreh Mekom ha-Moreh*, 3–4. Sarachek, *Faith and Reason*, 47–65.

[140] Ibid., 77–88.

[141] Graetz, VII, 36, n. 1; also ibid., 373–8. See *Ginze Nistarot*, IV, 10–3.

[142] See Renan's classic, *Averroès et l'Averroïsme*, 225 ff.

[143] *Kobez*, III, 2c, 6b, 8c, 10b.

[144] Ibid., III, 5.

[145] Ibid., III, 4.

[146] Ibid., III, 6.

[147] Ibid. III, 4.

[148] Ibid., III, 8 ff.

[149] Grayzel, op. cit., 33, n. 67; Zeitlin, *Maimonides*, 197.

[150] See Sarachek, *Faith and Reason*, 87–8, n. 34; *Kobez*, III, 14a.

[151] *Kobez*, III, 14, 17, 21; *Jeschurun*, VIII, 53, 89–94; Maimonides' son pictured the flame as a fiery chariot bearing his father's works to immortality even as Elijah was thus borne to heaven (Brody, *Moznaim*, no. 15). The locale of the auto-da-fé is given as Paris by Hillel of Verona, and Montpellier by Abraham son of Maimonides. Obviously the latter is the more reliable source.

[152] See above, I, 130 ff.

[153] Hillel of Verona in *Kobez*, III, 14a. Cf. *Jeschurun*, VIII, 51; Abraham Maimuni, *Kobez*, III, 17a; *Hemdah Genuzah* (1856).

[154] See Sarachek, *Faith and Reason*, 89–127.

[155] Graetz, VII, 54; cf. ibid., note 1.

[156] Graetz, VII, n. 5; Grayzel, op. cit., 29–32.

[157] *Kobez*, III, 14.

[158] See *Minhat Kenaot*, Letter 39, Introduction by Abba Mari, 'ר בראות החכם
יעקב בר מכיר כי הרב ר' שלמה בן אדרת החזיק בדבר ועודנו מחזיק להשתדל להוציא לפועל
מחשבתו הרצויה, עמד ושלח אליו כתבו ובא עליו בעלילות, כי הרב י"ץ הטיח דברים כנגד פי'
רמב"ם ז"ל בענין המרכבה ואל אלהים הוא יודע כי הוא י"ץ ממכירי מעלת רמב"ם ז"ל אשר
תורתו ומאוהבי חיים אנו מפיו. Cf. also Ibn Adret's retort to Jacob ibn Tibbon, ibid., 40:
ונעשית דלטור ביני ובין הרב (הרמב"ם) ז"ל . . . והנח לו להרב ז"ל כי הוא יריב לו, אם
חטאתי לו . . . ואין בכל בית הרב והנגיד בן בנו חכים ואהוב ובעל ברית כמוני וצא ושאול
לעוברי ימים ויגידו לך. Cf. also Letters 30, 84, 85, 89.

[159] The chief source for the following description is Abba Mari's collection of letters, entitled *Minhat Kenaot* (Pressburg, 1838). He omitted some of the most important documents representing the viewpoint of the liberals. Corrections and variants were published by Neubauer and by Halberstamm in *Israelitische Letterbode*, IV, 122–3, 160–73; V, 53–8, 71–83. See also J. Perles, *R. Salomo ben Abraham ben Adereth*, Breslau, 1863; Renan, *Les Rabbins Français*, 647–95.

[160] For the abortive agitation of Solomon Petit a decade earlier, see Sarachek, *Faith and Reason*, 141–8.

[161] Graetz and Perles erroneously designate him also as En Duran, passim. But En Duran was the surname of Simeon b. Joseph, one of Abba Mari's staunchest supporters. Gross, *Gallia Judaica*, 288.

[162] See especially *Minhat Kenaot*, pp. 5–19, 122–30.

[163] See Adret, I, 413; *Minhat Kenaot*, nos. 1, 3, 5, 7, 17, 36. Cf. Adret, I, 167, 772, 825.

[164] *Minhat Kenaot*, no. 1, p. 20.

[165] Ibid., no. 5, p. 32.

[166] Ibid., no. 5, p. 31; cf. also no. 12.

[167] Ibid., ס' הירח, Introd., 122.

[168] Ibid., no. 5, וחס ליה לזרעא דאבא להזכיר אותם כי לא דלמור אני להטיל גורלות;
ולא נלותי שמות הדרשנים ומי אביהם ואלה איפה הם רועים no. 19: Cf. also Letters 19, 56.

[169] Jean Astruc, *Mémoires pour servir a l'Histoire de la Faculté Médecine de Montpellier*, 168.

[170] *Minhat Kenaot*, no. 1.

[171] Ibid., no. 2.

[172] Ibid., no. 5; again at the critical moment, no. 34; and finally, with victory, no. 65.

[173] Ibid., no. 7; Adret, I, 414.

[174] Ibid.

[175] *Minhat Kenaot*, nos. 10, 15; cf. nos. 11, 16.

[176] Ibid., no. 12.

[177] Ibid., no. 20.

[178] Ibid., nos. 22, 23, 24.

[179] Ibid., no. 23.

[180] Ibid., no. 24.

[181] Ibid., no. 27.

[182] Ibid., nos. 25, 31.

[183] Ibid., no. 31.

[184] Ibid., no. 33.

[185] Ibid., no. 34.

[186] Adret described his correspondence later: ואם כמה דיו שפכתי כמה קולמוסים שברתי והתנפלתי כאשר התנפלתי וכמה נפתולים נפתלתי עם הגדולים לגדור גדר בבולם ולא ינעתי (ibid., no. 55).

[187] Ibid., nos. 35–8; cf. nos. 56–7.

[188] Ibid., no. 39.

[189] Ibid., no. 40.

[190] Ibid., no. 42.

[191] Ibid., nos. 44, 45, 47; cf. no. 60.

[192] Ibid., no. 50.

[193] Ibid., no. 51.

[194] Ibid., no. 53.

[195] Ibid., no. 54.

[196] Ibid., no. 55.

[197] Ibid., nos. 56, 57. The name *Nasi* is confused in the signature of no. 57 and is properly preserved in nos. 58, 63, 64, 65, etc.

[198] Ibid., no. 61.

[199] Ibid., no. 66.

[200] Ibid., nos. 61, 63.

[201] Ibid., no. 67. The same R. Samson had also been Ibn Adret's envoy to the communities of Castile, Navarre and other provinces in behalf of Maimonides' grandson and had collected 5,000 silver נודיניסי.

[202] Ibid., no. 65; see no. 62.

[203] Ibid., nos. 66, 70.

[204] Ibid., no. 70.

[205] Adret, I, 415.

[206] Ibid., I, 417, *Minhat Kenaot*, no. 81.

[207] Adret, I, 416: וזה כמשלש שנים חתרנו להוציא רצוננו אל הכוונה. Cf. *Minhat Kenaot*,
no. 82. ונשלוח ספרים מהגדולים אשר המה המחזיקים בתורן לא פעם ולא שתים, ולא יום
אחד ולא יומים כי זה שנתים.

[208] Adret, I, 416, 417.

[209] Ibid., I, 416: ועוד היום כל העדה כלם קדושים זולתי קצת אנשים קרואי עדה
ולמעלתם על העם ראשים.

[210] *Minhat Kenaot*, nos. 73, 78 (p. 150), 94.

[211] Ibid. p. 150: פתח דברי החרם ההוא: כל אשר יטיח כלפי הרב מורה צדק החכם
הגדול רמב"ם ז"ל וכל המונע בנו מללמוד חכמת הטבע והאלהות וחכמת האמת משום זמן נזירה
נגזרה מקירות העיר וחוצה לה, ובכלל החרם ההוא כל מוציא דבה על שום מחבר ספר לתומו.

[212] Ibid., no. 73.

[213] Ibid., nos. 73, 78; cf. 82, 84, 86, 89.

[214] Ibid., no. 78.

[215] Ibid., nos. 73, 78.

[216] Ibid., nos. 73–8.

[217] Ibid., nos. 83, 91–9. These letters, according to Abba Mari, were only a small part of the numerous letters he received. He planned to publish the entire collection as an independent volume (no. 97).

[218] Its contents have to be reconstructed indirectly through the reply which En Duran wrote at the bidding of Abba Mari. Published in *Zunz Jubelschrift* (1884) under the title "Hoshen Mishpat," 155–74 (Hebrew) and 143–51 (German).

[219] Adret, I, 418.

[220] *Minhat Kenaot*, nos. 82–89.

[221] Ibid., no. 97.

[222] Ibid., no. 100.

[223] Ibid.

[224] Ibid., nos. 99–101.

[225] *Israelitische Letterbode*, V, 73–6.

[226] Barfat, 45, 118. See Husik, *Hist. of Jewish Philosophy*, 328 ff.

[227] Ibid., 388 ff. M. Rosenmann, "Das Lehrhaus des R. Nissim Gerundi in Barcelona (ר״ן) als Ursprungsort der letzten anti-maimunischen philosophischen Richtung in Spanien," in *Festschrift Adolf Schwarz*, 489–98. Although Crescas' philosophy was opposed to Maimonides' system, the opposition was not predicated on an anti-rational basis. This applies equally to R. Nissim Gerundi, the teacher of Hasdai Crescas, who was described as the source of anti-Maimunist tendencies in the 14th and 15th centuries.

[228] Barfat, 45.

[229] See Steinschneider in supplement to Kayserling's *Bibliothek jüdischer Kanzelredner*, Berlin, 1870, I, 34–5.

[230] The great grandson of Asher b. Yehiel, Judah Asheri II, was engaged in the study of Avicenna's writings (Barfat, 240). Compare also the respective standpoints of the prominent Ibn Shem Tob family in the 15th century, viz., Shem Tob, Joseph and Shem Tob, father, son and grandson. The first was a violent opponent

of philosophy; the second appreciated its value but sensed its dangers; the third was as enthusiastic a philosopher as his grandfather was a cabalist. As to Isaac Shem Tob, see note 231, below.

[231] I am indebted to Prof. Harry Wolfson for the following notation from the colophon of a supercommentary on Averroes' *Intermediate de generatione* by Isaac b. Shem Tob at the Cambridge University Library, Cod. no. 6.3: והיתה השלמתו על ידי אברהם ן' אדרת בכאן באנולאר די קנפואה, בלמדי זאת החכמה המעיין הטתגבר החכם השלם הר' יצחק ן' שם טוב, ביום ראשון שבעה עשר ימים לחדש אדר שני, שנת מאתים ואחד ושלשים לפרט היצירה.

[232] Besides those who gained celebrity and distinguished themselves chiefly as philosophers, other names are mentioned in the responsa in connection with secular studies. Thus we learn that R. Nissim Gerundi was not only a famous halakist, but also a physician and an astronomer and enjoyed great prestige in non-Jewish circles (Barfat, 447). R. Isaac Barfat was conversant with philosophic questions (ibid., 45, 118, 157). He spoke with warm appreciation of his friend Don Joseph ibn Shoshan who was a talmudist, philosopher and cabalist (ibid., 157). He forwarded three commentaries of Avicenna to R. Judah Asheri which R. Isaac Alhadib, a disciple of R. Judah, had left with him for that purpose (ibid., 240). R. Judah was the head of a famous talmudic academy and was the great-grandson of R. Asher b. Yehiel, the foe of science. He was the author of an astronomic work, *Hukkot ha-Shammayim*, (Zacuto, *Sefer Yuhasin*, ed. Filipowski, 225. See Graetz, VIII, 58, n. 5). R. Isaac Alhadib was an astronomer of note. Before Barfat came to Saragossa, the *dayyan* of that city compiled a work on astronomical charts (ibid., 23 n. 1). R. Simon Duran prided himself on the study of all the secular sciences. See note 1, above; Duran, II, 52; cf. I, 163.

[233] Crescas; *Or Adonai*, preface.

[234] See Graetz, VIII, 114 ff.

[235] Cf. above pp. 100 f. and 192 ff. R. Shem Tob Shaprut, a correspondent of Barfat (210, 226, 515) translated parts of the four Gospels into Hebrew. See Graetz, VIII, 22. R. Simon Duran wrote a criticism of the Koran: Steinschneider, *A. L. J.*, xix, n. 1.

NOTES TO CHAPTER XVII

THE SYNAGOGUE AND ITS AUXILIARY INSTITUTIONS

[1] Adret, IV, 278; VIII, 268; Asher, V, 1.

[2] Adret, V, 222. Cf. Maim., 147; Asher, V, 1.

[3] Graetz, VII, 114.

[4] See below, pp. 149 ff.

[5] Cf. Adret, II, 134; Baer, I, 229, 368.

[6] It was not always feasible to carry out the talmudic injunction to set up the synagogue on the highest point of the city; but it was usually aimed to build the

house of God higher than the surrounding habitations. Cf. Shab. 11a and Prov. 1. 21; Grayzel, no. 123.

[7] Adret, V, 222.

[8] Ibid.; also III, 395, 443; Barfat, 331; Baer, II, 294.

[9] Adret, V, 222.

[10] Ibid.; Asher, V, 1.

[11] Adret, V, 222.

[12] Cf. Maim., 147.

[13] Adret, I, 96, 581; II, 52; III, 166, 434, 443; ZJ, 21; Abraham b. Nathan, Ha-Manhig, 19 §67. One of the synagogues in Toledo, known as *el midras de las vigas*, was probably noted for its beams (Baer, II, 390, p. 430).

[14] MGWJ, VI, 378–81; REJ, IX, 157–8; X, 245 ff.; BAH, V, 202 ff. See illustrations in JE, s. v. Spain, Cordova, Toledo.

[15] Barfat, 259. A structure without windows was unfit for public worship, according to the Talmud, Ber. 34b.

[16] Asher, V, 8. Allusion to Esther 8.16.

[17] Adret, II, 52; Maimonides (M. T., Hilkot Tefillah, XI, 5) observed: תנהגין כל
ישראל בספרד ובמערב בשנער ובארץ הצבי להדליק עששיות בבתי כנסיות ולהציע בקרקען
מחצלאות כדי לישב עליהם. ובערי אדום יושבין בה על הכסאות.
Cf. Barfat, 253: גם מה שאמרת אם יוכלו קצת אנשים שאין להם מקומות לתת כסאות
הנטלין באמצע בה'כ ולישב שם או שרצו לישב בארץ שורות שורות על מחצלאות נקיות...

[18] Adret, II, 52; Barfat, 249.

[19] Adret, I, 956; II, 52; III, 155; IV, 319; Asher, V, 3, 7.

[20] Ibid.; Barfat, 253.

[21] Adret, IV, 319; Barfat, 249.

[22] Asher, V, 5.

[23] Adret, IV, 319.

[24] Ibid.; cf. ibid., I, 939, 943, 956, 1156; II, 272; III, 158, 166; V, 250; VI, 7; VII, 189; Asher, V, 5. Cf. Adret, VIII, 26; Asher, V, 4.

[25] Adret, II, 182; III, 155; VI, 7; Baer, I, 351.

[26] Barfat, 253. Cf. Adret, I, 1156.

[27] Barfat, 253.

[28] Ibid., 249.

[29] Baer, I, 226. The *kahal* of Burgos passed a ban of excommunication against those who sought to bring outside pressure to bear on the synagogue authorities in the matter of seat distribution. Barfat, 249.

[30] The need for expansion is also indicated in Adret, III, 166.

[31] Graetz, VII, 114; Baer, II, 67.

[32] Rios, II, 359, n. 2. Graetz, VIII, 57. See Marx, 26, 31, n. 5. Among the synagogues of Seville were those known as "de Ihuda Abenxabal" and "de Alcoba" (Baer, II, 67, p. 50).

[33] Barfat, 331.

[34] Introd. to *Mekor Hayyim*, in Wiener, *Shebeṭ Yehudah*, 131; also Baer, II, 209.

[35] Ibid., I, 269, 272, 351. See Baer, I, 463, p. 729, and 527, p. 850. See also ibid.,

II, 397, where the last mentioned synagogue was known as *sinoga de vicorolim* and also *de los torneros*.

[36] Graetz, VI, 189. The fate of the Toledo synagogues was described by Fidel Fita in *BAH*, V, 396 ff. For reference to *xinoga del sofer* and *xinoga de barrio de Caleros* in Toledo, see Baer, II, 262; *REJ*, XXXVIII, 251 f.

[37] Grayzel, no. 123; Rios, I, 367–9, 556–7; *REJ*, IX, 157–8; Fita, *Actas Ineditas*, 214; *BAH*, V, 202, 241, 361–5.

[38] Fita, 382 ff.; *REJ*, IX, 157–8; X, 244–5; *BAH*, V, 234 ff.

[39] Barfat, 331. For a blacksmiths' synagogue in talmudic times, see Megillah 26a.

[40] Baer, I, 179, 351. See n. 32, above.

[41] References to מעות לבנין בה״כ applied to maintenance and repair funds. No mention is made in the Talmud of any tax for the building of a synagogue. Cf. Tosefta, B. B. 1. 6.

[42] Abraham b. Nathan, *Ha-Manhig*, 27 §22. See above, n. 36.

[43] Baer, I, 326, 351.

[44] Ibid., II, 167.

[45] Ibid., I, 300.

[46] Ibid., I, 272.

[47] Barfat, 331. For Seville see above, n. 32.

[48] Cf. Baer, I, 508.

[49] Graetz, VIII, 55–64; Rios, II, 349–96; Baer, II, 247, 249, 270, 278, 284. See also ibid., 300. The university of Salamanca also fell heir to some of the communal property of the Jewish *aljama*, including *una casa que dezian del midras*. King John II made this gift to the university *para fazer en ella hospital para el dicho estudio* (ibid., 280).

[50] See S. Katz, *The Jews in the Visigothic and Frankish Kingdoms of Spain and Gaul*, 73–5. Compare *REJ*, IX, 157, n. 1: *En cherchant bien, on trouvera probablement que très souvent la juiverie était attenante à une église ou très voisine de l'église, pour être plus dépendante du clergé ou mieux surveillée…*

[51] *Cod. Theod.*, 16.8.22 (415); 16.8.25 (Feb. 15, 423); 16.8.27 (June 8, 423); also *Nov. Th.*, III, 3. See J. Juster, *Les Juifs dans l'empire romain*, I, ch. IV, sect. IV §1, especially pp. 470–2.

[52] *Nov. Just.*, 131, §14; also *Novella* 37, of the year 535. Juster, op. cit., I, 472.

[53] Grayzel, no. 50.

[54] Ibid., no. 14.

[55] Ibid., no. 123. See above, n. 37.

[56] Baer, II, 221 §5.

[57] Rios, I, 451.

[58] *Las Siete Partidas*, ed. J. M. Martinez, VII, 24, 4; Rios, I, 467; Lindo, 99. The same attitude was taken by Islam toward the Church as well as the Synagogue since the Pact of Omar. See Graetz, V, 111. But although there were sporadic attacks upon these houses of worship, especially under the Almohades shortly after 1140, Islam did not develop a genius for repression and persecution. Moham-

medan countries therefore did not, in practice, present a parallel persecution of either the Synagogue or the Church.

[59] Baer, II, 221 §5, 222, 318. Cf. 266, 267, 283, 369.

[60] Jacobs, 241, 788, 900; Baer, I, 175, 326.

[61] Ibid., I, 229, 368. See above, notes 53, 55.

[62] Baer, I, 455 §2, 480 §2, 527 §4; p. 850; II, 247, 249. See also ibid., I, 508, 515; cf. I, 575.

[63] Ibid., I, 508.

[64] Ibid., I, 455 §2, 480 §2, 527, also p. 850; cf. I, 229.

[65] Ibid., II, 266, 267.

[66] Lindo, 214. See Baer, II, 318.

[67] Ibid.

[68] Ibid., II, 287 §3; Finkelstein, op. cit., 355. See above, p. 292, n. 1.

[69] Jacobs, 148; Baer, II, 391.

[70] *REJ*, XXXIX, 209–16.

[71] See *REJ*, IX, 157–8; X, 244–7; XXXIX, 209–16.

[72] Barfat, 259.

[73] See above, pp. 151 ff.

[74] Adret, III, 395, 443; V, 279.

[75] Baer, I, 175 §18.

[76] Ibid., §17; ibid., I, 579.

[77] Adret, I, 415, et passim.

[78] Ibid., III, 395; Baer, I, 463.

[79] Barfat, 331.

[80] Baer, II, 397. See above, I, 58 f.

[81] Cf. Maim., 17: ברוב השעות כשיתקבצו העם לשום דבר מצוה או על צרה שלא תבא הוא תמיד בבה"כ.

[82] Adret, I, 377, 433.

[83] Ibid., I, 377.

[84] Stern, *Urkundliche Beiträge über die Stellung der Päpste zu den Juden*, I, 48; Baer, II, 301.

[85] Lindo, 247; Rios, III, 287.

[86] The customary tax was twelve *maravedís*. At the Cortes of Toledo in 1480, it was increased to four *reales* of plate for each Torah (Lindo, 245).

[87] Ibid.

[88] Cf. above, I, 122.

[89] *ZJ*, 36; Baer, II, no. 287 p. 284; Finkelstein, 355–6; cf. Baer, I, 269.

[90] Adret, IV, 104. Cf. ibid., II, 108.

[91] Ibid., II, 95.

[92] Barfat, 388, 390.

[93] Adret, VIII, 275.

[94] Maim., 147.

[95] Adret, I, 469.

[96] Duran, II, 39.

⁹⁷ See above, pp. I, 123.
⁹⁸ Maim., 81; Adret, IV, 278; Abraham b. Nathan, *Ha-Manhig*, 64 §5.
⁹⁹ Cf. Barfat, 331.
¹⁰⁰ Asher, IV, 19.
¹⁰¹ Alfasi, 281.
¹⁰² Duran, III, 254. In Mohammedan countries, the *hazzan*, like the *talmid hakam*, was tax-exempt. See above, I, 102.
¹⁰³ Adret, I, 215, 300; Baer, I, 294.
¹⁰⁴ Alfasi, 281; Migash, 95; Adret, I, 300, 450; Nissim, 65.
¹⁰⁵ Baer, I, 294, 542.
¹⁰⁶ Barfat, 219.
¹⁰⁷ Baer, I, 374.
¹⁰⁸ Cf. Adret, I, 452; III, 288; Barfat 84, 334.
¹⁰⁹ Barfat, 37, 334. Cf. ibid., 369: אווירא דברצלונה מחכים בניה ובוניה כצוריאל בן אביחיל ובצלאל.
¹¹⁰ Adret, III, 289.

NOTES TO CHAPTER XVIII

CHARITIES

¹ Hebrew Prayer Book, ed. Singer, 5.
² Cf. Abot 1. 2.
³ Maim., *M.T.*, *Hilk. Mattenot 'Aniyyim*, IX, 3. Cf. Sanhedrin 17b: כל עיר שאין בה עשרה דברים הללו אין תלמיד חכם רשאי לדור בתוכה, ב"ד מכין ועונשין . . . וקופה של צדקה . . . Following talmudic terminology, Maimonides retained the distinction between the *kuppah*, or charity chest (the *arca* of the Roman Church), and the *tamhui*, the charity bowl (ibid., IX, 1–2). The former was a fund of money made up of weekly collections and was distributed among the poor every Friday; the latter consisted of daily collections of food which was rationed to the poor every evening. The *tamhui*, or relief in kind, was abandoned in many communities, according to Maimonides (ibid., IX, 3). It would appear that it was given up entirely in later generations.
⁴ Joseph Kimhi, *Sefer ha-Berit*, Constantinople, 1710.
⁵ Baer, II, 76; *BAH*, X, 465 f.; XII, 61 f.; *REJ*, XV, 125–8.
⁶ Baer, I, 434; II, 386, 390, 391. See ibid., I, 399.
⁷ Adret, I, 617, 669, 1103; II, 326; III, 129, 291, 380; IV, 173, 213, 239; V, 249, 269; Barfat, 207, 285; Nissim, 75; Baer, I, 179, 351, 362, 399, 434, 480 §13, 532, 533, et passim; II, 280.
⁸ Adret, IV, 55. Cf. Asher, XXXII, 6.
⁹ Neubauer, *MJC*, I, 68.
¹⁰ See Abrahams, 335–9.
¹¹ Adret III, 291; Asher, XIII, 5, 6; Baer, I, 532.

[12] Quoted in *Bet Yosef, Tur Yoreh De'ah*, 250; cited in Abrahams, 316, n. 1.

[13] Maim., *M.T., Hilk. Mattenot 'Aniyyim*, VII §5.

[14] Abrahams, *Heb. Ethical Wills*, II, 192.

[15] Ibid., 192–4.

[16] Ibid., II, 225. See Schechter, *Studies in Judaism*, 167; also Abrahams, *Jewish Life in the Middle Ages*, 318–9.

[17] Alfasi, 135, 247; Adret, I, 617, 654, 1100; III, 291, 297; IV, 239; Barfat, 207, et passim; Baer, I, 533.

[18] Adret, II, 326; III, 296; IV, 239; Asher, XIII, 7, 8, 9, 16, 17; Baer, I, 399, 434.

[19] Alfasi, 23; Adret, IV, 243; V, 265; Baer, I, 508; II, 283.

[20] Asher, XIII, 12, 13; Nissim, 75; Adret, V, 267–8; Baer, I, 179, 296, 351, 362, 508, 532, 543.

[21] Barfat, 331; Baer, I, 179, 351.

[22] Asher, XIII, 6.

[24] Adret, I, 669; III, 291; V, 249; Baer, I, 296.

[24] Adret, I, 617.

[25] Ibid., I, 669; Asher, XIII, 10, 17. Cf. above, I, 196.

[26] Adret, V, 267.

[27] Ibid., I, 617, 654; V, 269; Barfat, 207; Baer, I, 508; II, 157.

[28] Ibid., I, 179, 296, 362, 480; Adret, VIII, 275.

[29] Baer, I, 386, 447.

[30] Ibid., I, 543.

[31] See note 28, above.

[32] See note 7, above.

[33] Alfasi, 135, 247; Adret, I, 618, 656; IV, 150, 173, 213, 239.

[34] Ibid., IV, 150; Asher, XIII, 14.

[35] Alfasi, 6; Migash, 207; Adret, I, 604, 605; III, 291; V, 269; Asher, XIII, 5, 14; Barfat, 285.

[36] Cf. Asher, XIII, 8: אבל הקדש שבזמן הזה שהוא לעניים או לתלמוד תורה. See ibid., XIII, 17; Nissim, 1.

[37] Cf. Adret, III, 291; Asher, XIII, 5; Barfat, 285; Baer, II, 157, 287.

[38] Nissim, 1, 75; Baer, I, 362, 399, 508.

[38a] His name appears in the trust agreement in full as follows: יוסף הלוי בן דון אפרים בן דון יצחק הלוי בן שבת (*Yocef el Levi, fijo de don Frayme, nieto de don Çag Elevi aben Xabad*).

[39] Baer, II, 157.

[39a] For Joseph's brilliant career in the court of Alfonso XI and his tragic end, see Graetz, VII, 286–90.

[40] Maim., *M.T., Hilk. Mattenot 'Aniyyim*, IX and X. See also ZL, 68b, 70b.

[41] Maim., *M.T., Hilk. Mat. 'Aniyyim*, X.

[42] Adret, III, 380.

[43] Baer, I, 533; ZL, 109b–110a; cf. N. Coronel, *Zeker Natan*, 132b.

[44] Adret, III, 380.

[45] Ibid., III, 291; Barfat, 285, Baer, I, 532.

[46] Adret, III, 380; Asher, XIII, 6.

[47] Adret, III, 380.

[48] Shulhan ʿAruk, Yoreh Deʿah, 250 §5.

[49] Baer, II, 386, 390, 391; cf. 410; also REJ, XVI, 173, n. 1.

[50] Peʾah 1.1; Shab. 127a.

[51] Nissim, 75; Baer, I, 351, 463.

[52] Ibid., I, 351. See ibid., 436, p. 729; also II, 397, pp. 461–2.

[53] Abrahams, 330.

[54] See above, p. 109.

[55] Adret, V, 267–8; Asher, XIII, 12; Baer, I, 179, 296, 399, 508.

[56] Ibid., I, 179. Cf. Asher, XIII, 12; Adret, III, 291.

[57] See Abrahams, 326–8; Vogelstein-Rieger, Gesch. d. Juden in Rom, II, 316. Cf. JQR, V (1893), 514; Zion, V, 61–77. See Dinaburg in David Yellin Jubilee Volume, 157–82.

[58] Graetz, VII, 11–2; Zunz, "An Essay on the geographical literature of the Jews," §§44, 47, in Asher, The Itinerary of Rabbi Benjamin of Tudela; Steinschneider, Jüdische Schriften zur Geographie Palästina's, Jerusalem, 1892, no. 48.

[59] Cf. Asher, VIII, 13; XII, 7; XLV, 10; Nissim, 6; Barfat, 508.

[60] Asher, VIII, 13; XII, 7.

[61] Ibid., XII, 7.

[62] Ibid., VIII, 13.

[63] Ibid.

[64] The text adds also obscurely, ‏או אם [לא] חשׂין יד כל אחד ממנו לאלפים זהובים‎.

[65] See epilogue to Nahmanides' commentary on the Pentateuch; also letter appended to Nahmanides' Shaʿar ha-Gemul; cf. S. Schechter, Studies in Judaism, 131–3.

[66] Barfat, 508: ‏... וגם שבודאי ירושלים שיירות מצויות שם מכל העולם שהכל מעלין‎ ‏לירושלים‎. Writing a legal brief to a rabbi in Safed, R. Nissim, in conclusion, departed from his theme to express homage to the Holy Land: ‏הכותב משתחוה לארץ‎ ‏קדשנו מסקומו, עיניו ולבו שם, לילו ויומו מתפלל אל ד' להשיב את שבותם למען שמו ולהראות את‎ ‏כבודו במעון קדשו והדומו‎ (Nissim, 7. Cf. also Baer, I, 224a, §5).

NOTES TO CHAPTER XIX

SOCIAL RELATIONS BETWEEN JEWS AND CHRISTIANS

[1] See below, pp. 200 ff.

[2] Cf. above, pp. 98 ff. Even in exile the émigrés and their descendants preserved their Spanish tongue, the Ladino of the present day.

[3] Jews generally bore double names, Hebrew and Spanish, the latter being called Christian. The two names were not necessarily related. Joseph Jacob's famed identification of R. Moses b. Nahman (Nahmanides) with Bonastruc de Porta is a striking example. To force Jews to drop their Christian appellations was one of the objectives of the anti-Jewish legislation. Cf. below, p. 263.

[4] Cf. below, pp. 200 ff.

[5] See below, pp. 224 ff. Eighty slaves were included in the confiscated fortune of Samuel ha-Levi Abulafia, the fallen favorite of Pedro IV, who died under torture, in 1360 (Graetz, VII, 393). With regard to Don Abraham Señor and his retinue, see Marx, *JQR*, XX (1908), 250.

[6] See Régné, 376, 1343; Baer, II, 181 §32, 268; Lindo, 185.

[7] Cf. Régné, 8, 237; Jacobs, 267; Grayzel, no. 24.

[8] Cf. Régné, 1021, 1342; *BAH*, XXXVI, no. 30.

[9] Cf. above, I, 41.

[10] See above, ch. XV.

[11] See ch. XX, passim.

[12] Cf. below, pp. 266 ff., 271 ff.

[13] Cf. above, 99, 102 ff.

[14] See Baer, I, 400; cf. Barfat 60. See above pp. 214 ff.; also note 152, below.

[15] Cf. above, ch. IX.

[16] Cf. Maim., 237; Adret, II, 232; Barfat, 151.

[17] Adret, I, 783, 875; Asher, CIV, 3.

[18] Adret, V, 287. It is significant that as late as 1465 it was found necessary to forbid Christian clients the services of Jewish advocates (Baer, II, 318 §114).

[19] Adret, I, 715–6.

[20] Cf. ibid., IV, 125: ‏ראובן הביא נכרים אוהביו לחנותו של שמעון.‏

[21] Ibid., I, 178; Asher, XIX, 22; Barfat, 73; cf. *ZL*, 102b; cf. Baer, II, 148; Lindo, 130.

[22] Ibid., 182.

[23] Cf. Baron, II, 87–91; III, 116–7.

[24] Cf. above, I, 164 f.

[25] Cf. Adret, IV, 270, 325.

[26] Ibid., VIII, 16; Asher, XIX, 13; XCI, 4; Régné, 433; Baer, II, 117, 291, p. 304.

[27] Ibid., II, 117. This fact aroused the protest of the Council of Salamanca: ibid., II, 160.

[28] Adret, VIII, 207; Asher, XCVI, 6.

[29] Adret, V, 6; cf. Alfasi, 277.

[30] See above, I, 84 f.; Grayzel, 36–8.

[31] Adret, I, 163; Régné, 737, 771, 1761; Baer, I, 8, 12, 573 §3; also pp. 1036–7; II, 88, 133; Grayzel, nos. IX, XX, XXI, 17, 21, 33, 36, 60, 62, 66, 126.

[32] Ibid.; note especially Adret, I, 163.

[33] See Grayzel, 36 n. 1; cf. Baer, I, pp. 1036–7.

[34] Cf. *REJ*, LVIII, 203 n. 2.

[35] Grayzel, no. 66.

[36] Cf. ibid., no. 17.

[37] Régné, 737; cf. Baer, I, 12, 573; Rios, I, 409.

[38] Grayzel, no. 17; cf. no. 21.

[39] Ibid., nos. 33, 36, 60, 62.

⁴⁰ For the text of the concordat, see Baer, II, 7.   The following abstract is cited in Grayzel, 147:

1. Every male Jew of twenty or over, and if married, even below twenty, shall pay to the Archbishop an annual sum of one sixth of an *aureum*.

2. Every dispute regarding age shall be settled by two elders from the Jewish community of Toledo and two from another synagogue that the Archbishop may pick.

3. Jews shall be freed from the payment of tithes and offerings which the Lateran Council imposed.

4. The last provision shall apply to all property in Jewish hands at the time of the making of the Concordat.

5. It shall apply also to property sold by a Jew to a Christian, provided this property is within the diocese covered by the Concordat.

6. Property, however, sold by a Christian to a Jew after the establishment of the Concordat shall be subject to the tithe.

7. The above shall not include houses built or to be built.

8. The elders of the Synagogue shall be responsible for the payment of the tax by any Jew, so that the Archbishop may claim from the elders what any individual refuses to pay.

9. The tax shall be paid annually from the Feast of St. Michael to that of St. Martin (September 29 — November 11, hence immediately after the holiday of Succot).

10. The Archbishop promises in the name of God, and upon his own honor, to defend and help the Jews as much as will be in his power.

Rios, I, 357–9.   For a similar arrangement, half a century earlier, see Baer, I, 44; cf. 577 §3.

⁴¹ Ibid., II, 68; Fita, *BAH*, V, 369.

⁴² Baer, II, 88.

⁴³ Ibid., II, 133; Rios, II, 561 ff.; Lindo, 126–7.

⁴⁴ Ibid., 239.

⁴⁵ Grayzel, no. 85.

⁴⁶ Ibid., p. 13; also nos. 14, 16, 110; *REJ*, XXXV, 250.

⁴⁷ *Ep.*, I, 34; see also A. Lukyn Williams, op. cit., 243.

⁴⁸ Grayzel, no. 110; cf. L. Lucas, in Philippson's *Festschrift*, 26.

⁴⁹ Grayzel, 13–5.

⁵⁰ Cf. ibid., 14–5; also no. 12; *MGH, Reg. Greg.*, I, bk. I, no. 45; Wiener, *Regesten*, no. 29.

⁵¹ See Graetz, "Die westgotische Gesetzgebung in Betreff der Juden" in *Jahresbericht des jüdisch-theologischen Seminars, fraenckelscher Stiftung*, Berlin, 1858; Juster, *La condition légale des Juifs sous les rois visigoths*; Katz, *The Jews in the Visigothic and Frankish Kingdoms of Spain and Portugal*, Cambridge, Mass., 1937.

⁵² Katz, op. cit., 10–22. Cf. Pope Gregory I's observation on the outcome of forced conversion, cited above.

⁵³ An apostate created many religious and social problems which required rabbinic

adjudication. The relative paucity of such cases in the responsa prior to the whole-sale persecutions which commenced in the fourteenth century is proof that voluntary apostasy was an uncommon event in the *judería*. The non-Jewish sources also indicate the same relative dearth of Jewish conversions in Spain. Grayzel's collection of papal bulls covering the years 1198–1254 contain twenty letters relating to Jewish converts in whose behalf the popes intervened. Not one of these relates to Spain. Cases of converts in Baer, I and II, chiefly belong to periods of persecution.

References to apostates occur in the following responsa: Adret, I, 315, 661, 1091 = III, 401, 1162 (theoretical), 1176, 1180; III, 352; V, 66 (theoretical), 240; VII, 41 (theoretical), 179 (theoretical), 267, 292 (geonic and theoretical), 411 (theoretical), 434 = VIII, 224 (theoretical); VIII, 142 (theoretical), 180 (theoretical) Asher, XVII, 9 (theoretical), 10, 11, 12; XXXII, 4, 5, 6, 8 (these four responsa relate to women who became converted in captivity); XXXIV, 1 = XLI, 1. The responsa of R. Nissim and R. Isaac Barfat reflect the persecutions of 1348 and 1391, respectively. In reference to Nissim, 47, see Graetz, VII, 297. On the responsa dealing with *anusim*, or Marranos, following the persecutions of 1391, see *Ha-Kerem*, 1887, 18. For the subject of the Marranos in rabbinic literature, see H. J. Zimmels, *Die Marranen in der rabbinischen Literatur*, Berlin, 1932; S. Assaf, אנוסי ספרד ופורטוגאל בספרות התשובות, in *Zion*, V, 19–60.

[54] See below, pp. 194 f.
[55] Asher, XVII, 12.
[56] Ibid., XVII, 9.
[57] Ibid., XXXIV, 1.
[58] Adret, III, 352; cf. Régné, 2670; Baer, II, 228.
[59] Régné, 2529.
[60] Adret, VII, 292; Asher, XVII, 10.
[61] Cf. Grayzel, 18–9.
[62] See Régné, 2670.
[63] Grayzel, no. I.
[64] Ibid., 16–8. A century later, in 1322, the Council of Salamanca followed the same policy. An enactment was passed that converts were to be cared for in monasteries or other religious establishments. They were to be taught a trade and furnished with the necessary tools, unless they were otherwise well provided. Those who were qualified were to be instructed for the priesthood, if they so desired, and the bishops were requested to provide them with churches. Lindo, 130; Baer, II, 148.
[65] *Cortes*, I, 217 ff.
[66] Grayzel, no. 105. Innocent IV hailed the document as one of capital importance and incorporated it verbatim in the bull dated August 20, 1245, thus confirming it by his apostolic authority.
[67] Régné, 209, 215; cf. ibid., 723, wherein Pedro III, probably at the instigation of Pope Nicholas III, demanded that the Jews be forced to gather in the synagogues to hear missionary sermons by the monks; similarly James II: Baer, *Studien*, 37 n. 87, 38 n. 91; Jacobs, 920, 1033; Rios, II, 158.

[68] Régné, 216, 217, 386; Bofarull, 58 n. 34, 76-7 n. 73. For similar acts of Pedro III, see Régné, 731-6, 740, 746, 748; Baer, *Studien*, 37.

[69] Régné, 2670.

[70] Ibid., 2934.

[71] Baer, I, 390.

[72] *Partidas*, VII, 24, 6.

[73] Baer, II, 148.

[74] Ibid., I, 228.

[75] One of the early references to a Jewish convert to Christianity in Barcelona (July 13, 1023) was that of Isaac, son of Gento, who in the previous year had been convicted of adulterous relationship with a Christian woman and who had in consequence suffered the confiscation of his property. Baer, I, 4; see Adret, I, 315; V, 240; Régné, 3363. As to Nicholas Donin, see Grayzel, Appendix A, and the literature cited there.

[76] Régné, 3363.

[77] Adret, I, 1091 = III, 401.

[78] Cf. the letter of Jacob b. Eli to Pablo Christiani in *Jeschurun*, VI (1868), 29-30. Referring to Nicholas Donin, he wrote: "This apostate went before the king, superior to all kings in name and honor, and uttered lies and made false accusations concerning us, saying that on Passover nights we slaughter young boys not yet weaned from their mothers' breasts; that the Jews had adopted this custom; that merciful women cook these children and we eat their flesh and drink their blood ... This wicked man sought to destroy us and put a sword in the hands of the king to kill us. He lied to him. But God returned to him double his iniquity ... The honored king, in his piety and cleanness of hands, did not believe his words and paid no heed to him, knowing that they were folly and nonsense and vanity. Nor did all the kings of the world and the inhabitants of earth believe except that a learned wild man was speaking." Grayzel, 339; see *MGWJ*, XVIII, 102; *REJ*, LXXXII, 363 ff.

[79] Cf. Baer, II, 148; Lindo, 130; also Baer, I, 356, 525; see above, note 68.

[80] For the unusual case of a Jewish apostate who came to the defense of Judaism, see Bacher, *REJ*, XVII, 279 f.

[81] Cf. above, n. 78.

[82] See Baer, לבקורת הוויכוחים של ר' יחיאל מפאריש ושל רמב"ן, in *Tarbiz*, II, 172-87. Régné, 207, cites the important literature on the subject and gives a skeleton outline of the debate according to the Dominican *procès-verbal*. For the Hebrew version by Nahmanides, see Steinschneider, ed. *Sefer Vikuah ha-RaMBaN*, Stettin, 1860; see A. Lukyn Williams, op. cit., 244-7. The subsequent indictment of Nahmanides because of his written account of the disputation is outlined in Régné, 323, and the literature is there cited. See also ibid., 324.

In the non-Hebrew accounts, Nahmanides' name appears as Bonastruc (or Bonastrug) de Porta. During the same period, the records also contain references to Astrug de Porta who engaged in religious debates and suffered a fate similar to Nahmanides (Régné, 262, 315, 316). Astrug was a brother of the bailiff, Benveniste de Porta, one of the most important figures in the court of King James I. Astrug was himself a man of great wealth (cf. ibid., 302, 303). Whether Astrug was to be identified with Bonastruc, and hence with Nahmanides, gave rise to interesting speculation. See Baer, *Studien*, 34, n. 76.

[83] Cf. Baron, II, 70–8; III, 78–9.

[84] Steinschneider, op. cit., 21–2.

[85] Régné, 323, 324; Graetz, VII, 120–6.

[86] C. Roth, *A History of the Marranos*, 11–28. H. C. Lea, in *AHR*, I, 209–25.

[87] A. Lukyn Williams, op. cit., 252.

[88] Baron, II, 55–8.

[89] Régné, 2926, 2952, 2954, 2966, 2971, 3389, 3396, 3419; Baer, I, 166, 168; II, 351 (p. 375), 410; *REJ*, IV, 42 ff.

[90] See below, pp. 209 ff.

[91] See above, note 89.

[92] See below, pp. 196 f.

[93] Adret, I, 328.

[94] Ibid., I, 182, 328, 329, 1099 (Meir of Rothenburg); II, 252; IV, 139; VIII, 69; Asher, XV, 1, 2, 3, 4.

[95] For the laws against Jewish proselytism in the Theodosian and Justinian codes as well as in Visigothic Spain, see Katz, 42–4, 46, 48, 50–1.

[96] Régné, 9; Rios, I, 406 n. 1, 411 n. 4.

[97] Baer, II, 65.

[98] See ibid., II, 61. Lindo, 76.

[99] *Partidas*, VII, 24, 7; cf. VII, 26, 2; Lindo, 101; Baer, II, 63.

[100] *Partidas*, VII, 24, 2; Lindo, 98; Baer, II, 63.

[101] Régné, 2926; Baer, I, 166; Lea, I, 94.

[102] Régné, 2926, 2952, 2954, 2966, 2971, 3016; Baer, I, 166, 168.

[103] *REJ*, IV, 42 ff.; Fita-Llabrés, 24; Baer, *Studien*, 62.

[104] Régné, 3389, 3396.

[105] Ibid., 3419; Jacobs, 873; Baer, *Studien*, 62–3, Lea, I, 94.

[106] Baer, II, 351 (p. 375), 410.

[107] Grayzel, no. 5.

[108] Ibid., no. 87.

[109] Ibid., nos. 14, 70, 113, 117.

[110] See below, pp. 200 ff.

[111] Bishop Odo of Paris, c. 1200, expressed this view succinctly: *quorum enim dispar est cultus, nullus debet esse animarum consensus*, "Where the religions differ there ought to be no community of spirit," Grayzel, no. IV. For a detailed analysis of the church program in regard to the Jews, see ibid., part I, pp. 1–83. Part II comprises the text and translation of the papal letters and conciliar decrees of the period 1198–1254. The church program was incorporated in Alfonso's code, *Las Siete Partidas*. Baer, II, 63, contains the text concerning the Jews. For an English translation, see Lindo, 92–102; also S. P. Scott, *Las Siete Partidas*.

[112] Peter of Cluny, inciting the crusaders against the Jews, opposed their slaugh-

ter because they were "reserved for greater ignominy, for an existence more bitter than death."

[113] Innocent III thus sharply expressed this conception: "The Lord made Cain a wanderer and a fugitive over the earth, but set a mark upon him, making his head to shake, lest any finding him should slay him. Thus the Jews, against whom the blood of Jesus Christ calls out, although they ought not be killed, lest the Christian people forget the Divine Law, yet as wanderers ought they to remain upon the earth, until their countenance be filled with shame and they seek the name of Jesus Christ, the Lord. That is why blasphemers of the Christian name ought not to be aided by Christian princes to oppress the servants of the Lord, but ought rather be forced into the servitude of which they made themselves deserving when they raised sacrilegious hands against Him Who had come to confer true liberty upon them, thus calling down His blood upon themselves and upon their children." Grayzel, no. 24.

The same theory is worded more mildly in Las Siete Partidas: "The reason the Church, the emperors, the kings and other princes suffer the Jews to live among the Christians is this: that they might always live as in captivity and thus be a reminder to all men that they are descended from the lineage of those who crucified our Lord Jesus Christ." VII, 24, 1; cf. id., 3; Baer, II, pp. 44-5; cf. Grayzel, nos. 5, 8, 14, 18, 41, 49, 87, et passim.

[114] Partidas, VII, 24, 2.

[115] Ibid., VII, 24, 3; Grayzel, no. 49.

[116] Partidas, VII, 24, 8.

[117] Ibid.; Baer, II, 133, 148, 275, 295; Lindo, 127, 197, 203.

[118] Grayzel, no. XXXIII. The ecumenical council of 692 had made this prohibition apply to all Christendom. The Caliph Al-Hakim turned tables on the Christians and issued such an edict against Jews and Christians alike (Baron, II, 53).

[119] Baer, II, 8; also note 117, above; Grayzel, nos. 18, XXXIII, XXXIV, XXXVI.

[120] Intermarriage was evidently more "wicked" than promiscuous intercourse, according to Gregory IX (Grayzel, nos. 61, 73).

[121] Partidas, VII, 24, 9; Baer, I, 456.

[122] Partidas, VII, 24, 7.

[123] Ibid., VII, 24, 10.

[124] Grayzel, 60-70; concerning the origins of the badge, see the discussion, ibid., notes 97-8; for numerous references to the badge, note 99; Partidas, VII, 24, 11. On the general history and origin of the badge, see U. Robert, Les signes d'infamie au moyen age, Paris, 1891; F. Singermann, Die Kennzeichnung der Juden im Mittelalter, Berlin, 1915; cf. Fagnan, REJ, XXVIII, 294-5; H. C. Lea, History of the Inquisition of Spain, I, 68 n. 2; Rios, II, 198; Fernández y González, 16.

[125] See Grayzel, no. 27.

[126] Ibid., no. XXVII n. 1.

[127] Cf. ibid., no. 36.

[128] Barfat, 425; Asher, VIII, 8, שחייבים עליהם מיתה בדיניהם; Baer, I, 456, pp.

1037-8; II, 125 §72: *Todo judio que con christiana fallaren sea despennado y ella quemada.*

[129] Bofarull, 5, 6; Régné, 2517.

[130] Grayzel, no. 72.

[131] Ibid., no. 78.

[132] Cf. ibid., no. 18.

[133] Bofarull, 5, 6; Adret, I, 1187; IV, 257; cf. above, pp. 11 f.; also *ZJ*, 91; Régné, 1029, 1074, 2065; see Zacuto, *Sefer Yuhasin*, ed. Filipowski, 225a.

[134] Régné, 674; Barfat, 425.

[135] Grayzel, no. 120, also XX; cf. XLI: "And since by reason of the round capes which Jews generally wear, the respect due the clergy is seriously impaired, for they (the clergy) use round capes habitually, we decree, with the approbation of this Council, that in the future Jews shall not dare to wear round capes. They may, however, in the future wear capes with long sleeves, the sleeves being as long as the capes, but in these sleeves there must be no folds or creases."

[136] Cf. above, note 6.

[137] Grayzel, no. X; see ibid., p. 61 n. 98. Innocent's reference is to Num. 15.38.

[138] Singermann, op. cit., 9–10: Grayzel, p. 61 n. 97.

[139] Ibid., nos. XXIX, XXX.

[140] Ibid., nos. IX, X, XI, XIII.

[141] Ibid. no. 38; Rios, I, 361-2.

[142] Grayzel, no. 44.

[143] Ibid., no. 38.

[144] Ibid., no. 51.

[145] Ibid., no. 44.

[146] Ibid., no. 62; also no. 71.

[147] Ibid., nos. 72, 78.

[148] Ibid., no. 122.

[149] Bofarull, 34; see *REJ*, VI, 92.

[150] Concil. Tarraconens., an. 1238, cap. iv; an. 1282, cap. v (Martene, *Ampliss. Collect.*, VIII, 132, 280); Lea, I, 69, n. 5.

[151] Pella, *Hist. del Ampurdán*, 544, cited in Baer, *Studien*, 60 n. 5.

[152] Jacobs, 771; Régné, 390, 392, 394, 395, 1117, 2928; Adret, V, 183; Baer, *Studien*, 30, n. 64; ibid., I, 237, 265, 292 (p. 423), 303 note.

[153] Cf. Grayzel, no. 44.

[154] Jacobs, 771, 1088, 1147.

[155] Baer, *Studien*, 30 n. 63.

[156] *Partidas*, VII, 24, 11.

[157] Altamira, *Cuestiones de Historia del Derecho y de Legislación Comparada*, Madrid, 1914, §456.

[158] Baer, II,˙133; Lindo, 127; Lea, I, 69.

[159] Baer, II, 138.

[160] The Infante Juan, who presided over the Cortes as guardian of Alfonso XI,

withheld his sanction until he could determine what was for the good of the land: *Cortes*, I, 227; Lea, I, 69.

[161] Baer, I, 292, p. 423; ibid., II, 217.

[162] Ibid., II, 217; Lea, I, 69–70.

[163] Baer, II, 268; Rios, II, 419 ff.; Lindo, 184–5.

[164] Grayzel, nos. III, XVI, XXV, XXXIII; ibid., nos. 14, V, VI, XVIII.

[165] Ibid., no. VIII.

[166] Ibid., no. 15.

[167] Ibid., no. 14.

[168] Ibid., no. 69.

[169] Ibid., no. 104.

[170] Régné, 4, 5.

[171] Cf. Baer, II, 65, 72, 125, 138, 139, 181, 228.

[172] *El fuero real de España* (ed. *Los codigos españoles concordados y anotados*) I, 353 ff., Madrid, 1847; Baer, II, 61.

[173] Ibid., II, 125 §216.

[174] Cf. ibid., II, 181 §30.

[175] Cf. ibid., II, 228, 275 §4, 318 §102; Lindo, 197 §5.

[176] S. Assaf, עבדים וסחר-עבדים בימי הבינים, in *Zion*, IV (1940), 91–125 and 271–80. The lucrativeness of the trade is described in a geonic responsum, *Sha'are Zedek*, no. 27: וששאלתם רגילין במקומנו לקנות עבדים בזול ואין להם סחורה כמותה מהו למכרן לאלתר שאין עומדין בדין ישראל כלל אלא אחד ממאה ויש לנו ריוח הרבה. See *JQR*, N. S., X (1919–20), 144–51; Israel Abrahams, *Jewish Life in the Middle Ages*, 96–101; L. Lucas, "Judentaufen und Judaismus zur Zeit des Papstes Innocenz III," in Philippson's *Festschrift*, 34 ff.

[177] Biot, *L'abolition de l'esclavage*, 233.

[178] See note 173, above; cf. Régné, 101; Baer, I, 359, p. 546.

[179] Cf. Hai Gaon's responsum in *Sha'are Zedek*, no. 6, p. 23b, where מצריות is a misprint for נוצריות. Mann, *JQR*, N. S., X (1919–20), 147 n. 218; see also *Hemdah Genuzah*, 12, 13.

[180] Cf. Alfasi, 5, 14, 24, 60, 166, 231; Migash, 139.

[181] Adret, I, 68 (= VIII, 149) 99, 1205, 1240; III, 192; V, 242; VIII, 284 (Nahmanides); Asher, XIX, 18; XLV, 24; LXXVII, 2; RaMaH, 259; Barfat, 353; cf. Régné, 46, 177, 433, 562, 617, 620, 687, 792, 1097, 1197, 1401, 1918, 1996; Baer, I, 129, 164; II, 144, 221, §3; Grayzel, nos. 17, 19.

[182] Cf. Alfasi, 166, ראובן ואשתו יש להם צער אם ימכרו אותה. Very significant is the sentiment expressed in *Teshubot Geonim Kadmonim*, no. 118, probably by R. Kalonymous of Lucca, which although not issuing from Spain is expressive of the rabbinic attitude in general: ואפילו על העבדים שמשמרים את האמונה אומרים קדיש. Cf. Adret, III, 191; Asher, XLV, 24; RaMaH, 259.

[183] Cf. Adret, I, 1205, 1240; V, 242; see above, p. 11.

[184] See Adret, I, 68 = VIII, 149; VIII, 284 (Nahmanides).

[185] Ibid.

[186] Yeb. 48b.

[187] See above, n. 181; also *Sha'are Zedek*, no. 3.

[188] Cf. *Shulhan 'Aruk, Yoreh De'ah*, 267 §3; cf. Mann, *JQR*, N. S., X (1919–20), 146–8.

[189] Cf. *Teshubot ha-Geonim*, ed. Coronel, no. 78; *Sha'are Zedek*, no. 3; Mann, op. cit., 146, 151, n. 221.

[190] *Cod. Theod.*, XVI, 8, 22.

[191] See section XVI: *Ne christianum mancipium Iudaeus habeat*; cf. III, 1, 5; XVI, 9, 2–4; *Cod. Just.*, I, 3, 54 (56), 8 ff.; Gregory, *Ep.*, VI, 29; IX, 104. These sources as well as the Visigothic legislation are outlined in Katz, op. cit., 96–100. Juster, *La condition légale des Juifs sous les rois visigoths*, 48–54.

[192] See Katz, op. cit., 96–100. The principal sections in the Roman codes are *Cod. Theod.*, XVI, 9; *Cod. Just.*, I, 10. For further references in these codes, see Katz, op. cit., 96, notes 3 and 8. King Recared (586–601) prohibited even pagan slaves and thereby gained the warm commendation of Gregory I, but it was a vain gesture. Notwithstanding all the severities of Visigothic rule, Jews continued in the possession of slaves — even Christian slaves — who were sold to them by Christian priests, according to the declaration of the Tenth Council of Toledo in 656 (Lindo, 21). For sources, see Katz, 99 n. 5.

[193] *Partidas*, VII, 24, 10; also Baer, II, 318 § 108.

[194] Ingram, *History of Slavery*.

[195] Cf. above, p. 11.

[196] Grayzel, nos. 17 n. 2, 79.

[197] Ibid.; cf. no. 19.

[198] Ibid., nos. 17, 19.

[199] Régné, 46.

[200] Ibid., 687, 1097.

[201] Ibid., 433, 562, 1918.

[202] Adret, I, 99; Asher, XLV, 24; RaMaH, 259. A woman's will provided that her slave was to be manumitted either by accepting Judaism or by paying two hundred *sueldos*. The slave accepted the latter alternative (Adret, III, 192).

[203] Baer, I, 359, p. 546; II, 227.

[204] Ibid.

[205] Ibid., 221 §3.

[206] Ibid., II, 318 §108; cf. *Partidas*, VII, 24, 10.

[207] Cf. Grayzel, no. 24; also IV n. 3.

[208] Ibid., pp. 72–3 notes 138–41.

[209] Cf. ibid., IV, XVIII, XXXVII, XLI. James I refused to sanction such restrictions: Bofarull, no. 69; *Boletin de Madrid*, XXXVI, 26–7 n. 10; Régné, 388, 561; see Baer, II, 163.

[210] The Jewish wine trade was too important economically to be regulated by purely ecclesiastical considerations: cf. Baer, I, 250, 337, 496, 593; II, 163.

[211] The complete severance of trade in food and drink between Jews and Christians was finally decreed in the ordinance of Valladolid by John II in 1412 (Baer,

II, 275; Lindo, 198). Like most of the harsh provisions of this ordinance, it was probably not observed.

[212] On Jewish physicians in the Middle Ages, see S. Krauss, *Geschichte der jüdischen Ärzte vom frühesten Mittelalter bis zur Gleichberechtigung*, Vienna, 1930; Münz, *Die jüdischen Ärzte im Mittelalter*, Frankfort a. M., 1922; Carmoly, *Histoire des médecins juifs*.

[213] Grayzel, nos. XIX, XXXVII, XLI: cf. p. 74 n. 147. Similar legislation was passed by the Council of Constantinople as early as 706.

[214] Gratian, XIII, 28, 1. The policy of the Church toward the practice of medicine in general was strongly influenced by theological ideas. The Church was more concerned with the soul than with the body of the patient and it demanded the same attitude from the physician. The Fourth Lateran Council adopted as a universal rule in Christendom that the first duty of a physician was to provide the patient with a confessor, for the soul was more important than the body. At the same time, the Church did not look with favor upon the practice of medicine and surgery by ecclesiastics, except through prayer and exorcism: see Lea, I, 74.

[215] *Partidas*, VII, 24, 8; Baer, II, 63 p. 47; Lindo, 101.

[216] Baer, II, 133 §8; Lindo, 127; Rios, II, 561 f.

[217] Baer, II, 148; Lindo, 130.

[218] Baer, II, 160; Lindo, 139.

[219] Ibid., 214; Graetz, VIII, 123; see Rios, II, no. XX, 627 ff.

[220] Baer, II, 295; Graetz, VIII, 146–7.

[221] See below, pp. 242 ff.

[222] Baer, I, 591; cf. 605. For a striking example, see Grayzel, Appendix D, pp. 346–7.

[223] Idem; also nos. 41–3; cf. Baer, I, 149, 186, 204, 254, 591, 605; II, 429.

[224] Alonzo de la Espina, *Fortalitium fidei*, III, "crudelitas," 13.

[225] See below, pp. 217 ff.

[226] Cf. I, 13, above; Baer, *Studien*, 55–9.

[227] Ibid., II, 163 p. 162, 383 p. 415; cf. ibid., II, 340; also I, 400; see Graetz, VIII, 226 n. 2; Rios, III, 229.

[228] See Baer, I and II, index.

[229] Régné, 430, 505, 705.

[230] Grayzel, nos. 41–3.

[231] Baer, I, 149.

[232] Régné, 1009, 1042, 1048, 1065, 1182.

[233] Ibid., 2128; cf. 2296, 2365.

[234] Baer, I, 173; Régné, 3433; cf. ibid., 3128, 3129, 3447; see Gross, *Gallia Judaica*, 619; Steinschneider, *Hebräische Uebersetzungen*, 653, 973.

[235] Baer, *Studien*, 32 n. 69; *JQR*, VIII (1895–6), 491; *REJ*, LVII, 268, 274.

[236] Cf. Baer, I, 204, 206, 219, 224, 239, 246, 254, 258, 261, 374, 380, 382, 400; also 209, 242, 249, 252, 264, 267, 307, 350, 371. See also Miret y Sans, "Les médecins juifs de Pierre, roi d'Aragon," *REJ*, LVII, 268.

[237] Baer, I, 204, 206, 219.

[238] Ibid., I, 224; Rios, II, 299.

[239] Baer, I, 249.

[240] Ibid., I, 350.

[241] Ibid., 382; cf. Graetz, VIII, 21–2; *REJ*, XVIII, 219–26.

[242] Baer, I, 459.

[243] Ibid., I, 464; cf. I, 467, 475.

[244] Ibid., I, 459.

[245] Ibid., I, 513.

[246] Ibid., I, 527.

[247] Ibid., I, 539, 549 (p. 82), 555, 556, 558.

[248] Zurita, *Anales*, XVIII, c. 18; Lea, I, 75. As to the identity of the physician, see Baer, I, 539.

[249] Lea, I, 75; cf. A. Lukyn Williams, op. cit., 277.

[250] T. Ripoll, *Bullarium Ordinis FF. Praedicatorum*, IV, 44; Lea, I, 75.

[251] For Jewish physicians in Navarre, see Baer, I, 580, 584 (p. 947), 591, 596, 598, 600, 603, 605.

[252] Graetz, VI, note 4, pp. 354–6.

[253] Baer, II, 29; Graetz, VI, 72; Rios, I, 183.

[254] Graetz, VI, 73 f.

[255] Asher, XVII, 8; XVIII, 13; Baer, II, 146; see above, pp. 139 f.

[256] Baer, II, 241; see 244, also 258.

[257] Ibid., II, 289.

[258] Lindo, 152; Baer, II, 205.

[259] Rios, *Estudios*, 419–20; Graetz, VIII, 90.

[260] Baer, I, 602, p. 991; II, 246, 287, 293.

[261] Graetz, VIII, 89–93.

[262] See Baer, I, p. 991.

[263] Graetz, VIII, 95, n. 1.

[264] Cf. Grayzel, 74, n. 147, and Appendix D; Régné, 1065, 2296; also Baer, I, 464.

[265] Ibid., II, 275, 295, 296; Lindo, 224; Rios, II, 583 ff.; Graetz, VIII, 146–9.

[266] Cf. Solomon ibn Verga, *Shebet Yehudah*, ed. Wiener, 88.

[267] Baer, II, 205, 206.

[268] Ibid., II, 305 n. 1, 307, 311, 317, 323; also Graetz, VIII, 164–5.

[269] Ibid., VIII, 163–4 and note 4, 178–81; Baer, II, 305 n. 1.

[270] Ibid., II, 307.

[271] Ibid., II, 317, 422 p. 520, 432.

[272] Ibid., II, 422 p. 520, 432.

[273] Ibid., II, 429.

NOTES TO CHAPTER XX

IN THE SERVICE OF THE KING AND THE STATE

[1] See below, pp. 229 ff.

[2] See below, pp. 231, 233, 235, et passim.

[3] Thus Jafia of Monzon was bailiff of the bishop of Tortosa (Baer, I, 37). Joseph,

son of Jafia, was bailiff of the count of Cervera (ibid., I, 62). Bondia Gracian was bailiff of the count of Roussillon (ibid., I, 89). Abraham, son of Isaac Maimo, was bailiff of the Templars and of the count of Moncada in Tortosa (Régné, 61; Jacobs, 120).

[4] Cf. Régné, 661-3.

[5] See below, pp. 232 f.

[6] See below, pp. 239 ff.

[7] Baer, II, 82, 87, 185, 262, 269; cf. ibid., II, 318 §103.

[8] Cf. ibid., I, pp. 615, 993, 994; II, 223, 269.

[9] Régné, passim.

[10] Rabbi Jonah Gerundi: Baer, I, 116; cf. 309. Rabbi Solomon b. Abraham ibn Adret: Baer, I, 115, 116, 127, 132, 144, 154, 160, 162; Adret, I, 617; II, 229; Jacobs, 215, 713, p. 130; Régné, 712-3 et passim. Rabbi Nissim Gerundi: Baer, I, 260, 288, 309. Rabbi Isaac Barfat: ibid., 288, 375. Rabbi Hasdai Crescas: ibid., I, 309, 387, 390, 391, 396, 453, 460, 467, 477; cf. ibid., 338, 363, 418, 419, 422, 452, 462, 469, 487 and pp. 1000-1.

[11] Cf. Ibn Verga, *Shebet Yehudah*, ed. Wiener, 54, 108-10, 116.

[12] ZL, 122b.

[13] Barfat, 373; Alami, *Iggeret Musar.*

[14] *MGH, Epistolae*, 571; Mansi, *Concilia*, XX, 341, cited in Graetz, VI, 74 n. 2; Baer, II, 12.

[15] Grayzel, no. 45.

[16] Ibid.

[17] Ibid., no. 46.

[18] The signature was affixed in Latin and in Hebrew characters, viz., *Signum Perfecto hebreo* and שֹשת בר' שלמה נ'ג (Baer, I, 15). Hebrew signatures appear frequently in the early state documents: ibid., I, 7, 13, 15, 24, 25, et passim.

[19] Ibid., I, 24, 25, 32.

[20] Ibid.

[21] Baer, *Studien*, 174.

[22] Ibid., I, 37.

[23] Ibid.

[24] Bofarull, 13; Baer, *Studien*, 174.

[25] Ibid., I, 37.

[26] Ibid. The seal of Jafia, *iudei baiuli regis*, was affixed to a document dated May, 1170, in which King Alfonso II and the count of Urgel transferred a gift of a Jew and a Saracen to the Order of St. John (ibid., I, 38).

[27] Ibid., I, 40.

[28] Ibid., I, 37.

[29] The signatures appear variously as ברפית בן באנבנשת (Profet b. Benveniste) or ברפית (Profet), frequently with the title גובר, or bailiff (ibid., I, 45). The identification of Sheshet with Profet b. Benveniste is conclusively established by Baer who also cites the literature (ibid.). From nos. 46 and 63, it is clear that Profet b. Benveniste began service with Count Ramon Berenguer IV, father of

Alfonso, and that he therefore served under three successive rulers. Cf. I, 47; also 50, 61 and p. 1021.

[30] Cf. previous note; also Baer, I, 47, for Benveniste, brother of Profet. The Hebrew signature of still another royal bailiff of Alfonso II, Bonafos b. Judah, appears with that of the archbishop of Tarragona and the provost of the local chapter on a legal document dated December 1, 1192 (ibid., I, 54). He continued service under Pedro II, in whose behalf he signed an important constitutional privilege for the city of Fraga (ibid.). Other Jewish officials appear as administrators of crown property: ibid., I, 56. See ibid., I, 49.

[31] Cf. ibid., I, 59, 61, 62, 63, 86, 87; see also idem, *Studien*, 175.

[32] *Perfectus, baiulus Barchinone*: ibid., I, 61.

[33] Abrayim: Rios, I, 396. See Baer, *Studien*, 175 n. 11.

[34] *Bonafos, baiulus Llerde*: ibid.; see also idem, I, 63 and p. 1021.

[35] בונפוש בן יורה, *Bonafos, baiulus Tarrachone*: ibid., I, 54.

[36] Ibid., I, 52.

[37] בון דיאה רפושתיר: ibid., I, 85. Abraham b. Saadia was *repositar* of Saragossa: ibid.; see idem, *Studien*, 175.

[38] *The Chronicle of James I, King of Aragon*, tr. John Forster, 151, 212, 213, 441, 538, 559, 560.

[39] Cf. Régné, 1955. James conferred upon Solomon Alfaquim the right to act as judge over the Jewry of Saragossa and of Aragon (Baer, I, 104). For the status of royally appointed Jewish judges, see above, I, 114 f., 145 f.; see Baer, I, 136; cf. I, 92.

[40] Régné, 676, 782–3, 800, 810, 978, 1020, 1021, 1022, 1248, 1299, 1705, 1862, 1870, 1905, 1906, 1963, 2134, 2290, 2354; cf. Adret, VI, 224; Baer, I, 144.

[41] Régné, 4.

[42] Profet, ברפית נזבר: Baer, I, 86, 87; Régné, 2; Solomon Bonafos: שלמה בונפוש נזבר ברצלונה, *baiulus Barchinone*, and שלמה בונפוש נזבר קאטאלוניה, *baiulus domini regis in Catalonia*: ibid., I, 90; Vidal Salomo, וידל שלמה נזבר ברצלונה, Vitalis Salamon, *baiulus domini regis in Barchinona*: ibid., I, 94; Régné, 107; Jacobs, 158. Benveniste de Porta (ça Porta), בנבנשת ספרתה, *baiulus Barchinone*: Baer, I, 96; Régné, 188; Jacobs, 130, 168a; Bofarull, nos. XXXV, XXXVI. See n. 43, below.

[43] Bondia Gracian, *baiulus Gerunde*, בונדיאה נזבר: Baer, I, 89; Benvenist de Porta: ibid., I, 96; see n. 42; Joseph Ravalia, *bajulus Gerunde pro domino infante Petro*, יוסף רבאליה נזבר בר' יהודה אבן רבאליה צ'ב'י: Baer, I, 105, 109; cf. ibid., I, 118, 119, 120; Régné, 488; Jacobs, 723.

[44] Joseph b. Astrug Ravaya: Baer, I, 105, 109; Bofarull, no. LXXIV and p. 22; Régné, 393; Jacobs, 430; Salano d'en Salries: Régné, 404.

[45] Judah de Cavalleria: Baer, I, 104; Régné, 105; cf. 461, 662–8; Jacobs, 114, 220, 513, 630, 678; cf. ibid., 132, 165a, 183, 338, 352, 538; Bofarull, nos. LVI, LVII, LX, XCVIII, CXXI, CXXVIII, CXXXIV.

[46] Muça de Portella: Baer, I, 119; Régné, 548.

[47] Abraham son of Isaac Maimo, bailiff of the Order of Templars and of G. de Moncada in Tortosa: Régné, 61; Jacobs, 120; Astruc Jacob Xixo, appointed royal

bailiff: Bofarull, p. 21; also no. XXVII; Régné, 186; Jacobs, 201, 253, 326a. Cf. Baer, I, 102; Bofarull, LIV, XCIX and C; Régné, 1212, 1357.

[48] Salomón de Zaragoza: Bofarull, 21.

[49] Sulema (Solomon) de Monzon: Régné, 219; Moses Abinbinag: Bofarull, 21; also no. LXVIII; Régné, 382; Jacobs, 422.

[50] Judah de Cavalleria: Bofarull, CLXVII.

[51] Muçe de la Portella: Bofarull, 22 and no. CLXVI. Solomon de Cavalleria, son of Judah: Bofarull, no. CXXV; Jacobs, 517.

[52] Régné, 375, 466, 610, 2047; Baer, I, 102.

[53] Ibid., I, 90.

[54] Bofarull, 21. Twenty-five documents naming Xixon, and a similar number concerning Benveniste de Porta are cited in Jacobs, *Index Nominum.*

[55] He controlled the *bailía* of Barcelona, Gerona and Lerida: Jacobs, 142, 144, 162; Baer, *Studien,* 178 n. 23.

[56] See Bofarull, 17–20; Jacobs, p. XVIII; see also ibid., Index, citing over fifty documents; Baer, *Studien,* 178–9.

[57] Rios, I, 397; Tourtoulon, *Jacme le Conquerant,* II, 378; Baer, *Studien,* 178.

[58] Jacobs, 538; Bofarull, 19 and no. CXXXIV.

[59] Swift, 159 n. 1; Bofarull, no. 21; cf. Jacobs, 298.

[60] Bofarull, 18 and no. XXI; Baer, I, 104; Régné and Jacobs, passim.

[61] Swift, 159; Bofarull, 20, no. CLXVII.

[62] Tourtoulon, op. cit., II, 301–2; Swift, 159 n. 1, 224 n. 1.

[63] Régné, 800, 978, 1020–1. For other *alfaquims* during this brief reign, see ibid., 1122, 1297. Moses Alconstantin, bailiff of Saragossa, was also called by Pedro "our *alfaquim*": Baer, I, 114.

[64] Régné 661–8, 1053, 1063, 1079, 1131, 1134–5, 1164, 1174–5, 1207–8, 1214, 1281, 1358, 1406; Baer, I, 119, 122, 145; see also ibid., I, 153.

[65] Ibid., I, 120. See Régné, 661, 673, 677, 682, 799, 891. Cf. ibid., 1090, 1168, 1245, 2019.

[66] Baer, I, 122; cf. Régné, 682, 694. Baer's account of the downfall of the Ravaya family (*Studien,* 180) is not borne out in Régné, 1090, 1168.

[67] Baer, I, 114; cf. ibid., 104; see Régné, 680, 684, 709, 745.

[68] Ibid., 1311.

[69] Ibid., 807, 903, 907, 1120, 1253.

[70] Ibid., 810, 1020, 1022, 1248; cf. 1299.

[71] *Bolet. de Barcel.,* III, 138 n. 129; 174 nn. 154 and 156; Baer, *Studien,* 179 nn. 33, 34.

[72] Merriman, I, 433–7; Zurita, IV, 38; Baer, *Studien,* 180.

[73] Régné, 1100.

[74] Bondavio or Bondavin, *alfaquim*: Regne, 1602, 1906, 2278; Alaçar, *alfaquim,* ibid., 1860, 1871; Jahuda Almali of Alcañiz, *alfaquim*: ibid., 2134; Vives of Valencia, *alfaquim*; ibid., 2354; Bonanest was the *alfaquim* of the Infante Don Pedro, ibid., 2290.

[75] Ibid., 1747, 1774, 1780, 1804–5, 1843–4, 2128, 2365.

[76] Ibid., 1701, 1705, 1862, 1870, 1905, 1963.

[77] Ibid., 1701, 1862.

[78] Ibid., 1705, 1963.

[79] Ibid., 1880, 1881. Recognition of other Jews who rendered service to the king: Moses Castellan, ibid., 2193; Abrafim Abenamies and Abrafim El Jenet, who were attached to the royal house and therefore exempt from wearing the "Jewish hood": ibid., 2058; Aaron Abinafia: ibid., 1877; cf. 1885; Samuel Adenafia: ibid., 1885; Samuel Abenvives, who served the king daily: ibid., 2171. See also ibid., 1514, a reference to a group of Jews connected with the equipment of the fleet.

[80] Ibid., 548.

[81] Ibid., 661-3, 692, 1053.

[82] Klüpfel, *Verwaltungsgeschichte Aragoniens*, 9, 39, 100; Régné, 1487, 1493, 1525, 1538, 1653-4, 1660; cf. Carini, II, 125; Baer, *Studien*, 181.

[83] Merriman, I, 437-40.

[84] Zurita, IV, 83; Baer, *Studien*, 181.

[85] Cf. Régné, 1811. The flight of the family after Muça's death is indicated in Régné, 2608-12, 2634.

[86] Ibid., 1691, 1728, 1767, 1923, 2075, 2175, 2553. Klüpfel, 9, 36, 39, 102. The activities of another member of this family, Solomon de Portella, are indicated in Régné, 1598, 1606, 1617, 1621, 1635, 1728. Still another kinsman, Jusse de la Portella: ibid., 2068.

[87] Nevertheless, in 1290-1, Abraham Çaporta acted as judge over the inhabitants of San Antolin, while the vicar of Cervera executed his verdicts: ibid., 2294.

[88] Ibid., 2608-12.

[89] Baer, I, 153; Régné, 2880.

[90] Ibid., 2701. His attendance at the royal court is indicated: ibid., 2932, 2960, 3008.

[91] Ibid., 2837; Baer, I, 153; see Régné, 3380.

[92] Baer, I, 183-4; Régné, 3337. Her physician was Solomon of Calatayud (Baer, I, 186). See also Régné, 3250.

[93] Ibid., 3274, 3403, 3412, 3433, 3447; cf. Baer, I, 173; Régné, 3128-9.

[94] Ibid., 2386-7, 2390, 2481-3, 2513, 2524-6.

[95] Ibid., 3264, 3274, 3296.

[96] Ibid., 2613, 2886, 3068.

[97] Jacobs, 157.

[98] Baer, I, 285a, p. 413, 306.

[99] Ibid., I, p. 405. His leadership and official position in the *aljama* of Barcelona is indicated: ibid., I, 259, 338, 363. As to the quarrel between his son and Rabbi Isaac Barfat, or Perfet, see ibid., I, 288.

[100] Ibid., I pp. 442-4.

[101] Barfat, II, 9; Baer, *Studien*, 198. The responsa also allude to certain Jewish officers of state who exercised tyrannical power over their Jewish associates: Barfat, 261.

[102] Baer, I, 221, 278, 302 pp. 442–3, 384; Barfat, 261. For Jews who rendered service to the Crown, cf. Baer, I, 222, 295, 299, 301, 302, 335.

[103] Ibid., I, p. 603.

[104] Cf. ibid., I, 223, 284, 375 §2; Barfat, 373, 376, 377.

[105] Antoni Rubió y Lluch, *Documents per l'historia de la cultura catalana mig-eval*, I, nos. 137, 138, 295, 312, 319, 322; *Bolet. de Madrid*, IX, 309 n. 1; XIX, 357, 366 ff., cited in Baer, *Studien*, 33 n. 72. Cf. Steinschneider, *Heb. Übersetz.*, §404; *REJ*, LVII, 268 ff. See Baer, I, 373, 380.

[106] A. L. Isaacs, *Jews of Majorca*, 93–101; Rios, II, 201–4.

[107] Henry C. Lea, in *AHR*, I, 209–25; idem, *A History of the Inquisition of Spain*, I, 103–11; Graetz, VIII, 53–65, 73–99; Rios, II, 339–448, 487–526, 579–89, 592–604, 610–4.

[108] In addition to the preceding note, see the documents of this period, cited in Baer, I and II.

[109] C. Roth, *A History of the Marranos*, 14 ff.

[110] Baer, I, 450, 468.

[111] See note 14, above.

[112] Graetz, VI, 75–7, 354–6; Rios I, 182–4.

[113] The scattered, fragmentary references are assembled in Baer, II, 29; also in the Index, p. 552 n. 1. See also Graetz, VI, 72, 81.

[114] Baer, II, 29.

[115] Brody, *Dîwân des ... Jehuda ha-Levi*, I, no. 13; II, nos. 11–2.

[116] Baer, II, 18.

[117] Ibid.

[118] Ibid., II, 21.

[119] Ibid., II, 34; Neubauer, *MJC*, I, 80 f.

[120] Ibid.

[121] Judah continued in the royal service as *almoxarife*; also under Sancho III (Baer, II, 34).

[122] Grayzel, no. 17. It is farfetched to seek an explanation of Alfonso's pro-Jewish policy in his love of a Jewish mistress (Erler, in Vering's *Archiv*, XL, 397), but the amour, heightened by the tragedy of her cruel murder, undoubtedly left its traces.

[123] Following is the inscription on the tombstone of Alfonso's *almoxarife*, Joseph b. Solomon ibn Shoshan: וכל שרי המלך משתחוים לו אפים . . . החן משוך אליו והחסד נטוי עליו מטעם המלך וגדוליו. Cf. Rios, I, 346; Fita, *BAH*, XI, 441; Baer, II, 39, identified Çamal Falcon de Burgos as another Jewish *almoxerif del rey*. See also Baer's review of A. Gonzalez Palencia's *Los mozarabes de Toledo*, in *Tarbiz*, V, 232–4, for other Jews of eminence during this reign. For a reference to Alfonso's *alfaquim* Abenlahazer: Baer, II, 35. Abraham ibn Alfakhar was Alfonso's ambassador at the court of the Almohade prince at Morocco. His ready wit and literary skill are described in Graetz, VI, 189–90.

[124] Grayzel, no. XI.

[125] Ibid., nos. 45, 46.

[126] Baer, II, 18.

[127] *Con. Tol. IV*, §65.

[128] See n. 124, above.

[129] Grayzel, no. 71. Ferdinand's physician Judah al-Fakhar is well known in Jewish literature as an anti-Maimunist in the famous religious controversy (Graetz, VII, 46 f.; Sarachek, *Faith and Reason*, passim). Another royal physician, Don Sisa, may be identified with ויזא הרופא בן שושן, the subject of Todros b. Judah ha-Levi's poem in *Gan ha-Meshalim*, ed. Yellin, no. 522. Baer, II, 67. Don Çulema, father of Don Zag de Malea, attained importance under Alfonso X; but Ferdinand, too, addressed him as *mio mandadero* (Baer, II, 67). Yuçef, *alfaquim* (ibid., II, 55), may possibly be the one who later was a collaborator in astronomy at the court of Alfonso X.

[130] *Partidas*, VII, 24.3.

[131] Zacuto, *Sefer Yuḥasin*, 221–2; Graetz, VII, 115, and note 6; *The Legacy of Israel*, 222–5.

[132] Graetz, VII, 101, 115; Steinschneider, *Heb. Übersetz.*, 979; Baer, II, 76.

[133] M. Rico y Sinobas, *Libros de saber de astronomia del rey don Alfonso el Sabio*, I, 149, cited in Baer, II, 67.

[134] Graetz, VII, 115, 408.

[135] Ibid.

[136] Baer, II, 67, 76. Don Todros, referred to as *el rab*, was evidently appointed by the court as chief rabbi over the *aljamas* of Castile (cf. ibid., I, 292; II, 287, introd.). Abraham Bedersi described him thus in his poem, חרב המתהפכת, v. 201 f.: ראש גלות ספרד . . . רועה מלכים רב פעלים. Another interesting reference to Todros Halevi by Abraham Bedersi is appended to *Maskiyyot Kesef* by Mordecai b. Isaac Thamah, Amsterdam, 1765, fol. 23b.

ראיתי לכתוב פה כתב אשר נכתב מהרב אברהם בדרשי ז'ל ואותה ראיתי בתכלית
הצחות ויופי המליצה שמתיה פה כי היא ישרה בעיני.   עבר בגבולינו זה שנים רבות, המלך
הגדול מלך קאשטילייא ונטה אהלי כבודו בעיר הזאת תקופות ימים, ובא בקרב מחנהו השר
הגדול הנשיא נשיא נשיאי הלוי מרנא ורבנא טודרוס הלוי ז'ל והיה גדול ונשוא פנים לפני הנבירה
מלכת קאשטילייא ההולכת אז עם המלך והיה הנכבד הזה חכם ונעים זמירות . . .

[137] Cf. Merriman, op. cit., I, 112.

[138] Baer, II, 84.

[139] Ibid., II, 67; Régné, 309; Jacobs, 319.

[140] Cf. *Cortes*, I (Madrid, 1861), for the years 1252, 1258 and 1268. See Yellin, nos. 393–4; Baer, II, 84; cf. ibid., II, 72.

[141] See below, p. 246 et passim.

[142] See note 140. Cf. Mondéjar, *Memorias del rei Alfonso el Sabio*, 373 f.

[143] See above, note 139; also Baer, II, 82.

[144] Ibid., II, 67.

[145] Ibid., II, 84; cf. 67, 76. In particular, see Brody, *Encycl. Judaica*, I, 654, and Baer, II, pp. 67–8.

[146] Yellin, nos., 390, 393–4, 398, 405–6, 422–3, 595, 646–55.

[147] Cf. *Crónica de Alfonso X*, chs. 71–2, 74, and Yellin, nos. 405–6, 422–3, 595, 646–55; see Baer, II, 84; Graetz, VII, 140 f.; Rios, I, 492.

[148] Yellin, no. 405; Baer, II, p. 68.

[149] Ibid., II, 67, 76, 84; see above, note 145; Yellin, no. 569 f.; cf. Graetz, VII, 140 f.; Rios, 488 f.

[150] Baer, II, 67, 76. In the latter reference mention is made of Jews who were the king's archers or porters, a significant office concerning which more information would be valuable. Jewish tax farmers were engaged by the Order of Santiago (ibid., II, 82). For Yucef Pimetiella, see ibid., II, 85.

[151] Graetz, VII, 116.

[152] Ibid., VII, 141; cf. Adret, I, 1159: ראובן היה נזבר המלך ולבסוף תפסו המלך והרגו ותפס כל אשר לו, ולאחר שהמית אותו קם מלך חדש ושמעון בן ראובן נכנס בעבודת המלך . . . .

[153] Baer, II, 93.

[154] *Gan Hammeshalim we-Haḥidoth, Diwan of Don Tadros Son of Yehuda Abu-el-ʿĀfiah*, ed. Yellin; H. Brody, "Gurtelgedichte des Ṭodros Abu-lʿAfija," *Mitteilungen des Forschungsinstituts für Hebräische Dichtung*, I, 1–93. Baer, II, 98. From these sources it appears that he served under Alfonso X, Sancho IV and also the Infante Enrique.

[155] Yellin, nos. 636–40, 642, 644; Baer, II, pp. 93–4. Brody, in *Encycl. Judaica*, I, 653.

[156] Mose aben Crespin was *almoxerife* of Toledo (Baer, II, 87). Don Abrahem Abenxuxen was the queen's *almoxarife* (ibid.). Likewise, Don Yehuda (ibid., II, 98). Mosse Aventuriel was *almoxarife* in Murcia under Sancho and, when the political fortunes changed, he served in the same office under James II of Aragon (ibid., p. 90, n. 1; Régné, 2619, 2681–2). Samuel de Vilforado was Sancho's diplomatic emissary to Granada; also receiver of taxes and tolls; and, in addition, the *almoxarife* of Don Fernando, later Fernando IV (Baer, II, p. 89 nn. 1, 2). Mose Falcon was an important factor in supplying the army with provisions (ibid., II, 87). He was associated with Abrahem el Barchilon, Todros el Levi and the *almoxarife* Abrahem Abenxuxen (ibid., II, 98). Other names of court personages, *alfaquims* and physicians appear in the lists: ibid., II, 87, 98.

[157] Ibid., II, 100 §9.

[158] Merriman, I, passim.

[159] Baer, II, 103.

[160] Ibid., II, 111.

[161] Ibid., II, 113 §14, 115.

[162] Ibid., II, 119, 123. It is significant that the name of Don Mahomat Abenazar, *rey de Granada, vasallo del Rey*, heads the list of those who confirmed the ordinances passed at the Cortes of Medina del Campo. The king of Granada attended the Cortes as vassal of the Castilian king. Attendance upon summons was obligatory. Absence, if not previously excused, was considered a declaration of revolt. Cf. Merriman, I, 220–1.

[163] Cf. Baer, II, 122: Don Çag Abenays, *almoxarife de la reyna, mi madre.*

[164] Graetz, VII, 273.

[165] Baer, II, 128.

[166] Graetz, VII, 250.

[167] Rios, II, 113–7, 561–6; Lindo, 126–7; Baer, II, 133.

[168] Ibid., II, 138, 139.

[169] Ibid., II, 138 §7.

[170] Ibid., II, 142 §6.

[171] Ibid., II, 144 §8.

[172] Ibid., II, 147 §§6 and 18.

[173] Ibid., II, 148 §70; Lindo, 130.

[174] Baer, II, 144; Lindo, 128.

[175] Asher, XVII, 8; XVIII, 13; Baer, II, 146.

[176] Ibid., II, 146, pp. 139–40.

[177] Baer also cites a document, dated 1319, which alludes to an *almoxarife*, Don Çag Moro, and to Jaco Cavallero, a fiscal agent of the Regent Don Juan Manuel (ibid.).

[178] *Crónica de Alfonso XI*, chs. 39, 41–2, 61, 68–71, 80, 82–3; Rios, II, 128–35; Graetz, VII, 286–90; Baer, II, 150.

[179] *Crónica de Alfonso XI*, ch. 71.

[180] Ibid., chs. 80, 82.

[181] Cf. Baer, I, 193; II, 150.

[182] Ibid., II, 153.

[183] Ibid., I, 193.

[184] *Crónica de Alfonso XI*, chs. 95–6, 98.

[185] Baer, II, p. 142; cf. Baer, in *Festschrift für D. Yellin*.

[186] Graetz, VII, 293 f.

[187] Ibid.

[188] Moses Abzaradiel, described in *Shebet Yehudah*, no. 10, as הסופר הגדול למלך, was secretary of the royal chancellory. His signature appears on a series of official documents of great variety and importance (Baer, II, pp. 143–4; cf. *JQR*, N. S., XIX, 145 ff.). Samuel el Levi, who played a prominent role subsequently under Pedro, was during the latter part of Alfonso's reign the *almoxarife* of Juan Alfonso de Albuquerque (Baer, II, 171, 187). Mosse Marguan was described by Alfonso XI as *chanceller de don Tello, mio fiio* (ibid., II, 175). According to a tombstone inscription, Samuel ibn Mazah wielded great influence at the court: אשר אור בכה מחנים לעמוד בעד עם ה' בפרץ עם כל גויי הארץ, פאר העדה והדרתה ויוצא ובא לכל עבודתה ישב במושב וזקנים . . . : Luzzatto, *Abne Zikkaron*, no. 2; Moïse Schwab, "Les Inscriptions Hebraïques de l'Espagne," *Nouvelles Archives des Missions Scientifiques et Littéraires*, XIV, Paris, 1907, 53. Cf. Asher, LV, 10; Baer, II, 174.

Alfonso XI requested the vassals of the monastery and the Order of the Knights in the bishopric of Burgos to submit to the regulations of the *cogedores*, or tax collectors, Don Ebrahem el Levi, Don Yuçaf Cordiella and Don Çag Abenbeniste (ibid., II, 169). For a long-term lease on church revenue farmed to a Jew, see ibid., II, 162. Cf. ibid., II, p. 168, for an interesting agreement entered into by the representatives of the city of Toledo with *los judíos de Toledo que andan aqui en la corte de nuestro sennor el rey.*

[189] Rios, II, 232–4, 254–6; Graetz, VII, 356.

[190] Baer, II, 171, 187 and 205; Ayala, *B. A. E.*, 66, 410, 434 f., 452, 458 f.; Rios, II, 218–47; Graetz, VII, 356 ff.

[191] Baer, II, 187 p. 179.

[192] See above, 147 f.

[193] See the facsimile of the inscription in the Toledo synagogue: Lindo, Appendix VIII; Luzzatto, op. cit., 19 f.; Schwab, op. cit., 47 f.

[194] The Cortes complained of him *que era grant privado de aquel tirano que se llamava rey: Cortes*, II, 158 §9, cited in Baer, II, 205.

[195] His nephew Don Yuçaf el Levi was *almoxarife* of Seville and also *dispensero mayor del rey* (ibid., II, 187). Another, Samuel el Levi, and one Yuze Abenhala also appear as *almojarifes* of Seville (ibid., II, 182).

[196] Lopez de Ayala, *Crónica*, ch. 16.

[197] Graetz, VII, 362 n. 3.

[198] Ibid.

[199] Lopez de Ayala, ch. 17; Rios, II, 234–46; Graetz, VII, 363.

[200] Don Yuhuda was a member of the royal council (Baer, II, 181, end). Çag Garcom represented King Pedro and the Infante Alfonso (ibid., II, 201). Yhuda Abenatabeb was the *almoxerife* of the Infante Alfonso (ibid.). Mayr Abenhamias was *almoxerife* of Toledo and, together with Yhuda Mohep, he farmed part of the church revenue of the chapter of the Toledo cathedral (ibid., II, 185). Zulema Alfahar was an important farmer of taxes (ibid., II, 194). Mosen Cohen was the *almoxarife* of a noble (ibid., II, 200). In Valladolid, the *alcavala*, which was a blighting tax on commercial transactions, was controlled by Jewish tax farmers (ibid., II, 197). Likewise, the tax on cattle was largely in Jewish hands (ibid., II, 202). Samuel Abravalla was *recaudador mayor* of the marquis of Villena and count of Ribagorza (ibid., II, 207; cf. ibid., I, 295). A certain David appears as *contador* — one of the first Jews to hold this title (ibid.).

[201] Graetz, VII, 366–72; Rios, II, 571–3; cf. Baer, II, 210.

[202] Graetz, VII, 372 n. 3.

[203] Immanuel Aboab, *Nomologia o Discursos Legales*, 290: *Estimó en mucho el prudente Rey don Henrique la constancia de los Hebreos, y dixo: que tales vasallos come aquelles devian los reyes amar mucho y premiarlos, quales tenian mas respecto à la fidelidad de vita a su Rey aunque vencido y muerto, que no á la presente fortuna del vencedor, y despues se le entregaron con partidos muy honrosos.* Cited in Graetz, VIII, 16 n. 3.

[204] Baer, II, 205, pp. 10, 11.

[205] Ibid., II, 211.

[206] Ibid., I, 281.

[207] *Nuestro almojarife mayor e facedor de las rentas de todos los nuestros reinos* (ibid., II, 223).

[208] Ibid.

[209] Ibid., II, 211.

[210] See above, 1, 136; Graetz, VIII, 40; Rios, II, 333–7, based on Ayala, *Crónica de don Juan I, año* 1, ch. 3; Baer, II, 223; cf. 227.

[211] The main source is Ayala, *Crónica de D. Enrique III, año* 1, ch. 7; cf. Neubauer, *MJC*, I, 98; *Sefer Yuhasin*, ed. Filipowski, 224. See Graetz, VIII, 17 and appendix, note 4. Baer, II, 262, where the literature is cited, mentions documents tending to prove that the conversion took place before 1391 (p. 246 n. 2), but the proof is not conclusive.

[212] The names of Mayr and Mose appear as officials on state documents (Baer, II, p. 205). Joseph Abravanel (Juce Abrabanell) was accorded recognition in Aragon because he belonged to the court of "the illustrious Henry, King of Castile" (ibid., I, 277). Çag aben Maçah and Don Ihuda Dalva were farmers of taxes; also, Don Salomon Abenlup (ibid., II, 223). The following also appear as *arrendadores*: Don Sisa and Don Samuel in Guadalajara, Don Hayn Abdali in Murcia and Don Abrahem in Madrid (ibid.). The highly important office of royal treasurer (*tesorero del rei*) was held by Don Samuel Altavalla in 1374 (ibid.). Nothing further is known concerning him.

[213] Ibid., II, 217; Lindo, 154–5; Graetz, VIII, 18; Rios, II, 315–7.

[214] To Don Sisa and Don Samuel in Guadalajara; to Don Hayn Abdali in Murcia and to Don Abrahem in Madrid (Baer, II, 223).

[215] Baer, II, 220; Lindo, 157; Rios, II, 318.

[216] It is possible that his attitude was influenced, in part, by the manner in which the execution of Joseph Pichon was brought about. Ayala (*Crónica*, II, 127–8) attributed the withdrawal of the rights of criminal jurisdiction from the *aljamas* to this event.

[217] At the Cortes of Sória, Sept. 18, 1380: Baer, II, 228.

[218] Ibid., II, 234 §9; Lindo, 166, where Saragossa is an error and should read Valladolid, as Graetz, VIII, 42 n. 3, pointed out. Besides the narrative accounts in the standard histories of Graetz, VIII, 55–64, and Amador de los Rios, II, 349–96, see the documents and the literature cited by Baer in both volumes for the years 1391–1400, passim. See letter of Hasdai Crescas in *Shebet Yehudah*, ed. Wiener, 128–30; ibid., nos. 45–9; also the anonymous elegy edited by Adolph Neubauer in *Israelit. Letterbode*, VI, 33 ff. and noted by David Kaufmann, ibid., 80 ff., re-edited by Enelow, with notes, in the supplement to his edition of the *Menorat ha-Maor* by R. Israel ibn al-Nakawa, II, 444–53. Cf. Lea in *AHR*, I, 209–25.

[219] Baer, II, 234 §3; Lindo, 166.

[220] Graetz, VIII, 45.

[221] Ibid., VIII, 45 f.

[222] Ibid., VIII, 46; cf. Baer, II, 230.

[223] For names of *arrendadores*, *recabdadores* and *cogedores*, see ibid., II, 246; also 249.

[224] Besides the narrative accounts in the standard histories of Graetz and Amador de los Rios, see the documents and the literature cited by Baer in both volumes for the years 1391–1400, passim.

[225] Cf. Solomon Alami, *Iggeret Musar*: ורוב הטוכסים המחסים יצאו משם בהמנע בהם והחכירות והמכסים.

[226] He was described as משנה למלך קאשטילייא: Baer, II, 269. Cf. Kobak's *Jeschurun*, IX, 1, n. 1; Brüll, *Jahrb. f. jüd. Gesch. u. Lit.*, VIII, 58.

[227] Ibid.

[228] Graetz, VIII, 74, 83, 89, 93, 95.

[229] *Thesorero mayor del rey en el regno de Toledo con Estremadura* (Baer, II, 269). Another Ibn Verga had farmed the *monedas*, voted to the king by the Cortes of Burgos in the previous reign.

[230] Ibid.

[231] In Baer, II, 269, the following members of well-known families appear jointly as *arrendadores mayores* of special revenues: Yuçaf aben Çaçon of Toledo, Don Mayr aben Megas of Burgos and Don Semuel Alguadix of Vitoria. Don Yuçaf aben Resq was *arrendador mayor* of similar revenues in the bishopric of Burgos. Mose Priego and Don Semuel Varroso were *arrendadores* of the *alcavala de la palata* in Valladolid. Juda Abenhemir was *recaudador mayor*. Don Çag Alhavate and Çulema aben Arroyo were tax farmers. Additional names of similar officials appear: ibid., II, 262.

[232] Don Mosen de aben Arias and Don David aben Alphahar: ibid.

[233] Ibid., II, 268.

[234] Graetz, VIII, 109; Rios, II, 493 f.; Lea; *AHR*, I, 209–25.

[235] Cf. Baer, II, 275 p. 272.

[236] Ibid., II, 273; Lindo, 186–8.

[237] Baer, II, 275; Lindo, 196–201.

[238] Ibid.

[239] Lindo, 201–7.

[240] See Baer, II, 280, 282, 283, 285.

[241] Rios, II, 404–7, 424–32, 489 ff.; Graetz, VIII, 106–11, 121.

[242] *Crónica de don Juan II*, cap. XXII, cited in Rios, II, 490, n. 2.

[243] Alami, op. cit., 23: וינזרו עליהם שנוי המלבושים וימנעו מהם המסחר והחכירות והאומניות . . . נגזר עלינו לו̇דל שער ראשנו וזקננו . . .

[244] Ibid.

[245] Cf. Baer, II, 271–2, 276, 278, 280–2, 285; Rios, 397–448; Graetz, VIII, 105–25.

[246] Cf. Baer, II, 271–2, 276, 278–9.

[247] Lindo, 213–5; Rios, II, 504–10, 627–53.

[248] Baer, II, 286; Rios, III, 32, 573–82; Graetz, VIII, 141.

[249] *Shebet Yehudah*, ed. Wiener, nos. 8, 67; cf. Graetz, VIII, 419–20.

[250] See Graetz, VIII, appendix, note 5; ibid., VIII, 141–5; Baer, II, 286–7, 292–3; Rios, III, 22–3, 32.

[251] Baer, II, 286.

[252] Lindo, 218; Baer, II, 286.

[253] Rios, III, 22–3.

[254] Cf. Zacuto, *Sefer Yuhasin*, ed. Filipowski, 226.

[255] In this official capacity, he convened the conference of the Castilian Jewries at Valladolid in 1432. See above, ch. XV, n. 1.

[256] Baer, II, 292–3.

[257] Ibid.

[258] Ibid. See also ibid., 305.

[259] Ibid., II, 292–3.

[260] Ibid., II, 292 n. 1. Associated with the Benvenistes in many of their undertakings may be found the names of Joseph the Barcelonian and Solomon de Cavalleria: ibid., II, 292–3.

[261] Ibid., II, 305 n. 1; Graetz, VIII, 163–4, 178–80; ibid., note 4, II.

[262] Baer, II, 305 n. 1.

[263] Munk, *Mélanges de philosophie juive et arabe*, 507–9.

[264] Joseph ibn Shem Tob records this episode in his ms. work, '*En ha-Kore*, quoted by Graetz, VIII, 421–22.

[265] See Graetz, VIII, 422.

[266] Munk, op. cit., 508 n. 1; Steinschneider, *Heb. Uebersetz.*, §§107–8, 110–1.

[267] Graetz, VIII, 164. He also translated into Hebrew Hasdai Crescas' polemic work written in Spanish, published by Deinard, Kearny, N. J., 1904.

[268] See note 261.

[269] Reynaldus, *Ann. eccl.*, 1442, no. 15; Graetz, VIII, 146–8; Rios, III, 42–43; Baer, II, 295; cf. M. Simmsohn, *Die kirchliche Judengesetzgebung im Zeitalter der Reformkonzilien von Konstanz und Basel*, Breslau, 1912.

[270] See Rios, III, 583–9; ibid., 44–7; Lindo, 221–6; Graetz, VIII, 148–9; Baer, II, 296.

[271] Cf. Baer, II, 305–7, 309; Rios, 131 n. 3; Graetz, VIII, 228 n. 1.

[272] Baer, II, 318; Lindo, 235–6; Rios, III, 164–5.

[273] Lindo, 239; cf. Graetz, VIII, 226 n. 1.

[274] Baer, II, 336, 359, 362, 363, 364, 370, 372; cf. ibid., 329 note, 337 note.

[275] Baer, II, 309.

[276] Ibid., II, 322; A. de Palencia, *Crón. de Enrique IV*, trad. Paz, III, 183 f.

[277] See Capsali, in *Likkutim Shonim*, ed. Lattes, 60 f.; Mariana, *De Rebus Hispaniae*, XXIV, ch. 1; Kayserling, *Christopher Columbus*, 24–7; Graetz, VIII, 232–3.

[278] M. Kayserling, *Christopher Columbus*, 25.

[279] Rios, III, 279–80.

[280] Baer, II, 329; cf. ibid., 347, 350, 352, 355, 358, 365, 373, 379, 387.

[281] Rios, III, 280; cf. ibid., 347.

[282] Cf. Baer, II, 322, 336, 372.

[283] Ibid., II, 363.

[284] Ibid., II, 348, 352.

[285] Rios, III, 298 f.; Graetz, VIII, 296, 337; Baer, II, 366–7; Lindo, 272; Neubauer, *M. J. C.*, I, 100, 111; *Shebet Yehudah*, p. 108; Capsali, in *Likkutim Shonim*, ed. Lattes, 65 f.; cf. Baer, II, 376; Zacuto, *Yuhasin*, ed. Filipowski, 227.

[286] Baer, II, 348.

[287] Ibid., II, 360; cf. Marx, in *JQR*, XX (1907–8), 247.

[288] Abravanel, *Commentary on Joshua*, Introduction; idem, Introduction to *Commentary on Kings*; Rios, III, 296; Baer, II, 362, 380, 381; Graetz, VIII, 330.

[289] Rios, III, 280, 295–6; Graetz, VIII, 332.   For the role of Leo Hebraeus see Abrabanel, *She'elot Shaul*, X, 20b.

[290] Baer, II, 380.

[291] Graetz, VIII, 344–5.

[292] Marx, op. cit., 11, 15, 22 n. 26; Graetz, VIII, 348.

GLOSSARY

ADELANTADO (ADELANTADOS, ADELANTATI); ADENANTADO (ADENAN-
TADOS, ADENANTATI) — elected representative, or member of com-
munity council.
AGGADA (HAGGADAH) — ethical or homiletical portion of rabbinic litera-
ture.
'AGUNAH — deserted wife.
ALBALÁ — royal seal, royal letters patent.
ALBEDINUS — royal officer; commissar of Jews.
ALCALDE (ALCAIDE) — minor judicial official, representative of the king.
ALCAVALA — tax on commercial transactions.
ALFAQUIM — scholar, physician; also scribe and personal attendant of
Spanish king.
ALJAFERIA — an old, picturesque Moorish palace.
ALJAMA — congregation or community; also Jewish (or Moorish) quarter.
ALMAHONA — excise on wine and meat.
ALMOJARIFE (ALMOXARIFE) — taxgatherer for the king; customhouse
officer.
ARCA — chest or coffer.
ARRELDE — weight of four pounds.
ARRENDADOR — tax farmer.
ASIGNACIÓN — assignment of revenue to a person or institution.
AUREUM — mediaeval gold coin.
'AZARAH — open court of synagogue.

BAILÍA — jurisdictional district of a BAILE or bailiff.
BARUR (BERURIM) — secretary or deputy of communal board; also known
as MUKDAM and NE'EMAN.
BEDINAGE — tax.
BET DIN — Jewish court.
BET HA-KENESET — synagogue.
BET HA-MIDRASH — chapel, schoolhouse.
BIKKUR HOLIM — visiting the sick.

CABEÇA DEL PECHO — poll tax.
CALLE — street, Jewish quarter.
ÇALMEDINA — royal official.
CAPA ROTUNDA — cloak, or mantle prescribed for Jews.
CARCELAJE — prison-fee.

345

Carta maledictionum — chart of curses.
Casas del almidras — chapels of prayer or study.
Casas de la merced — houses of mercy or charity.
Castellano — ancient Spanish coin.
Cena (Cens) — tax for housing the king and his retinue.
Cena de ausencia — tax for housing royal family, payable in coin.
Cena de presencia — tax for housing royal family, payable in kind.
Clavario (Clavari; Clavarium) — treasurer.
Cogedor — tax collector.
Collecta — tax district.
Commissari per lo senyor rey — royal commissioners.
Concilium or Concejo — civic body of a small town or village.
Confrade — member of a brotherhood or fraternity.
Confraria — fraternity, benevolent brotherhood.
Contador — controller.
Contador mayor — controller general.
Converso — convert.
Cornado — old copper coin.
Corredor — broker.

Dayyan — judge.
Demanda — annual tribute.
Dinero — medieval copper coin.
Dineros Burg.— dineros coined at Burgos.
Dineros Jac. — dineros coined at Jaca.
Dirhem — an ancient coin.
Dispensator — dispenser, one who grants exemption.
Dispensero mayor del rey — chief royal dispenser.

Empréstito — levy in the form of a compulsory loan.
En cabeza (En cabeça) — poll or head-tax.
Erusin — betrothal.
Escribano (Escrivano) publico — notary public.

Familiar — royal attendant.
For (Fuero) — charter, privilege.

Gabbai — treasurer, trust officer.
Gaon (Geonim) — title of head of Babylonian Jewish academy.
Gizbar — treasurer.
Get — bill of divorce.

Haburah (Haburot) — association.
Haggadah — see Aggada.
Hakam — scholar, rabbi.

HALAKÀH (HALAKOT) — law or legal literature of Judaism.
HALIZAH — ceremony liberating a childless widow from the levirate marriage (Deut. 25.5–11).
HALLEL — psalms of praise.
HASKAMAH (HASKAMOT) — communal enactment.
HAZAKAH — claim to possession based on undisputed occupancy.
HAZMANAH — summons.
HAZZAN — public reader; precentor.
HEBRAT EREZ YISRAEL — Palestine league.
HEBRAT KEBARIM — burial society.
HEBRAT TALMUD TORAH — educational society.
HEBRAT YERUSHALAYIM — Jerusalem league.
HEKDESH — dedicated to a sacred purpose; funds or property belonging to a religious or charitable institution.
HEREM — excommunication.
HERMANDAD — brotherhood.
HIDALGO —Spanish nobleman.
HIDDUSHIM — novellae.
HOKMAT HA-'IBBUR — science of intercalation.
HONRAS — funeral honors.
HUPPAH — marriage canopy.
HEKAL — Shrine or ark which contains the sacred scrolls of the Torah.

INFANZON — nobleman.

JUDERÍA — Jewish quarter.
JURISPERITO — judicial crown officer.
JUSTICIA — a justice, a high-ranking judicial officer.

KAHAL — community, community council.
KENAS — fine.
KETUBAH — marriage contract.
KOHEN — descendant of the priestly tribe of Aaron.
KUPPAH — charity chest.

LA'AZ — foreign language.
LEGATO — deputy.
LEONERIUS (LEONER) — keeper or trainer of lions.
LEZDA — toll on merchandise.
LUISMO — feudal transfer tax.

MA MAJOR — upper class.
MA MIJANA — middle class.
MA MINOR — lower class.
MALSÍN (MALSHIN) — informer.

MANEH — Bible coin or weight.

MARAVEDÍ — Spanish coin.

MARRANO — Spanish word meaning damned, accursed, and applied to Jews who under compulsion accepted baptism but secretly practiced Judaism.

MASOR — informer.

MAYORDOMO — major-domo.

MAYORDOMO MAYOR — chief steward of the court.

MERKABAH — divine chariot of the vision of Ezekiel (Ezek. 1).

MERINO (MERINUS) — royal official exercising judicial powers.

MIDRASH — schoolhouse.

MINHAG (MINHAGIM) — usage, customary practice or ritual.

MOHAR — the wife's settlement.

MONEDA — special tax voted by the Cortes for the king.

MONTAZGO — toll for cattle.

MORABATIN — Moorish coin current in Spain.

MUKDAM (MUKDAMIM, MUKDAMIN) — deputies or officials of administrative boards.

MUSAPH — the additional service on Sabbaths and holidays.

NASI — prince.

NE'EMAN — trustee.

NIDDUI — ban, mild form of excommunication.

NISSU'IN — wedding ceremony.

PARNAS — leader of a community or congregation.

PATRIMONIO REAL — Crown estate.

PECHO — general tax in Aragon.

PEITA (PEITE) — general tax in Castile.

PILEGESH — concubine.

PINKAS — register of tax payers and their accounts.

PONTAZGO — toll over a bridge.

PRAESCRIPTION — see HAZAKAH.

PRIVADO — member of the privy council.

PROCURADOR — representative or emissary of the community.

PROHOMBRE — notable or member of the community council.

PROSBOL (PROSBUL) — document nullifying the Sabbatical cancellation of debts.

RAB DE LA CORTE — court rabbi.

RAB E JUES MAYOR — rabbi and chief justice.

REAL — a Spanish coin.

RECABDADOR DE LAS RENTAS DEL REY — collector of the public revenue; controller of the treasury.

RECAUDADOR MAYOR — chief tax controller.
RECEPTOR COMPOTORUM — receiver of accounts.
REGIDOR — member of inner communal council.
REGISTRO — a register.
RESPONSA — written rabbinic replies to questions of Jewish law.
RICO HOMBRE — peer of the first rank in Spain.
ROSH YESHIBAH — head of a Talmudic academy.
ROTULUS — scroll.

SALVA LA FÉ DEL SEÑOR — "Saving our allegiance to the lord," a clause inserted in some Hebrew communal statutes in order to make possible an appeal to the king without the threat of excommunication.
SECRETARIO — secretary; officer of council.
SELA' — a biblical coin or weight equal to one sacred or two common shekels.
SERVICIO — a service tax; an extra grant over and above the regular annual tax, variously known as PECHO, CABEÇA DEL PECHO, EN CABEÇA.
SHADKAN — marriage broker.
SHEMITTAH — release, cancellation of debts and rest of the soil in the Sabbatical year.
SHEMITTAT KESAFIM — release of loans (during Sabbatical year).
SHETAR — writ, document.
SHOFAR — ram's horn, trumpet.
SIRSUR — broker.
SIRSURIA — brokerage.
SISA — excise on wine and meat; also called *almahona* in Castile.
SUELDO — ancient Roman coin; also Spanish coin. In Aragon, the SUELDO was worth half a REAL of plate.
SYNDIC (SINDICO) — an official of the Jewish community council.

TAILLE — tax levied by the king, or feudal lord, on his subjects or on land held under him.
TAKKANAH (TAKKANOT) — communal enactment or statute.
TALLIT — prayer shawl.
TALMID HAKAM — sage, scholar.
TALMUD TORAH — study of Torah or school where Torah is the subject of study.
TAMHUI — charity plate.
TANNA — Palestinian teacher, or rabbi, of the Mishnaic period (prior to 200 C. E.).
TARGUM — Aramaic translation of the Bible.
TESORERO — treasurer.
TESORERO DEL RE — royal treasurer.

THESAURAR — treasurer.
TORNADIZO — turncoat, renegade.
TOSAFOT — glosses.

VECINO — citizen, property owner.
VERGUER — high constable.
VIEJO — elder.
VIRI BONI — "good men," guardians of the sacred property.

YABAM — husband's brother, or levir, upon whom devolved the duty of marrying the former's widow, if left without issue.
YIBBUM — marrying the wife of a brother who died without issue.
YESHIBAH — Talmudic academy.
YO'AZIM — councilors.

ZUZ — ancient silver coin.

BIBLIOGRAPHY

BIBLIOGRAPHY*

ABBA MARI BEN MOSES YARHI, see ASTRUC DE LUNEL.

ABOAB, IMMANUEL, Nomologia ó Discursos legales. Amsterdam, 1629.

ABRAHAM BAR HIYYA HA-NASI (Savasorda), "Iggeret Rabbi Abraham bar Hiyya ha-Nasi." *Festschrift Adolf Schwarz*, Hebrew section, 23–36, Berlin, 1917.

———, Sefer megillat ha-megalleh. Ed. by A. Poznanski, with an introduction by Julius Guttmann, Berlin, 1924.

———, Zurat ha-arez. Offenbach, 1720.

ABRAHAM BEN NATHAN YARHI, see YARHI, ABRAHAM BEN NATHAN.

ABRAHAM IBN DAUD, see IBN DAUD, ABRAHAM.

ABRAHAMS, ISRAEL, ed., Hebrew Ethical Wills. 2 parts, Philadelphia, 1926.

———, Jewish Life in the Middle Ages. London, 1932.

ABRAVANEL, see ISAAC BEN JUDAH ABRAVANEL.

ABULAFIA, MEIR HA-LEVI, Kitab al-rasa'il. Letters, collected by Jehiel Brill, Paris, 1871.

———, She'elot u-teshubot, in Sefer or zaddikim. Saloniki, 1799.

ADLER, E. N., Auto de Fé and Jew. London, 1908.

ADRET, SOLOMON BEN ABRAHAM IBN, She'elot u-teshubot. Vol. I, Bologna, 1539; vols. II, III, Leghorn, 1657, 1778; vol. IV, Wilna, 1881; vol. V, Leghorn, 1825; vols. VI, VII, Warsaw, 1868.

———, Teshubot ha-RaShBA ha-meyuhasot le-ha-RaMBaN. Warsaw, 1883.

AGUILO, E. K., "Una carta esponsalica hebrea, 1328." *Boletin de sociedad Luliana*, 1891, 169–70.

AGUIRRE, JOS. SAENZ DE, Collectio maxima conciliorum omnium Hispaniae. 6 vols., Rome, 1753–5.

AHAI, RAB, She'iltot. Venice, 1546.

ALBO, JOSEPH, Sefer ha-'ikkarim. Translation and notes by I. Husik, 4 vols., Philadelphia, 1929–30.

ALFASI, ISAAC BEN JACOB, Sefer ha-halakot. In Vilna edition of the Babylonian Talmud.

———, Sefer she'elot u-teshubot. Leghorn, 1781.

Alfonsine Tables, Libro de las tablas Alfonsies. Ed. with notes by M. Rico y Sinobas, Madrid, 1867.

AL-HARIZI, JUDAH BEN SOLOMON, Tahkemoni. Amsterdam, 1729.

ALMANZI, JOSEPH, Abne zikaron. Published by Samuel David Luzzatto, Prag, 1841.

ALPHONSO DE SPINA, Fortalitium Fidei ... Lyons, 1525.

ALTAMIRA, RAFAEL, Cuestiones de Historia del Derecho y de Legislación Comparada. Madrid, 1914.

AMADOR, DON JOSÉ DE LOS RIOS, see RIOS.

*For additional references, dealing especially with local history, the reader is referred to the bibliography in Baer I and II.

Anatolio (Anatoli), Jacob ben Abba Mari, Malmad ha-talmidim. Lyck, 1866.

Araujo, Oscar d', "La grande synagoge de Ségovie." *REJ*, XXXIX (1899), 209–16.

Asher ben Yehiel, She'elot u-teshubot. Venice, 1607.

Asheri [Judah ben Asher ben Yehiel], Zikron Yehudah. Berlin, 1846.

Ashkenazi, Eliezer ben Solomon, Ta'am zekenim. Ed. by R. Kirchheim, Frankfurt a. M., 1854.

Assaf, Simhah, " 'Abadim u-sechar 'abadim ezel ha-Yehudim bi-yeme ha-benayim." *Zion*, IV (1940), 91–125.

——, "Anuse Sefarad u-Portugal be-sifrut ha-teshubot." *Zion*, V (1933), 19–60.

——, Bate ha-din ve-sidrehem ahare hatimat ha-talmud. Jerusalem, 1924.

——, Ha-'onashin ahare hatimat ha-talmud. Jerusalem, 1922.

——, Mekorot le-toledot ha-hinnuk be-Yisrael. 3 vols., Tel-Aviv, 1925–36.

Asso y del Rio, J. T. de, El ordenamiento de leyes que Alfonso XI hizo. . . Madrid, 1847.

Astruc de Lunel [Abba Mari ben Moses Yarhi], Sefer minhat kenaot. Pressburg, 1838.

Astruc, Jean, Memoires pour servir à l'histoire de la Faculté de medicine de Montpellier. Paris, 1767.

Atlas, Eliezer, "Ha-yareah ve-ha-kokabim, o ha-RIBaSh u-bene doro." *Ha-Kerem*, I (1887), 1–26.

Ayala, Pedro Lopez de, Crónicas. Pamplona, 1591.

Azemard, E., Étude sur les Israélites de Montpellier au moyen-âge. Nimes, 1924.

Bacher, Wilhelm, "Matériaux pour servir à l'histoire de l'exégèse Biblique en Espagne dans la première moitié du XII° siècle." *REJ*, XVII (1888), 272–84.

Baer, Fritz, "Abner von Burgos." *Korrespondenzblatt . . . Akademie für die Wissenschaft des Judenthums*, X (1929), 20–37.

——, "Die Disputation von Tortosa." *Spanische Forschungen der Görresgesellschaft*, III (1931), 307–36.

——, Die Juden im christlichen Spanien, I: Aragonien und Navarra; II: Kastilien, Inkquisitionsakten. Berlin, 1929–36.

——, "Eine jüdische Messiasprophetie auf das Jahr 1186 und der dritte Kreuzzug." *MGWJ*, LXX (1926), 113–22, 155–65.

——, "Ha-mazab ha-politi shel yehude Sefarad be-doro shel R. Yehudah ha-Levi." *Zion*, I (1935–36), 6–23.

——, "Le-bikoret ha-vikkuhim shel R. Yehiel mi-Paris ve-shel R. Moshe ben Nahman." *Tarbiz*, II (1931), 172–87.

——, "Probleme der spanisch-jüdischen Geschichte." *Korrespondenzblatt . . . Akademie der Wissenschaft des Judenthums*, VI (1925), 5–25.

——, "Review of 'Los Mozárabes de Toledo en los siglos XII y XIII,' por Angel González Palencia." *Tarbiz*, V (1934), 228–36.

——, Studien zur Geschichte der Juden im Königreich Aragonien während des 13. und 14. Jahrhunderts. Berlin, 1913.

——, Untersuchungen über Quellen und Komposition des Schebet Jehuda. Berlin, 1923.

——, "He'arot hadashot le-sefer Shebet Yehudah." *Tarbiz*, VI (1934–35), 152–79.

Bahya ben Joseph ibn Pakuda, Duties of the Heart. English translation by M. Hyamson, New York, 1925.

BAHYA BEN JOSEPH IBN PAKUDA, Kitab al-hidaya ila faraid al-qulub. Ed. in Arabic by A. S. Yahuda, Leyden, 1912.
———, Sefer hobot ha-lebabot. Hebrew translation by Yehudah ibn Tibbon, with an introduction and notes by A. Zifroni, Jerusalem, 1928.
BALAGUER, V. DE., Las calles de Barcelona, 1866.
BARFAT, ISAAC BEN SHESHET [Profet or Perfet], Sefer she'elot u-teshubot [Sefer bar Sheshet]. Riva di Trenta [1559].
———, Sefer she'elot u-teshubot ha-RiBaSh ha-hadashot. Ed. David Frankel, Munkacz, 1901.
BARON, SALO W., A Social and Religious History of the Jews. 3 vols., New York, 1937.
———, "The Historical Outlook of Maimonides." *Proceedings of the American Academy for Jewish Research*, VI (1935), 5–113.
BARZILAI, *see* JUDAH BEN BARZILAI OF BARCELONA.
BÉDARRIDE, I., Les Juifs en France, en Italie, et en Espagne. Paris, 1861.
BERLINER, ABRAHAM, Censur und Confiscation hebräischer Bücher im Kirchenstaate, auf Grund der Inquisitions-Akten in der Vaticana und Vallicellana dargestellt. Frankfurt a. M., 1891.
BENJAMIN OF TUDELA, The Itinerary of Rabbi Benjamin of Tudela. Translated and edited by A. Asher, 2 vols., London and Berlin, 1840–41.
BERNALDEZ, ANDRES, Crónica de los Reyes Católicos. Ed. Lafuente, Granada, 1856.
BERNSTEIN, BELA, "Die Schrifterklärung des Bachja ben Ascher ibn Chalawa und ihre Quellen." *MWJ*, XVIII (1891), 27–47, 85–118, 165–96.
BIOT, EDOUARD C., De l'abolition de l'esclavage. Paris, 1840.
BLAU, LUDWIG, Das altjüdische Zauberwesen. 2nd edition, Berlin, 1914.
BOFARULL Y SANS, FRANCISCO DE, Los Judíos en el territorio de Barcelona (Siglos X al XIII) reinado de Jaime I, 1213–1276. Barcelona, 1910.
BRAUNSTEIN, B., The Chuetas of Majorca: Conversos and the Inquisition of Majorca. Scottsdale, Pa., 1936.
BRODY, HEINRICH, "Gürtelgedichte des Todrōs Abu-l'Āfija." *Mitteilungen des Forschungsinstituts für hebräische Dichtung*, I (1933), 1–93.
———, Beiträge zu Salomo Da-Piera's Leben und Wirken nebst Auszügen aus seinem Diwan. Berlin, 1893.
BURKE, ULICK RALPH, A History of Spain from the Earliest Times to the Death of Ferdinand the Catholic. Third Edition, edited by Martin A. S. Hume, 2 vols., London, 1900.

CALVIN, JOHN, "De usuris responsum." *Economic Tracts*, IV, New York, 1881.
CAMPANTON, *see* ISAAC BEN JACOB CAMPANTON.
Cambridge Mediaeval History. Vol. VI., New York, 1929.
CANTERA BURGOS, FRANCISCO, El Judío Salmantino Abraham Zacut: Notas para la historia de la astronomía en la España medieval. Madrid, 1931.
———, La conversión del célebre talmudista Salomon Levi (Pablo de Burgos). Santander, 1933. Reprinted from *Boletín de la Biblioteca de Menendez y Pelayo*, vol. XV.
———, "La usura judía en Castilla." *La Ciencia Tomista*, XLIII (1931), 5–26.
CAPMANY Y DE MONTPALAN, A. DE, Memorias históricas sobre la Marina, Comercio y Artes de Barcelona. 4 vols., Madrid, 1779–92.
CARINI, I., Gli archivi delle biblioteche di Spagna, II. Palermo, 1884.

CARMOLY, ELIAKIM, Histoire des médecins juifs. Bruxelles, 1842.

CARO, GEORG, Sozial- und Wirtschaftsgeschichte der Juden im Mittelalter und in der Neuzeit. 2 vols., Frankfurt a. M., 1908–20.

CASTRO, AD. DE, Historia de los judíos en España. Cadiz, 1847.

CASTRO, RODRIGUEZ DE, Biblioteca española. Madrid, 1781.

Codex Theodosianus: Theodosiani libri XVI cum constitutionibus Sirmondianis et leges novellae ad Theodosianum pertinentes. Ed. by Th. Mommsen and Paulus M. Meyer, 2 vols., Berlin, 1904–05

COHEN, BOAZ, Kuntres ha-teshubot. Budapest, 1930. Reprinted from Ha-Zofeh, vol. XIV.

———, "Une légende juive de Mohammet." REJ, LXXXVIII (1929), 1–17.

Colección de documentos inéditos del Archivo general de la Corona de Aragón. 41 vols., Barcelona, 1847–76.

Colección de las crónicas y memorias de los reyes de Castilla. 7 vols., Madrid, 1779–87.

COLMEIRO, MANUEL, Curso de derecho politico. Madrid, 1873.

———, Cortes de los antiguos reinos de León y de Castilla. 2 vols., Madrid, 1883–84.

———, Historia de la economía política en España. 2 vols., Madrid, 1863.

CORONEL, NAHMAN NATHAN, Sefer zeker Natan. Vienna, 1872.

Corpus iuris canonici. Ed. by E. L. Richter, revised and annotated by E. Friedberg. 2 vols., Leipzig, 1879–81.

Cortes le los antiguos reinos de León y de Castilla. 2 vols., Madrid, 1882–1903.

CRESCAS, HASDAI BEN ABRAHAM, Sefer bittul 'ikkare ha-nozerim. Reprinted by Deinard, Kearny, N. J., 1934.

———, Sefer 'or adonai. Ferrara, 1555.

CUNNINGHAM, WILLIAM, An Essay on Western Civilisation in its Economic Aspects. 2 vols., Cambridge, 1898–1900.

DENIFLE, O. P., "Quellen zur Disputation Pablos Christiani mit Moses Nachmani zu Barcelona, 1263." Historisches Jahrbuch der Görres-Gesellschaft, 1887, 225–44.

DEPPING, G. B., Les Juifs dans le Moyen Âge. Paris, 1845.

Derek tobim. Published by Hirsch Edelmann, London, 1852.

DINABURG, BENZION, " 'Aliyato shel Rabbi Yehudah ha-Levi le-Erez Yisrael." Minhah le-David (David Yellin Jubilee Volume), Jerusalem, 1935, 157–82.

———, Yisrael ba-golah. 2 vols. in 3 parts, Jerusalem, 1926–31.

DÖLLINGER, JOHN J., "Die Juden in Europa." Akademische Vorträge, Nördlingen, 1890.

DOZY, REINHART, Spanish Islam: A History of the Moslems in Spain. Translated with a biographical introduction and additional notes by Francis Griffin Stokes. London, 1913.

DUKES, LEOPOLD, Ehrensäulen und Denksteine zu einem künftigen Pantheon hebräischer Dichter und Dichtungen. Wien, 1837.

———, Literaturhistorische Mittheilungen über die ältesten hebräischen Exegeten, Grammatiker und Lexicographen. Stuttgart, 1844.

DUBNOW, SIMON, Weltgeschichte des jüdischen Volkes. 10 vols., Berlin, 1925–29.

DURAN, ISAAC BEN MOSES HA-LEVI [known as Profiat Duran], "Al tehi kaaboteka." Kobez vikkuhim, collected by Isaac ben Abraham Akrish. 2nd edition, Breslau, 1844.

DURAN, ISAAC BEN MOSES HA-LEVI [known as Profiat Duran], Sefer ma'aseh efod. Edited by J. Friedländer and J. Kohn, Vienna, 1865.
DURAN, SIMEON BEN ZEMAH, Sefer magen abot. Ed. by A. Jellinek, Leipzig, 1855.
——, Sefer ha-tashbaz. 3 parts, Amsterdam, 1738.

EBERT, ADOLF, Quellenforschungen aus der Geschichte Spaniens. Kassel, 1849.
EISENSTEIN, J. D., Ozar wikkuhim: A Collection of Polemics and Disputations. New York, 1928.
ELLIOTT, CALVIN, Usury: A Scriptural, Ethical and Economic View. Millersburg, Ohio, [1902].
ENELOW, H. G., ed., Israel ibn Al-Nakawa's Menorat ha-Maor. 4 vols., New York, 1929–32.
EPSTEIN, ISIDORE, The Responsa of R. Solomon ben Adreth of Barcelona (1235–1310) as a Source of the History of Spain. London, 1925.
——, The Responsa of R. Simon b. Zemah Duran as a Source of the History of the Jews in North Africa. London, 1930.
EPSTEIN, LOUIS M., The Jewish Marriage Contract: A Study in the Status of the Woman in Jewish Law. New York, 1927.
EYMERIC, N., Directorium inquisitorum. Edited and annotated by F. Pegna; revised ed., Venice, 1607.

FAGNAN, E., "Le signe distinctif des Juifs au Maghreb." REJ, XXVIII (1894), 294–98.
FERNANDEZ Y GONZALEZ, DON FRANCISCO, Institutiones juridicas del pueblo de Israel: Introducción histórico-crítica. Vol. I, Madrid, 1881.
——, Los Mudejares de Castilla. 1866.
——, Ordenamiento formado por las procuradores de las aljamas hebreas. Madrid, 1886 (reprinted from BAH, VII).
FINKE, HEINRICH, Acta Aragonensia. 3 vols., Berlin, 1908–22.
——, Konzilienstudien zur Geschichte des 13ten Jahrhunderts. Münster, 1891.
FINKEL, J., "An Eleventh Century Source for the History of Jewish Scientists in Mohammedan Lands (Ibn Said)." JQR, XVIII (1927–28), 45–54.
FINKELSTEIN, LOUIS, Jewish Self-Government in the Middle Ages. New York, 1924.
FITA, FIDEL, Actas inéditas de siete concilios españoles. Madrid, 1882.
——, Estudios históricos: colección de articulos escritos y publicados en el Boletín de la real academia de la historia. 8 vols., Madrid, 1882–1887.
——, "Guadatich en favor de Salomon Gracian, Juheu de Barcelona (20 Jan. 1395)." La Vue de Monserrat, August 13, 1881.
——, Lápidas hebreas de Gerona. Gerona, 1871.
——, La España hebrea. 2 vols., Madrid, 1891.
——, "La synagogue de Cordoue." REJ, IX (1884), 157–58; X (1885), 244–47.
——, and GABRIEL LLABRÉS, "Privilegios de los Hebreos mallorquines en el códice Pueyo." BAH, XXXVI (1900), 15–35, 122–48, 185–209, 273–306, 369–402, 458–94.
FITER Y INGLÉS, JOSÉ, Expulsión de los Judíos de Barcelona. Barcelona, 1876.
FLOREZ, E. ET AL., ed., España Sagrada. 51 vols., Madrid, 1747–1879.
FRANCK, A., The Kabbalah or the Religious Philosophy of the Hebrews. New York, 1926.

358 JEWS IN SPAIN

FRANKEL, ZECHARIAH, Die Eidesleistung der Juden in theologischer und historischer Beziehung. Dresden, 1847.

——, "Ein Pseudo-Messias im 14ten Jahrhundert." *MGWJ*, XXVIII (1879), 78–81.

——, Entwurf einer Geschichte der Literatur der nachtalmudischen Responsen. Breslau, 1865.

FREIDUS, A. S., List of Works Relating to the History and Condition of the Jews in Various Countries. New York, 1914.

FREIMANN, A., "Die hebräischen Inkunabeln der Druckereien in Spanien und Portugal." *Gutenberg Festschrift zur Feier des 25-jährigen Bestehens des Gutenberg-Museums in Mainz*, ed. by A. Ruppel, Mayence, 1925, 203–6.

——, "Kopisten hebräischer Handschriften in Spanien und Portugal." *Zeitschrift für hebräische Bibliographie*, XIV (1910), 105–12; XV (1911), 26–7.

Fuero real de España, El, *Los códigos españoles concordados y anotados*, I, 353 ff., Madrid, 1847.

Fuero del reino de Navarra. Pamplona, 1815.

GABIROL, SOLOMON BEN JUDAH IBN, Choice of Pearls. Translated into Hebrew by Judah ibn Tibbon, with English translation by B. H. Ascher, London, 1859.

——, Mekor hayyim. In Latin translation entitled "Avencebrolis Fons vitae," ed. by C. Baeumker, Münster, 1892–95.

——, The Improvement of the Moral Qualities. Translation and an essay on "The Place of Gabirol in the History of the Development of Jewish Ethics," by S. S. Wise, New York, 1901.

——, Mekor hayyim. A Hebrew translation from the Latin by J. Bluvstein, Jerusalem, 1926.

——, Selected Religious Poems. Translated into English verse by Israel Zangwill from a critical text ed. by Israel Davidson, Philadelphia, 1923.

——, Shire Shelomoh ben Yehudah ibn Gabirol. Ed. by C. N. Bialik and I. H. Ravnitzky, 7 vols., Tel Aviv, 1927–32.

GANDZ, SOLOMON, "The Astrolabe in Jewish Literature." *HUCA*, IV (1927), 469–86.

——, "The Dawn of Literature." *Osiris*, VII (1939), 261–522.

——, "The Mishnat ha-Middot." *Quellen u. Studien zur Geschichte der Mathematik*, II, Berlin, 1932.

——, "Studies in Hebrew Mathematics and Astronomy." *Proceedings of the American Academy for Jewish Research*, IX (1939), 5–55.

——, "Studies in the History of Mathematics from Hebrew and Arabic Sources." *HUCA*, VI (1929), 247–76.

GARCIA VILLADA, Z., Historia eclesiástica de España. 2 vols., in 4 parts, Madrid, 1929–33.

GERONDI, *see* MOSES BEN NAHMAN GERONDI [NAHMANIDES].

GERSHENFELD, LOUIS, The Jew in Science. Philadelphia, 1934.

GERSONIDES, *see* LEVI BEN GERSHON.

GERUNDI, *see* NISSIM BEN REUBEN GERUNDI.

GINSBURG, JEKUTHIEL, "Enbalshem Efrayim Girondi." *Hadoar*, IX (1928), 22–3, 41, 54–5, 71–3.

GIRBAL, E. C., Los Judíos en Gerona. Gerona, 1870.

GOLDE, M., "Familienleben der spanischen Juden vor ihrer Vertreibung 1492." *Jüdische Familienforschung*, II (1929), 110–14.

González Palencia, C. Angel, Los Mozárabes de Toledo en los siglos XII y XIII. 4 vols., Madrid, 1926–30.

Gottheil, Richard J. H., "Some Spanish Documents." *JQR*, O. S., XVI (1904), 702–14.

Graetz, Heinrich, "Der Minister-Rabbi Samuel Ibn-Nagrela." *Wertheimer Jahrbuch*, Vienna, 1860.

——, "Die westgothische Gesetzgebung in Betreff der Juden." *Jahresbericht des jüdisch-theologischen Seminars, Fränckelscher Stiftung*, Breslau, 1858.

——, Geschichte der Juden von den ältesten Zeiten bis auf die Gegenwart. 11 vols., Leipzig, 1853–76. Also 3rd edition, vols. VI, VII; 4th edition, vol. VIII.

——, History of the Jews. 6 vols., Philadelphia, 1891–98.

——, Leket shoshanim; Blumenlese. Breslau, 1862.

Grayzel, Solomon, The Church and the Jews in the XIIIth Century. Philadelphia, 1933.

Gross, Henri, Gallia Judaica. Paris, 1897.

Grunwald, M., "Aus Spanien und Portugal: Bemerkungen zu Fritz Baer, Die Juden im christlichen Spanien." *MGWJ*, LXXIII (1929), 366–76.

Güdemann, Moritz, Das jüdische Unterrichtswesen während der spanisch-arabischen Periode. Wien, 1873.

——, Geschichte des Erziehungswesens und der Cultur der abendländischen Juden während des Mittelalters und der neueren Zeit. 3 vols., Wien, 1880–88.

Guia histórica y descriptiva de los archivos de España. Madrid, 1921.

Gulak, A., Le-heker toledot ha-mishpat ha-'ibri bi-tekufat ha-talmud. Vol. I. Jerusalem, 1929.

Guttmann, Jakob, Das Verhältniss des Thomas von Aquino zum Judenthum und zur jüdischen Litteratur. Göttingen, 1891.

——, "Die Religionsphilosophie des Abraham ibn Daud aus Toledo." *MGWJ*, XXVII (1878), 361–76.

——, Die Scholastik des dreizehnten Jahrhunderts. Breslau, 1902.

Guzman, Perez de, Crónica de Juan II. Valencia, 1779.

Halevi, see Judah ben Samuel Halevi.

Halevy, I., Dorot ha-rishonim. 4 vols., Berlin, 1918–22.

Harkavy, Abraham Y., Zikkaron la-rishonim ve-gam la-aharonim. Berlin, 1887.

Hasdai ben Abraham Crescas, see Crescas.

Hefele, C. J., Histoire des Conciles. 9 vols., Paris, 1907–31.

Hemdah genuzah ve-hu teshubot ha-geonim. Jerusalem, 1863.

Heschel, A., Maimonides. Eine Biographie. Berlin, 1935.

Himyari, ibn 'Abd al-Mun 'im al-, La Péninsule ibérique au moyen âge d'après le kitab ar-rawd al-mi'tar fi habar al-aktar d'Ibn 'Abd al-Mun 'im al-Himyari. Publié par E. Lévi-Provençal, Leiden, 1938.

Hoffmann, M., Der Geldhandel der deutschen Juden während des Mittelalters bis zum Jahre 1350. Leipzig, 1910.

Hurter, Fr., Innocenz III und seine Zeitgenossen. 3 vols., Hamburg, 1838.

Husik, Isaac, "Joseph Albo, the Last of the Medieval Philosophers." *Proceedings of the American Academy for Jewish Research*, I (1928–30), 61–72.

——, A History of Medieval Jewish Philosophy. 2nd ed., Philadelphia, 1930.

IBN DAUD, ABRAHAM, Emunah ramah. Ed. in Hebrew and translated into German by S. Weil, Frankfurt a. M., 1852.

——, Sefer ha-kabbalah. Ed. by A. Neubauer, Oxford, 1887. (*M. J. C.*, vol. I.).

IBN EZRA, *see* MOSES BEN JACOB IBN EZRA.

INGRAM, JOHN K., History of Slavery. London, 1895.

ISAAC BEN JACOB ALFASI, *see* ALFASI.

ISAAC BEN JACOB CAMPANTON, Sefer darke ha-gemara. Wien, 1891.

ISAAC BEN JOSEPH ISRAELI, *see* ISRAELI.

ISAAC BEN JOSEPH PULGAR, *see* PULGAR.

ISAAC BEN JUDAH ABRAVANEL, Commentary on Joshua. Pesaro, [1511?].

ISAAC BEN MOSES HA-LEVI DURAN, *see* DURAN.

ISAAC BEN SHESHET BARFAT, [Profet, Perfet or Barfat], *see* BARFAT.

ISAACS, A. LIONEL, The Jews of Majorca. London, 1936.

Israelietische Letterbode. Vols. 4–6, Amsterdam, 1878–81.

ISRAELI, ISAAC BEN JOSEPH, Musar le-rofe'im. Ed. by David Kaufmann, Odessa, 1866.

——, "Isak Israeli's Propädeutik für Aerzte." Uebersetzt von David Kaufmann, *MGWJ*, XI (1884), 97–112.

——, Sefer yesod 'olam. Ed. by D. Cassel and B. Goldberg, 2 vols., Berlin, 1848.

ISSERLES, MOSES BEN ISRAEL, She'elot u-teshubot. Amsterdam, 1711.

JABEZ, JOSEPH BEN HAYYIM, Or ha-hayyim. Amsterdam, 1781.

JACOB BEN ASHER OF TOLEDO, Tur orah hayyim. 4 vols., Warsaw, 1882.

JACOB BEN JUDAH, OF LONDON, *see* Shibe'ah 'enayyim.

JACOB BEN MEIR OF RAMERU [RABBENU TAM], Sefer ha-yashar. Frankfurt a. M., 1850.

JACOBS, JOSEPH, Sources of Spanish-Jewish History. New York, 1894.

JELLINEK, ADOLPH, Auswahl kabbalistischer Mystik. Erstes Heft, Leipzig, 1853.

——, Beiträge zur Geschichte der Kabbala. 2 parts, Leipzig, 1852.

JOSEPH BEN EPHRAIM CARO, Shulhan 'aruk, Hoshen Mishpat.

JOSEPH BEN HANAN EZOBI, "Ka'arat kesef." Translated by D. I. Freedman, *JQR*, O. S., VIII (1896), 534–40.

JOSEPH BEN HAYYIM JABEZ, *see* JABEZ.

JOSEPH BEN ISAAC KIMHI, Sefer ha-berit. Excerpts reprinted in J. D. Eisenstein, *Ozar Wikkuhim*, 66–78.

JOSEPH BEN JOSHUA HA-KOHEN, Emek ha-bakah. With notes by S. D. Luzzatto and M. Letteris, Cracow, 1895.

JOSEPH BEN MEIR HA-LEVI IBN MIGASH, Sefer she'elot u-teshubot. Salonica, 1791.

JOSEPH BEN SAMUEL TOB ELEM, Teshubot geonim kadmonim. Ed. by S. L. Rapoport, Berlin, 1848.

JOST, I. M., Geschichte der Israeliten seit der Maccabäer bis auf unsere Tage, nach den Quellen bearbeitet. Vols. I–IX, Berlin, 1820–28; vol X, Berlin, 1846–47.

Jubelschrift zum neunzigsten Geburtstag des Leopold Zunz. Berlin, 1884.

JUDAH BEN ASHER and JACOB BEN ASHER, Zavaot ha-Rab Yehudah ben ha-Rosh we-ahiv ha-Rab Ya'akob ba'al ha-turim. Ed. by S. Schechter, Pressburg, 1885.

JUDAH BEN ASHER BEN YEHIEL, *see* ASHERI.

JUDAH BEN BARZILAI OF BARCELONA, Sefer ha-shetarot. Ed. by S. J. Halberstamm, Berlin, 1898.

JUDAH BEN SAMUEL HALEVI, Das Buch Kusari des Jehuda ha-Levi. Translated and edited by D. Cassel, Leipzig, 1853.

JUDAH BEN SAMUEL HALEVI, Kitab al-Khazari. Translated and ed. by H. Hirschfeld, with a preface to the new edition by M. M. Kaplan, 2nd ed., New York, 1927.
———, Diwan. Ed. by H. Brody, 4 vols., Berlin, 1894–1930.
JUSTER, JEAN, La condition légale des Juifs sous les rois visigoths. Paris, 1912.
———, Les Juifs dans l'empire romain. 2 vols., Paris, 1914.

KAHN, SALOMON, "Documents inédits sur les juifs de Montpellier." REJ, XIX (1889), 259–81.
KATZ, SOLOMON, The Jews in the Visigothic and Frankish Kingdoms of Spain and Gaul. Cambridge, Mass., 1937.
———, "Pope Gregory the Great and the Jews." JQR, XXIV (1933–34), 113–36.
KAUFMANN, DAVID, Gesammelte Schriften. Ed. by M. Brann, 3 vols., Frankfurt a. M., 1908–15.
———, "Jewish Informers in the Middle Ages." JQR, O.S., VIII (1895–96), 217–38.
———, "Simeon ben Josefs Sendschreiben an Menachem ben Salomo: ein Beitrag zur Geschichte der jüdischen Exegese und Predigt im Mittelalter." Zunz Jubelschrift (1884), 143–51; Hebrew Section, 142–74: "Hoshen mishpat."
———, "Zur Geschichte der Khethubba." MGWJ, XLI (1897), 213–21.
KAYSERLING, MEYER, Biblioteca Española-Portugueza-Judaica. Strasbourg, 1890.
———, Christopher Columbus and the participation of the Jews in the Spanish and Portuguese discoveries. Translated by Charles Gross, New York, 1894.
———, "Das Castilianische Gemeinde-Statut." Jahrbuch für die Geschichte der Juden und des Judenthums, IV (1869), 263–334.
———, "Die Juden in Mallorca." Jahrbuch für die Geschichte der Juden, I (1860), 67–100.
———, "Don Pedro und sein Schatzmeister Samuel Lewi: ein historischer Versuch." MGWJ, VI (1857), 365–81.
———, "Ein Verein der jüdischen Schuhmacher in Saragossa." Allgemeine Zeitung des Judenthums, LVI (1892), 438.
———, Ein Feiertag in Madrid: Zur Geschichte der Spanisch-Portugiesischen Juden. Berlin, 1859.
———, Geschichte der Juden in Spanien und Portugal: I. Die Juden in Navarra, den Baskenlaendern und auf den Balearen. Berlin, 1861.
Kebuzat hakamim ... Wissenschaftliche Aufsätze in hebräisch-talmudischer Sprache ... Gesammelt von W. Warnheim. Wien, 1861.
KIMHI, JOSEPH BEN ISAAC, see JOSEPH BEN ISAAC KIMHI.
KISCH, A., "Die Anklageartikel gegen den Talmud und ihre Vertheidigung durch Rabbi Jechiel b. Joseph vor Ludwig dem Heiligen in Paris." MGWJ, XXIII (1874), 10–18, 62–75, 123–30, 155–63, 204–12.
———, Papst Gregors IXten Anklageartikel gegen den Talmud. Leipzig, 1874.
KISCH, GUIDO, "The Landshut Jewry Oath." Historia Judaica, I (1939), 119–20.
———, "Studien zur Geschichte des Judeneides im Mittelalter." HUCA, XIV (1939), 431–56.
———, "Research in Medieval Legal History of the Jews." Proceedings of the American Academy for Jewish Research, VI (1934–5), 229–276.
———, "The Jewry-Law of the Medieval German Law-Books." Part II, Proceedings of the American Academy for Jewish Research, X (1940), 130–63.
KLÜPFEL, L., Verwaltungsgeschichte des Königreiches Aragon zu Ende des 13. Jahrhunderts. Stuttgart, 1915.

KOBAK, JOSEPH ISAAC, Sefer ginze nistarot. 4 pts., Bamberg, 1868–78.

KRAUSS, SAMUEL, Geschichte der jüdischen Ärzte vom frühesten Mittelalter bis zur Gleichberechtigung. Vienna, 1930.

LATTES, ISAAC BEN JACOB, Sha'are Zion. Ed. and annotated by S. Buber, Jaroslaw, 1885.

LATTES, MOSES BEN ABRAHAM, Likkutim shonim, memoir of Elijah Kapsali, and extract from his unpublished Sefer debe Eliyahu. Padua, 1869.

LEA, HENRY CHARLES, An Historical Sketch of Sacerdotal Celibacy in the Christian Church. Second edition, Boston, 1884.

———, A History of the Inquisition of the Middle Ages. 3 vols., New York, 1908–11.

———, A History of the Inquisition of Spain. 4 vols., New York, 1906–07.

———, "Ferrand Martinez and the Massacres of 1391." *AHR*, I (1896), 209–25.

Legacy of Israel, The. Ed. by E. R. Bevan and Charles Singer, Oxford, 1927.

LEVI B. GERSHON [GERSONIDES], Die Kämpfe Gottes. Translation of parts I–IV by B. Kellermann, 2 vols., Berlin, 1914–16.

———, Milhamot Adonai. Leipzig, 1866.

LEVY, RAPHAEL, The Astrological Works of Abraham ibn Ezra. Baltimore, 1927.

LEWIN, A., "Die Religionsdisputation des R. Jechiel von Paris 1240 am Hofe Ludwigs des Heiligen, ihre Veranlassung und ihre Folgen." *MGWJ*, XVIII (1869), 97–110, 145–56, 193–210.

Libro verde de Aragón, E. Ed., with an introduction by R. Amador de los Rios. *Revista de España*, CV (1885), 547–78; CVI (1885), 249–88, 567–603.

LINDO, E. H., The History of the Jews of Spain and Portugal. London, 1848.

LLABRÉS, GABRIEL, see FITA, FIDEL AND LIABRÉS, G.

LOEB, ISIDORE, "Joseph Haccohen et les Chroniqueurs juifs." *REJ*, XVI, 28–56, 211–25; XVII (1888), 74–95, 247–71.

———, "La controverse de 1263 à Barcelone entre Paulus Christiani et Moise ben Nahman." *REJ*, XV (1887), 1–18.

———, "La correspondance des Juifs d'Espagne avec ceux de Constantinople." *REJ*, XV (1887), 262–76.

———, "Le nombre des Juifs de Castille et d'Espagne au moyen âge." *REJ*, XIV (1887), 161–83.

———, "Liste nominative des Juifs de Barcelone en 1392." *REJ*, IV (1882), 57–77.

———, "Une inscription hébraique de Calatayud." *REJ*, XVI (1888) 273–75.

LUCAS, LÉOPOLD, "Innocent III et les Juifs." *REJ*, XXXV (1897), 247–55.

———, "Judentaufen und Judaismus zur Zeit des Papstes Innocenz III." *Festschrift zum siebzigsten Geburtstage Martin Philippsons*, 25–38, Leipzig, 1916.

Ma'aseh Book: Book of Jewish Tales and Legends. English translation by M. Gaster, 2 vols., Philadelphia, 1934.

MAIMONIDES, see MOSES BEN MAIMON.

MAIMUNI, ABRAHAM, see ROSENBLATT, S.

MAIMUNI, ABRAHAM, Sefer milhamot Adonai. Hannover, 1840.

MANN, JACOB, The Jews in Egypt and in Palestine under the Fatimid Caliphs. 2 vols., Oxford, 1920–22.

———, "Ha-tenu'ot ha-meshihiyot bi-yeme mass'e ha-zelab ha-rishonim." *Ha-tekufah*, XXIII (1925), 243–61; XXIV (1926), 335–58.

MANN, JACOB, Texts and Studies in Jewish History and Literature. 2 vols., Cincinnati and Philadelphia, 1931–35.

———, "Une source de l'histoire juive au XIII° siècle: La lettre polémique de Jacob b. Elie à Pablo Christiani." *REJ*, LXXXII (1926), 363–77.

MANSI, GIOVANNI DOMENICO, ed., Sacrorum conciliorum nova et amplissima collectio. 53 vols., Paris, 1901–27.

MARCU, V., Expulsion of the Jews from Spain. New York, 1935.

MARCUS, JACOB RADER, "Notes on Sephardic Jewish History of the Sixteenth Century." *HUC, Jub. Vol.* (1925), 279–96.

———, The Jew in the Medieval World: A Source Book. Cincinnati, 1938.

MARGOLIOUTH, D. S., "Responses of Maimonides in the Original Arabic." *JQR*, O. S., XI (1899), 533–50+ facsimile.

MARGOLIS, MAX L., AND ALEXANDER MARX, A History of the Jewish People. Philadelphia, 1927.

MARIANA, P. JUAN DE, Historia general de España. English translation, abridged, by J. Stevens, London, 1699.

MARTINI, RAYMOND, Pugio fidei. Paris, 1651.

MARX, ALEXANDER, see MARGOLIS, MAX L. AND MARX, ALEXANDER.

———, "The Correspondence between the Rabbis of Southern France and Maimonides about Astrology." *HUCA*, III (1926), 311–58.

———, "The Expulsion of the Jews from Spain." *JQR*, O. S., XX (1908), 240–71; N. S., II (1911–12), 257–58.

———, "The Scientific Work of Some Outstanding Mediaeval Jewish Scholars." *Essays and Studies in Memory of Linda R. Miller*, New York, 1933, 121–22.

MAS Y CASAS, T. M., Memoria histórica de los Hebreos y de los Arabes en Manresa. Manresa, 1837.

MEIR BEN BARUK OF ROTHENBURG, She'elot u-teshubot MaHaRaM. Prague, 1608; Lemberg, 1860; Budapest, 1895.

———, Sefer sha'are teshubot MaHaRaM. Berlin, 1891.

MEIRI, MENAHEM BEN SOLOMON, see MENAHEM BEN SOLOMON HA-MEIRI.

MENAHEM BEN AARON IBN ZERAH, Zedah la-derek. Sabionetta, [1567?].

MENAHEM BEN SOLOMON HA-MEIRI, Magen abot. Ed. by Isaac Last, London, 1909.

———, Sefer bet ha-behirah. Vienna, 1934.

MERRIMAN, ROGER B., The Rise of the Spanish Empire in the Old World and in the New. 2 vols., New York, 1918.

MICHEL, F., Histoire des races maudites de la France et de l'Espagne. 2 vols., Paris, 1847.

MIGASH, see JOSEPH BEN MEIR HA-LEVI IBN MIGASH.

MIRET Y SANS, IOACHIM, "Les Médecins juifs de Pierre, roi d'Aragon." *REJ*, LVII (1909), 268–78.

MOCATTA, F. D., The Jews of Spain and Portugal and the Inquisition. London, 1877.

MONDEJAR, G. IBANEZ, MARQUES DE, Memorias históricas del Rey Don Alfonso el Sabio, Madrid, 1777.

MORDECAI BEN ISAAC TAMAH, Maskiyyot kesef. Amsterdam, 1765.

MOSES BEN JACOB OF COUCY, Sefer mizvot gadol. Kopys, 1807.

MOSES BEN ISRAEL ISSERLES, see ISSERLES.

MOSES BEN JACOB IBN EZRA, Sefer shirat Yisrael (Kitab al-muhadhara wa-almudhakara). Tr. into Hebrew with intr. and notes by B. Halper, Leipzig, 1924.

Moses ben Jacob ibn Ezra, Selected Poems of Moses Ibn Ezra. Ed. by H. Brody and translated into English by Solomon Solis-Cohen, Philadelphia, 1934.

———, Shire Moshe ben Ya'akob ibn Ezra. Ed. by Ch. N. Bialik and W. H. Ravnitzky, Tel-Aviv, 1929.

———, Shire ha-hol. Ed. by H. Brody, vol. I, Berlin, 1935.

Moses b. Maimon [Maimonides], Dalalat al-Ha'irin (Moreh nebukim or The Guide of the Perplexed). Ed. in Arabic with French translation by S. Munk, 3 vols., Paris, 1856–66.

———, "Brief des R. Moses an seinen Jünger Josef b. Jehuda ibn Aknin." Ueber-setzt von Heinz Wolff, *MGWJ*, LXXIX (1935), 81–9.

———, Iggeret Teman. Ed. by David Holub, Vienna, 1873.

———, Kobez teshubot ha-RaMBaM ve-iggerotav. Ed. by A. L. Lichtenberg, 3 parts, Leipzig, 1859.

———, Mishneh Torah, or Yad hazakah. Amsterdam, 1702.

———, Sefer ha-mizvot (The Book of Precepts). In Arabic, ed. by M. Bloch, Paris, 1888.

———, Sefer moreh nebukim. Hebrew text of the Ibn Tibbon translation, with commentary, by J. Kaufmann, vol. I, Jerusalem, 1935.

———, Sefer moreh nebukim. Translated into Hebrew by Judah b. Solomon Alharizi, with notes by S. Scheyer, 3rd ed., Vilna, 1912.

———, The Guide for the Perplexed. English translation by M. Friedlaender, 3 vols., London, 1881–85; in one vol. [without notes], London, 1928.

———, Teshubot ha-RaMBaM. Ed. by Abraham Freimann, Jerusalem, 1934.

———, "Texts by and about Maimonides." Ed. by Alexander Marx. *JQR*, XXV (1935), 371–428.

Moses ben Nahman Gerondi [Nahmanides], Perush ha-Torah. Venice, 1545.

———, Sha'ar ha-gemul. Naples, 1490.

———, Torat ha-adam. Warsaw, 1841.

———, Vikkuah (Disputation with Pablo Christiani). Ed. and annotated by M. Steinschneider, Stettin, 1860.

———, Vikkuah. Hebrew text with Latin translation, Altdorf, 1681. In J. C. Wagenseil, *Tela ignea Satanae*.

Moses Mordecai Meyuhas, *see* Sha'are teshubah.

Moses the Priest, of Constantinople, Sefer kehunat 'olam. 2 parts, Con-stantinople, 1740.

Müller, Joel, Die Responsen der spanischen Lehrer des 10. Jahrhunderts, R. Mose, R. Chanoch, R. Joseph ibn Abitur. *Siebenter Bericht der Lehranstalt für die Wissenschaft des Judentums in Berlin*, 1881.

———, Responsen der Lehrer des Ostens und Westens, nach Handschriften heraus-gegeben und erklärt. Berlin, 1888.

Munk, Solomon, Mélanges de philosophie juive et arabe. Paris, 1857–59.

———, Notice sur Joseph Ben-Iehouda, ou Aboul' Hadjadj Yousouf Ben-Ya'hya al-Sabti al-Maghrebi, disciple de Maïmonide. Paris, 1842.

Münz, Isak, Über die jüdischen Ärzte im Mittelalter. Frankfurt a. M., 1922.

———, Maimonides (the Rambam): the story of his life and genius. Translated from the German, with an introduction, by Henry T. Schnittkind, Boston, 1935.

NAHMANIDES, see MOSES BEN NAHMAN GERONDI.

NEUBAUER, ADOLF, ed., Mediaeval Jewish Chronicles and Chronological Notes. 2 vols., Oxford, 1887–95.

NEUMAN, ABRAHAM A., "Some Phases of the Conditions of the Jews in Spain in the Thirteenth and Fourteenth Centuries." *Publications of the American Jewish Historical Society*, XXII (1914), 61–70.

NEUMARK, D., Essays in Jewish Philosophy. Vienna, 1929.

———, Geschichte der jüdischen Philosophie des Mittelalters. 3 vols., Berlin, 1907–28.

———, Toledot ha-pilosophia be-Yisrael. 2 vols., New York and Phila. 1921–29.

NEWMAN, LOUIS I., Jewish Influence on Christian Reform Movements. New York, 1925.

NISSIM BEN HAYYIM MODAI, see Sha'are zedek.

NISSIM BEN REUBEN GERUNDI, She'elot u-teshubot. Metz, 1786; Warsaw, 1907.

ORTEGA, MANUEL L., Los Hebreos en Marruecos: estudio histórico, político, y social. Madrid, 1919.

PALENCIA, ALFONSO FERNANDEZ DE, Crónica de Enrique IV. Trad. Antonio Paz y Melia, 4 vols., Madrid, 1904–08.

PALQUERA, SHEM-TOB BEN JOSEPH, see SHEM-TOB BEN JOSEPH PALQUERA.

PARKES, J. W., The Conflict of the Church and the Synagogue: A Study in the Origins of Antisemitism. London, 1934.

———, The Jew in the Medieval Community. London, 1938.

PELLA Y FORGAS, Historia del Ampurdán. Barcelona. 1883.

PERLES, JOSEPH, "Beiträge zur rabbinischen Sprach und Altertumskunde." *MGWJ*, XXXVII (1892), 356–78.

———, R. Salomo ben Abraham ben Adereth. Breslau, 1863.

PIRENNE, HENRI, "The Stages in the Social History of Capitalism." *AHR*, XIX (1914), 494–515.

PFLAUM, H., "Shire ha-nizzuah ha-datiyim shel yeme ha-benayim." *Tarbiz*, II (1930–31), 443–76.

POOLE, R. L., The Papal Chancery. Cambridge, 1915.

POZNANSKI, SAMUEL, Babylonische Geonim im nachgaonäischen Zeitalter. Berlin, 1914.

PULGAR, HERNANDO DEL, Crónica de los Reyes Católicos. Valencia, 1780.

PULGAR, ISAAC BEN JOSEPH, 'Ezer ha-dat. London, 1906.

RAIT, ROBERT S., Life in the Medieval Universities. Cambridge, England, 1912.

RASHDALL, H., Universities of Europe in the Middle Ages. 3 vols., Oxford, 1936.

RAYNALDUS, O., Annales ecclesiastici. 15 vols., Lucca, 1747–56.

RÉGNÉ, JEAN, "Catalogue des actes de Jaime Ier, Pedro III et Alfonso III, rois d'Aragon, concernants les Juifs." *REJ*, LX (1906), 161–201; LXI (1907), 1–43; LXII (1908), 38–73; LXIII (1909), 245–68; LXIV (1910), 67–88, 215–35; LXV (1911), 61–88, 196–223; LXVI (1912) 252–62; LXVII (1913), 53–81, 195–224; LXVIII (1914), 198–221; LXIX (1919), 135–220; LXX (1920), 74–87, 195–208. Reprinted, vol. I, part 2, Paris, 1911; vol. II, part 2, Paris, 1914.

Régné, Jean, Étude sur la condition des Juifs de Narbonne du V° au XIV° siècle. Narbonne, 1912.

Remedios, J. Mendes dos, Os Judeus em Portugal. 2 vols., Coimbra, 1895-1928.

Renan, Ernest, Averroès et l'Averroïseme: Essai historique. (Sixième edition). Paris.

————, "Les rabbins français du commencement du quatorzième siècle." L'Histoire Littéraire de la France, XXVIII (1877), xxii +431-764.

Rios, Don José Amador de los, Estudios históricos, polítcios y literarios sobre los Judíos de España. Madrid, 1848.

————, Historia social, política y religiosa de los Judíos de España y Portugal. 3 vols., Madrid, 1875-76.

Rivkind, Isaac, "Mas ha-kubya, lekorot mas ha-kalon." Zion, I (1935-36), 37-48.

————, "Mishpete kubyustusim." Horeb, II (1935-36), 60-66.

Robert, Ulysse, "Étude historique et archéologique sur la roue des Juifs depuis le XIII° siècle." REJ, VI (1882), 81-95.

————, Les signes d'infamie au moyen âge. Paris, 1891.

Rodocanachi, Emmanuel, Le Saint-Siège et les Juifs. Paris, 1891.

Rosenblatt, Samuel, The High Ways to Perfection of Abraham Maimonides. New York, 1927.

Rosenmann, Moses, "Das Lehrhaus des Rabbi Nissim Gerundi in Barcelona als Ursprungsort der letzten antimaimunischen philosophischen Richtung in Spanien." Festschrift Adolf Schwarz, 489-98.

Rosin, David, "Die Religionsphilosophie Abraham Ibn Esra's." MGWJ, XLII (1898), 17-33, 58-73, 108-15, 154-61, 200-14, 241-52, 305-15, 345-61, 394-407, 444-57, 481-505.

Roth, Cecil, A History of the Marranos. Philadelphia, 1932.

Rubió y Lluch, A., Documents per l'historia de la cultura catalana mig-eval. 2 vols., Barcelona, 1908, 1921.

————, "Notes sobre la ciencia oriental a Catalunya en el XIVen siglo;" Appendix, "Metjes y cirurgians juheus," by Jordi Rubió y Balaguer. Estudis Universitaris Catalans, Barcelona, III (1909).

Samter, N., "Der 'Jude' Aristoteles." MGWJ, XLV (1901), 453-59.

Samuel ben Moses de Medina, She'elot u-teshubot. 3 vols., Salonica, 1595.

Samuel ben Çarça [Ibn Sana], Sefer mekor hayyim. Mantua, 1559.

Sarachek, Joseph, The Doctrine of the Messiah in Medieval Jewish Literature. New York, 1932.

————, Faith and Reason: The Conflict over the Rationalism of Maimonides. Williamsport, Pa., 1935.

Sarton, George, Introduction to the History of Science. 2 vols., Baltimore, 1927-31.

Sassoon, D. S. D., ed., Diwan of Shemuel Hannagid, published for the First Time in its Entirety According to a Unique Manuscript. London, 1934.

Schechter, Solomon, "A Jewish Boswell." Studies in Judaism, I, London, 1896, 173-8.

Scherbel, Simon, Jüdische Ärzte und ihr Einfluss auf das Judentum. Berlin, 1905.

BIBLIOGRAPHY 367

Scholem, G., Bibliographia cabbalistica. Leipzig, 1927.
———, "Kabbala." *Encyclopaedia Judaica*, IX (1932), 630–732.
———, "Zur Frage der Entstehung der Kabbala." *Korrespondenzblatt ... Akademie für die Wissenschaft des Judentums*, IX (1928), 4–26.
Schorr, Joshua, "Dibre ha-berit asher ba'u bo ezeh kehilot Sefarad b-shenat 1354." *He-Haluz*, I (1866), 15–29.
Schreiner, Martin, "Die apologetische Schrift des Salomon b. Adret gegen einen Muhammedaner." *ZDMG*, XLVIII (1894), 39–42.
Schwab, Moïse, Rapport sur les inscriptions hébraiques de l'Espagne. Paris, 1907.
Sedgwick, Henry D., Italy in the Thirteenth Century. 2 vols., Boston, 1912.
Sha'are zedek. Ed. by Nissim b. Hayyim Modai, Salonica, 1792.
Sha'are teshubah. Ed. by Moses Mordecai Meyuhas, Salonica, 1802.
Shem-Tob ben Joseph Palquera, Sefer ha-mebakkesh. Ed. by Mordecai ben Isaac Tamah, Hague, 1778.
Shibe'ah 'enayyim. Ed. by Jacob ben Judah of London, Livorno, 1745.
Shohet, D. M., The Jewish Court in the Middle Ages. New York, 1931.
Siete Partidas, Las, del Rey don Alfonso el Sabio. Madrid, 1807.
———, Ed. by J. M. Martinez, 2 vols., Valladolid, 1875.
———, English translation and notes by S. P. Scott, Chicago, 1931.
Silva Rosa, J. S. da, Die spanischen und portugiesischen gedruckten Judaica in der Bibliothek des Jüd. Portug. Seminars "Ets Haim," in Amsterdam: eine Ergänzung zu Kayserlings "Bibliotheca Española-Portugueza-Judaica." Amsterdam, 1933.
Simeon ben Zemah Duran, *see* Duran.
Simmonsohn, M., Die kirchliche Judengesetzgebung im Zeitalter der Reformkonzilien von Konstanz und Basel. Breslau, 1912.
Singermann, Felix, Die Kennzeichen der Juden im Mittelalter. Berlin, 1915.
Sirah, The Wisdom of Ben Sirah. Ed. by S. Schechter and C. Taylor, Cambridge, 1899.
Smith, A. L., Church and State in the Middle Ages. Oxford, 1913.
Solomon Alami, Iggeret musar. Leipzig, 1854.
Solomon ben Abraham ben Parhon, Mahberet he-'aruk. Pressburg, 1844.
Solomon ben Abraham ibn Adret, *see* Adret.
Solomon ben Judah ibn Gabirol, *see* Gabirol.
Solomon ibn Verga, Shebet Yehudah. Ed. with German translation by M. Wiener, Hannover, 1924.
Sombart, Werner, The Jews and Modern Capitalism. English translation with notes by M. Epstein, London, 1913.
Steinschneider, Moritz, An Introduction to the Arabic Literature of the Jews. London, 1901.
———, Die arabische Literatur der Juden. Frankfurt a. M., 1902.
———, Die hebraeischen Uebersetzungen des Mittelalters und die Juden als Dolmetscher. Berlin, 1893.
———, Die jüdischen Mathematiker und die jüdischen anonymen mathematischen Schriften. Frankfurt a. M., 1901.
———, Jewish Literature from the Eighth to the Eighteenth Century with an Introduction on Talmud and Midrash. Translated from the German, London, 1857.

STEINSCHNEIDER, MORITZ, "Jüdische Literatur." Ersch u. Gruber Encyklopädie, XXVII, Leipzig, 1850.

——, Jüdische Schriften zur Geographie Palästina's (X–XIX. Jahrh.). Jerusalem, 1892.

——, "Moreh mekom ha-moreh." *Kobez 'al yad*, I (1885), 1–32.

——, "Notices sur les tables astronomiques attribuées à Pierre III d'Aragon." *Bulletino di bibliografia delle scienze matematici*, XIII (1880).

——, "Perush Rab Yehudah ben Bal'am 'al ha-torah bilshon 'arabi." *He-Haluz*, II (1853), 60–63.

——, "Philosophische Prediger im XV. Jahrhundert und ihre Gegner." *Bibliothek jüdischer Kanzelredner*, I (1870), 34–5.

——, Polemische und apologetische Literatur in arabischer Sprache, zwischen Muslimen, Christen und Juden. Leipzig, 1877.

STERN, MORITZ, Urkundliche Beiträge über die Stellung der Päpste zu der Juden. Kiel, 1893.

STRAUSS, L., "Quelques remarques sur la science politique de Maïmonide et de Fârâbí." *REJ*, C (1936), 1–37.

SWIFT, E. D., The Life and Times of James the First, the Conqueror, King of Aragon. Oxford, 1894.

TAM, [RABBENU] JACOB BEN MEIR OF RAMERU. *see* JACOB BEN MEIR OF RAMERU.

TAYLOR, HENRY OSBORN, The Mediaeval Mind. 2 vols., London, 1938.

TEJADA Y RAMIRO, Coleccion de canones y todos los concilios de la Iglesia española. 5 vols., Madrid, 1859.

Teshubot geonim kadmonim: Rechtsgutachten der Geonim. Hrsg. von D. Cassel, Berlin, 1848.

Teshubot ha-geonim. Ed. by Nahman Nathan Coronel, Vienna, 1871.

TAMAH, *see* MORDECAI BEN ISAAC TAMAH.

THORNDIKE, L., History of Magic and Experimental Science. 4 vols., New York, 1929–34.

TODROS HALEVI IBN ABU-L'AFIAH, Gan Hammeshalim we-Hahidoth: Diwan of Don Tadros son of Yehuda Abu-l-'Āfiah. Ed. by David Yellin, 2 vols., Jerusalem, 1932–36.

TORQUEMADA, TOMAS, Compilación de las Instrucciones del Officio de la S. Inquisición. Madrid, 1630.

——, "Spanischer Text mit deutscher Uebersetzung mitgeteilt von E. Schaefer." *Archiv für Reformationsgeschichte*, V (1904), 8–53; VI (1905), 109–75.

TOURTOULON, CH. DE, Jacme Ier, le conquérant., Montpellier, 1863.

URBACH, E., "Études sur la littérature polémique au moyen-âge." *REJ*, C (1935), 49–77.

USQUE, S., Consolaçam as tribulaçoens de Israel. Ed. by M. dos Remedios, Coimbra, 1906.

VIDAL, PIERRE, "Les Juifs de Roussillon et de Cerdagne." *REJ*, XV (1887), 19–55; XVI (1888), 1–23.

VILLANUEVA, J. L., Viage literario á las iglesias de España. Madrid, 1803–52.

VOGELSTEIN, HERMANN AND RIEGER, PAUL, Geschichte der Juden in Rom. 2 vols., Berlin, 1895–96.

WAXMAN, M., A History of Jewish Literature from the Close of the Bible to Our Own Day. 4 vols., New York, 1930–41.

——, "The Philosophy of Don Hasdai Crescas." *JQR*, VIII (1917–18), 305–37, 455–75; IX (1918–19), 181–213; X (1919–20), 25–47, 291–308.

WEILL, JULIEN, "Notes sur les Maranes d'Espagne aprés l'edit 1492." *REJ*, LXXXVIII (1929), 59–61.

——, "Source de la formule du serment juif codifié dans les "Partidas" d'Alphonse X." *REJ*, LXXXVI (1925), 58–60.

WEISS, ISAAC HIRSCH, Dor dor ve-doreshav. 5 vols., Wilna, 1904.

WIENER, MEIR, Regesten zur Geschichte der Juden in Deutschland während des Mittelalters. Part I, Hannover, 1862.

WILLIAMS, A. LUKYN, Adversus Judaeos: A Bird's-Eye View of Christian Apologiae until the Renaissance. Cambridge, 1935.

——, "The Jews and Christian Apologists in Early Spain." *Church Quarterly Review*, C (1925–26), 267–87.

WOLF, LUCIEN, Report on the "Marranos" or Crypto-Jews of Portugal. London, 1926.

WOLFSON, HARRY AUSTRYN, "The Classification of Sciences in Medieval Jewish Philosophy." *Hebrew Union College Jubilee Volume*, (1925), 263–315.

——, Crescas' Critique of Aristotle. Cambridge, Mass., 1929.

——, "Maimonides and Halevi." *JQR*, II (1911–12), 297–337.

——, "Note on Maimonides' Classification of the Sciences." *JQR*, XXVI (1935–36), 369–77.

XIMÉNEZ DE EMBUN, TOMAS, Descripción histórica de la antigua Zaragoza. Zaragoza, 1901.

YAARI, A., Reshimat sifre Ladino ha-nimza'im be-bet ha-sefarim ha-le'umi ve-ha-universitai bi-Yerushalayim (catalogue of Judaeo-Spanish books in the Jewish National and University Library). Jerusalem, 1934.

YAHUDA, A. S., "Contribución al estudio del Judeo-Español." *Revista de Filogia Española*, II (1915), 339–70.

YANGUAS Y MIRANDA, JOSÉ, Diccionario de antigüedades de Navarra. Pamplona, 1842.

YARHI, ABRAHAM BEN NATHAN, Sefer ha-manhig. Constantinople, 1519.

YELLIN, DAVID AND ABRAHAMS, ISRAEL, Maimonides. Philadelphia, 1903.

ZACUTO, ABRAHAM BEN SAMUEL, Sefer yuhasin. Ed. by Herschell Filipowski. London, 1857.

ZEITLIN, SOLOMON, Maimonides: A Biography. New York, 1935.

ZEUMER, KARL, ed., Leges Visigothorum (*Monumenta Germaniae Historica*, Legum, sectio I, tom. I). Hannover and Leipzig, 1902.

ZIEGLER, A., Church and State in Visigothic Spain. Washington, 1930.

ZIMMELS, H. J., Beiträge zur Geschichte der Juden in Deutschland im 13. Jahrhundert, insbesondere auf Grund der Gutachten des R. Meir Rothenburg. Wien, 1926.

——, Die Marranen in der rabbinischen Literatur. Berlin, 1932.

ZIMMELS, H. J., "Erez Israel in der Responsenliteratur des späteren Mittelalters." *MGWJ*, LXXIV (1930), 44–64.

ZINBERG, ISRAEL, Di Geshichte fun der Literatur bei Yidn (A History of Jewish Literature in Europe). Vols. I–VIII, Vilna, 1929–37.

ZUNZ, LEOPOLD, "An Essay on the Geographical Literature of the Jews." §§44, 47, in *The Itinerary of Rabbi Benjamin of Tudela*, ed. and translated by A. Asher, London and Berlin, 1840–41.

———, Die Vorschriften über Eidesleistung der Juden. Berlin, 1859.

———, Zur Geschichte und Literatur. Vol. I, Berlin, 1845.

ZURITA Y CASTRO, J., Anales de la Corona de Aragon. 6 vols., Saragossa, 1610–70.

INDEX

INDEX

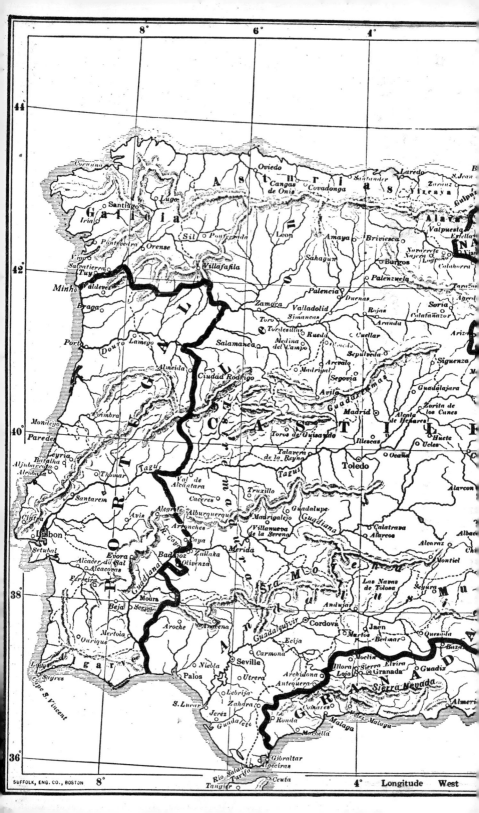